SEE IT

FEELINGLY

THOUGHT IN THE ACT

A series edited by Erin Manning and Brian Massumi

· RALPH JAMES SAVARESE ·

SEE IT
FEELINGLY

Classic Novels, Autistic Readers,

and the Schooling of

a No-Good English Professor

Duke University Press   Durham and London   2018

Printed in the United States of America on acid-free paper ∞
Designed by Courtney Leigh Baker
Typeset in Garamond Premier Pro and Futura by
Westchester Publishing Services

Library of Congress Cataloging-in-Publication Data
Names: Savarese, Ralph James, author.
Title: See it feelingly : classic novels, autistic readers, and the schooling
of a no-good English professor / Ralph James Savarese.
Other titles: Thought in the act.
Description: Durham : Duke University Press, 2018. | Series: Thought
in the act | Includes bibliographical references and index.
Identifiers: LCCN 2018015605 (print) | LCCN 2018013140 (ebook)
ISBN 9781478001300 (hardcover : alk. paper)
ISBN 9781478002734 (ebook)
Subjects: LCSH: Autistic people—Psychology. |
Autistic people—Language. | Autistic people—Education. |
English fiction—Study and teaching.
Classification: LCC RC553.A88 S296 2018 (ebook) |
LCC RC553.A88 (print) | DDC 616.85/882—dc23
LC record available at https://lccn.loc.gov/2018015605

COVER ART: Photo by Robert Cushman Murphy taken aboard
the whaleship *Daisy*. Courtesy of the Whaling Museum & Education
Center of Cold Spring Harbor.

FOR THE SIX IN THE BOOK

· · ·

And in memory of F. D. Reeve, my former teacher,
and Mando Montaño, my former student

LEAR:

. . . No eyes in your head, nor no money in your purse?
. . . Yet you see how this world goes.

EARL OF GLOUCESTER:

I see it feelingly.

William Shakespeare, *King Lear*

· contents ·

· foreword ·

Sooner or later in a reading life, one finds words are living things. Whether this knowledge comes by writing or reading, via reader-response theory or neuropsychoanalysis, hardly matters—a word or stanza (in the case of a poem) starts up from its page, extends broad wings, and reader and writer never forget it. In my case I read poems by D. H. Lawrence during a severe adolescent illness, a near-death experience, and found these simple lines to a torn pomegranate:

> For my part, I prefer my heart to be broken.
> It is so lovely, dawn-kaleidoscopic within the crack.

Later I'd learn of Lawrence's long struggle with tuberculosis and know him as a lyric poet of the body in crisis, but first encountering his pomegranate, I only knew the words were sharp as broken glass, cryptic, and then lifting. I'd never seen anything like it. That a man's heart could be preferably broken was interesting enough to a disabled teen fighting to stay alive, but then the poem's living words flew up and away from custom: it is so lovely, dawn-kaleidoscopic within the crack. Wounds, I saw, could be the cracked doors of hope.

No adult had ever shared so much sharpened intimacy with me, not my teachers, not our local priest, certainly not my parents who held my blindness as something unmentionable whether in emotional or practical terms.

Lovely dawn-kaleidoscopic; torn skin of the fruit-heart-man; one who's implicitly survived the night. If prior to this discovery words were quiescent, passive, easy to overlook, they were no longer.

In disability there are innumerable obstacles to having what we often call an empowered life—Helen Keller comes immediately to mind. When she sought admittance to Radcliffe College she was compelled to demonstrate her literacy and she endured tests designed to prove that her written words and her inner life were not her own. How could a blind-deaf woman who used an amanuensis to communicate have an authentic and self-directed capacity for language? In Keller's case her natural talent with language was so far beyond the skills of her "teacher," Annie Sullivan, the matter was settled, if not quickly, speedily enough.

My reception as a blind writer who can speak has been less onerous than Keller's, though it's not without its cringeworthy moments. During an interview for a teaching position at a major American university, a professor in the creative writing department asked how I could write so clearly about the world if I can't see? Aside from its borderline illegality (did he think I was faking blindness?), the question revealed how little some contemporary writers understand what language does at its most fundamental level. That all nouns are images had never occurred to my questioner, a well-regarded fiction writer who presumably should have recognized what I said next: "I say strawberry, you see a strawberry; I say battleship, you'll see it. Whether I've seen the poxy thing myself has no bearing on your reception—this is why poets were believed to be magical in ancient times." Of course, blind people produce mental imagery just like sighted people, as contemporary neuroscience has demonstrated. A working retina is not required.

But literary language is often as much about the unseen as the seen. Accordingly, Milton was the right poet to describe the vaults of hell. But what's more interesting is the evident and often mysterious joy that comes from sensing the unseeable or unnameable in our reading. Joy is not always or invariably concerned with custom. Pablo Neruda, who spent many years alone as a young man traveling with the Chilean Foreign Service, wrote,

> I grew accustomed to stubborn lands
> where nobody ever asked me
> whether I like lettuces
> or if I prefer mint
> like the elephants devour.
> And from offering no answers,
> I have a yellow heart.

In literary consciousness solitude is always instructive. Filtered through Neruda's imagination, it's both figuratively improbable and unforgettable.

There's a growing acknowledgment among readers familiar with writers like Oliver Sacks and Steve Silberman that people with autism (who prefer, rightly, to be called autistics or autists) innately grasp the elephant's mint and its influence on the yellow heart with nary a wink. Or with many winks. Like the blind, they haven't been asked too many questions either and, until recently, have offered few answers. But the times, as Bob Dylan famously sang, "they are a-changin.'"

In *See It Feelingly: Classic Novels, Autistic Readers, and the Schooling of a No-Good English Professor*, the poet and memoirist Ralph James Savarese has engaged with people on the spectrum, not to study them, not to inflict upon them the Keller test, but to explore classic literature with men and women who know a great deal about solitude, the crack in the pomegranate, the dawn-kaleidoscopic, and the silent wounds in lovely hearts. One can't help but feel while reading this remarkable book the wonder of reading truly. I was reminded of Paulo Freire's dictum: "Nobody studies authentically who does not take the critical position of being the subject of curiosity, of the reading, of the process of discovery." Emily Dickinson put it like this:

He ate and drank the precious words,
His spirit grew robust;
He knew no more that he was poor,
Nor that his frame was dust.
He danced along the dingy days,
And this bequest of wings
Was but a book. What liberty
A loosened spirit brings!

This is a volume about reading unlike any I've ever encountered. Put away those pernicious clichés and stereotypes of autism. Autistics lack theory of mind. . . . Autistics suffer from linguistic impairment. . . . Autistics cannot engage in imaginative play. . . . Follow along as a nonspeaking man from Austin, Texas, swims through *Moby-Dick* to tell his own sensory story. Or watch a cyberpunk writer and computer programmer from Portland, Oregon, track the empathetic failings of Rick Deckard, a bounty hunter in *Do Androids Dream of Electric Sheep?* who "retires" six escaped androids. Like these androids, autistics are said to lack empathy.

What do neurodivergent minds bring to novel reading? Plenty. Their oft-reported talent for "thinking in pictures" may even provide a leg up in literature's "cinema of emotions."

W. H. Auden once remarked that "as readers, most of us, to some degree, are like those urchins who pencil moustaches on the faces of girls in advertisements." But what if we're the pencil, the urchin, the girl, the advertisement, the mustache, without the drag anchor of uncertainty? That is, what if no reader is neurotypical? Wouldn't masterful neuro-atypical readers then become mentors in whose authority we can derive much profit? This is at its very core one of the most probative and imaginative recognitions we can "brave"—that all writers and readers are more complicated and surprising than we've customarily known.

Stephen Kuusisto

· acknowledgments ·

Annie Dillard once wrote, "I think that the dying pray at the last not 'please,' but 'thank you,' as a guest thanks his host at the door." Finishing this sort of book has been a little bit like dying, and I, too, wish to thank my gracious hosts: DJ, Tito, Jamie, Dora, Eugenie, and Temple. What a dinner party of ideas they each put on! Their remarkable generosity gave life to this project. What I did with it—well, that's my responsibility, not theirs. I hope, at the very least, that I have honored their participation by foregrounding their own words and by dramatizing repeatedly the intractable problem of any anthropological endeavor. Mistakes are inevitable, but interpretive humility is not.

I want to thank Erin Manning, whose belief in this book made all the difference, and Ken Wissoker and Elizabeth Ault at Duke University Press. My agent, Deirdre Mullane, performed her duties with great skill and gusto. Thanks as well to Gillian Silverman for considerable help with the Grandin chapter and to Lisa Zunshine, to whom that chapter is dedicated. Meeting Lisa and working closely with her on a project about literature and autism turned out to be the sort of coincidence that changes one's life. Nancy Barber read the whole book and offered invaluable feedback; her friendship of almost thirty years lifted me up when I fell down. Pilar Martinez Benedi read every word (in multiple drafts), offering both warm encouragement and invaluable guidance. I profited enormously from talking to her about literature and neuroscience.

I am very grateful to the Mellon Foundation for granting me a Humanities-Writ-Large fellowship, which funded a year at Duke University's Institute for Brain Sciences. Special thanks to Michael Platt, Zab Johnson, Tanya Schreiber, Lasana Harris, Len White, Laura Eastwood, Chris Chia, Geri Dawson, and, especially, Deborah Jenson. I learned so very much from Deborah about cognitive literary studies—no one could have been more generous with her time or more enthusiastic about my work. I now count her and her husband, Jim Jenson, as dear friends. While I was at Duke, Priscilla Wald and Joe Donahue befriended me— and housed me as well! I drafted the Mukhopadhyay chapter in their guest room. I am indebted, in addition, to the book's anonymous, external reviewers, whose comments were extremely useful, and to the National Endowment for the Humanities, which awarded me a summer research fellowship.

I also received tremendous support from Grinnell College, and I wish to thank both the president, Raynard Kington, and the dean, Mike Latham, for helping to make Grinnell a place where research and teaching symbiotically thrive. I owe the students in a recent independent study and those in my "neuro-lit" seminars, where I first began to try to reconcile the insights of disability studies and cognitive literary studies, a great deal. I owe my colleague Johanna Meehan and her partner, Maura Strassberg, even more. They opened up their house to me—I commute to Grinnell from Iowa City—and their hearts. They've heard more about this project than any friends should have to. I feel the same way about two other couples: Mark Montgomery and Tinker Powell and Maria Tapias and Xavier Escandell. Writing is lonely; comrades in the endeavor help a great deal. Even closer to home, my in-laws, Phil and Rachel Thornton, have offered unflagging love and support. My son, DJ, once said of them, "You're old enough to be my grandparents but young enough to be my friends." By not only embracing difference but also unreservedly relishing it, they have taught me much. Their gentle spirits are balm for a hostile world.

My colleagues in the Grinnell English department offered significant assistance while I was chair of the department—half of the book was drafted, and all of it was revised, during that time. Erik Simpson was especially helpful. Dean Bakopoulos and Alissa Nutting ran the department's reading series, Writers@ Grinnell. They did so skillfully and cheerfully while sending their own books out into the world. Their devotion to the daily practice of writing steered me through the waters of despair. Without De Dudley and Lisa Mulholland, the department's support staff assistants, I would be worse than lost. Their good humor is a life raft; their competence, a rescue helicopter! I'm grateful to my colleague Shanna Benjamin for providing some research guidance for chapter 4.

I'm also grateful to Mary K. Bercaw Edwards for graciously conducting a tour of the *Charles W. Morgan* at Mystic Seaport and to Will Garrison, the curator of the Berkshire Historical Society at Arrowhead, and Will Demick, guide, for conducting a tour of Melville's homestead. The first "Will" was a 1985 graduate of Grinnell.

I could not have written this book without the example, input, and/or encouragement of so many writers, scholars, artists, activists, and friends across the country—and indeed the globe. A woefully incomplete list will have to suffice: Sara Maria Acevedo, Kazim Ali, Melanie Almeder, Diane Alters, Mel Baggs, Julia Bascom, Jill Bennett, Tammy Berberi, Michael Bérubé, Doug Biklen, Larry Bissonnette, Sonia Boue, Maria Brincker, Lydia X. Z. Brown, Victoria Brown, Brenda Brueggemann, Mike Burke, Sheree Burke, David Campbell, Joy Castro, Kerima Cevik, Geoff Hume Cooke, David Coster, Tom Couser, Lennard Davis, Selene DePackh, Marty Dobrow, Elizabeth Donaldson, Anne Donnellan, John Duffy, Marshall Duke, David Dunbar, Paula Durbin-Westby, Judy Endow, Eva Feder-Kittay, Angus Fletcher, Stephen Forssell, Chris Foss, Chris Gabbard, Susannah Goodman, Ibby Grace, Mike Guenther, Elizabeth Hamilton, Laura Hans, Bev Harp, Aeron Haynie, Andy Hazucha, Judith Hill-Weld, Monica Huerta, Paweł Jędrzejko, Dan Kaiser, Julie Kane, Estee Klar, Kevin Kopelson, Jennifer Krohn, Martha Leary, Dawn-Joy Leong, Cynthia Lewiecki-Wilson, Heather Lobban-Viravong, Janet Lyon, Brian Massumi, John Matteson, Harley McIlrath, Bobbie and Shirley McKibbin, Karen McRitchie, Celeste Miller, Susannah Mintz, Mario Montano, Cal Montgomery, Soma Mukhopadhyay, Stuart Murray, Nico Ian Nicolson, Christina Nicolaidis, Keith Oatley, Laura Otis, Nick Pentzell, Martina Pfeiler, Jeff Porter, Lynn Powell, Elizabeth Prevost, Dawn Prince, Chammi Rajapatirana, Scott Robertson, Julia Rodas, Rachel Rottenberg, Sue Rubin, Dani Alexis Ryskamp, Becky Saletan, Carrie Sandahl, John Schaut, Carlos Schaut, Phil Schwarz, Sue Schweik, Amy Sequenzia, Jenn Seybert, Stephen Shore, Steve Silberman, Olga Solomon, Chris Sten, Laura Stevenson, Jane Thrailkill, Tracy Thresher, Sarah Thwaites, Emily Titon, Elizabeth Torres, Jason Tougaw, James Trent, Nick Walker, Brent White, Marco Wilkinson, Amy Williams, Donna Williams, James Wilson, Tilly Woodward, Melanie Yergeau, Zhenyu Yuan, Martin Zelder, and Mary Zournazi.

A few people deserve special thanks. Ben Reiss and Rosemarie Garland-Thomson reminded me, when I needed it most, that what I was writing was both important and distinctive. The novelist Elizabeth Graver, with whom I went to college, has, for almost forty years, been a lighthouse of encouragement and fine sentence making. David Blake, with whom I taught high school English some three decades ago, has offered continual instruction in artful thinking and writing—I've learned much from him and his work. John

Bryant, Melvillean extraordinaire and fellow adoptive father, has tutored my very soul. Suzanne Paola alerted me to the possibilities of writing about neurodiversity in both factual and creative ways. Her friendship has been sustaining. In his poems and conversation, the poet Rick Kenney has repeatedly demonstrated that literature and science, like Ishmael and Queequeg, belong in the same bed. Peter Sokol is the kind of friend that one dreams of having (and that one can never come close to equaling). Let me put John and Elaine Mahon in that category as well. I sometimes think that my friend Michael Hofmann exists in order to prove that extraordinary achievement and extraordinary humility can sometimes go hand in hand. He, like his partner, Barbara Hofmeister, is also extraordinarily kind. I count it a lucky blessing that the Internet brought the poet Chris Martin into my life; we had each been teaching poetry writing to autistics without knowing of the other's activities. The comedian Henny Youngman once joked that his brother worked as a lifeguard in a carwash. Steve Kuusisto and David Weiss work there as well. Again and again, they rescue me in my convertible! I feel the same way about Jeremy Mindich, my oldest friend. His wife, Amy Smith—let me call her a brother-guard, too. Their remarkable generosity has no expression in language. For thirty-five years, John and Leslie Paoletti have been like much-needed parents, and Sarah and Rebecca Paoletti like much-needed sisters. Emily Thornton Savarese has been my partner for almost three decades, the last two parenting DJ. Would that I were as filled with such steady and unassuming wisdom as she. Would that I were as indefatigably generous.

Finally, since this is a book about teaching—autistics teaching me, me (sort of) teaching autistics—I'll conclude with a short list of teachers who made a difference in my life. From middle school and high school: Charles Campbell, Tad Cavuoti, Bill Doswell, Rod Dulany, Gail Nields, Ed Sundt, Peter Swineheart, and Fred Zirm. From college: George Creeger, Annie Dillard, Sherman Hawkins, Gertrude Hughes, Priscilla Meyer, John Paoletti, F. D. Reeve, Richard Stamelman, and John Tivenan. From graduate school: Don Ault, Marsha Bryant, Michael Hofmann, David Leverenz, John Murchek, Robert Ray, Robert Rothstein, Stephanie Smith, and Phil Wegner. These teachers showed me what a life of the mind (and body) could be.

Grateful acknowledgment is made to the editors of *Fourth Genre*, who published a version of the prologue, and to the editors of *Thinking in the World*, who published an earlier version of chapter 2. The prologue was a "Notable Essay" selection in the *Best American Essays* series of 2013.

· introduction ·

Donald Barthelme once described "the aim of literature" as "the creation of a strange object covered with fur which breaks your heart." Like a creature birthed in a basement study, a creature at once preposterous and terrifying, literature cannot be fully domesticated. It will not sit; it will not roll over; it will not greet you at the door. However firm the leash—or shackles—of form, this Adam of the writer's labors takes the reader for a walk.

When Barthelme says that the hirsute entity should break our hearts, he is in part alluding to an effect of narrative. "All stories are about wolves," writes Margaret Atwood, and wolves bring conflict and loss. Of course, a majority of the time, the wolves in life are human, as when I opened my computer this morning and saw a photograph of a rhino—a living rhino— whose face had been hacked off by poachers wanting its horns. Because the poachers had removed most of the rhino's underlying bones, leaving only soft tissue, veterinarians used elephant skin, which is tough, to close the gaping wound. One of the news accounts I read reported, "As clients pay top dollar for rhino horns, poachers have become more brutal and sophisticated, forcing veterinarians to come up with innovative ways of treatment." If the writer is a kind of Dr. Frankenstein, she is also a sympathetic and experimental veterinarian.

But what does literary creation have to do with autism? The disorder's well-known "triad of impairments" (in communication, imagination, and social interaction) suggests that reading literature, let alone writing it, would be a considerable challenge for autistics. Indeed, studies from the last three decades have consistently presented evidence of deficits in two key areas: theory of mind (ToM) and the apprehension of figurative language. Simon Baron-Cohen, chief purveyor of the ToM hypothesis, says of autistics that they are unable "to develop an awareness of what is in the mind of another human." If the mental states of others are beyond their reach, how can they possibly manage that moody jungle gym of make-believe conflict called a novel? And, further, how can they ascertain the undisclosed and indirect meaning of irony or metaphor? An obdurate, self-contained literality plagues autistic consciousness, the experts maintain. This view of autism has become so prevalent that a bestselling novel, *The Curious Incident of the Dog in the Night-Time*, makes social and metaphoric bafflement a central aspect of the protagonist's characterization.

Yet the proliferation of autistic autobiography—in print, on the web, in presentations at conferences—reveals a very different picture of autism, one more in line with what I have experienced with my son, DJ, and with the many autistics I know. Literary reading and writing are by no means too alien or demanding for them. Even a figure like Temple Grandin, who conceives of herself as an overly logical animal scientist, turns out to be much more sensitive to literature than we were led to believe. In his 1993 *New Yorker* profile of Grandin, "An Anthropologist on Mars," Oliver Sacks presented a portrait of conspicuous psychological and aesthetic impairment that came to shape popular conceptions of autism. The piece is slippery, and at times he almost puts words in Grandin's mouth.

Consider, for example, the passage in which he asks her about Greek mythology and Shakespeare:

> "I understand Nemesis and Hubris," she said. But the loves of the gods, *I ascertained* [my italics], left her unmoved—and puzzled. It was similar with Shakespeare's plays. She was bewildered, she said, by Romeo and Juliet ("I never knew what they were up to"), and with *Hamlet* she got lost with the back-and-forth of the play. *Though she ascribed these problems to "sequencing difficulties," they seemed to arise from her failure to empathize with the characters* [my italics], to follow the intricate play of motive and intention.

Like a wrangler corralling cattle, Sacks maneuvers Grandin into the autistic pen. Dismissing her own account of her challenges, he "ascertains" a more fundamental and debilitating lack. Yet one needn't have autism to be confused by, or to be uninterested in, Shakespeare, as anyone who has taught college literature courses knows.

Not half a page later, Sacks quotes from the very article in which she blames sequencing difficulties for her struggles with literature: "My interests are factual and my recreational reading consists mostly of science and livestock publications. I have little interest in novels with complicated interpersonal relationships, because I am unable to remember the sequence of events. Detailed descriptions of new technologies in science fiction or descriptions of exotic places are much more interesting." Sequencing difficulties may prevent identification with characters in longer literary works—think, for instance, of how intricate some nineteenth-century British novels are—but it doesn't mean that Grandin lacks empathy, as her profound feeling for livestock shows, or that she is incapable of responding to shorter works.

At the same time, Grandin herself suggests that beauty—in art or nature—doesn't make her "swoon." "Her inability to respond deeply, emotionally, subjectively, is not confined to music," Sacks writes in the profile. "There is a similar poverty of emotional or aesthetic response to most visual scenes: she can describe them with great accuracy but they do not seem to correspond or to evoke any strongly felt states of mind." While in some ways Grandin contributes to the stereotype of unfeeling, Spock-like detachment in autism, Sacks pushes the idea too far, once again straining to reconcile what he observes as a progressive "neuro-anthropologist" with what he has learned as a conventional doctor. Because he is such a fine writer and because he seeks to explore the "paradox of disease," what he calls its "'creative' potential," the profile of Grandin is alive with humanizing complexity and contradiction. But the reader must look for moments when autism appears simply as another form of life and not as lamentable pathology.

When I interviewed Grandin—Temple—in the summer of 2016, I discovered that one of her favorite classes in college had been "Western Civilization," which she described as a "great books" course. With fondness, she remembered reading Keats's "Ode on A Grecian Urn" and Dante's *Inferno*. That the center of hell appears in this latter work as a frozen wasteland, with Satan emerging mid-breast from the ice, had remained fixed in her mind. She found the paradox intriguing. She said that she especially enjoyed the way the professor helped to elucidate the deeper meanings of the text, and more than once she spoke about the value of ambiguity, a key element in literature. She conceived of ambiguity as an antidote to simplistic thinking. She also reported that literature helped her to understand her own and others' feelings.

But did it affect her? Did it stir her emotions? Although she specifically cited the movie *Titanic* and the song "The Widow Maker" as examples of things that had made her cry, she said that literature had also elicited emotion from her in the past, though not to the same degree. Interestingly, both of the above-mentioned "disaster romances" turn on the gallant sacrifice of a male lover. (Temple is celibate and has claimed repeatedly that she doesn't understand the subtle nuances of romance.) In "The Widow Maker," a truck driver purposefully swings his rig off the road in order to save ten kids in a pickup. When, in ethnographic researcher mode, I dryly asked why the end of *Titanic* had moved her, Temple was incredulous: "The lovers can't ever be together!" Tragedy—of Jack and Rose or Billy Mack and Wanda Ann—did in fact wound her.

But my point isn't simply that autistics can "do" literature. In a number of key ways literature lines up nicely with an autistic neurology. Here, Barthelme's quip about "strange objects covered with fur" anticipates my argument. Famous for redesigning the chutes at cattle-processing plants—rounded chutes, it turns out, are much more soothing to livestock awaiting slaughter than rectilinear ones—Temple has gone so far as to propose that autistic cognition resembles animal cognition. "The thing is I don't think in language," she says, "and animals don't think in language. It's sensory based thinking, thinking in pictures, thinking in smells, thinking in touches."

If, as studies have demonstrated, autistics disproportionately rely on posterior sensory regions of the brain to think, then neurotypicals disproportionately rely on their frontal lobes. Neurotypicals, Temple believes, are "abstractified in their sensory perceptions as well as their thoughts." "Animals don't see their ideas of things," she stresses. "They see the actual things themselves." Temple illustrates the difference between the two groups by pointing to what their brains look like in a scanner when performing an embedded figure task. In this protocol, subjects must find a figure hidden within a complicated picture—autistics tend to find the figure much more quickly than neurotypicals. Using a remarkable poetic analogy, Temple compares the visual center of autistic brains during the test to "a little bright cabin out in the snowy wilderness." "Everything else is shut off, but [it] is turned on really bright," she says. Neurotypical brains, by contrast, remind her of a lamp store: "There's so much stuff turned on that the visual stuff gets obscured." For Temple, the unfiltered visual concentration of autistics resembles that of animals.

Of course, all of that "other stuff" in the lamp store is crucial for understanding literature. The point is that literature partially corrects for the "abstractification" of neurotypical cognition just as it partially corrects for the resolute concreteness of autistic cognition. As Temple herself makes clear, autistics accomplish higher order thought in a different way. To explain the distinction between the two neurotypes, she must move beyond the sensory, even as she uses a concrete image to make her point. As literature explores its larger themes, it, too, thinks in pictures, smells, and touches. "That's right," Temple said when I described how its diction sets off sensory fireworks. While obviously word-based, literature aims to simulate embodied experience by activating nonlinguistic areas in the reader's brain, and it may be as close to an autistic way of engaging with the world as any form of language will allow. Literature may even constitute, as I have come to believe, a wordy haven or home. (Or, with Barthelme in mind, we might say a wordy burrow or lair.)

In act IV, scene VI, of Shakespeare's tragedy *King Lear*, the Earl of Gloucester, whose eyes have been gouged out, begs to be led to the cliffs of Dover so that he may jump off and kill himself. While on the heath, he runs into Lear, who foolishly bequeathed his kingdom to his conniving daughters and has himself plunged into madness. As Lear decries the failure of ordinary sight to uncover ruthless deception, Gloucester invokes a different—and, in the end, superior—kind of vision. "Your eyes are in / a heavy case, your purse in a light; and yet you see how / this world goes," the king says. "I see it feelingly," Gloucester replies. While the blind may lack images generated by the retina, they do not lack images generated by the visual cortex, as research has shown. Gloucester's remark uncovers the neurological basis of the familiar *in*sight trope: mental imagery. Literature, we might say, actively cultivates the condition of Gloucester's blindness so as to enable the reader to feel beyond or beneath what her eyes merely see. Think of a novel or a play or a poem as a visual limbic system, a verbal cinema for the emotions. The poet Anne Sexton gets at the idea, albeit in an inverted form, when she writes in a letter, "I like you. Your eyes are full of language."

. . .

SEE IT FEELINGLY is about my experience discussing classic American novels (and a couple of short stories) with autistic readers across the spectrum. From the so-called "high-functioning" to the so-called "low-functioning"; from those who might "pass" as neurotypical, at least some of the time, to those whose perseverative behavior and inability to speak encourage others to dismiss them as intellectually incompetent. My son, for example, carries the latter label—"low-functioning"—though he is presently a college student with a 3.9

grade-point average. (That, for the record, is a lot better than his old man's undergraduate GPA!) My intention from the beginning of this project has been to eschew the customary focus on autistic deficits and to explore instead how a talent for sensory engagement—and, yes, strong feeling—might contribute productively to the reading process. If my son and other autistic people have taught me anything, it is to look for competence in unexpected forms and, when thwarted, to try again.

What, you might ask, are my qualifications for writing this book? First and foremost, I am a reader, an unapologetic lover of books. My attention, like my hands, is constantly divided. I read while eating; I read while doing the laundry; I even read while bathing myself. I am also a writer and English professor whose scholarly work falls largely into two categories: disability studies and cognitive approaches to literature. The latter involves the application of neuroscientific insights to literary understanding. The former tries to look at physiological distinctiveness—being blind or deaf, using a wheelchair—as just another way of existing in the world and not an occasion for pity. With the advent of a difference model in autism, self-advocates (and increasingly doctors and scientists) speak not of pathology but of neurodiversity.

In 2012–13 I was awarded a neurohumanities fellowship at Duke University's Institute for Brain Sciences. Before the academic year began, I participated in a boot camp for incoming doctoral students in neuroscience. For two weeks, from 8:00 A.M. to 7:00 P.M., I learned about the brain—I even touched one during a neuroanatomy lab! I also learned firsthand about some of the discipline's tools for probing the mysteries of human thought and action, such as event-related potentials (ERP), functional magnetic resonance imaging (fMRI), and transcranial magnetic stimulation (TMI). During my fellowship year, I took science classes, attended lectures, and taught a neurohumanities course. My fellowship project tried to account for what Ilona Roth has termed the "conundrum of autistic poetry." As Roth explains, "Prose and poetry written by people with ASD [autism spectrum disorders] call for investigation because to write a poem without imagination, or to write about oneself without awareness, would seem an oxymoron." I had had success teaching my son and other autistics to write poetry, and I wanted to try to square what the research literature said about autistic impairment with significant evidence to the contrary.

The project may sound academic, but what motivated it was the sheer joy of poetry—my own and that of the autistic poets with whom I worked. Here's how I once described the project to the six-year-old son of a colleague in Durham, North Carolina, who had precociously asked me about my "research." "Remember Eeyore, from *Winnie-the-Pooh*, who believes the other animals in the forest to be 'brainless'? There's 'only grey stuff . . . blown into their heads by mistake,' he whines, while of course celebrating his own intelligence. Eeyore writes poetry that Pooh says is superior to his own. Well, I'm trying to teach the other animals in the forest how to write poems. I want poetry to be as plentiful as the leaves on the trees!"

My other qualifications for writing this book? I talk about strange objects covered with fur for a living. My students at Grinnell College are very bright young people from all over the United States and, in fact, the world. Like playful puppies, they love to chew on texts, and they come to class prepared. At least a few times a semester, I get to witness the transformative power of literature. It's like reenacting my own awakening as an undergraduate: the son of a lawyer and an economics major becomes a bookworm. Picture me as Bill Murray in *Groundhog Day*, blissfully stuck in a time loop. I, too, am a weatherman of sorts, trafficking in the future, waiting for Punxsutawney Phil to emerge from his den, coaxing the flowers that he might herald from the ground.

Over the years, I've increasingly found myself teaching students at Grinnell who have what the medical community used to call Asperger syndrome, a relatively "mild" form of autism. (Now there's just a single diagnosis: ASD.) While the stereotype would look for students only in those disciplines that foreground logical thinking—in the aforementioned *Curious Incident of the Dog in the Night-Time*, the protagonist, though clearly deficient in most academic subjects, is studying to take his A-levels in math—at my college we don't allow this sort of rigid specialization. We glorify the liberal arts: we want our students to be well rounded. The economics majors take painting; the biology majors take anthropology; and the lit majors take calculus. And so even if an Aspie kid has failed to ascertain what kind of college he is attending and longs to take nothing but computer science, he's steered toward classes in the humanities, at least a few of them anyway.

I remember one young man who was in my introductory poetry-writing course. He seemed the epitome of the quiet math nerd—until, that is, he put pen to paper and out poured exquisite figures of speech and strangely elegantly rhythms. He used to walk the railroad tracks, which bisect the campus, before class, counting the ties. Back and forth he'd go, his head down, ostensibly oblivious to the world above and around those wooden timbers. I could see him from my office in the English/History building. The higher-ups in Student

Affairs were concerned that he might get hit by a train, but if anyone knew the railroad's schedule—the line moved corn sweetener from one end of the state to the other—it was this young man. "Counting ties calms my anxiety," he told me. "I love their symmetry."

Because the college itself is quite quirky, he was able to make it through. (We tend to attract the alienated bohemian type. As a colleague once joked, "It's a place where misfits thrive.") Because the college is also quite small, we are able to get to know our students and provide support. Sadly, this is far from the rule in higher education, and many with Asperger syndrome or "high-functioning" autism fall through the cracks. And those with much more significant autism never make it to college in the first place. By some estimates, my son will be just the tenth nonspeaking person with autism ever to earn a bachelor's degree.

This book is in part a response to this predicament. While I'm generally not a fan of distance learning—I prefer an actual classroom—I started to use Skype with a few autistics who had been much less fortunate in their educational pursuits than my son or the young man mentioned above. They lived in other states, and Skype seemed our only chance for regular, half-bodied connection. We'd read a novel—Tim O'Brien's *The Things They Carried*, say—and talk about it. Although an ardent inclusion advocate, I quickly noticed an advantage of this technology (once you overlooked its occasional fitfulness). Because autistics take in so much detail, they tend to become exhausted in unfamiliar places. A kind of hypervigilance reigns, which brings anxiety. Being able to work in their home environments allowed them to relax and to concentrate. They could also take a break when necessary and tic or stim as much as they wanted. Such actions wouldn't be deemed "disruptive."

After several years of conducting regular Skype tutorials, I began to ponder the idea of a narrative about my experience. Why not share the compelling insights of autistic readers? Perhaps it would inspire people to view autism differently. Chatting with eager, neurodivergent minds had certainly invigorated my own love of literature. Again and again, books I knew quite well had come alive in fresh ways. For instance, reading Mark Twain's novel *The Adventures of Huckleberry Finn* with DJ compelled me to think more deeply about its adoption conceit and the kind of emotion that a novel can elicit in readers. I remember being astonished as much by DJ's ferocious identification with the runaway slave Jim as with the lonesome river itself. The latter's melancholy intelligence seemed akin, he said, to that of a nonspeaking autist—both remain unrecognized.

When I discussed Herman Melville's novel *Moby-Dick* (1851) with Tito Mukhopadhyay, a nonspeaking young man from Austin, Texas, he identified so intensely with the book's cetacean hero that he began to view the current obsession with finding a cure for autism as a kind of whale hunt. In the novel, of course, a megalomaniacal ship captain named Ahab seeks to avenge the loss of his leg at the hands—or, rather, the *jaws*—of Moby Dick, a huge white Leviathan. By the time Tito and I were done reading, even I thought the novel, that strange object encased in blubber, was an allegory of the present-day autism wars. Interestingly enough, Tito found an actual autistic character in the book. When he called my attention to how Melville describes the carpenter who fashions Ahab a leg, I was shocked, though perhaps I shouldn't have been. Autism is by no means a new condition, even though it wasn't officially recognized until the early 1940s. With the novel's elaborate evocation of the sperm whale's sensing, *Moby-Dick* turned out to be an excellent way of exploring sensory-processing differences in autism. Whatever the challenges that autistics face, one thing is clear: their sensory lives are much richer and more immediate than our own. Tito, who has authored a number of well-received books but never been included in a regular school, is wildly and uncommonly synesthetic. Both auditory and tactile stimulation have a visual, and sometimes even an olfactory, component.

And so, deciding to write a book, I recruited some additional conversation partners. Because I have my doctorate in American literature, I opted to stick with American classics. Whenever I could, I tried to pick a novel that might resonate with a particular partner. For example, I knew that Jamie Burke was keenly interested in Native American history and culture, so I chose Leslie Marmon Silko's novel *Ceremony* (1977), which tells the story of a Laguna-Pueblo veteran who suffers from posttraumatic stress disorder and gradually journeys back to wholeness. The novel promotes a Native understanding of health, and I was curious to see how Jamie conceived of his own therapeutic journey to better sensory integration, movement, and speech. With the intervention of an innovative occupational therapist, he had learned to type independently and then, at the age of thirteen, to read aloud what he was typing. He can now speak conversationally. More and more, scientists are viewing autism as a complex sensorimotor condition and not some innate defect of imagination or sociality. Silko's *Ceremony* presents something like a Native American version of occupational therapy with its emphasis on whole body healing through ritualistic movement. Jamie's visuospatial prowess and his acute appreciation of pattern illuminated both the novel's spiritual geography and the subtle key to the protagonist's recovery.

Sometimes I got lucky. I'd read online that Dora Raymaker had once worked as a computer programmer. She circumvented her dyscalculia (or difficulty making sense of numbers) by seeing code as a series of colorful, interlocking 3D shapes. She is now a community-based researcher, despite sometimes being unable to speak for periods at a time. We had both appeared in an autism documentary, *Loving Lampposts, Living Autistic*, and in the film she typed everything she said. Dora was apparently interested in artificial intelligence, so I proposed that we read Philip K. Dick's novel *Do Androids Dream of Electric Sheep?* (1968), in which a bounty hunter tracks down and kills six rogue androids. Although she hadn't read the novel before, she'd seen *Blade Runner*, its filmic adaptation, at least twenty-five times—indeed, it was her favorite movie.

Incredibly, she was also a budding cyberpunk writer whose own futuristic novels feature autistic heroes who must work around their poorly understood disabilities while, at the same time, exploiting their unique abilities. A classic of science fiction, Dick's *Androids* hinges on the question of whether the replicants, who are said to lack empathy, are really less human than the empathy-challenged humans who hunt them. For years, of course, scientists have claimed that autistics lack empathy. Codirector of the Academic Autism Spectrum Partnership in Research and Education, Dora read the novel as if she were adhering to the principle of community-based participatory research. According to this principle, research subjects—in this case, androids—should be given a chance to weigh in on questions about their essential nature. Approaching the novel like this, she fruitfully unpacked Dick's coruscating ironies.

Eugenie Belkin describes herself as "White. Japanese. Mongolian. Black. Cherokee. Indonesian. Female. Autistic. Deaf. Jewish." She is also the mother of an autistic child. All too frequently, autism is conceived of as a "white" disorder, and it is rarely discussed in relation to another race or ethnicity, let alone another disability. Nor is it discussed in relation to parenting—indeed, the operative assumption is that people with disabilities shouldn't parent. With Eugenie, I chose to read Carson McCullers's novel *The Heart Is a Lonely Hunter* (1940), which features, among other characters, two deaf individuals, a labor agitator, a teenage girl on the cusp of sexual awakening, and an African American doctor, all of whom are psychologically alienated. In the novel, one of the deaf characters becomes mentally ill and is sent to an institution. Set in Georgia, which had the fifth highest rate of sterilization of the mentally ill and "deficient" in the first half of the twentieth century, the novel maps a terrain of immense isolation and repression. "The most fatal thing a man can try to do is stand alone," the doctor says, and yet how to stand together? (The word "autism" can be translated as "the person alone.") How to communicate across insurmountable divides?

Like many people with Asperger syndrome, Eugenie received an autism diagnosis in adulthood, and she represents an especially intriguing example of what academics like to call intersectional identity. What would a sense of connectedness mean for a mixed-race, deaf, autistic woman whose hearing, yet autistic, son passes as white? A classically trained ballerina and ice-skating coach who is fluent in American Sign Language and who has one cochlear implant, Eugenie "thinks in feelings," as she puts it. For her, the translation of fluid emotion into something mechanically cognitive remains a challenge, though she is a quick thinker and an effective writer. Although she struggles with motion dyslexia, her dedication to ballet, a historically white art form, suggests an antidote to the clumsiness of narrow identity labels and politics.

In the book's final chapter, I converse with Temple, about whom much has been written and yet about whom much is apparently still to be known. When she recited lines by heart from William Wordsworth's "Ode: Intimations of Immortality from Recollections of Early Childhood," I was stunned. Nobody had ever really asked about her experience with literature. Temple did seem less emotionally engaged as a reader, but that judgment is relative, not absolute, and anyway she brought other strengths to the discussion table. The old adage about autism—"When you've seen one person with autism, you've seen exactly one person with autism"—very much applies to autistic reading. While DJ, Tito, Burke, Dora, Eugenie, and Temple share some notable similarities, what distinguishes them is just as interesting and important. Autism, like so-called neurotypicality, is conspicuously heterogeneous.

In an effort to be sensitive to Temple's sequencing challenges, busy schedule, and avowed interests, I suggested that we read two short stories from a recent anthology, *Among Animals: The Lives of Animals and Humans in Contemporary Short Fiction*. The first is about a family that ethically raises the animals it eats. Narrated from a young child's point of view, it presents a father who insists on naming a new pig "Meat" so that everyone will be reminded of its fate. The second is about a female researcher whose devotion to gentoo penguins in Antarctica leads to a kind of lonely misanthropy.

Eschewing romantic relationships, she finds herself drawn into a brief sexual relationship with a tourist who was left behind by his boat.

I must admit that I tipped the scales of readerly engagement with Temple. I was confident she would respond to a story about the politics of meat consumption. But would she appreciate what the medium of fiction can do with this familiar topic? I predicted that she would identify with the solitary researcher in the second story, yet here she surprised me. Like any other reader, she brought her personal experiences to bear on the central conflict. Instead of lamenting her own steadfast celibacy, however, she offered a quasi-feminist defense of it. She related that her aunt, at whose ranch she was introduced to livestock as a teenager, had an abusive husband and that she'd never seen a single marriage she admired. In fact, she had witnessed too many women, including some of her students, sacrifice their own ambitions for love. "I'm all about my career," she said. Suddenly, what many, including Temple herself at times, presented as a nearly inevitable consequence of autism seemed anything but. Neurological explanations for remaining celibate gave way to psychological and social ones. As in literature itself, complex motivation reigned.

"Will such a book prove anything?" a friend of mine recently asked. No, it won't *prove* anything. My data set, if you can call it that, is ridiculously small, and I strategically chose the books and participants. What is more, the project is intentionally, if casually, ethnographical. I spend time with my conversation partners, report what they have to say. In the process, I become their friend and, yes, their champion. I also become their student—not only of autism, but also of literature. The poet Robert Graves reminds us, "In love, as in sport, the amateur status must be strictly maintained." In this book, I try desperately not to be an expert, or at least one who refuses to learn anything himself and who alienates all but fellow English professors with his recondite discourse. Instead, I tell a story, pitched halfway between memoir and literary criticism, about neurodiverse brains. I look at the emerging science of autism, and I compare it to what we know about how neurotypical brains read poems and novels. In the end, the book is about loving literature—truly, madly, deeply, as it were—and I hope at least some of that love is contagious.

Readers who have a horse in the autism race may be tempted to label my conversation partners anomalies. If I generalize about competence or potential competence, it is because so many people generalize about incompetence, and that negative generalization serves as yet another barrier to achievement, to say nothing of autistic fulfillment and happiness. When no one expects an autistic child to be good at language arts, he is found anywhere but in the language arts classroom. A few years back, I wrote to the authors of a study on metaphoric comprehension in autism to object to their sweeping claim of impairment. When I presented evidence of comprehension in individual autistics, the authors dismissed it as statistically meaningless. "Probabilistically," they said, autistics have great difficulty with metaphor.

But is it wise to reject such evidence out of hand, especially when we still don't know much about autism (and the many subtypes that comprise it) and when access to education and therapy is so uneven? Lisa Zunshine has pointed out that we don't describe Henry James, William Shakespeare, or Jane Austen as "outliers on the neurotypical spectrum." No, "we feel that they are 'like us,' only more intensely so, glorifying the community of 'us,' by showing 'us' what 'we' are capable of." Let's think of exemplary autistics like this. And while we're at it, let's imagine a more expansive and inclusive "us": people who, as Umberto Eco once put it, "live for books."

· prologue ·

RIVER OF WORDS, RAFT OF OUR
CONJOINED NEUROLOGIES

> I looked at my hands, to see if I was the same person now that I was free. There
> was such a glory over everything; the sun came like gold through the trees . . .
> and I felt like I was in heaven.
>   If you hear the dogs, keep going. If you see the torches in the woods, keep
> going. Don't ever stop. Keep going. If you want a taste of freedom, keep going.
>   — HARRIET TUBMAN

In the eighth grade, my son, DJ, who is autistic and who uses a text-to-voice
synthesizer to communicate, became so distraught while learning about Harriet Tubman and a little Polish boy whom the Germans murdered that he
couldn't continue reading. His breathing was heavy; his eyes had glazed over;
his heart pounded in the narrow cage of his chest. In response to his ninth-
grade English teacher's question "What are your strengths as a reader?" he
replied, "I feel characters' feelings." He then added, "Dread very scary books
and wish I took breathing easy mom to class to create more security."

In the often sterile language of literary critics, DJ can be said to have
identified with these historical figures. Having been abandoned by his birth
mother at the age of three and subjected to unspeakable abuse in foster care,
he experienced a similar barbarism. In the case of Tubman, the identification was particularly intense. DJ saw in this leader of the Underground Railroad what he calls "political freedom fighting," and he imagined working
on behalf of his "people": namely, those with autism who cannot speak and
who have been assumed to be intellectually disabled.

Consider what DJ wrote about Moses, as Tubman was called, a few days after first learning about her. The process of composition was no less physiologically agitating than reading had been; indeed, he periodically let loose with shrieks and headbanging. So that you understand the first line of the piece, let me say that "breaking the barriers" is the official motto of a disability rights group whose website features a speech by my son. Let me also say that "frees" refers to those who don't have autism and, thus, who claim a privileged position in society.

Estimating Harriet Tubman Respectfully

If we're breaking the barriers, great freedom fearfully awaits. Harriet realized, until freedom treated her people with respect, her intestines seemed unsettled, her heart beat resentfully, and her fear never disappeared. The challenges she faced each day were far greater than anything you and your people have ever endured; breathing resentful air, great very hard breaths, undermines heartfelt feelings and deeply effects the western world. Pedestals rest on hurt, estimated dressed not great human beings deserted by frees. I heartily entreat you to help my unfree, treated responsibly, great, hip, jumping self to walk the trail. You kind, responded easy breathing frees don't understand how terrifying seemingly fresh freedom is.

It should be clear that a term like "identification" can't convey this sort of readerly cathexis. We might instead speak of "intimate history" or "relational time" and note just how visceral the engagement seems. DJ feels Tubman's "unsettled intestines," "very hard breaths," and "racing heart" because his own walk down freedom's trail, as the only fully included high school student with classical autism in Iowa, was equivalently "terrifying." As he morphs into her, so she morphs into him: a fellow traveler in need of respectful estimation. I've come to think that my son has borrowed the language of educational assessment and deployed it ironically. In the chapter he wrote for my book *Reasonable People*, he remarked of his former special-ed instructors, "No one was assessing me as sweet." It's as if the flawed judgment of ability (and thus of human worth) at the hands of the powerful has become the primary lens through which he views experience.

His frustration with the dominant majority can be seen in a piece from the fifth grade that he wrote for an Elks Club writing contest:

The great United States of America is breathtakingly not free. Equality is not as sacred because not everyone has access to it. Freedom is not as available as many people think. First, free people treat my people, very smart people who type to communicate, as mindless. Second, they underestimate us as very bad instead of reaching out to us. The creators of everyone's very important Declaration of Independence wasted their breath.

Needless to say, DJ didn't win the contest, as the Elks were hoping for something a bit more positive. I frankly love the repetition of "breath"—the way the paragraph begins and ends with this word. It's as if DJ had condensed the primary physical symptom of his anxiety—heavy breathing—into a political modifier. My son was demanding his place in America. I remember taking note of the signature trope, which rediscovers the body as a way of reviving the cliché, and picturing democracy itself in respiratory distress.

The concern with breathing shows up repeatedly in his writings, particularly in the sixth grade when he composed the final chapter of *Reasonable People*. In that chapter he includes a letter he wrote to his middle school principal after a meltdown threatened to have him expelled: "It's very important to me to be at Grinnell Middle School. . . . I very much value teachers who give nice instructions breathing easily." "You ignored the resentment in my young breath," he says, grateful for another chance to prove himself. "As long as I treat people resentfully, I will miss out on telling people that kids who don't talk deserve to be in a real school." "Respect for others," he concedes, "is important. Respect for underestimated kids is important, too, because they read and resent testing that mistakenly identifies them as retarded." At the end of the chapter, punning off of the book's title, he declares, "Reasonable people promote very, very easy breathing."

While there's no doubt that the fight-or-flight impulses of posttraumatic stress disorder have contributed to DJ's anxiety, the experience of inclusion and the literacy at its core have—paradoxically—as well. Learning to read empowered him to become a disability rights activist, and yet it also awakened him to the story of his early childhood and the often negative meaning of his difference. Like a boy learning to lift himself out of the deep end of a pool, he emerged from the sensory murk of an alternative neurology only to be clobbered by the sunlit clarity of what had been wrought upon him. He found himself running to, and from, words—as if they were, interchangeably, a police officer and an assailant. Reading became both a form of survival as he bonded with characters like himself and a kind of traumatic channeling of their injuries.

After being utterly alone as a small child, he demanded, as a twelve- and thirteen-year-old, the constant company of his adoptive parents, especially while doing work for English or history class, his hand often resting in one of ours as we read with him a particular assignment. At times we wondered if he would survive literacy, which he had achieved in the fourth and fifth grades, long after most schoolchildren, and then mastered, rocketing forward—to the point that he graduated from high school with a straight A average and is currently attending Oberlin College as its first nonspeaking student with autism. During these middle school years, a tense narrative would invariably elicit a full-blown flashback and the ashen visage of the war veteran. Sometimes we'd have to restrain him to prevent self-injury, his legs and arms flailing.

Of course, in many ways, DJ's emergence into literacy was no different from a typical child's, however belatedly it occurred. In "Children Selecting Books in a Library," the poet Randall Jarrell captures the mythic danger of this unsuspecting skill:

With beasts and gods, above, the wall is bright.
The child's head, bent to the book-colored shelves,
Is slow and sidelong and food-gathering,
Moving in blind grace . . . yet from the mural, Care,
The grey-eyed one, fishing the morning mist,
Seizes the baby hero by the hair
And whispers, in the tongue of gods and children,
Words of a doom as ecumenical as dawn
But blanched like dawn, with dew.

Drawn like an animal to a baited trap, the child feels the spring-loaded words come down upon him. And yet, this violence, this "doom," seems strangely pleasurable; it is the force of what I previously called identification—and what might as well be thought of as a kind of compassion. "Read meanwhile . . . hunt among the shelves, as dogs do, grasses / . . . ," Jarrell writes, "we live / by trading another's sorrow for our own." As the child grows up, whatever was unnerving about this activity falls away.

Not so for autistics who, even after they've been reading for some time, cannot trade sorrow as nonchalantly as their counterparts. Though you wouldn't know it from prevailing stereotypes, autistics *do* experience this emotion and quite intensely. In fact, it often overwhelms them. Stephen Shore, for example, speaks of "fusing" with another's suffering, whether real or imagined, of being so attuned to the pain that it becomes his own.

Rita Rubin has told me that her daughter Sue, star of the Academy Award–nominated *Autism Is a World*, watched the film *Malcolm X* from another room—the violence and oppression were just too much for her. Neurotypical engagement seems, in contrast, to be much less full or dynamic; it involves moving toward the sufferer-who-is-not-me while vigilantly preserving a sense of separateness. My son's autism, I came to believe, was acting as a second accelerant, igniting the timber-frame of narrative and turning it into a four-alarm fire. Along with his trauma, it prevented a more stable or removed reading experience.

Call this autist if not an ideal reader, then a most invested one. DJ had taught me much about our deepest emotions and their centrality to literature—to all of the arts. Admonishing the painters of his time, the eighteenth-century critic Denis Diderot wrote, "First, move me, surprise me, . . . make me tremble, weep, shudder; outrage me. Delight my eyes afterward if you can." But whenever DJ and I sat down with a book, I found myself playing the part of the ancient Chinese philosopher Lao Tzu: "Do you imagine the universe is agitated? Go into the desert at night and look at the stars. This practice should answer the question." Truth be told, equanimity wasn't my strong suit. Once, in a discussion of the autism spectrum, DJ remarked, "Hoping that fresh thinking, very nervous dad is autistic."

Literature had saved me as a young man. When I was growing up, any sign of emotion was considered a weakness. Like those Chilean miners in the Copiapó mining accident, feelings *belonged* some 2,300 feet underground. While other families clumsily confronted their unhappiness, my family walked away from the mine and sat down to dinner. Literature, in contrast, drew me into myself. It handed me a shovel and said, "Dig." It offered safe passage to and from a complex inner life. (When, after seventeen days, a borehole reached the miners, the men taped a message to the end of the drill: "We are well in the shelter the 33 of us.")

DJ, of course, had the opposite problem: he didn't need to locate his emotions; he needed to subdue them. While he loved encountering great fictional and historical heroes, it took too much out of him. His mind was like a cast-iron stove that lacked a dampener, burning so hot it shook and turned ominously red. Or his mind, as Herman Melville wrote, was like "a bit of wreck in the mid-Atlantic." My son needed a future in words, words that wouldn't drive him under and fill his lungs with dread.

By the time tenth grade approached, I devoted myself to making reading more manageable for DJ. I knew that the key text in his multigenre, multitradition literature class would be *The Adventures of Huckleberry Finn*, which famously presents an adopted—and abused—child protagonist. "Pap got too handy with his hick'ry, and I couldn't stand it. I was all over welts" (33), Huck tells us at the beginning. As if this weren't worrisome enough, the novel explores the issue of slavery, subjecting Jim to the worst sort of comic shenanigans. DJ might resent the lighthearted approach or ignore it all together, "feeling," in his word, the grave danger of a runaway slave.

I decided to create a ritual to cushion the impact: we'd do his reading for English in the master bedroom. A recent addition to our one-and-a-half story Queen Anne home, the room has five skylights but no windows. With its sloping roof and picturesque purchase on the heavens, it feels as snug as a well-lit cave. Or a raft with a wigwam on it, "to get under in blazing weather and rainy, and to keep things dry" (89), as Huck says. I told DJ that the bed was our floating haven; the novel, our wide and meandering Mississippi. Whenever he'd get that ashen look on his face or threaten to bang his head, I'd declare in the best Missouri twang I could muster, "There [ain't] no home like a raft, after all. Other places do seem so cramped up and smothery, but a raft don't. You feel mighty free and easy and comfortable on a raft" (162).

I figured I'd encourage my son to allegorize the reading process itself, to dedicate his considerable imagination to becoming not Huck honey but an exemplary reader, lighting out for the territory of crafted sentences and alternative values. I wanted him to feel at home in literature: to regard the current of a writer's prose, to hear its swirling cadences—not as an escape from life but as a beautiful refraction of it. "The sky looks ever so deep when you lay down on your back in the moonshine" (49), Huck notes, and lying on our backs in that comfortable queen-sized bed, we discovered a depth that could sustain us, an expanse of vision in, or under, which we could never feel "cramped up and smothery." Adoptive father and son, nonautistic writer and autistic high school student—what were these supine lumps but conjoined neurologies encountering the splendor of a classic book?

My distancing strategy proved effective if only because DJ had started saying that he wanted to be a writer and because I frequently interrupted whatever book I was reading aloud to ask how a particular scene had been staged or how an image was resonating. "As the author," I'd say, "you're the one behind the magic. How's it done here?" I also encouraged DJ to be critical, to take Twain or any other writer to task for their questionable aesthetics or politics. By junior year he could calmly critique fiction's use of suspense to "string the reader along." "Many people joyfully succumb to this form of entertainment," he wrote in a paper. "Having never experienced hopeless terror in their own lives and knowing that the author will ultimately resolve the tension, they enjoy reading books that terrify them." (Years before, he had complained about my memoir, which tracks his evolving literacy through a series of verbatim exchanges, because it had turned his life into a kind of pleasure. "I resent these very hurtful conversations being easy reading for others," he declared. Although he granted me permission to publish the memoir—"Kids need our help," he reasoned—neither the content nor the way that it was typically consumed sat well with him.)

Don't get me wrong: reading remained a real challenge. Trying to get through Jon Krakauer's *Into Thin Air*, one of the assigned texts the following summer, may have been as difficult as the Everest descent the book so effectively describes. By the time Rob Hall speaks to his wife for the very last time, patched through on the satellite phone, low on oxygen, his hands and feet horrifically frostbitten, telling her, "Sleep well, my sweetheart. Please don't worry too much," DJ was screaming at the top of his own oxygen-depleted lungs. I, to be fair, wasn't doing very well either. Reading truly was like making it down that blizzard-effaced col: each sentence a step you didn't think your feet could take. At one point, DJ typed out "foster care," his analogical mind knitting together two experiences of extreme helplessness. How could I not recall what he had written about his years as a wordless and, in some sense, fingerless little boy? "When I lived in fear, I yearned to urge just one especially humane free gesture to tell someone, 'Just hear me. I really need help.'" Imagine being so plagued by fine-motor impediments that you can't even command your hands to act out what was happening to you.

There was simply no way to render this read a lazy river float, and yet DJ *did* get through it. Even more impressive, he got over it quickly. Was he maturing? Was his brain—o wonderful plastic thing!—actually becoming a bit more typical? Had an emotional dampener begun to assert itself? All I knew for sure was that reading had become unambivalently important to him, as a paper he wrote at the end of his senior year shows. It begins like this:

> Last Thursday night was the Academic Excellence Award ceremony at my school. I yearned to walk up on stage and shake the principal's hand without flapping my arms, but I did not succeed. At first I felt disappointed, but when I saw my dad waving to me with a huge smile on my face, I felt proud. I looked great *and* autistic at the same time. I realized in my own life something I had begun to learn from the books

I was reading: simply conforming to the dominant culture is not always a worthy goal. In fact, real change is only possible when different thinkers free people to open their eyes to new ways of being.

Just after this paper, my curly-haired nonconformist wrote a personal essay about the challenges, both physiological and psychological, of his inclusion experience—what he called, invoking Tubman once again, "my reassessed as smart self's walk down freedom's trail." Noting that he "look[s] to her for encouragement every day," he described his sensory dislocations: losing functional hearing and sight, especially when anxious; needing the heaviest of backpacks to locate his body in space; having occasionally to jolt his senses by purposefully crashing to the ground. All of this he conveyed while narrating a typical morning's journey to school—his heart a flock of pigeons in his chest, freedom still a distant mirage. Up to the front doors and through the swirling mass of students in the halls, he moves, trying to reach, as he put it, "dear Mr. Rudolph and the safe house of my Honors American Literature classroom."

one

FROM A WORLD AS FLUID
AS THE SEA

You must learn to heed your senses. Humans use but a tiny percentage of theirs. They barely look, they rarely listen, they never smell, and they think that they can only experience feelings through their skin. But they talk, oh, do they talk.
— MICHAEL SCOTT, *The Alchemyst*

"Hands in your pocket, Tito! Hands in your pocket!" Soma said in her customary manner. We had just climbed the stairs of Arrowhead, Herman Melville's farmhouse-turned-museum in western Massachusetts, and we were about to enter the great author's study. Tito struggles with perseverative behavior, especially around books, and Soma, his mother, feared that he might touch something he wasn't allowed to touch. Like a cage for small birds, the pockets of his pants would offer some resistance to his fluttering fingers.

Melville had lived at Arrowhead from 1850 to 1863, and he had written the epic tale for which he is famous, *Moby-Dick*, along with the novel *Pierre* and stories such as "Bartleby, the Scrivener" and "Benito Cereno," just a few feet from where we were standing. The writing table, we learned from our guide, wasn't original, but the view from the window certainly was. Mount Greylock, of the Taconic mountain range, loomed in "excellent majesty," as Melville once wrote. Though it was only late October and nothing but fallen leaves blanketed the ground, I could imagine the scene in winter: snow-covered Greylock breaching the treeline like the hump of a giant, white sperm whale.

To the right of the table, an iron harpoon leaned against the wall; to the left, a door led to a small bedroom in which Nathaniel Hawthorne had slept when visiting Melville. Hawthorne's proximity to the study seemed terrifically apt. Melville had once thanked the older writer, who some believe encouraged him to turn a typical whaling yarn into a gloomy metaphysical adventure, for "dropping germanous seeds in [his] soul." On the writing table itself lay a copy of *Moby-Dick*, opened to the "Mast-head" chapter. "There you stand," Ishmael tells us in the chapter, "a hundred feet above the silent decks, striding along the deep, as if the masts were gigantic stilts, while beneath you and between your legs . . . swim the hugest monsters of the sea" (151). Masthead watchmen must "sing out every time" (153) they see a whale or a ship or an approaching storm. Skilled watchmen, I had read, could not only spot a whale some eight miles away, but also discern what kind of whale it was by virtue of the spout.

Before Soma or I could stop them, the birds in Tito's pockets got loose. They flitted above the desk, lifting up the book and encouraging his nose to inspect the contents. If one sensory modality predominates in Tito, it is smell, which is often the case in autism. The senses are generally heightened in the condition and not conventionally integrated. In a bit of daily writing produced while reading *Moby-Dick* with me, he had blithely reported, "Whenever I get hold of a book, I sniff through the pages. After that I look at what those pages show. Some people question my unique engagement with books. I answer them by sniffing more books, inviting them to join me in the search for a whale-like smell."

In the same piece of writing, he had recalled auditioning for a job at a bookstore. Because he was a published author and loved to read, some higher-up in his school district—Tito was a nonspeaking, special-ed student with classical or "severe" autism—had thought he should spend his adult days around books. "All senses riding the one sense of smell, I entered the store," he'd recounted. "Rowing my nose, I halted in front of a shelf. The smell of books intensified. There was plenty to do with my nose." As his potential employers looked on, he proceeded to sniff volume after volume—from *Horticulture for Professionals* to *Tax Law for Dummies*. He was the Russian writer Gogol's man without a nose, Major Kovalyov. Rather, he was the nose itself, insisting on a readerly life for nostrils.

In a nod to the biblical story of Jonah, Tito had written, "The vital smell of those books kept me alive in the stomach of the store." He breathed in the glorious odor of the pages and breathed out what he called "unnecessary social consciousness." By that he meant his knowledge of proper comportment. "The thought that I was somewhere being observed by curious sets of eyes, which pondered my ability to work at a bookstore, was breathed out, too," he'd added. The young man was lost—or, maybe from another perspective, found—in smell.

"It wasn't my idea to work there," Tito had explained, annoyed as much by his lack of employment possibilities as by the fact that he was always at the mercy of other people's ideas—whether those people were school administrators, autism professionals, or the average, gawking Joe on the bus. How could he work in a bookstore? That would be like having an arsonist work in a match factory or a harpooner work in the Boston Aquarium! "Why can't I just be a writer?" he'd complained, which was, of course, the lament of many a scrivener before him.

Needless to say, Tito didn't get the job. His nose had been too much in the product, even if that product was a book and even if certain books—novels, say, or volumes of poems—demand of both writer and reader profound sensory engagement. As we stood in Melville's study, that very same nose was too much in the "Mast-head" chapter. It was sniffing out whales beneath the surface of the page. Who needs vision when you have a schnoz! Soma gasped and quickly took the tome out of Tito's hands. Although I had arranged the trip, including this private tour of Arrowhead, and was in theory responsible for Tito's actions, I secretly relished his olfactory panache. My friend was excited. We had just spent seventeen months reading and discussing *Moby-Dick* by Skype, two chapters a week, and here we were in Melville's house, the book of books before us.

. . .

I FIRST MET Tito Rajarshi Mukhopadhyay in the summer of 2008, when he was nineteen years old. I was interviewing him for a project on neurodiversity at his home in Austin, Texas. Anyone who knew anything about the classical form of the "disorder" knew about Tito. If Temple Grandin had become the face of relatively minimal impairment in autism, then Tito had become the face—the promising face—of significant impairment. His story is really quite extraordinary.

He grew up in Mysore and Bangalore, India, where at the time autism was considered a form of psychosis. Repeatedly refused admission to school, he was educated at home by his mother. As a boy, he traveled to England to be evaluated by scientists affiliated with the National Autistic Society—in particular, Lorna Wing and Judith Gould, "legends of autism research," as Tito once referred to them. A significant challenge to the notion of "mental retardation" in the "severely" autistic, he quickly became something of a sensation. At age twelve, he published his first book, *Beyond the Silence*, in the United Kingdom. (In its American publication three years later, it would have the title *The Mind Tree*.) On the back cover of the book, the neurologist Oliver Sacks gushed, "Amazing, shocking, too, for it has usually been assumed that deeply autistic people are scarcely capable of introspection or deep thought, let alone of poetic or metaphoric leaps of imagination. . . . Tito gives the lie to all of these assumptions, and forces us to reconsider the condition of the deeply autistic."

A writer friend of mine has labeled the book "Mozartian"—it's that precocious. In the section that gives the American edition its title, a banyan tree, with no way of communicating its awareness, yearns to ask a man who sits in the shade it provides why he is sad. "I have been gifted this mind," the tree says. "I can hope, I can imagine, I can love, but I cannot ask." Clearly a figure for the nonspeaking autist, the tree has trouble relating thought to embodiment: "My concerns . . . are trapped . . . somewhere in my depths, maybe in my roots, maybe in my bark or maybe all around my radius." While the prose is quite lyrical, the book is peppered with actual poetry—sometimes Tito stops midsentence to offer a verse. At the conclusion of *The Mind Tree* appear poems that he wrote for a BBC documentary about his life. In one, Tito the tourist wittily takes in the sights:

Tower of London
Strong as death
Breathing the echoes of last breaths
Of those punished by the law
Their misty breath is what I saw
And there's Big Ben. Big Ben
Telling us now is when
And Churchill Churchill standing there
In the chill

After describing the typical London tumult—"people of busy mood / . . . under the cloudy skies"—the poem concludes:

I did not manage to see the Queen
Yet her palace with grave discipline

Stood since yonder ages thus
I saluted it from the red bus

With the success of his book and the BBC documentary, the autism world saluted Tito. He received an invitation from Cure Autism Now (CAN; it would later merge with Autism Speaks) to come to Los Angeles. The plan was for him to serve as a high-profile figure for the organization and for his mother to help other nonspeaking children with autism learn to communicate. Although not the first classical autist to demonstrate his intelligence, he was marketed as such, and because Soma had taught him how to write and to type with his own hand unaided, the experts took notice. "Tito is for real," Dr. Michael Merzenich, a neuroscientist at the University of San Francisco Medical School, insisted in a *New York Times* article from 2002. "He unhesitatingly responds to factual questions about books that he has read or about experiences that he has had in . . . high fidelity." "I've seen Tito sit in front of an audience of scientists and take questions from the floor," Dr. Matthew Belmonte, an autism expert at Cambridge University, reported in the same article. "He taps out intelligent, witty answers on a laptop with a voice synthesizer. No one is touching him. He communicates on his own."

Soma called the technique that she had pioneered with Tito the "rapid prompting method" (RPM). As her website puts it, "RPM uses a 'Teach-Ask' paradigm for eliciting responses through intensive verbal, auditory, visual and/or tactile prompts." It shouldn't be thought of as "mere pointing at a letter board," she says, though learning to put a pencil through the board's cut-out letters is what the technique has come to be associated with. In order to overcome significant sensory-processing disturbances as well as profound motor planning (and initiating) challenges, Soma first employs a range of exercises designed to capture the nonspeaking autist's attention, to engage him or her cognitively, and to ground the idea of volition in the body. The constant verbal commands, issued at a pace that matches the person's self-stimulatory behavior (rocking, say, or finger-flicking), plug into and override that rhythm. Once the autist is using the letter board and has mastered spelling out words, Soma begins to ask him or her questions: at first, simple fact-based questions and then more complicated, open-ended ones. Ultimately, the goal is independent writing and typing—the letter board lays a kind of communicative foundation.

Eventually Soma and Tito left CAN; Tito loathed its cure agenda. While the organization was all too happy to champion his "miraculous breakthrough," its primary mission was to eradicate autism, and it knew no bounds in deploying fear as a fundraising vehicle. In *The Mind Tree*, Tito wrote, "I dream that we can grow in a matured society where nobody would be 'normal or abnormal' but just human beings, accepting any other human being—ready to grow together." He would later recount, "I was astonished by Mother's involvement with the belief that autism is a disease and needs a cure. Mother had always believed in my thoughts and judgment before. How could she participate in a system that classified me as sick? Did mother really think I was less of a person?" When they at last extricated themselves from CAN, they moved to Austin and established HALO, an RPM clinic.

While Soma offered instruction at HALO, Tito spent the day in a self-contained, special-ed classroom—basically a holding pen for people with cognitive disabilities. There was no place else for him to go when she was at work: he needed an aide to support him, and Soma, a single mother who hadn't yet become a U.S. citizen, couldn't fight to include him in regular education or manage that inclusion once it had been established. It seemed preposterous that someone this talented—this well known in the autism world—could be consigned to such a fate. With a sort of heartbreaking pragmatism, he acceded to the indignities of special education. Before leaving for work, and after returning, Soma would tutor Tito. They would do an hour and a half of humanities and then an hour and a half of science. They would make of necessity a virtue. Who needed a typical education when a more rigorous one could be provided at home?

If my son's inclusion had taught me anything, it was that it hugely benefited from, if not demanded, two parents and enormous economic and cultural capital—things that Tito lacked. My wife, Emily, had given up her career as an inclusion specialist to manage DJ's own inclusion. No one knew better than I how chancy life could be: my son, who had lived in poverty and who had been diagnosed as "profoundly mentally retarded," was now an upper-middle-class honors student at our local high school. Some kids get lucky, and some do not—there was no ignoring this simple, unforgiving truth. The fact that DJ had in effect won the lottery only mocked the ordinary failure of our educational and economic systems. In a poem called "Hap," the British poet Thomas Hardy writes, "Crass Casualty obstructs the sun and rain, / And dicing Time for gladness casts a moan. . . ." For nearly a year after we adopted DJ, the Florida Department of Children and Family Services would call at dinnertime to see if we might take another kid. My exasperated "no"s were a course in bitter realism.

Homeschooling had obviously worked for Tito—at the time of our interview he had just published a third book—but I sensed that he still pined for the social acceptance and stimulation that come with a typical education. While other young people were off at college, he was aging out of special education, and it wasn't clear what he would do during the day while Soma worked. In response to an interviewer's question about the essential attributes of a welcoming school, he had once declared in verse:

My school is the open dream
    My words find hard to say.
My school is the doubt in your eyes
    And my withdrawing away.
My school is the summer dust grain
    I saw coming through my window,
Trying to find a way to my room,
    Then disappearing in an obscure shadow.

"What happens to a dream deferred?" Langston Hughes famously asked. Behind Tito's lines lurked a long history of rejection—what the blind writer Stephen Kuusisto calls "the hourly ache of not belonging."

In *The Mind Tree*, Tito had recounted any number of humiliating scenes with potential educators. I remembered one as we conversed in his living room:

"Here we go again," I told myself and pushed aside the words by wiping the air. . . . Why should boys like me need schools? After all, how can we be taught, since we have lost our minds? . . . I watched the words toss in the air like bubbles of soap all around me. They arranged and rearranged themselves . . . and I laughed aloud. "See why I told you," the teacher [said] . . . pointing towards me. . . . I walked out of the school, with a tail of words following me. Words made of letters, crawling like ants in a disciplined row.

By giving the teacher's words a visual presence, Tito plaintively gestured at the education he was denied; it's as if the air were a blackboard. He also revealed the sensory basis of autistic thought—just how palpable language is to him. For many an educator, comportment, sadly, means everything. And yet, as the woman's demeaning words followed him into his life, they became, I thought to myself, the very words that, through his tenacious homeschooling, now fill his books.

How to describe the peculiar expression of Tito's sorrow? His was an orderly disappointment. Like the verbal insolence of a soldier, it hid beneath a uniform, manifesting itself only in a slight perturbation of tone. At one point in our interview, he called me a Marxist. I had been lamenting the plight of poor families whose children have autism. Drawing a distinction between the two of us, he scribbled, "Activists revolt while I explain." I reminded him of the passages in his work that argue against the cure proponents and instead insist on opportunities for those with autism. "I explain passionately," he clarified. I got the impression that he was doing a kind of dance, a "Texas two-step," in which the leader, Resignation, and the follower, Hope, move counterclockwise around the floor.

About his relationship with Soma, who was both sun and moon, earth's everlasting companion, Tito had offered the aforementioned interviewer this couplet: "Me and Mother a fine pair / In the world a strange affair." He'd then added, "How we manage, how we fare / As we bargain with despair." Soma had a reputation for being a taskmaster, someone who really pushed Tito to achieve—Tito himself had said as much in print. As I would get to know her, I would certainly see this aspect of her personality. Her tough, no-nonsense exterior met the world head-on and either maneuvered around, or compensated for, its ignorance. A chemist in India, she had been on the verge of a promising university career when Tito was diagnosed with autism. She had clearly taught herself not to complain but instead to labor and then labor some more.

While Tito was accustomed to the demand for emotional candor in his writing, Soma did not waste time on feelings, either positive or negative. The latter, of course, were the natural response of a parent whose child had autism in India. Stigma swirled around that child like a stubborn monsoon, and services, if they existed at all, were woefully inadequate. No one had worked harder to educate her son, and yet, in some ways, she had taught him to expect so little. He would write books, he would "be somebody," in her words, but would he have friends or a life in the world? I know, easy for me to say. Many would contend that I have taught my son to expect too much. When DJ would start thinking about college and would end up falling in love with Oberlin, my wife and I would figure out how to make his dream happen, even if it meant living apart so that she could support him in Ohio. Empowering one's child is a privilege, a hugely expensive one.

. . .

AS THE INTERVIEW in Austin ended, Tito stunned his mother and me by making a request. "I want to be your student," he wrote. Feeling the pathos of the moment, yet not knowing how to respond, I was initially flippant. "Well, come to Iowa," I said. I knew full well that he couldn't come to Iowa. I also knew that he was taking a chance: he risked being disappointed again. The fact that he was directly asking a stranger—not any stranger, of course; I'd adopted DJ and written a lot about neurodiversity, but still someone he didn't know—to be his teacher must have felt like jumping out of a plane: the sturdy floor of pride giving way to plunging want. After a long and somewhat desperate pause, I suggested that we could work together by Skype. Truth be told, I had no idea what I was proposing: I had never taught by Skype; in fact, I rarely used it personally.

Moreover, it wasn't clear that Tito could sit for an hour (or longer) in front of a computer screen. He had great difficulty controlling himself. Temple Grandin describes her first encounter with him—Tito was twelve at the time—as a contest between his "acting self" and his "thinking self." Wanting to see how Tito used language, Grandin showed him a photograph of an astronaut-equestrian. "What is that?" she asked him.

> *Apollo II on a horse*, he typed rapidly.
> Then he ran around the library flapping his arms.
> When he returned to the keyboard, I showed him a picture of a cow.
> *We don't eat those in India*, he typed.
> I asked him another question, but I no longer remember what it was. Still, you know what happened next, Tito answered it, and then he ran around the library flapping his arms.
> And that was it for the conversation. Tito had done as much writing as he could in one session. He needed to rest, because even answering three short questions required tremendous effort.

Tito's thinking self had lost out to his acting self, "the self," as Grandin puts it, "that the outside world sees: a spinning, flailing, flapping boy."

In a composition inspired by the white whale, Tito would describe the obstacle to distance learning in his own way. Painting the land, with its reliable solidity, as the terrain of neurotypicals, and the sea, with its continuous tumult, as the terrain of autistics, he would lament his shipwrecked body—in particular what he called his "tactile defensiveness":

> The Moby Dick of disorders swims within you. No see-saw can be as intense as the see-saw of hyper- and hyposensitivity, rocking you from one end to the other, lifting you up, dropping you down, then lifting

you up again—throughout the ocean of days, months and years that we call life. Awake, you feel the fish under your feet; asleep, you feel the slimy eel under your back. No matter how much you pace yourself or rock your body to compensate, the see-saw finds your nerves and rocks you ever more furiously into an exhausted self. You grow old as a wave—fluid and always displaced.

As anyone familiar with the autobiographical literature knows, autistics have been reporting inadequate or excessive sensory input for years, and many have pointed to this fact (and the anxiety it causes) as the reason for their purportedly bizarre behavior, such as stimming, rocking, or flapping. Grandin explains, "Auditory and tactile input often overwhelmed me. Loud noises hurt my ears. When noise and sensory stimulation became too intense, I was able to shut off my hearing and retreat into my own world." According to her, nine out of ten autistics struggle with at least one sensory disorder—often multiple disorders. Tito struggles at times with sound, but touch and vision—in particular, a propensity to see too much detail—drive him mad. While smell is a delight, it is frequently too much of a delight. "I think very few people see the sensory connection," he would later tell me in one of our Skype sessions. Instead, experts have postulated a series of innate deficits—from impaired awareness of self and others to impaired communication and imagination—that may in fact be attributable to sensory disturbances. Remediating such difficulties, many autistics contend, can facilitate skills in these areas.

Although she had taught him how to do all sorts of exceedingly difficult things, such as to write and to type independently, even Soma doubted whether Tito could manage regular Skype sessions. But he had done well during the interview, getting up only a few times and remaining admirably focused. I kept thinking, *Maybe he will get comfortable.* Recalling the times that I had underestimated my son and knowing that the possible always depends on the imagination and inventiveness of those who would presume to define it, I said, "Let's give Skype a try." Tito remembers the moment like this: "My high school years passed with the tides—high and low. My education continued at home through books in philosophy and science. Then there was opportunity. Professor Savarese saw me differently and agreed to accept me as his student." Little did I know that I would be embarking on one of the most rewarding teaching experiences of my career, an experience that continues to this day.

We began with a private, weekly tutorial and, over the course of several years, read and discussed all manner of essays, stories, novels, and poems. After the success of the private tutorial, I proposed that Tito join an actual creative-writing course at Grinnell. "I'll project your face onto the wall," I told him. "That way the other students can see you, and you can feel like you're part of the class." Aside from some nervous gestures, such as twirling a pencil and occasionally taking a book off of a shelf and smelling it while I spoke, he was commendably composed. I could tell how much effort it took to suppress the wilder habits of classical autism, but I could also tell how much he wanted a taste of inclusive education. Clearly, the engine of desire has more horsepower than we think. Tito loved the experience—almost as much as my students. They found his workshop comments, which he typed on the Skype sidebar, to be quite helpful, and after reading his published work, they relished the opportunity to study "next" to him. The class went so well that he ended up taking two more creative-writing courses by Skype. He even established email friendships with a number of the students. In between, and after, these courses, we continued with our private tutorial.

When he later reflected on being included—we had just set out on the *Pequod* with Ishmael and Queequeg, and he had begun to appropriate the novel's watery setting to evoke his experience of autism—he remarked, "Where there is a will, there is a way. I wasn't sure how my senses would cope with a two-hour long class. But when the wind is calm and assurance floats in the air, the sea grows calm. I lasted in front of the computer screen and all boats sailed smooth. Students accepted me, and finally I found the coast." With our little virtual classroom anchored just offshore, we forged a compromise. "Students accepted me"—in that simple statement you can hear the answer to a prayer.

I remember, very early on, becoming terrifically excited: He could take an actual class! He could get a bachelor's degree or a master's of fine arts! Why wasn't he attending the University of Iowa Writers Workshop? While I was drunk on possibility, Tito was parceling out hope the way a hiker lost in the wilderness parcels out a candy bar. He was still doing that Texas two-step—maybe the follower was now Resignation, but the leader, Hope, understood the limitations of the dance. The more we read of Moby Dick, the more inclusion seemed to him a question of natural habitat:

> Let me tell you the reason why I am not the right person to be educated in a classroom. I am an isolated whale for reasons beyond my

control. I have autism and learning with typical mammals will not work for me. I need more territory due to my tactile-defensiveness. Even the rising temperature of the bodies around me in a classroom might cook me up. There is also the problem of my auditory sensitivity: if I were to hear a breathing sound from someone on my left or perhaps a secret gulp from someone on my right, I might not have any control over those sounds boring deep into my cerebrum. They might expand inside me, their decibel-level increasing, beginning a butterfly effect—dragging me from the coast like a riptide, then dumping me on a distant island resembling the smooth back of a white whale. Between me and the continent called a classroom far away would be the sea and its rolling waves. Above, would be questions like gulls hovering in the sky.

Actual inclusion would be too disruptive, Tito suggests. It could provoke a meltdown at once embarrassing to him and incomprehensible to his teacher and classmates. Summing up his sensory distortions, he once joked, "Strange is truther in autism."

When I pressed him, he conceded that there were other obstacles to inclusion besides sensory overload: "I long ago gave up on the terrestrial world of an inclusive classroom because I was unwelcome and because I was too proud to beg. To the principals of the various schools who closed their doors to me, I was a sea mammoth. They could not recognize anything but typical: their zoos were spilling over with typical students." Because he was "from a world as fluid as the sea," he would need "special accommodation to fit in the classroom-land of promises." That accommodation would have to be both material—Tito, for example, despite his auditory sensitivity, prefers to have his assignments read aloud—and attitudinal. His teachers would have to be able to see talent in another form and want him in the classroom. They would have to be willing to overlook autistic idiosyncrasies and the occasional bad day. Without these things, inclusion won't work.

With a mixture of pride and regret, Ishmael tells us in *Moby-Dick*, "A whale ship was my Yale College and my Harvard" (114). (Melville, too, was denied a secondary education and took to sea as a common sailor.) Tito adopted Ishmael's cheerful stoicism, turning the limitations of our virtual relationship into a kind of advantage: "And so I began to sharpen my harpoons behind the computer screen. There are harpooners who chase college degrees. Harpooners like me chase whales, hoping to catch the perfect whale in the shape of literature." Skype became a marvelous way to encounter *Moby-Dick*, especially as Tito settled on the novel's phantom antagonist as his primary figure of identification. It was as if I were a mast-head watchman and he a leviathan, each of us spotting the other at a great distance and singing out with enthusiasm: "Hello, Tito"; "Hello, professor." When the connection faltered and the picture blurred, this seemed especially true— the wavy lines like seas in rough weather.

Our tutorial, though, was not so much a hunt as a cooperative undertaking between man and whale, neurotypical and autist. We were rewriting the story of Captain Ahab's demonic quest as we read it, page by blustery page. Tito described our process:

> We each have Skype accounts and use them to discuss the novel face to face. Once a week, we spread the worded whale out in front of us; we dissect its head, eyes, and bones, careful not to hurt or kill it. The Professor and I are not whale hunters. We are not letting the whale die. We are shaping it, letting it swim through the Web with a new and polished look. I see the Professor's face floating on the computer screen; I see my face in a smaller box below, wondering about its projected image. Perhaps my face like Moby Dick floats on his computer screen.

Students sometimes complain that studying literature kills it. Tito understood the purpose of our discussions, which he wittily contrasted with the whale's gruesome slaughter and dismemberment. The reassembled novel moved in our conversations like the great mammal itself. Breaching the surface, its complexity glistened in the light of our shared engagement. This was precisely the sort of critical appreciation that I try to teach my students at Grinnell.

. . .

WHEN OUR TOUR of Arrowhead was complete, we descended the stairs and walked out to the barn behind the house: there were t-shirts to buy in the gift shop. The one that Tito chose said, "I Prefer Not To," which was, of course, a line from "Bartleby, the Scrivener." Mine said, "What Would Queequeg Do?," which was, of course, a twist on the popular Christian saying "What would Jesus do?" For me, part of *Moby-Dick*'s appeal lay precisely in Ishmael's decision to befriend the Polynesian harpooner—over and against what his culture, and importantly his religion, told him about "savages."

In the beginning of the novel, as the *Pequod* is being prepared for its voyage, the two must share a bed at the Spouter Inn, and after getting riled up about the "wild cannibal [with] tomahawk between his teeth" (39), Ishmael declares, "What's all this fuss I have been making about . . . the man's a human being just as I am" (40). The next morning, he comically awakens to find "Queequeg's pagan arm thrown round [him]" (42); try as he might, he can't "unlock his bridegroom clasp" (42). The harpooner "hugged me tightly" (42), Ishmael says, furthering the matrimonial conceit, "as though naught but death should part us twain" (42). Some ten chapters (and a few adventures) later, he cryptically alludes to the *Pequod's* demise—Ishmael, of course, was the only survivor: "I clove to Queequeg like a barnacle, yea, till poor Queequeg took his long last dive" (72). The novel makes a powerful case for embracing differences of all kinds.

After snapping some final photographs and conversing with the Arrowhead staff, we drove to the Berkshire Athenaeum in Pittsfield to see the library's Melville Room. Among other things, it contained a pair of Turkish slippers, which the author had used as a kind of tobacco pouch and which had originally hung from a hook on the fireplace at Arrowhead. Tito did some more book-sniffing at the Athenaeum—it was a library, after all—and I continued to marvel at the accoutrement of Melville's life. We then got back in the car and drove several hours to Mystic, Connecticut, where we had an appointment to see the *Charles W. Morgan*, the world's only remaining wooden whaling vessel and a close approximation of the *Pequod*. Mary K. Bercaw Edwards, a historian of whaling, Melville scholar, and Mystic Seaport staff member, had kindly offered to give us a tour.

I had promised Tito that we would take such a trip after we finished *Moby-Dick*. I longed not only to celebrate our readerly adventure but also to give him something to which he could look forward. In addition, I thought that seeing the *Charles W. Morgan* would make the novel come to life. When I later reflected on this assumption, I recognized both its neurotypical bias and its undercutting of the very premise of imaginative literature. With respect to the latter, wasn't it the writer's job to evoke the *Pequod*, to make the reader feel as if he were walking its decks or rigging its sails or manning its boats? Who needed to board an actual whale ship? With respect to the former, wasn't it the neurotypical, always greeting the world with the prow of his frontal lobes, and not the autist, who required such sensory enhancement? I don't want to make these points too strenuously—I understand the value of historical appreciation—but nor do I want to ignore what contemporary neuroscience is beginning to tell us about autism, on the one hand, and about the reading of literature, on the other.

Autistics struggle to subdue the sensory; I hope that much is clear. The reason that Soma took so many photographs of Arrowhead and would take still more of Mystic Seaport was to aid Tito in processing what he encountered. In a new environment, he can't readily establish "global coherence." He sees bits and pieces of things, micro-facets. By looking at the photographs after the fact, the categorical elements—what both subordinate and organize the sensory for neurotypicals—can begin to emerge. Imagine Tito scrutinizing a picture of Melville's bedroom: *Yes, that was the bed in which Herman and his wife, Lizzie, slept. That was the cradle beside the bed. The mattress, I now remember, rested on ropes. The guide said, "That's where the phrase 'Sleep Tight' comes from."*

Here's an actual example: "Fallen leaves and scarecrow sculptures surrounded Arrowhead. The house floated on a sea of chilled air, anchored like a ship to the end of October. Mount Greylock in the distance was the tomb of Moby Dick." In this particular photograph, Soma had captured the grounds around the house—an artist had populated the lawn with lifelike people made of straw.

In another, photocopies of the author's work, in his own difficult script, lay scattered on a table: "Pages saved between then and now like shreds from the sails of a ship that constantly fought the storm of rejection." I had reminded Tito, as we stood there looking at those "shreds," that one reviewer had called *Moby-Dick* "so much trash." (Later, after our trip, I would ask him what he had learned: "I can feel the rejection, the determination, and all that we heard about Melville, and I realize I'm not the only person in the world whom I must pity.")

For Tito, looking at something unfamiliar thus required a series of steps. Experience set the process in motion; photographs allowed him to calmly and patiently reconstruct the scene; writing allowed him to make sense of what he saw. These lyrical reflections were not something projected retrospectively onto visual facts; they helped to bring these facts into existence.

So, what might contemporary neuroscience tell us about Tito's visual proclivities? A team at the University of Montreal led by Laurent Mottron has proposed a theory of enhanced perceptual functioning (EPF) in autism. By "perceptual," Mottron means the low-level mechanics of sensing, not what the brain does with that input. According to the theory, in autism "perception . . . play[s] a prominent, if not always beneficial, role across a range of areas of functioning, including language and problem-solving and reasoning." A relative lack of "top-down processing influences on perceptual systems" allows these systems to operate with a kind of autonomy. Imagine your nose or your eyes or your ears commandeering your mind: "It's a sensory hijacking! Nobody move!" If you recall, autistics disproportionately use posterior sensory regions of the brain to think.

One result is what Tito terms "hyperfocusing." He sees an immense amount of detail, so much more detail than his nonautistic counterparts, which can overwhelm him. "Hyperfocusing makes the world seem shattered," he explains: "I would say the world *is* shattered. Underlooking makes it seem whole." It's easy to understand how "underlooking" would constitute an advantage in most contexts—who wants, for example, to inspect the wood grain of the planks that make up the *Morgan* to the exclusion of the masts and sails—but it does come at a cost, one that neurotypicals admittedly don't think too much about. Our capacity for generalization depends on abstraction, which is to say, "the act of considering something as a general quality or characteristic, apart from concrete realities." We let our categories—our homogenized, frontal-lobe sense of the world—do much of our seeing, hearing, smelling, and touching for us. Particularity gets lost. In this way, trying to enliven a whaling narrative by showing Tito the *Morgan* made little sense, at least until he had become comfortable with what he was seeing.

As important, the novel didn't need enlivening, if by enlivening we mean a palpable alternative to the abstraction of language. Language, scientists are learning, is far more embodied than anybody previously thought, especially literary language, which strives less to denote experience than to re-create it. Indeed, literature might be defined as purposefully simulative sensing. There is little difference in the brain, it turns out, between organic and artificial sensory stimuli. "Visual imagery," write Vittorio Gallese and Hannah Wojciehowski, "is somehow equivalent to . . . an actual visual experience, and motor imagery is also somehow equivalent to . . . an actual motor experience." Accordingly, the distinction between the world as it is presented to us in reality and the world as it is presented to us in a novel becomes harder to maintain. Autistics, who excel at thinking in pictures, sounds, touches, and smells, bring to linguistic comprehension an obdurate attachment to mental imagery. Call it the upside of "liv[ing] in the sensory," as Donna Williams puts it. Might autistics, in this respect, be the perfect readers of literature?

A study from 2006 helps to clarify the attachment to mental imagery in autism. In the study, researchers compared how autistics and neurotypicals process high- and low-imagery sentences. For example, "The number 8, rotated 90 degrees, looks like a pair of glasses." To comprehend this high-imagery sentence, you must activate not only your traditional language centers but also your parietal lobes, which integrate sensory information and facilitate spatial awareness, and your occipital lobes, which enable both sight and the production of visual mental imagery. You must, in effect, pull John Lennon—or, rather, the kind of spectacles he wore—out of the picture-making, three-dimensional hat that is your head! In the high-imagery setting, autistic and neurotypical brains looked most alike to the functional magnetic resonance imaging (or fMRI) scanner, though the former activated sensory regions more than the latter.

In the low-imagery setting, however, where "sentences . . . did not refer to spatial objects or relations"—for instance, "18 minus 11 equals 7"—autistics continued to rely on mental imagery. They continued to read, that is, in 3D mode, though the sentences themselves did not present visuospatial images. Neurotypicals, in contrast, activated only their traditional language centers. Although scientists found no difference in the error rate or response time of the two groups, they interpreted autistic processing as underconnected and inefficient. It never occurred to them that there might be different ways of skinning a higher order cognitive cat or that diminished sensory thinking in neurotypicals could ever be a problem, let alone a kind of disability.

For neurotypicals, a wealth of neuroimaging data has confirmed "a greater involvement of sensory . . . areas in concrete word processing . . . and a more focal activation of . . . 'language' areas for function words as well as abstract nouns." This distinction in part underlies the pleasure, and indeed the power, of literature, which by eschewing abstract diction encourages the reader to produce mental imagery and thus to feel the story with her body. When reading literature, your brain is like an old-fashioned movie house: the words on the page are the nerdy yet film-loving projectionist. As one literary critic has argued, appealing to the work of Elaine Scarry, "The 'great sensory writers' endow their visual images with the vivacity of live perception. . . . Readers mentally produce images 'under the instruction'" of the writer.

Could there be a better description of the experience of reading *Moby-Dick*? Virtually every line contains an imagistic feast. Listen, for example, to Ishmael's description of a sunset, which hints at the whaleman's long estrangement from family: "The starred nights seemed haughty dames in jeweled velvets, nursing at home in lonely pride, the memory of their absent conquering Earls, the golden helmeted suns!" (127). (In his notes for the day's discussion, Tito wrote, "Another great visual picture for the occipital cortex.") Or listen to his description of the air, which, like the biblical Delilah, plots to rob the sea of its physical strength: "The firmaments of air and sea were hardly separable in that all pervading azure; only the pensive air was transparently pure and soft, with a woman's look, and the robust and man-like sea heaved with long, strong, lingering swells, as Samson's chest in his sleep" (474).

"The writer who merely goes for meaning does nothing but calculate," Michel Serres insists. "He can only be said to write when all the senses tremble within the flesh of language, . . . a double variety for sight, touch, smell and taste." Literature is our linguistic lifeline to the body: it not only simulates the real, but it also re-presents it in ways that disrupt our habits of perception. We might even say that literature is the autistic version of language, whose spoken and written forms become more abstract as the typical person ages.

Even figures of speech, that important staple of literature, elicit mental imagery. A recent study found that, when processing metaphors, we recruit the appropriate sensory cortex in the back of our heads, not simply our traditional language centers in the front. In the study, sentences containing textural metaphors—"I had a rough day"—activated the parietal operculum, a region responsible for sensing texture, whereas literal sentences matched for meaning—"I had a bad day"—did not. "I had a rough day," in other words, took hold in the body. The day was like skinning your knee on an asphalt road, or it was like curling up in a sandpaper blanket. What was aggravating could only be fully communicated when it was actually felt.

If, in the words of Julian Jaynes, "language and its referents climbed up from the concrete to the abstract on the steps of metaphors, even . . . created the abstract on the bases of metaphors," then autistics appear to reflect how knowledge is perpetually borne out of the sensing body and neurotypicals, how it is perpetually freed from it. Nothing at its root lacks flesh. The word "bad" can apparently be traced back to the Old English word for hermaphrodite, *baeddel*. To have a bad day, according to this (offensive) logic, would be to give birth to a child who is neither male nor female. Abstract words, writes Jaynes, are merely "ancient coins whose concrete images in the busy give-and-take of talk have worn away with use." Whereas literate neurotypicals fill their pockets with such coins, autistics seem to crave freshly minted currency. Thus, for them, reported difficulty understanding metaphor may be less a function of sensory association than self-consciously mining the association for its cognitive implications. Indeed, studies from 2012, 2013, and 2014 have shown that autistic children can be taught the cognitive aspects of metaphor.

In my creative-writing courses at Grinnell, I'm consistently presented with a paradox: very bright students who can't seem to use language concretely and who haven't a clue how to devise fresh analogies. "Pick nouns that you can see, hear, taste, or touch," I say. "If you're going to modify these nouns, choose unexpected modifiers. With metaphor, don't think categorically; think perceptually. Look for resemblances that hide beneath what the dictionary insists makes objects distinctive. For example, *The streetlights, those dimming dominoes*. . . . Ignore the fact that the latter don't illuminate anything or that the former never fall (except in a storm or earthquake), and instead focus on their shared, precategorical properties—in this case, verticality and roughly comparable sequentiality." Sometimes, when I'm frustrated, when I'm ready to pull out whatever's s left of my diminished hair, I quote Percy Bysshe Shelley: "Reason respects the differences, and imagination the similitudes of things." And sometimes I tell my students a story.

A researcher once tested an autistic child on object recognition. When shown a picture of a decorative bedroom pillow with gold-colored welt cord and asked to identify what was in the picture, the boy said, "Ravioli." Now, this is not a consciously deployed metaphor, in which a visual similarity serves a larger cognitive and emotional purpose, but it's taken the first big step. I can well imagine a poem in which the speaker—namely, me!—remembers his Italian grandmother's Bronx apartment: in particular, her cooking and her bed. I used to sleep in that bed with just such a pillow whenever I visited her, and she always treated me to my favorite dish: ravioli and meatballs. A metaphor, we might say, is cooking in the memory pot. The first line of the imagined poem might go like this: *Even her bed was a meal you could savor.* That in English "pasta" and "pillow" both begin with "p" could well be enough to send the poem on its musical and semantic way.

Melville was a genius at this kind of analogy. In the novel's penultimate chapter, for instance, after the white whale has destroyed two of the harpooners' boats, Ishmael reports, "For a space, the odorous cedar chips of the wrecks danced round and round, like the grated nutmeg in a swiftly stirred bowl of punch" (488). How, the reader might ask, can such a disaster be compared to a festive drink? One almost wants to side with the nineteenth-century reviewer who fulminated against Melville's "implausible associations," claiming that he "allowed his mind to run riot amid remote analogies." But when you remember that Ishmael is telling his story of survival after the fact, you can begin to fathom how an image of fragrant, swirling punch might trigger a memory of the disaster and his deceased comrades. Trauma, too, heightens the sensory, unmooring it from frontal-lobe control and giving it a terrifying life of its own.

Exploring the neuroscience of autism and literary reading and writing, I began to think that literature might serve as a corrective—maybe even a kind of accommodation—for *both* autistics and neurotypicals. With the former, sensation overwhelms thought; with the latter, thought overwhelms sensation. Literature, of course, combines the two, as in this passage where Ishmael presents Ahab's festering resentment of the white whale as something utterly tangible: "His steady, ivory stride was heard, as to and fro he paced his old rounds, upon planks so familiar to his tread, that they were all over dented, like geological stones, with the peculiar mark of his walk. Did you fixedly gaze, too, upon that ribbed and dented brow; there also, you would see still stranger foot-prints—the foot-prints of his one unsleeping, ever-pacing thought" (136). Ahab's manic brooding grows legs; it "turn[s] in him as he turned, and pace[s] in him as he paced"—to the extent that "all but seemed the inward mould of every outer movement" (136).

This perfect alignment of thought and action reflects how literature works in the extreme. Ideas without embodiment are preposterous. It's almost as if Melville provided an allegory for the generation of mental imagery: just as Ahab's ruminations palpably appear on the strange projection screen of his brow, so the image of Ahab palpably appears on the strange projection screen of our minds. A megalomaniacal ship captain, who is really nothing more than some graphic marks on a page, suddenly begins to move. In his novel *Pale Fire*, Vladimir Nabokov comments, "We are absurdly accustomed to the miracle of a few written signs being able to contain immortal imagery, involutions of thought, new worlds with live people, speaking, weeping, laughing. . . . I wish you to gasp not only at what you read but at the miracle of its being readable." He's right, but the miracle is less the regular conversion of water into wine than the taste and smell of that wine in our heads.

Yet sensory knowing in autism doesn't end with a preference for language that elicits mental imagery; it extends to the medium of communication itself—what Alberto Manguel calls, from the point of view of a child learning to read, "that string of confused, alien ciphers." The aforementioned study involving high- and low-imagery sentences is thought to corroborate a study from 2005, which found that autistics possess a "non-verbal, visually oriented processing style" and tend to remember printed letters as though they were shapes and not the phonological symbols that nonautistics immediately take them to be. The control group "coded each stimulus letter verbally to facilitate memory," whereas the autistic group left them unnamed, showing less activation in left-hemispheric prefrontal regions associated with language and more activation in the right hemisphere generally and in posterior regions.

This evidence led researchers to postulate a "greater reliance on visual feature analysis" when processing printed language. From the point of view of most experts, there is too much seeing in autistic reading, just as there is too much hearing in autistic listening to speech: the medium of communication refuses to disappear. The graphic or sonic properties of the words direct attention away from their ordinary function as signifiers. As a result, language behaves less like a mule than a rearing circus horse: something to behold as much as to unpack (or decode).

As a young boy, Tito treated words strictly as an "auditory toy." When Soma recited poems to him, he would invent his own rhymes and acoustical patterns. "Designs can be visual," he has said, "and designs can be formed in sound." The pattern makes it "more than a thing to ignore." Although he obviously learned how to use language semantically, he still thinks of literature as "an ambition to please the ear." He has even compared saying a poem over and over again in his head to "self-stimulating action": that state when an autist seems utterly consumed, at times even cornered, by his senses. Through trancelike repetition, the words lose their meaning and become mere marbles in the mouth.

A study from 2008 found that autistics exhibit "superior perceptual processing of speech relative to controls." In other words, they actually hear speech sounds more precisely and robustly than neurotypicals, but they do not as effectively convert those sounds into usable phonemes. A phoneme, of course, is "any of the distinct units of sound in a specified language that distinguish one word from another." With respect to neurotypicals, the study speculated that attention to meaning degrades perceptual awareness. As soon as the "p" in "purple" becomes a phoneme, it no longer sounds like the rain on your roof. Indeed, its wetness in the ear evaporates. The instrumental use of language depends, in part, on ignoring the sensuous materiality of the signifiers.

It also depends on effacing difference. As Reuven Tsur notes, unlike the processing of environmental sounds, "where the shape of the perceived sound is similar to the shape of the sound wave," the processing of speech sounds requires active distortion. "We hear a unitary phoneme that is very different," he says, "from the stream of auditory information that conveys it." We learn to generalize, to produce an abstract and thoroughly homogenized phonetic category, one capable of working across all manner of voices and words. In the process, "precategorical auditory information" is lost. To the neurotypical ear, the "p" of "purple" resembles the "p" of "popcorn" or the "p" of "potato." While the words may be different as a result of the letters that follow, the "p" functions in the domain of sound the way common nouns function in the domain of sense. Once again, the prow of our frontal lobes haughtily parts the waters of particularity.

In contrast to the generalizing talent of neurotypicals, the "enhanced discrimination skills" of autistics make "extracting the common, invariant features characterizing all exemplars of a given phoneme" difficult. They simply hear too much specificity. The "p" of "purple" is *not* the "p" of "popcorn"; moreover, a Southern man's "p" is different from a Southern woman's "p." In fact, each of a hundred Southern women's "p"s is different from all of the others' "p"s! In addition, autistics do not appear to have a "primary, or 'default,' speech-processing mode." Unlike neurotypicals, they neither automatically listen for meaning when in the presence of speech sounds nor automatically privilege such sounds over all other sounds in the environment. To an autistic child, the wind in the birch trees is just as compelling as a friend's comment on the playground.

All of these things render oral comprehension a Herculean task for many autistics. "I doubt whether the typical person's talking voice and my listening ears cooperate," Tito remarks, "because those ears are also scooping up noises with their remote spatula-shaped lobes—not just from the talking voice but also from the sound of my own breathing, the humming of the refrigerator, and perhaps even the scratching of my hands around my cheek as I anticipate other noises in the environment, like a spoon dropping somewhere to stir a new vibration of sound in the air." Whereas neurotypicals can easily block out such auditory information, autistics cannot. "My ears are like sinking, overloaded boats," Tito says in a nod to *Moby-Dick*. "There is simply too much to scoop up and pour into my ears." Of course, the issue of attention works both ways. As the authors of another study comment, the "reduction of the surrounding environment" in neurotypical attention is "a great simplification, if one . . . consider[s] the richness of what is constantly available for an agent to see, hear and otherwise experience." Such richness gets overlooked when people strictly pathologize autism.

A passage from Tito's second memoir, *How Can I Talk If My Lips Don't Move?*, nicely captures the tension between autistic richness and impairment. In it, he recalls trying to prove his competence to a researcher who doubted that the "severely" autistic can master language. Instructed to listen to a book being read aloud by an aide and to report on what it says, Tito found himself focusing on the man's voice, not on the meaning of his words:

> Claude read.... I saw the voice transform into long apple green and yellow strings, searching under the table for who knows what? Threads like raw silk forming from Claude's voice.
>
> Claude read. I watched those strings vibrate with different amplitudes as Claude tried to impress the silent beholders and serious researchers of autism with the varying tones of a near-to-perfection performance.
>
> Claude read. I watched those strings with stresses and strains, reaching their own elastic limits and snapping every now and then, when his voice reached a certain pitch. I saw those snapped strings form knots like entangled silk, the color of apple green and yellow.

When the researcher asked, "So, what was he reading?" Tito responded with a sentence about "the beauty of the color green, when yellow sunshine melts its way through newly grown leaves." ("Take that, Mr. Bigwig!" I want to shout from the bleachers of my reading—I've had my own encounters with arrogant autism professionals.)

Like his nose at Arrowhead, Tito's ears wouldn't settle for a conventional relationship to language. His synesthesia, which neuroimaging has documented, suggests a complete immersion in the sensory and a further loosening of categorical bonds: as hearing becomes sight, sound becomes silk. The researcher, of course, interpreted the answer as a failure to comprehend what was read—not as a lucid and indeed artful description of the voice's alternative registration. (This god of science, let us say, is hardheaded and hard-nosed, sensible without being sensitive. He has banished irony from the lab!) Tito has had to teach himself not to respond to spoken language in this fashion, but when emotions run high—after all, his very personhood was at stake—ordinary understanding proves challenging.

"But why praise sensory richness?" some would ask. "People with autism need jobs. They need to be able to care for themselves. They need to be able to understand what's being said to them." Diane Sawyer, the former host of *Good Morning America*, once dismissed the concept of neurodiversity as "a beautiful way of justifying heartbreak." She was interviewing Ari Ne'eman, cofounder of the Autistic Self-Advocacy Network (ASAN). No one with any judgment would minimize the hardships of autism, yet, as a literature professor and writer, I see strength in the condition's sensory orientation. (At faculty meetings, when my colleagues drone on and on, I positively pine for an apple green and yellow distraction!) As a human being, I marvel at autistic joie de vivre—call it neurological carpe diem. Robert Frost once wrote, "The present / Is too much for the senses, / Too crowded, too confusing." But if the present is where we live, we neurotypicals should ask ourselves, "How much life are we missing?"

After reading the "Mast-head" chapter, Tito sent me a poem—he would often send poems or mini-essays along with his notes for our weekly discussions—in which he cleverly deployed Ishmael's failure to look for whales on the mast-head of the *Pequod* as a metaphor for his own failure to listen for meaning on the mast-head of speech. Ishmael, as readers of *Moby-Dick* know, was a terrible mast-head watchman:

> Let me make a clean breast of it here, and frankly admit that I kept but sorry guard. With the problem of the universe revolving in me, how could I—being left completely to myself at such a thought-engendering altitude,—how could I but lightly hold my obligations to observe all whale-ships' standing orders, "Keep your weather eye open, and sing out every time." . . . I say: your whales must be seen before they can be killed. (153)

On the mast-head "the young philosopher," as our narrator humorously refers to himself, is "lulled into such an opium-like listlessness of vacant, unconscious reverie . . . by the blending cadence of waves with thoughts, that . . . he loses his identity" (154). Indeed, he forgets his job as watchman, forgets even the concept of *whale* or *water* or *mast-head*. When this occurs, Ishmael says, "there is no life in him . . . except that rocking life imparted by a gently rolling ship, by her borrowed from the sea" (155).

For Tito, a better description of how autistics lose themselves in the sensory doesn't exist. While the sensory frequently exasperates, it just as frequently enchants, and it can have a "drug-like addictive effect," according to Donna Williams. For her this sort of pleasure resembles "merging with God because [she] would resonate with the sensory nature of [an] object with such an absolute purity and loss of self that . . . [she would] become part of the beauty itself." Literary critics have traditionally understood the "Mast-head" chapter—really the novel as a whole—as expressing Melville's own search for God, and there's more than a hint that a deliberate, frontal-lobe assault won't find her.

The poem's occasion, Tito explained, was an ordinary conversation. Up with the seagulls and the wind, clinging to that spar we call a human voice, he once again struggled to make phonemes, but something mysterious and ennobling, he suggests, is at least the equal of semantic comprehension.

I Kept but Sorry Guard

There must have been shoals of them in the far horizon.
—HERMAN MELVILLE

His voice was a mere frequency of sound.
Like any other voice, it carried a wave in sound.
I saw the wave come bouncing around.

There might have been words moving along that wave,
Moving past me, sailing down that wave,
Lingering a little before they escaped.

The voice before me—its frequency was blue.
Light as the light, the spreading of that blue.
Lulled into listlessness, I was lulled into blue.

He asked me questions—maybe one or two—
As I manned the mast-head but failed to pursue
Those shoals of meaning in a faraway blue.

Is there a better way to describe the two competing forms of attention? Whereas autistics "keep sorry guard" over meaning, neurotypicals "keep sorry guard" over precategorical sensation. In literary writing, especially poetry, we're hunting two kinds of whales—or, rather, one hybrid one.

In life, of course, we're ruthlessly utilitarian. "What is my contribution to society?" Tito asks in *How Can I Talk If My Lips Don't Move?* "With my physical and neurological limitations, I am unable to do certain kinds of work. But I can think," he says. "And I can write. I can write down my stories on paper with my pencil." But then his words turn darker as he ponders "the humiliation he will face" when his mother is gone and "[he is] at the mercy of others":

Perhaps my mere presence will be a contribution because it will remind some stray hearts that they have enough reasons to be thankful to the Maker of the Universe because they are not like me. And by my mere presence . . . I can remind the Creator . . . that all that He has created may not be perfect . . . and forgive [Him] for every distortion in which I exist. And I am not worried about Hell because I have experienced it here on earth.

At the end of the "Mast-head" chapter, Ishmael jokes that the problem with "the young philosophers" is that "their vision is imperfect" (154). "They are short-sighted; what use, then, to strain the visual nerve? They have left their opera glasses at home" (154). Of course, the penchant for precategorical sensory information in autism is itself a kind of near-sightedness. Fingering visual impairment as the cause of poor job performance, Melville slyly satirizes a narrow economic sense of value. What good is a mast-head watchman who can't spot whales or a writer who can't sell books or an autistic person who can't always decipher speech? Who needs esoteric wonders? Like a foghorn on the coast, life intones its constant warning: "You must make money!" In a letter to Nathaniel Hawthorne, Melville once complained, "Dollars damn me.... Try to get a living by the Truth—and go to the Soup Societies." At the age of ten, my son, who was nearly killed by his birth mother and then horrifically abused in foster care, typed on his computer, "Autism sucks, Dad, but I see things that you don't see."

. . .

WHEN WE ARRIVED at Mystic Seaport, I immediately spotted the *Morgan*'s masts. As we waited for our guide near the entrance, the ship's grandeur unabashedly declared itself. Whatever equivalence existed between actual sight and the vision afforded by literature, the orbs that flanked my nose behaved like Oliver Twist: "May I have some more, sir?" they cried after a first helping of the visual. Perhaps seeing anything out of the ordinary allows neurotypicals to at least partially cast off the yoke of the categorical and return to the sensory.

Built in 1841, the *Morgan*, we learned, is roughly 107 feet long, twenty-seven feet wide, and fourteen feet deep. Its main mast, on which the young philosopher stood precariously perched, rises 110 feet above the deck. During our tour, some interns demonstrated climbing up to the mast-head—they looked like gulls circling a church spire. In its time, the ship boasted seven thousand square feet of sail, and it carried a crew of between thirty and thirty-six men and four whaleboats. Because the ship was so slow, smaller craft were lowered for the chase and kill. The large try-works, the brick furnace used for turning blubber into oil, sits toward the bow. The *Morgan*'s first voyage yielded fifty-one whales—about 850 barrels of oil. Eighty years later, at the conclusion of its thirty-seventh and final commercial voyage, it had processed 55,000 barrels of whale oil and 153,000 pounds of whalebone.

Before we toured the ship, Mary K. showed us one of the whaling boats, which lay in the water, its oars on the dock. I was surprised by how big the boat was and yet how little room there must have been with one man operating the long steering oar, several men paddling furiously, and at least one harpooner at the ready with his iron spear. With so many moving men and parts, the chances of getting caught in the whale line or being yanked from the boat and lost were high. "When the line is darting out, to be seated . . . in the boat," Ishmael reports, "is like being seated in the midst of the manifold whizzings of a steam engine in full play, when every flying beam, and shaft, and wheel, is grazing you" (253).

If reading Moby-Dick with Tito had done anything, it had made me think less about the fate of the whaleman, however, and more about the fate of the whale. In preparing for our trip, I had found on the New Bedford Whaling Museum website an account of the marine mammal's typical slaughter:

> When the whale tired, the crew pulled on the line to draw the boat close to their prey, while . . . the boatheader carried a lance forward and plunged it into a vulnerable spot, such as the heart or lungs. With each breath, the whale spouted blood. . . . As the whaleboat backed off again, the crew observed the awesome spectacle of the death of the whale. The great beast swam violently in ever smaller circles, a pattern known as the "flurry." The end came when the whale beat the water with its tail, shuddered and . . . turned over on its side.

In Moby-Dick the moment of the kill is even more dramatically—and analogically—rendered: "The red tide now poured from all sides of the monster like brooks down a hill. His tormented body rolled not in brine but in blood, which bubbled and seethed for furlongs behind in their wake" (256–57).

Ishmael depicts a truly hellish enterprise, one whose cruelty is unmistakable: "Stubb slowly churned his long sharp lance into the fish, and kept it there, carefully churning and churning, as if cautiously seeking to feel after some gold watch that the whale might have swallowed. . . . But that gold watch he sought was the innermost life of the fish" (257). After Stubb's assault, the whale, Ishmael tells us, "surg[ed] from side to side; spasmodically dilating and contracting his spout hole, with sharp, cracking, agonized respirations. At last, gush after gush of clotted red gore, as if it had been the purple lees of red wine, shot into the frighted air. . . . His heart had burst!" (257).

Because Tito identified with the creature whose liquid life seemed analogous to his own sensory one, he, too, felt hunted. Encountering Ahab, he compared the captain's obsession with killing Moby Dick to our culture's obsession with vanquishing autism. Just as Ahab believes that the white whale maliciously took his leg, so people believe that autism maliciously takes their children. Of his phantom antagonist, Ahab says, "I see in him outrageous strength, with an inscrutable malice sinewing it. That inscrutable thing is chiefly what I hate" (159). Like Moby Dick, the classically autistic represent a lamentable enigma. Try as you might, you cannot crack the mystery of their strange behavior. You cannot penetrate their wordless gaze—or so the stereotype contends. At the very end of the novel, just before delivering to Moby Dick what he hopes is a fatal blow, Ahab screams, "To the last I grapple with thee; from hell's heart I stab at thee; for hate's sake I spit my last breath at thee" (499).

Tito's conceit may seem hyperbolic until you consider the kind of fundraising advertisements that Autism Speaks supports. "I am autism," a particularly infamous one declares. "I am visible in your children, but if I can help it, I am invisible to you until it's too late. . . . I work faster than pediatric AIDS, cancer, and diabetes combined." Becoming louder and more demonic, the voice in the ad sneers, "If you're happily married, I will make sure your marriage fails. Your money will fall into my hands, and I will bankrupt you for my own self-gain." With glee, it then alludes to the plight of underfunded researchers, the heroes in this implied drama of good and evil: "Your scientists don't have the resources, and I relish their desperation."

As Tito well knew, ferociously negative depictions of autism have consequences. Like a kind of awful clockwork, the news regularly coughed up stories of parents murdering their autistic children. In 2015 alone, seventy autistics died at the hands of family members. Just this morning, a wealthy, New York businesswoman was convicted of manslaughter in the death of her six-year-old, nonspeaking son. After trying all manner of quack treatments and still not finding a cure, she forcibly fed the boy a lethal concoction of painkillers and anti-inflammatories. To be certain that he consumed this concoction, she stuck a syringe—I want to say a harpoon—down his throat. And not three days ago, a woman in Oregon parked her car on a bridge and threw her six-year-old, nonspeaking son into the waters of Yaquina Bay. When I try to picture this boy—the wind on his face, that orange spider perched in the sky, his mother yanking him toward the rail—I shudder at how perilous the mast-head of autism really is. "And . . . with one half-throttled shriek," Ishmael says, "you drop through that transparent air into the summer sea, no more to rise forever" (155).

Even scientists, no matter how dispassionate their work, play into a narrative of relentless pathology. "You have calculated the intelligence of an autistic person," Tito wrote in one of his essays. "You have measured his skull and found it bigger than others, you have measured the white matter over grey matter, you have measured his emotions, but could you please help me to calculate the number of steps to the moon?" He would rather live on that desolate, rotating orb than perpetually engage with the medical and education establishments, to say nothing of the autism alarmists. In a satire of the rising incidence rate of autism, he teased, "Beware! Beware! One out of eighty-eight! Or eighty-eight out of something, or something out of eighty-eight, or perhaps I am getting confused because eighty-eight looks like two giant infinities: heads down, bodies up—they have no legs to run."

"Is Ishmael complicit in the whale slaughter?" I asked during one of our Skype sessions. We had both been uneasy about his macabre accounts of dismemberment, as he almost seemed to delight in the great mammal's demise. At one point in the novel, the crew takes apart a sperm whale and then, a couple of days later, a right whale. Severed from their bodies, the gargantuan heads of these creatures hang from the two sides of the ship. "As before," Ishmael recalls, "the *Pequod* steeply leaned over toward the sperm whale's head, now, by counterpoise of both heads, she regained her even-keel; though sorely strained" (295). One head he mischievously calls the philosopher John Locke; the other, Immanuel Kant. "Here, now, are two great whales, laying their heads together," he says, "let us join them and lay together our own" (297).

In the end, we decided that Ishmael is a bit like an environmentalist who works at Exxon. A whaling vessel is no place for a cetacean advocate, but that's where Ishmael found himself. Tito and I took note of how he compares the anatomical features of humans and whales and mounts an argument in support of the latter's physiology. "The position of the whale's eyes corresponds to that of a man's ears," he says, "and you may fancy for yourself, how it would fare with you, did you sideways survey objects through your ears" (297). While such vision most certainly has its drawbacks—among other things, a considerable gap at the center of the visual field—it also has its advantages. By working in monocular fashion, each eye retains its autonomy. As a result, the whale's brain, according to Ishmael, "can at the same moment of time attentively examine two distinct prospects, one on one side of him, and the other in an exactly opposite direction" (298). Imagine a man, he boasts, "simultaneously go[ing] through the demonstrations of two distinct problems in Euclid" (298).

Ishmael also celebrates the virtues of the whale's ear and, pointing out how "wondrously minute" it is, comments,

> Is it not curious, that so vast a being as the whale should see the world through so small an eye, and hear the thunder through an ear which is smaller than a hare's? But if his eyes were broad as the lens of Herschel's great telescope; and his ears capacious as the porches of cathedrals; would that make him any longer of sight, or sharper of hearing? Not at all. Why then do you try to "enlarge" your mind? Subtilize it. (299)

In this way, it required no effort at all to link Ishmael's defense of the whale with neurodiversity's defense of autism.

Tito especially appreciated Ishmael's understanding of the whale's lack of speech: "Seldom have I known any profound being that had anything to say to this world, unless forced to stammer out something by way of getting a living" (332). Ahab, in contrast, rails against the creature's silence. In the aforementioned scene with the severed heads, he approaches the sperm whale and issues a command: "Speak thou vast and venerable head . . . ; speak . . . and tell us the secret thing that is in thee" (282). The whale, of course, cannot speak; moreover, it is dead. The absurdity of Ahab's wish points to his fundamental narcissism: he wants the animal to conform to his own physiology, indeed his own cognition. Any departure is maddening defect. Approaching the sperm whale once again, he cries in frustration, "O head! thou hast seen enough to split the planets . . . and not one syllable is thine!" (282).

Precisely because speech is considered the quintessential mark of the human, Tito has despaired of his inability to speak. "Did you ever wonder how so much sound can hide in the inch and a half of a typical person's mouth?" he asks. "I guess you notice things like this when your own mouth contains but a few limited sounds." In a poem titled "Harpoons," he mapped the slaughter of whales onto a typical scene with a "severely" autistic child, ghoulishly suggesting that violent death might be a form of speech therapy:

Harpoons

With harpoons they queried—they lacked finesse.
He voiced no response except some noisy breaths,
Excavating sound from deep in his chest.

What pointed questions! They injured his head!
He breathed to explain how he talks with that head:
Great blubbery words that rise from his chest.

Is there a mind, they wondered, inside that head?
The sound of his answers? Those cumbersome breaths.
Let blood uproot what's locked in his chest.

Imagining a time when both whales and autism have vanished, he wrote in a prose piece, "Your voice is an extinct animal—too primordial and fossilized. All you will hear from that fossil are a few gurgles, fathoms deep, beneath the rolling waves."

"Are we imposing autism on the novel?" I asked some thirteen months into our discussions. "No," Tito replied. "It is the hidden image that lurks in the sea. Sometimes it shows up as Ahab's mania and obsession; sometimes it shows up in the way Ishmael sees the world from the mast-head; and sometimes it shows up in Moby Dick himself." In at least one respect, my question was unfair. After all, readers make sense of a book in relation to their own experiences. As important, Tito insisted that autism itself exists in the novel: in the figure of the carpenter, who fashions a second prosthetic leg for Ahab when the original prosthesis fails. Admittedly, it is something of a cottage industry identifying literary and historical figures that may have been autistic, yet Tito is definitely onto something.

The carpenter, Ishmael says, was as "uncompromised as a new-born babe; living without premeditated reference to this world or the next" (409). "You might almost say," Ishmael continues, "that this strange uncompromisedness in him involved a sort of unintelligence; for his numerous trades, he did not seem to work so much by reason or instinct, or simply because he had been tutored to it, or by any intermixing of all of these, . . . but merely by a kind of deaf and dumb, spontaneous literal process" (409). The carpenter was a "pure manipulator; his brain . . . must have early oozed along into the muscles of his fingers" (409). The portrait is indeed highly suggestive of one form of autism—the "intelligence," in the words of Leo Kanner, "scarcely touched by tradition and culture"; the inexplicable and automatic technical abilities; the infamously one-sided conversations. Whatever was different about the carpenter, Ishmael notes, it "kept him a great part of the time soliloquizing; but only like an unreasoning wheel, which also hummingly soliloquizes; or, rather, his body was a sentry-box and this soliloquizer on guard there" (410).

As an author, Melville witnessed the rise of professional medicine. By 1851, the date of the novel's publication, however, what we think of as psychiatric disorders hadn't even begun to congeal into something like official diagnoses. In fact, it would take another ninety years before the term "autism" would come into existence. In many ways, the world of 1850 was much more neurodiverse than our own, particularly on whaling vessels, which tended to collect those who didn't fit into ordinary society. Diagnosing the carpenter with "high-functioning" autism, Tito took pleasure in his gainful employment and extraordinary craftsmanship, while also mourning his own lack of possibilities.

But if he wasn't imposing autism on the novel, surely Tito was responding to it autistically, perseverating on it, perhaps even turning it into a cognitive version of stimming. After all, most of the writing by him that I've presented in this chapter has some connection to it. Yet we were reading the novel slowly, as if under a microscope, which paradoxically allowed it to expand—beyond, much beyond, its already appreciable heft. Suddenly, all manner of things became visible: from clever historical references to subtle thematic patterns. I came to believe that every great novel should be encountered this way. As Tito said toward the end of our adventure, "We will let it swim back and forth for a few more weeks, discussing two chapters at a time because slow cooking brings out the best of the whale flavor." What literature professors call "close reading" might as well be called "autistic reading," I decided, for the kind of careful attention and full-bodied engagement that Tito evinced are exactly what literature deserves.

Even more than what such reading did for our understanding of *Moby-Dick*, the story did something for—or, rather, *to*—our lives. *Moby-Dick* was everywhere; we couldn't escape it. "For nearly seventeen months, I navigated the novel with my teacher and captain, Ralph Savarese," Tito wrote:

Sitting in my room, I saw Moby Dick through the eyes of Jonah in Father Mapple's sermon—my room the hollow stomach of the whale. Flapping my hands, I saw whale flippers. No wonder it took me a long time to isolate my fingers and learn to write with a pencil! Looking at the Walmart parking lot, I saw a concrete sea. The abandoned trolleys were boats waiting for the wind to knock them against someone's car—and I, I was a cautious whale swimming toward the front door. I saw Moby Dick trapped in a wall clock, the *Pequod* pursuing it. And I saw time as a slippery fish chasing its own future. Working through the pages of *Moby-Dick*, I spotted Ahab's frown in the folds of billowing clouds just before it started to rain; I heard Starbuck's whispers in a hotel air-conditioner; and I recognized Stubb's laughter in my own voice when my very existence seemed absurd. One day, there was Moby Dick in the sickle moon; around it blue-green clouds. Another day there was Moby Dick in an airplane—we were the passengers stepping inside.

As Ahab ruled the *Pequod*, so Melville's novel ruled Tito's ship of days.

I, too, saw *Moby-Dick* everywhere. Whatever else I was reading I read in relation to that mysterious tome. I was like the mad captain at the end of the novel: I'd gotten my harpoon into Moby Dick but was "taken out of the boat by the line" (253) and "dragged down after him into the profundity of the sea" (252). Waxing existential, Ishmael says, "All men live enveloped in whale-lines. All are born with halters round their necks. . . . And if you be a philosopher, though seated in the whale-boat, you would not at heart feel one whit more of terror, than though seated before your evening fire with a poker, and not a harpoon, by your side" (253). And if you be a reader of *Moby-Dick*, well, grab hold of that poker, for the "most dreaded creatures glide" beneath your easy chair, "treacherously hidden" by "the loveliest tints of azure" (248).

"There is no Frigate like a Book / To take us Lands away," Emily Dickinson once opined, but it can just as easily transmogrify your house. In a letter to the New York publisher Evert Duyckinck, composed while writing *Moby-Dick* at Arrowhead, Melville commented,

> I have a sort of sea-feeling here in the country, now that the ground is all covered with snow. I look out of my window in the morning when I rise as I would out of a port-hole of a ship in the Atlantic. My room seems a ship's cabin; & at nights when I wake up & hear the wind shrieking, I almost fancy there is too much sail on the house, & I had better go on the roof & rig in the chimney.

I'd put the wind in Iowa up against the wind in western Massachusetts any day—it's not for nothing that the wagons making their slow way across the Midwest were called prairie schooners! Many a night before my own evening fire or tossing in bed, I'd want to rig in the chimney myself. And from that slippery perch, I'd look up suddenly, finding an even bigger theater for my imagination. "Nor when expandingly lifted by your subject, can you fail to trace out great whales in the starry heavens, and boats in pursuit of them" (245), Ishmael says.

. . .

AFTER GIVING US a thorough tour of the *Morgan*'s deck, Mary K. took Tito, Soma, and me below and showed us the captain's stateroom and the crew's very cramped quarters. It was hard to believe how tiny the sleeping berths were and how little privacy they offered. Climbing into one of the berths, I thought of how Ishmael characterizes the sailor's sleep: "under his very pillow rush herds of walruses and whales" (74). Another set of stairs and we were in the very bowels of the ship—where the crew kept its supplies and barrels of whale oil. When we had finished with the *Morgan*, Mary K. showed us the Charles Mallory Sail Loft, where the sails for the *Morgan* and other ships were repaired. We also visited the Cooperage and the James Driggs Shipsmith shop, in whose working forge harpoons were made. Mary K. invited Tito to work the giant, suspended bellows that fanned the fire. I have a wonderful picture of him doing so.

Leaving Mystic Seaport, we felt the way that we felt at the end of our readerly voyage. We had lived with this story, these characters, for nearly a year and a half. "It's sad to see them go," Tito said.

"We could read *Moby-Dick* again," I joked.

"How about another book?"

"Yes, another book," I replied.

When I returned to Iowa and opened my email, I saw that a whale or perhaps a mast-head watchman had left me a message: "We are home. And I am eager. Are we meeting this evening?"

two

THE HEAVENS OF THE BRAIN

The body is a big sagacity. . . .
— FRIEDRICH NIETZSCHE

In a short essay from high school, Jamie Burke offered a whimsical approach to adversity. "Struggles are the vegetables of life," he wrote. They "do not appear the tastiest, but are necessary to attempt good health." With a flair for the figurative, he described both his sensorimotor challenges and the therapies and accommodations that have allowed him to flourish. Take, for example, his sensitivity to smell and hearing. From the moment he began his inclusion journey as a young boy with classical autism, he dreaded the malodorous mosh pit of the cafeteria. He dreamt of lunch "being served in a room far from cooking, so smells are not sickening." Lunch should be "a time for peaceful eating and not loud talking and annoying bells and whistles, which split my ears as a sword in use of killing monsters." "My ears hear colossally well," he noted, "so noise can be difficult."

Anxiety could be difficult, too—very difficult. It arrived, the burly, six-foot-seven Jamie said, "as a constant visitor, just as breathing." He believed his "cells have a nucleus filled with it." Pacing offered some relief, but he felt as if a porcupine were constantly prodding his nerves. "Sensory integration has been like a giant Band-Aid to my body," he reported. "It wraps up the stingers as a ball of cotton and makes things more comfortable for me." Such therapy took many forms, either striving to subdue his overperforming senses or to draw out his underperforming ones, all the while working to blend them in a manner that neurotypicals take for granted. For instance, Jamie used—in fact, still uses—an augmentative communication device called a Lightwriter, which allowed him to "both see the words and hear them in a constant voice that was always the same . . . in speed and tone." The simultaneity stitched vision and hearing together, making each more useful.

Samonas ("spectral activated music of optimal natural structure") listening therapy promoted better auditory processing of speech. According to Jamie, "It gives your ears the feeling of reaching the bridge over the missing meaning of sounds." It helped, he said, with both "distinction" and "connection." Heavily patterned classical music, adapted to emphasize high-frequency overtones at targeted moments and shifting strategically from ear to ear, is thought to aid the listener in taking in the full auditory spectrum and processing it more efficiently. Suddenly, Jamie could hear "whole words." "Before," he commented, "I would lose certain sounds, and the words seemed as garbage to be thrown out with no use to them."

Other therapies focused on his proprioception, or the awareness of his body in space. Not only is there demonstrable dysfunction in the brain's motor areas in classical autism but also the two cerebral hemispheres don't communicate as well as they might. Therapies like neurological drumming and figure-eight movements on a rope swing facilitate midline crossing, which in his case worked to integrate the two sides of his body. With the former, the patient alternates hitting a drum with his left and right hands as the clinician moves the drum and forces him to reach on a diagonal. These therapies, Jamie contended, "gave me faster speed in typing with both hands, and helped me to organize my body when I cut food, ate, shaved and washed my hair."

Basic, improvised accommodations made a difference as well. "In elementary school, beanbag seats, rocking chairs, headphones with music, net swings, and being squeezed between two mats in the physical therapy room allowed me my upsets," he wittily explained, "but . . . never . . . the request to leave the school." To make lunch bearable, he would collect his loaded tray at the entrance of the cafeteria, having ordered it in advance, and thereby avoid the "ordeal of looking at and smelling all the many foods." Although he lamented eating by himself in a quiet place, he knew that he had to manage stress. Henry David Thoreau, that paragon of primitive solitude, once remarked of his aversion to comfortable urbanity, "I would rather sit on a pumpkin and have it all to myself, than be crowded on a velvet cushion." He, too, had his quirks, and, some believe, may have been on the spectrum. Or, as one of Aesop's fables advises, "Better to eat a crust in peace than to partake of a banquet in anxiety."

Some of these accommodations fell away as Jamie grew older; others took their place. When he matriculated to Syracuse University, which was just a short drive from his house, he had to acquaint professors with the kinds of needs most had never encountered before. (Jamie is thought to be only the eighth or ninth student with classical autism ever to earn a college degree.) For one thing, he had a classroom aide, as he did in elementary, middle, and high school. The aide helped him to remain on task, oversaw his augmentative communication devices, and studied with him. For another, he frequently stimmed in class—this allowed him to vent nervous energy and, paradoxically, to take in the lecture. Albert Einstein once quipped, "A man who can drive safely while kissing a pretty girl is simply not giving the kiss the attention it deserves." In autism, however, the postures of attention are different: driving can facilitate, as it were, the ardent movement of lips. "Really, I think my stims may help my management to absorb information at times," Jamie has said.

Because anxiety often inhibited word retrieval and rendered auditory processing difficult, he made sure that his professors didn't leap to conclusions about his ability. "I feel stronger when you get to know me and my autism. Your knowledge is my power," he explained. If he struggled to respond to a question, it wasn't necessarily because he didn't know the answer or was like other distracted (or hungover) college students. Jamie much preferred a classroom with windows, and he wished to sit near natural light rather than "in the middle of the crush of desks." He asked his professors not to speak too quickly and requested that course materials be available in alternative formats so that he could both see and hear them. Fairly typically, he needed extra time on tests, but he also needed them in a larger font. And he wanted to take tests in a private room so as to be able to read them aloud to himself. In labs, he needed a stereohead (what Jamie called a "dual-eyed") microscope and time to do the labs alone. His motor impairments made the process excruciatingly slow, and he didn't want the other students to have to wait for him.

About inclusion, the young man with a chinstrap beard and auburn hair was at once starry-eyed and pragmatic. "Certainly students like me struggle at times, but when we struggle . . . I see the lowering of expectations," Jamie remarked at an autism conference in Vermont in 2013. "I have been truly fortunate with people who respect me and . . . try to help my success . . . as a student. Passionate, creative ways are sometimes necessary." He was especially appreciative of teachers who believed in his "potential as a true possibility." "I am not planning a segregated life for myself," he told the audience, but "our bodies need . . . support in order to live in the world." Speaking directly to educators, he pleaded, "Do not just give us the desk then leave us to only fill the seat. We are certainly worth your efforts."

At the same time, he fully acknowledged the disabling aspects of autism, which couldn't always be circumvented, and he knew his own sensory limits. "I am greatly perplexed when I see young students' systems being overwhelmed trying to be what is 'normal,'" he warned. The summer before my son, DJ, embarked on his own college adventure, he asked Jamie about living in the dorm. "Not a chance," he replied. "It's too long in the day." It was all he could do to keep it together from 9 to 5. He needed to be able to return from campus at night to the familiar space and rituals of home. For him autism was "a balance straddling the gulf between what is desired and what is."

But lest you hear too much resignation in that statement, consider the fact that Jamie desired to speak, and at the age of thirteen, to the astonishment of many an expert, including Albert Galaburda at Harvard University, he accomplished this feat. As a small child, he had been taught to type on a keyboard using that much-maligned technique called facilitated communication (FC). With FC (or supported typing), the person with autism is offered resistance at the hand, elbow, or shoulder as he manipulates a keyboard. Eventually, Jamie learned how to type independently and then started to speak what he pecked out, two fingers at a time, like an oilfield pumpjack or "thirsty bird," as that contraption is sometimes called. "I decided to take a risk and began to try just one word," he recounted. "I know my voice sounded foolish, but it felt ok to try."

"The voice is a wild thing," Willa Cather wrote. "It can't be bred in captivity. It is a sport, like the silver fox. It happens." And yet Jamie's voice was indeed bred in captivity. "When I was growing up . . . I could see the words in my brain," he recalled, "but . . . they died as soon as they were born. What made me feel angry was . . . that I knew exactly what I was to say and my brain was retreating in defeat." An innovative occupational therapist used a range of movement therapies, including rhythmic drumming and a metronome, to mechanically coax a voice from Jamie's fingertips. At first, he could only speak while typing; then he could only read aloud something that he himself had typed, the memory of having produced the words with his fingers somehow guiding his mouth. Now he can read aloud another person's text and even speak without first typing what he wants to say. As the Zen adage puts it, "Leap and the net will appear." When he is nervous, however, he still prefers to prime his voice motorically. "This is the journey I am on," Jamie told the Vermont conference audience, "from a boy in his tender years with no voice, to a boy who could begin to find his voice and formulate useful language." "It has taken many, many people who presumed me to be competent and who held my dreams," he said gratefully.

I recount the story of Jamie's eggplant or green pepper response to adversity because the novel we read together by Skype—Leslie Marmon Silko's *Ceremony*—features a protagonist who must similarly find his way to health. Not health in the strictly narrow, Western, medical sense but in the much broader Native American sense, where an individual's illness or dysfunction can only be healed in relation to the health of his or her community. Of the protagonist Tayo, the medicine man, Betonie says, "The becoming must be cared for closely" (120). This becoming turns out to be a rich, sensorimotor odyssey, one that Jamie could very much relate to. His own sensorimotor odyssey began at the Jowonio School in Syracuse, an institution devoted to the principle of inclusion. In the language of the Haudenosaunee, a group of Native American tribes in the Northeast and Great Lakes areas of the United States, "Jowonio" means "to set free." "I was a little boy with luck," Jamie recalled, "because Jowonio was a joyous . . . place of community."

. . .

PUBLISHED TO GREAT ACCLAIM in March of 1977, *Ceremony* tells the story of a World War II veteran of mixed Laguna-Pueblo and white ancestry who returns from combat in the Philippines with a severe case of battle fatigue, or what we now call posttraumatic stress disorder. After convalescing for a period at a VA hospital, Tayo travels to the impoverished Laguna reservation in New Mexico where his aunt and grandmother reside, still haunted by the death of his cousin Rocky during the infamous Bataan Death March of 1942. He had promised to look after Rocky, whose head a Japanese soldier had sadistically cracked in two. Western medicine fails to help Tayo, who, like many Native Americans, was encouraged to leave the old customs behind in favor of the material promises of assimilation. In his case, he joined the army.

The novel tracks Tayo's agonizing descent into alcoholism and destructive behavior as he fleetingly recalls, through his grandmother and the New Mexico landscape itself, a long forgotten way of relating to the world. Eventually, the ministrations of the mixed-race medicine man Betonie and a phantom woman (or spirit figure) bring about Tayo's recovery. That recovery coincides with the return of rain to the drought-plagued reservation. During combat in the Philippines, Tayo cursed the jungle's unending deluge; the curse, he comes to realize, worked too well. At the end of the book, he completes a ceremony that "restores harmony with [his] natural surroundings and . . . with [his people]," Silko remarked in an interview.

Considered by some to be the first Native American novel by a woman, *Ceremony* won its author many honors, including an inaugural MacArthur (or "genius") Award in 1981. The book is widely taught in high school and college and is considered a seminal text in Native American literature. As the Western writer Larry McMurtry notes, it "has been startling and moving readers in their thousands for more than a quarter-century." It isn't, however, your typical novel—not by a long shot. The Native writer N. Scott Momaday has labeled it "a telling" because it is so filled with, and shaped by, the mythic creation stories of tribal culture, which is a distinctly oral, as opposed to print, phenomenon. The book also seems to present a Native version of magical realism, one that paradoxically amplifies the gritty verisimilitude of reservation life while also making palpable the living force of the Laguna past and land. Some scholars have read the novel as an early and powerful ecological statement; others have called the land, which has been contaminated by nuclear testing, the novel's primary storyteller.

I'm embarrassed to admit that I hadn't read *Ceremony* before I did so with Jamie by Skype. I'd simply not gotten around to it; nor had I assigned it for a class, which is sometimes the motivation I need to fill such professional lacunae. Jamie and I had been friends for a decade by the time we began our collaborative discussions. I had met him and his parents, Mike and Sheree, at an autism conference about a year or so after he had learned to speak. Mike was a former corrections officer who traveled the country selling baseball memorabilia; Sheree was a former administrative assistant who worked part-time and supported her son's inclusion—Jamie was the third of three truly strapping Burke boys. (The oldest is six-foot-nine.) In every sense, my son, DJ, looked up to Jamie, and because they shared the experience of being inclusion pioneers, the two grew quite close.

I knew that, having now graduated from Syracuse, Jamie missed what he called "structured learning." I also knew of his fascination with Native American culture. *Maybe he could participate in my project*, I thought; *maybe we could read* Ceremony *together*. At SU, he had majored in Religion and Society and minored in Native American Studies, yet his interest in the latter long predated his postsecondary pursuits. As he pointed out, his home-town sits "on Native lands but most don't know it."

Lake Onondaga, the birthplace of the Haudenosaunee, borders Interstate 690 as it heads southeast from the New York Thruway to the western sub-urbs of Syracuse and then into the city itself. On the shores of Onondaga, in the thirteenth or fourteenth century—the date is still in question—the Peacemaker Dekanawidah founded a political and cultural union, a confed-eracy, of five previously warring nations: Oneida, Mohawk, Cayuga, Onon-daga, and Seneca. (The Tuscarora were added in the eighteenth century.) The Great Law of Peace, which Jamie studied in the fourth grade, lays out in wampum symbols a kind of storied constitution, along with rules and pre-scribed ceremonies. *I have uprooted the Great White Pine Tree. In this cavern we shall toss our weapons of war and bury the hatchets of hatred as we replant the Tree of Peace. On top of this tree I will place an eagle to watch for any dan-gers that may come to endanger this peace. I will also send out four white roots of peace. If anyone seeks peace, they can trace the roots back and find shelter here.*

If you grew up in Syracuse, you couldn't miss the befoulment of Lake Onondaga, even if you knew nothing about its importance to the Haudeno-saunee. In the seventeenth century, a group of Jesuits set up a mission on the northeast shore of the lake. The Onondaga welcomed them, and an agree-ment was ceremonially proclaimed: *We shall call each other Brother, as we are equal. In one canoe is our way of life, laws, and people. In the other is your ship with your laws, religion, and people. Our vessels will travel side by side down the river of life. Each will respect the ways of the other and will not interfere with the other, forever.* As in any good contract, the terms were meticulously spelled out: *Forever will be as long as the grass is green, as long as the water runs down-hill, and as long as the sun rises in the east and sets in the west.* In Mario Puzo's novel *The Godfather*, Don Corleone tells a rival family, "We are all honorable men here. We do not have to give each other assurances as if we were lawyers."

The discovery of salty brine springs at the southern end of Onondaga soon attracted the interest of settlers. Salt was not only a prized seasoning but also a crucial preservative. It had value. After the War of Independence, New York State took control of the lake, and commercial salt production burgeoned—to the point that throughout the eighteenth and nineteenth centuries, Syracuse was referred to as the "Salt City" and Onondaga as "Salt Lake." The mineral was so central to the region that when the Erie Canal opened in 1825, someone dubbed it "the ditch that salt built." Between 1797 and 1917, nearly twelve million tons of finished salt were produced. The waste from this process was dumped directly into Lake Onondaga, but the environmental damage was only just beginning.

The real culprits would turn out to be soda ash, which was needed to make industrial products, such as glass, and mercury, which was needed to make chlorine. By the mid-1970s, Allied Chemical was responsible for releasing an estimated twenty-five pounds of mercury into the lake each day. It was as if Skyholder himself, the high god of Haudenosaunee mythology, had been poisoned, and the lake eventually succumbed: ice harvesting was outlawed in 1901, swimming in 1940, and fishing in 1970. The very place where, more than half a millennium before, the confederacy had been consecrated, was now a superfund site, the most polluted lake in America. An old Cree saying warns, "When all the trees have been cut down, when all the animals have been hunted, when all the waters are polluted, when all the air is unsafe to breathe, only then will you discover you cannot eat money."

In English we speak of a man being worth his salt—but not his lake. As he grew up, Jamie followed the environmental protests in Syracuse. He loved to read about the different Indian nations—both in school and on his own. A favorite teacher, who "felt the sadness in dear destruction," exposed him to the history of conquest. She also exposed him to Native American creation stories, unleashing a veritable obsession—what the typical autism expert would term, without irony, a "restricted interest." (As one website puts it, "Restricted and repetitive interests and activities are . . . [a] key feature[] of autism. Watching a fan spin around for hours; flipping the flag on a toy mailbox up and down again and again; taking a spoon or other inanimate object everywhere as though it were the most special thing in the world.") Looking back, Jamie said, "I simply love the idea of the earth as the valuable essence of life. I feel comfortable in this culture." He especially appreciated contemporary efforts at tribal rebirth—what he called "developing the hope of living in liberation after being devastated in fundamental life."

At Syracuse he was able to take a number of classes with Native American professors, and he was pleased by "the respect he received as a learner." He felt not only welcomed, which is rare enough in inclusive education, but also treasured. "I have noticed," Jamie wrote, "that in the study of the Native Americans, there seems to be a calling for . . . demonstrating the life-worth of all communities of people, whether they are the Nations of the Haudenosaunee, Iroquois, or Mohawk, or communities of people who . . . struggle with communication, motor dysfunction, or sensory regulation. [Everyone] deserves to be valued just for being the humans they are." Imagine a philosophy so organically accepting that it didn't need the contemporary concept of neurodiversity to honor people who are cognitively different.

Jamie knew how lucky he was: if he hadn't grown up in Syracuse, where the university has an especially progressive college of education, a commitment to facilitated communication, and a close relationship with the public school system, he may never have escaped the predictable life trajectory of someone with classical autism. From the moment he could type, he worried about kids less fortunate, and he longed for them to have a shot at their dreams: "My joy on this journey wants to include so many others who should have the opportunity to be at a college or university, where worlds of odd literature and explanations of staying safe in sex and dating, and soulful revelations of an Ojibwa professor regarding the truth of the destruction of the Native Americans, are boldly open to all."

This is the context in which Jamie and I read *Ceremony*, roughly twenty pages a week for twelve weeks. I knew going into our Skype discussions that autistic readers tend to wonderfully scramble typical patterns of identification. When I had discussed *Moby-Dick* with Tito, I was astonished by how much he identified with the book's central mammal—he especially loved Ishmael's descriptions of the very different ways that whales hear and see, linking these descriptions to his own neurodiverse sensing. And when I had discussed *Adventures of Huckleberry Finn* with DJ, I was astonished as much by his ferocious identification with the runaway slave Jim as by his identification with the lonesome river.

Jamie, in contrast, was more conventional. He naturally identified with the Native American protagonist and immediately empathized with Tayo's debilitating fear. (I say "conventional" because a novel encourages the reader to get behind its hero, even as, in the case of *Ceremony*, it may tamper with the conceit of a strictly individual or human one.) "I have journeyed in my own system of terror to a dimension of peace," Jamie said. For him, the terror was the recognition of "being abnormal in the social world" and the possession of a sensory system so differently integrated and intense as to produce constant anxiety. "Many are lost in fear. Fundamental to know others suffer and greatly emerge," he commented. When I asked him how he had vanquished his terror, he replied, "The contribution of therapies is paramount to my value of calm."

The connection to the novel's protagonist was strengthened by his father's service in Vietnam. A marine, Mike had fought in the Battle of Hamburger

Hill, so named for the way that men had been ground up like beef. Part of Operation Apache Snow, this ill-advised assault on the North Vietnamese Army resulted in the deaths of seventy-two Americans; five times that number were wounded. A quiet, dependable man, Mike had a granite dignity about him. "My father," Jamie explained, "effected love as a natural discourse to leave the memories behind." In the novel, of course, Tayo also finds love and in the process begins to heal.

Jamie's understanding of traumatic recovery seems profoundly astute: it involves, in his words, "not vitally destroying the emotion of fear but moving through the connection it brings to life." When we discussed the difference between the white man's medical response to trauma and the Native American's ceremonial response, we lingered over the medicine man Betonie's remark: "In that hospital they don't bury the dead, they keep them in rooms and talk to them" (114). In Jamie's analysis, "White people deem pills as returning to health, but Native Americans believe that the soul of the past within the physical must be healed first. The body will follow." "When the mind and the soul are in illness, the physical," he clarified, "can be recuperated but not whole. It is as a living death." The ceremonial response to trauma, which is at once communal and somatic, seeks to heal a failure of relation—between body and mind, past and present, individual and group, people and land.

In this way, to identify with Tayo was to identify with other entities as well. The Acu, or "place that always was," if not a character per se, is certainly a presence, even a conscious being, in *Ceremony*, and Jamie shared both the author's nonlinear sense of time and her ecological politics. The novel, to put it simply, doesn't have a setting: the Laguna people don't live *on* the land; rather, they live *in* and *through* it. Because Silko refuses all manner of dichotomies and instead insists on dynamic simultaneity, Jamie's identification with Tayo wasn't finally a conventional gesture at all. Rather, by identifying with him, he was identifying with the Native dream of wholeness in which the alienated individual falls away and a place and a people, along with its vital history, stand proud.

· · ·

WE HAD BEGUN to discuss *Ceremony* in April 2014, a few weeks after my spring break, and I was already feeling the crush of late semester obligations. We'd Skype at the end of a workday when I was typically tired and a tad irritable. I have terrific students at Grinnell, but when they get stressed, many of them become scattered, even downright spacey. And because the college tries to cram too many events and meetings into that cruelest of months, it compounds the frenzy of the school year's conclusion. With confidence, and more than a bit of sass, Walt Whitman exclaims in *Song of Myself,* "My words itch at your ears till you understand them." In April and early May, itching frankly won't cut it. A professor's words need to burrow like a cockroach into the auditory canal. (Cockroaches, according to experts, crawl into peoples' ears more than any other bug. I read this on Yahoo last week. "Positively thigmotaxic," they like tight-fitting spaces.)

And yet, no matter how tired or irritable I was—to think of one's pedagogy as an insect invasion is pretty irritable—Jamie would snap me out of it. "Hi, friend, good to see you," he would say. "Fun to engage this most enjoyable time." His dedication to the novel and our discussions moved me greatly; it went so far beyond mere diligence or enthusiasm. "Really, I feel the reality of having a strong obligation to read this," he said, though he often found the novel "highly distressing to the emotions." He wondered about how DJ manages "deep upset": "Can he shed tears and express this? I cannot myself and strongly carry the dependent emotion of crying in my mind." In one conversation, he proclaimed, "Literature is very vital to my knowledge." And then he asked, "How do kids search in their hearts when they cannot read these books?"

A Native American professor at Syracuse had once described Jamie's writing as "dreamy." There was indeed something to this description, but the *Brigadoon* quality often seemed more diagrammatic than pictorial, more math than mist. Imagine a kind of divine geometry: all manner of shapes floating in the air, the cathedral of life rendered as a set of three-dimensional plans. An aficionado of complex symmetry, Jamie attempted to translate his formidable spatial perceptions, which are governed largely by the right cerebral hemisphere, into language, which is governed largely by the left, with all of the syntactical and usage challenges this entailed. For example, he called the business of talking about how a book intersects with our lives "dimensional truth." Laguna chants were "harmonies of elevation." Human voices "carry visual form." Ceremonies "can structure visual connection with the grounding of the past." When he liked something I said, he would respond with "cool as ice" or "highly structural." There was no greater compliment he could give than to appreciate an entity's essential organization.

In *The Autistic Brain,* Temple Grandin provides a clue as to what may be going on. Whereas in her groundbreaking work *Thinking in Pictures* she simply conceived of neurotypicals as verbal thinkers and autistic thinkers as visual ones, in this book she ruffles the binary in order to account for autistics who are verbal thinkers and autistics who are visual thinkers but in ways very different from herself. "What I called a *picture thinker*," she reports, "[the new research] called an *object visualizer*, and what I called a *pattern thinker*, [it] called a *spatial visualizer*." Grandin excelled at the former but was surprisingly poor at the latter. Spatial visualizers can manipulate objects in their heads, moving them at will in a kind of organic calculus, as though they were determining the volume of a solid of revolution without equations. Grandin can see these objects in astonishing detail, but to map them she must move around the object herself, as though she were holding a video camera.

Neuroimaging has shown that there are two visual pathways in the brain: the ventral, which handles the appearance of objects, and the dorsal, which handles the position and relation of objects in space. As Grandin notes, "People obviously use both pathways, relying more on one or the other depending on the task." But in autism a particular path may be dominant, exceedingly so. In the 1920s, a German psychologist noticed that hallucinations—from drugs, migraines, flickering lights, and other causes—took one or more geometric forms: tunnels, spirals, lattices, or cobwebs. In the 1980s, a mathematician at Cal Tech hypothesized that "because hallucinations moved independently of the eye, the source of the images was not on the retina but in the visual cortex itself." In other words, the hallucinations were a reflection of the fractal geometry that undergirds functional sight, a geometry that turns out to be ubiquitous in nature. When you hallucinate, you see seeing. It's quite possible that in autism, where bottom-up processing is the norm, spatial visualizers behave a bit like a computer, a natural one, synthesizing and manipulating visual information to discover the living essence of objects in space. They see an object, at least initially, the way that a dorsally driven visual cortex, and not the eye in service to the frontal lobes, would "see" it.

Whenever I applauded Jamie's insights and spoke more generally about cognitive strengths in autism, he would say, "You are a wonderful man." But he could also tease me about being too professorial. Sometimes I'd lose track of what I was doing. I'd think I was at the annual Modern Language Association conference blathering away with my colleagues. "You are engaging the academic," he would say cheerfully. "A professor is someone who talks in someone else's sleep," the British poet W. H. Auden quipped. Even more devastating is this remark by the Danish philosopher Søren Kierkegaard: "Take away paradox from the thinker and you have a professor."

Jamie reminded me of one of the reasons I had fallen in love with literature in the first place: it is a sanctuary for paradox, a Jurassic Park where roaring contradictions thrive—long after, we might say, an asteroid struck the human mind with such force that it sent a cloud of rationality into the frontal lobes and precipitated their extinction. A paradox doesn't need to be resolved; it is a way of thinking multiple things at once, a way of moving beyond the restrictive categories of language. Take the word "disability," for example. Is autism a disability? Perhaps it is a disabling ability? Or even an enabling disability? Literary language, as Tito demonstrated, is as fluid as the sea, and it allows us to swim around or under the terms that constitute thought. In my teaching, I try to analyze a text without mastering it, and I try to hold back as much as I can so that my students discover things on their own. With Jamie I strove less to be a professor than an older, book-loving comrade. "There are two kinds of teachers," wrote Robert Frost, "the kind that fill you with so much quail shot that you can't move, and the kind that just gives you a little prod behind and you jump to the skies."

Increasingly Jamie believed that the novel welcomes an autistic neurology. While *Ceremony* obviously presents a story, it dramatizes space, not time, the customary engine of narrative. In fact, it does away with the latter altogether, or at least its unidirectional version, because it has come to signify inexorable ruin. At one point in the novel, as Tayo searches for some cattle that white ranchers have stolen, he muses, "The ride into the mountain had branched into all directions of time.... Rocky and I are walking across the ridge in moonlight.... This night is a single night; and there has never been any other" (179). By treating time as space, Tayo begins to escape the iron logic of loss. He experiences the fullness of the past through something like radical stereopsis, or depth perception. The image of Rocky gestures at unseen dimensions, including the "four worlds below," where the spirits of the dead reside, and the space of mythological figures such as Corn Mother and Thought-Woman.

When I inquired as to why Silko interrupts the story with Native legends and poems, Jamie replied, "Through the poems, memories and ceremonies are slowly returned to Tayo's mind. They are the voices of the past seeking connection to the present. They exist outside of the novel and must somehow be brought in." "Tayo," he remarked in a startling figure, "is listening with more than ears." And Jamie, it seemed to me, was reading with more than eyes. He was using his considerable visuospatial prowess to illuminate the novel's spiritual geography. Betonie's counsel that "the becoming must be cared for closely" thus applies as much to the protagonist as to the reader who is asked to think like a spatial visualizer and to piece together—dynamically—the novel's own "becoming."

"How would Silko understand autism?" I asked, intrigued by the prospect that Jamie's affinity for Native American culture was as much a matter of cognitive style as it was hospitable feeling or political conviction. Although he certainly experienced the equivalent of "the Native American world of challenges," something about his own sensing lined up with what he had encountered in his studies at Syracuse and in reading *Ceremony* with me. Pointing to the mute boy Shush who lives with Betonie and who is said to have been raised by bears—think of him as a Native twist on the feral child—Jamie believed Silko would reject the prevailing stereotype of autistics as "deeply tuned out." She would view the condition not only as a potential shamanic gift, he maintained, but also as a mark of profound connection with nature. "Perhaps Shush is autistic," he speculated, "in that he sees beyond the purely physical."

In a conceit that reflected Silko's desire to preserve the endangered values and traditions of an oral culture in a print medium, Jamie presented autism as a kind of literacy instructor. "Autism plays ideas as a mother in the reading of books," he said, "meaning that the mother, or earth, formulates connection in the strong sense of the Indian language." I remember being perplexed by this statement but also having a sense of what he meant. The irony of associating autism with parenting, let alone teaching, did not, however, escape me. Autism, according to Jamie, is at once a mother instructing her children to read and Mother Nature herself, a source of interpretable, life-sustaining lessons. Literacy in this understanding becomes a way of being in the world as much as a phonological, orthographical, semantic, syntactical, and morphological technique; the book of life, as reflected in the language of the Laguna people, emerges from the land. Like Silko, Jamie refused to accept a strict dichotomy between reading and living or between thinking and seeing.

Although autism is a profoundly visuospatial intelligence, it doesn't preclude verbal ability—that should go without saying. Just as Grandin learned to express herself in language, so, too, did Jamie, though he acknowledged that the translation of the visual into the verbal continues to be frustrating. My point is that certain works of literature seem especially to reward a visuospatial intelligence. When Jamie reported that he "really enjoys the strong visual emotions that Silko extends to readers" or references her "words of visual courage," he could be said to confirm what cognitive scholars already know: that literature's concrete diction elicits mental imagery in the minds of readers. But when he says, "I enhance the process of interpreting the patterns of language in order to demonstrate the progress of movement in the visual" or "I work in the beauty of the production of image evolving in my world of interpretation," he points to something conspicuously autistic: the kind of videographic imagination that Grandin and others have talked about.

Grandin's seminal book *Thinking in Pictures* begins like this: "I think in pictures. Words are like a second language to me. I translate both spoken and written words into full-color movies, complete with sound, which run like a VCR tape in my head. When somebody speaks to me, his words are instantly translated into pictures. Language-based thinkers often find this phenomenon difficult to understand, but in my job as an equipment designer for the livestock industry, visual thinking is a tremendous advantage." Jamie hasn't yet found employment that would allow him to exploit his own capacity to think in pictures, but he would agree with Grandin. "My creation of visual mind is something I am passionate about," he emphasized. To him, reading literature is akin to watching a 3D (or even 4D) film in his head. While the typical reader seems to connect a novel's images like a primitive, flip-book animator, Jamie connects them like an award-winning Hollywood producer! He "enhances," as he says, the "process of interpreting the patterns of language" by giving words not only more flesh but also more motion. Such enhancement proved especially useful when he began to explore Silko's idea of reparative becoming through ceremonial movement.

Scholars of modernist literature speak of a literary style called "stream of consciousness" in which, as a common dictionary definition puts it, "a character's thoughts, feelings, and reactions are depicted in a continuous flow, uninterrupted by objective description or conventional dialogue." Images run into each other like entities in a flood: lawn chairs collide with trashcans; strollers collide with bicycles. It's a constant, cerebral ampersand in which the non sequitur reigns! Silko no doubt uses this technique to convey Tayo's anguished state of mind, but she is finally interested in something else, something much more ambitious. She wants to convey, as Jamie helped me to understand, an evolving relationship between the land, the past, and a people—an evolution that in no way sacrifices that past or renders it defunct. Call it "stream of geography" or the spatial visualizer's antidote to linear history.

Jamie's movie-making mind dedicated itself to the project of vitally seeing Tayo's slow passage back to wholeness. In a Western context, the poet Wendell Berry remarks, "The concept of health is rooted in the concept of wholeness. To be healthy is to be whole. The word *health* belongs to a family of words, a listing of which will suggest how far the consideration of health must carry us: *heal, whole, wholesome, hale, hallow, holy*." Jamie was intimately familiar with this broader notion of health, which for him involved not only the many therapies and accommodations he had received but also, and just as important, the community of support he had worked to establish. From that community emerged a kind of palpable spirituality. His "creation of visual mind" and his love of Native American culture fueled his identification with Tayo, and, as will become clear, it encouraged him to map his motor challenges onto Silko's hero.

In chapter 1, Tito explained the phenomenon of hyperfocusing. One consequence of local overconnectivity and a greater reliance on posterior sensory regions of the brain to think is a preference for details over categories and the concrete over the abstract. Jamie experienced this phenomenon as well, and it, too, seemed—uncannily—to serve the needs of the novel. Before thinking *tree*, for example, he takes in "the molecular structure of the good freedom of the natural world." "Details are my friends," he explained. Like a poststructuralist of the visual, Jamie celebrates each tree's irreducible particularity, noting, "The wood of the forest of trees perhaps engages the brain to connect with the work of differences." The category *tree* and the even bigger category *forest* emerge slowly. "I believe it's seeing the tree in the process of creation," he remarked. With this kind of seeing, the world doesn't exist in advance as something to be used or mastered.

"Delayed decoding," to borrow another scholar's memorable phrase, facilitates extraordinary pattern detection in autism. In fact, the ability to think beneath the category is crucial for seeing how ostensibly discrete things might connect or how ostensibly linked things might connect differently. The researcher Tim Langdell found that autistics excel at "pure pattern" whereas neurotypicals excel at "social pattern"—"pure pattern" hides in plain sight, as in the test where the autistic boy called that decorative pillow a ravioli. It contradicts the socially assigned and accepted meaning of things, and in this way it can foster creativity. As Grandin writes, "The trick to coming up with novel uses for a brick is not to be attached to its identity as a brick. The trick is to reconceive it as a non-brick." Imagine a mason doing just that by using his beloved materials to shatter the plate-glass tyranny of his employer. In this scenario, the mason becomes a matador and the boss a bull—both see red.

Hans Asperger, the doctor who separately discovered autism in Austria during the late 1930s, believed that "the enhanced pattern-recognition of his autistic patients would make them valuable code-breakers for the Reich."

In bravely stating this view, Asperger, according to the recent book *NeuroTribes: The Legacy of Autism and the Future of Neurodiversity*, was trying to save them from the Nazi T-4 program, which ended up euthanizing some 300,000 people it deemed "life unworthy of life." Asperger looked beyond the disabling aspects of autism and discerned otherwise imperceptible ability. Pure pattern recognition can thus have a paradoxically social use: it can protect against coagulated prejudice.

Over the course of our discussions, Jamie revealed his considerable ability to "sequence the pattern"; "the pattern is what I see in the first look," he said. "I like following it. Truly I am summoning the answers and revealing what the information connects." Unlike Grandin and other so-called "high-functioning" autistics, he doesn't attribute his advanced patterning skills to a Spock-like repudiation of emotion; his seeing isn't strictly logical, however bottom-up it may be. Nor is it a-social, not in the least. What Jamie describes above sounds a lot like motif tracing, a staple of literary study. A motif, as any first-year literature student knows, is a reoccurring image or theme that musically structures a novel, poem, or play. This structure is subtle, and it requires not only searching for it in unexpected places but also recognizing it in unexpected forms. I took note of how Jamie had translated a nonconceptual autistic propensity—to see patterns—into a conceptual neurotypical one. In literature he had found a meeting point for the two processing styles. "Books are patterning on thoughts," he said confidently.

Ceremony makes great use of patterns—and not just in the way that a skilled author does. Rather, the ritual that restores Tayo to health literally requires improved pattern detection. Tayo is said to be "involved with other things [than words]: memories and shifting sounds heard in the night, diamond patterns, black on white; the energy of the designs spiraled deep, then protruded suddenly into three-dimensional summits, their depth and height dizzy and shifting with the eye" (212). The woman with whom he makes love wears a blanket. Tayo "did not miss the designs woven across the blanket in four colors: patterns of storm clouds in white and grey; black lightning scattered through brown wind" (165). When I asked Jamie about this passage, he replied, "The pattern is of the universe and through her he will receive the heavens of the brain." To be certain that I hadn't missed the import of this insight (or his miraculous phrasing), he added, "I mean that this pattern will open the thought to remembering what Betonie has spoken of and seen as vision."

In *Ceremony*, an actual picture of "the pattern of stars the old man drew on the ground that night" (165) appears. "Why would a novel, which is an art form made of words, include a drawing of a constellation?" I asked. "It is important to reveal the vital process of emotion, especially when those stars will passionately interpret a pattern of return. To me the drawing looked simply as a thought of pure energy," he replied. How interesting: Jamie seemed to put his finger on Silko's need at this moment for something like an autistic, which is to say visuospatial, intelligence. The patterning of words alone, she hints, is inadequate: the writer's tiny graphic signifiers can't quite depict the volumetric depth or annulated shape of prophecy.

Neurobiological accounts of trauma, interestingly enough, reveal an analogous overreliance on the brain's posterior sensory regions and right-hemispheric limbic structures. What matters to such an intelligence and what seems more likely to initiate healing in trauma is not language alien-ated from the body—the so-called talking cure—or language alienated from the patient's environment, but embodied, communal activities such as yoga and dance that holistically incorporate language. Traumatic images become healing ones, Silko implies in a Native American context, through ceremonial movement. But new patterns are paramount. They bring new thoughts, new possibilities.

In this way, a multiracial author insists on a multimedia form. The future depends, as Betonie understood, on adapting the old ways, including the transformation of oral storytelling into print narrative. Burke called this sort of "changing with the present" "intelligent continuation," and the phrase can be applied as much to Tayo's "journeying into the place of memory" as to his own journeying into the place of typing and speech.

. . .

IT WAS A TYPICAL February morning in Grinnell—cold, gray, and, above all, windy. The plains writer Greta Ehrlich once titled a book *The Solace of Open Spaces*, but I've never found such openness to be a balm. As I drove to the public radio station in Iowa City, I kept looking at the scraggly pines that served as a windbreak for the farmhouses I passed. Facing west, stoop-ing in spite of themselves, they struggled in the late-winter gale. The fronts that come through, their endless histrionics, mock the tight-lipped stoicism of these trees. It's as if they are trying to offset some embarrassment of sky—some nimbostratus aunt, say, who descends upon the house and pours out her intimate miseries. The weather in Iowa, I once told a friend, is like a Sharon Olds poem: it's entirely too confessional.

In 2011, my wife, Emily, and I had coedited a collection of writings about the concept of neurodiversity, and I had convinced the host of Iowa Public Radio's noon show *The Exchange* to have us on—not only us but also two of the volume's contributors: a graduate student at Penn State named Scott Robertson and Jamie. Robertson, who was vice president of the Autistic Self Advocacy Network and who had contributed an essay titled "Neurodiversity, Quality of Life, and Autistic Adults: Shifting Research and Professional Focuses onto Real-Life Challenges," would phone into the program from State College. Jamie, who had contributed to the self-advocate roundtable and whose words in an email to me became the volume's epigraph, would participate via the public radio station in Syracuse. ("I must send forward my bold appreciation for taking the soul of this topic . . . to be shared among the many and diverse hearts who will attempt a new understanding," the epigraph reads. "It can be very lovely when curious old patterns of comprehension shift to a more connected and true demonstration of the improved focus. My deep thanks, then, for the spirit of change and challenge.")

To make things still more complicated, Emily would phone in from Grinnell—only I would be in the IPR studio in Iowa City. I had told the host, Ben Kieffer, that Jamie would need to type his remarks before speaking them, which presented a problem: dead air, a period of near-silence in which listeners would be treated to the faint sound of fingers on a keyboard. But since this was a show about neurodiversity, Kieffer went with it, explaining periodically to the audience what they were hearing. In 1964, a writer for *Life* magazine commented on the many improbable things that Guglielmo Marconi's contraption had spawned: "Radio tried everything, and it all worked. It invented a new kind of singer whose voice wasn't even loud enough to carry across a hotel bedroom, and Americans, as it turned out, would rather hear these 'crooners' than any big-bellied tenor who ever shook an opera house chandelier." Jamie's voice could certainly carry, but it needed motoric priming before it could make the light fixtures swoon.

As far as we knew, this was the first live radio interview with a formerly nonspeaking autist—or at least one who'd learned to speak at thirteen. I was apprehensive, to put it mildly. In fact, as I donned the IPR headphones and positioned my mouth in front of the microphone, I thought of Ronald Reagan's ill-conceived mic-test joke: "My fellow Americans, I am pleased to tell you I just signed legislation which outlaws Russia forever. The bombing will begin in five minutes." What might I say? "I have just signed legislation that outlaws normalcy forever. Inclusion will begin in five seconds."

The social psychologist Carol Gilligan, whose 1982 book *In a Different Voice* sparked a much-needed consideration of gender in the field of ethics, trenchantly observes, "Speaking and listening are a form of psychic breathing." My son, DJ, would love this notion—the ears and mouths of people operating as lungs, the body politic and all of its ethnic, racial, gender, class, and neurological differences striving for homeostasis. I thought of how labored psychic breathing can become when a particular group hasn't been invited to join the conversation. *Whatever happens on air will be fine*, I told myself. Indeed, it would be an improvement upon the constant palaver of nonautistics about autism. Let the majority listen for a while. After all, "listening," as autist Dawn Prince once pointedly remarked, "is the superior half of speaking."

For as long as I had known Jamie, I had marveled at his ability to type independently, which is rare in classical autism, and to speak aloud what he had typed, which is even rarer. Jamie had distinguished himself in these (and other) respects, but how exactly had he done so?

I was, of course, familiar with the research that conceived of autism as a sensorimotor disorder. That view had emerged when the stranglehold of mechanistic thinking about the brain began to relax. Scientists abandoned modular notions of brain functioning (this controls that, etc.) in favor of complex networks that connect otherwise distinct regions in intricately patterned ways. Even the oldest, most primitive, "reptilian" regions, such as the basal ganglia and cerebellum, which had been thought to contribute narrowly to motor function, were implicated in higher-order thought. (The basal ganglia enable voluntary motor actions whereas the cerebellum ensures "coordination, precision and accurate timing.") In fact, Gerald Edelman coined the phrase "basal syntax" to emphasize the fundamental relationship between movement and language.

Speaking, to be sure, is one of the most complicated motoric things that humans do—speaking as the act of making discernible sounds but also the act of stringing such sounds together in a fluently sequential way. Language, argued Marcel Kinsbourne, is an "elaboration, extension and abstraction of sensorimotor function." It evolved from "utterances that were coincident with and driven by the same rhythm as the movement in question." Or as Iain McGilchrist put it more recently, "The deep structure of syntax is founded on the fixed sequences of limb movement in running creatures." These researchers point to the fully integrated and embodied nature of human cognition: it is neither modular in its operation nor cut off from the flesh. Indeed, the brain depends on a body—a very active body—to think. (Even—or especially—when it claims to be a kind of self-made man!) "A voice cannot carry the tongue and lips that gave it wings," the Lebanese poet Kahlil Gibran once lamented. "Alone it must seek the ether. And alone and without his nest shall the eagle fly across the sun."

This is not to say that impairments in the "nest"—in the basal ganglia and cerebellum—fail to manifest themselves in specific ways. Rather, it is to insist on a holistic understanding of both dysfunction and potential remediation. Over the last five or six years, the scientific literature has confirmed what autistics, parents, and clinicians have known for quite some time: that autism spectrum disorders (ASD) are "associated with significant and widespread alterations in motor performance," as a meta-analysis from 2010 concluded. This study went so far as to propose that motor differences, particularly in the basal ganglia and cerebellum, constitute a "core element" of autism and that "interventions aimed at improving . . . motor coordination (i.e., gait and balance, arm functions and movement planning)" should be developed.

But what is at stake in such interventions? Nothing less than being itself. If we remember the pithy formulation of two systems scientists—that "to move is to perceive, and to perceive is to move"—then we might begin to fathom the extraordinary dynamism of this constant feedback loop. We might also be less tempted to conceive of impaired social interaction in autism, for example, or perseverative "behavior" as evidence of innate cortical dysfunction than as "downstream effects of . . . various noisy, unpredictable and unreliable peripheral inputs." This last bit is researcher-speak for disturbances in sensory processing and action broadly construed. If such disturbances can be corrected or circumvented, the reigning narrative of ASD falters dramatically.

Listen to the editors of a groundbreaking book on movement differences in autism. I quote Elizabeth Torres and Anne Donnellan at length because they effectively depict what typical maturation accomplishes and, in turn, help us to see the hidden challenges that autistics face:

> When the sensations from our ever changing physical motions emerge
> as a stable percept that we can reliably predict, we begin to anticipate

the sensory consequences of our impending actions with remarkable certainty.... We begin to understand cause and effect in the physical world that we interact with, a world that includes others in social motion as well. The understanding of our own actions through their sensations helps us scaffold social cognition by establishing first the sense of self as an anchor, and then the sense of others and their relative motions.... It is through the sensations of our own movements and through those of the movements of others as we sense them kinesthetically and visually that we learn to mentally navigate actions, to acquire a sense of agency and autonomy, and to eventually imagine, in a disembodied way, what it would be like to perform a physical action without actually having to do it.

Analyzing the movements of typical toddlers, Torres discovered that three-year-olds "do not yet have statistical predictability of temporal features of their limb movements." It's not only that they lack the control and motor fluency of four-year-olds but also that their movements are still conspicuously random: there's too much noise, and too little signal, as they respond with their bodies to a moving and endlessly variable world.

Even when they attempt to produce the same movement, the movement is different—that's the point. The organism must be able to adapt spontaneously to the demands of the present, which in all of its swirling specificity only vaguely resembles the moment just before it. These toddlers haven't yet assimilated what the philosopher Maria Brincker and Torres call "sensorimotor priors": a sturdy, "probabilistic expectation about the variability itself." In this key respect, classical autistics operate motorically like typical three-year-olds.

Brincker views "'sensorimotor priors' ... as a kind of predictable probabilistic body, an abstract body that we can 'bring into' counterfactual scenarios and thus use to navigate and make decisions in spaces we do not stand in current embodied relations to." In contrast, autistics must "rely on their 'here & now' body and world sensation." They are beautifully stuck in the present, unable to leverage the past to create an immediate, if less captivating because motorically homogenized, future. They are like Adam and Eve taking their first entrancing step in the Garden. They are living quite literally *in the moment*—again and again and again. I am unaware of anyone who has proposed a link between "weak central coherence"—the business of sensing so much detail as to make forming conceptual generalizations difficult—and a lack of "sensorimotor priors." In both cases, as probabilistic expectation offers little guidance, perception and movement stall, like a stunt plane whose angle of attack has exceeded maximum lift. They remain immured in mesmerizing intensity, not propelled by the customary procedures—the flight plan—of temporal abstraction.

For this reason, another researcher in the collection, Pat Amos, argues that autism should be considered a temporo-spatial processing disorder akin to Parkinson's syndrome or certain traumatic brain injuries. She writes,

> It is often observed that the sense of time appears to work differently for many people with autism. That would not be surprising, given the increasing evidence that autism involves challenges to neural connectivity and different ways of assembling experiences. What has to be connected in order to accurately sense time is something even more complicated than, for example, connecting speech sounds with facial movements. Time is not a mode or channel of sensory experience, but an amodal property that unites the perceptions of different senses. We sense time through comparisons of our experiences, bootstrapping from events of known duration to establish expectations about other events; repeated events in the world and familiar rhythms of the body come to stand for intervals of time, with which new events can be compared.

Amos concludes, "If these embodied experiences are unreliable for people on the autism spectrum, it might make sense that the comparison process also would prove challenging, resulting in a panicked feeling of being adrift in a sea of time."

Enter the drum and metronome. As the authors of yet another essay in the volume report, not only does auditory rhythm activate a person's motor systems, but there is also "evidence of rapid motor synchronization to an external rhythmic cue in persons with and without neurological disability." As anyone who has ever attended a dance or tapped their fingers to a song on their iPod knows, a particular beat can physiologically commandeer our bodies, prompting us to move in concert with it. Scientists call this phenomenon "entrainment," and it has far-reaching implications for rehabilitative interventions. Research has demonstrated that auditory rhythmic cueing offers a "temporal template for [the] organization of motor output." It affects both "the timing of movement and the total movement pattern" by "add[ing] stability in motor control immediately (within two or three stimuli) rather than through a gradual learning process." It's like a referee, or the shot clock at a basketball game: it imposes itself on the action. By "influencing motor anticipation . . . the [listener's] response pattern gradually becom[es] automatized."

In this way, such cueing can compensate for irregularities in the basal ganglia or cerebellum and perhaps even encourage cortical plasticity. As the authors note, the cerebellum has been shown to aid "in computing the temporal parameters of incoming sensory stimuli and outgoing movements as well as in novel, temporally precise motor movements." It is the organic "comparator" of which Amos speaks. It "predicts the timing of an upcoming movement, utilizes sensory feedback from the current movement, compares ongoing performance to an internal model, and then adapts responses such as force and/or trajectory." Like a kind of motorized auditory wheelchair, rhythmic cueing can move the struggling autist along. It can do much of the work of "sensorimotor priors."

Neurological drumming and a metronome helped Jamie to type independently and eventually to speak. Samonas listening therapy helped him to tie his shoes. "So many things were hard for me to learn," he reported. About that latter milestone, which he had achieved at the age of fifteen, he said, "My brain moved into hiding the reason for not being able to do it." "Like saying letters, mostly there was no pattern to follow in my brain for tying my shoelaces. After much practice . . . it seemed a pattern moved into my brain, giving directions to my hands. I think my music therapy gave help with this." By pattern, Jamie means something like a path or continuum, a kind of impetus that helps to string a series of motor actions together. His body needed the conviction of a moving sidewalk at the airport or a bowling ball that's kept out of the gutter by bumpers—momentum and direction driving intentionality forward and instilling confidence. The authors of the aforementioned article write, "Building an anticipatory means of motor control in autism might . . . facilitate the development of internal models for motor planning." This seems to be what happened with Jamie.

Like him, Tito also used auditory motor cueing to learn how to tie his shoes, except that his cue of choice was metrical poetry—in particular, a poem by the eighteenth-century British romantic poet William Blake. Wrapping, in his words, the tetrameter of the poem around his fingers, he coaxed them to execute the necessary movements. If we should no longer think of the brain as modular (but, rather, as a fully embodied, plastic, and integrated network, one capable of neural accommodations and workarounds), perhaps we should no longer think of the arts as narrowly modular, too. They are not simply effete refinement—an unimportant evolutionary inheritance, a kind of "auditory cheesecake," as Stephen Pinker once described music. Auden famously lamented, "Poetry makes nothing happen," but that's not true, as least with respect to its effects on the body and, as we will see, its ability, through the phenomenon of motor coupling, to foster community.

"The predictability of musical stimuli and the use of stimuli to improve motor planning may have additional effects on cognitive, communicative, and social functioning." Indeed! Tito was so plagued by anxiety as a young boy and Soma had so run out of ways to mollify him that one day she popped into her eight-track recorder a tape of British metrical poetry and he stopped dead in his tracks, becoming quite calm. The way some people leave the TV on all day, Tito leaves poetry on—"as a background to [his] sound environment." "It gives me a secured feeling because of the predictability formed by the pattern in words," he explained.

I had heard of clinicians using poetry to help patients understand their emotions, but that is largely a content-based endeavor. I had never considered the psychological benefits of rhythm and rhyme. When I pressed Tito on this notion, he replied, "A rhyme is a very linear auditory experience. And so is the beat—be it in tetrameter or in pentameter. It arouses the cortical mind with certain meaningful language experience and arouses the subcortical mind with the expectation of the mechanical beat that is offered by the lines of the poem. Anxiety is subcortical. Anxiety gets diluted by the experience." Delving into the matter more deeply, I discovered that he was right. A study from 2013 found that metrical patterning and phonological resonance between words "help to structure a verse line in time." Such structuring, I reasoned, may work to pull the autistic listener into the future. There was even evidence that these things "led . . . to more positively perceived and felt emotions." With its loud and regular horn, the sonic train of verse may provide precisely what the proverbial psychologist orders: the *feeling* of moving forward.

It may also aid in what Frederick Turner calls the brain's "synthetic and predictive activity of hypothesis construction." By that he means our ability to answer the question "What's next?" without overly taxing the system. "By ruling out certain rhythmic possibilities," Turner writes, "meter satisfies the brain's procrustean demand for unambiguity and clear distinctions. By combining elements of repetition and isochrony [the rhythmic division of time into equal portions] on the one hand with variation on the other, it nicely fulfills the . . . habituative need for controlled novelty." That need, as I have shown, is overwhelming in classical autism.

I came to think that formal poetry had served as a kind of prosthesis for Tito—the equivalent of Ahab's ivory leg or "the auger hole [on the *Pequod*'s quarter deck], bored about half an inch or so into the plank" (125–26). "His bone leg steadied in that hole," Ahab, Ishmael tells us, could "st[and] erect, looking straight out beyond the ship's ever-pitching prow" (126). Tito, too, needed a way to stand erect—to captain the heaving ship of his senses. Like Ahab's, his was a homespun accommodation, something worked up out of necessity, in the absence of formal help from professionals. All across the country, parents of autistic children—usually the mothers—tinker in this way. Sometimes, as in Jamie's case, they're aided by innovative occupational therapists, psychologists, and speech-language pathologists. Rarely do parents or clinicians or autistics themselves(!) get the recognition they deserve as the experimental vanguard of scientific knowledge.

With Sheree sitting quietly beside him and offering the "grace" he said he needed to engage in the autism wars, Jamie performed magnificently during the program on neurodiversity. The *Exchange* host began by asking him why he needed to type his answers before speaking them. As he hunted and pecked in the background, I tried to establish a context for his answer, explaining the problem of poor sensory integration in autism and noting the way that Jamie's Lightwriter device joined the visual and the auditory in real time. "It's seeing and hearing together," he had once said to some education professors. When he typed, the word would dutifully emerge on the screen and then just as dutifully be voiced by the mechanical synthesizer. Both print font and voice remained stable.

Whereas typical children move from speech to literacy by connecting the sounds they produce with ease to the graphic marks on a page, Jamie moved in the opposite direction by connecting the graphic marks on his Lightwriter to the sounds coming out of the synthesizer. The Lightwriter served as prompt and model; the metronome, as external motor-planning device. With his eyes, in effect, being asked to move his tongue, and his ears, in effect, being asked to move his limbs, he jerry-rigged a voice, one whose nest most certainly travels with it as it flies across the sun! Aggressive auditory-visual and auditory-motor coupling overwhelmed the considerable obstacles to speech.

"The patterns are powerful only when brains are given a thoughtful way of exchange," Jamie told the IPR audience. I sensed that the host didn't quite know what to make of this answer, for he immediately said, "To your knowledge, Ralph, this doesn't happen every day on radio or in the media very much?" "*Ever*," I replied, both stressing the word and drawing it out. What was most intriguing to me (and what obviously couldn't be explored on the radio) was that motor memory in one domain (typing) could facilitate motor performance in another (speech). On a basic level that made sense: movement has to be translatable from one form to another—in this case, from arm and hand movements to tongue and voice-box movements. But how could the *memory* of the former aid the performance of the latter?

A recent study revealed that listening to unfamiliar music activates the listener's motor systems. Even more interesting, the interstices between songs on a *familiar* CD do the same. The researchers hypothesized that motor areas support sequential mastery and, in the process, provide a memory boost. This is why we all know which song is coming next on our favorite CD. It is as if our motor systems create an essential continuum by constantly anticipating— we might even say, by constantly remembering—the future. They listen, in Jamie's phrase, "with more than ears." They listen when technically there is nothing to listen to and, in so doing, provide "intelligent continuation." Perhaps Jamie's tongue and voice box moved with more than arms. Perhaps, in perfect stillness, they remembered how to talk.

"What has full inclusion meant for you, Jamie?" the host then asked. "How has it made you different from how you would have been had you not been included in regular education?" With a kind of spiritual gusto, he replied, "Perhaps it's the power of belief in the soul of the independent individual." "Inclusion is important initiation to life," he added, repeating the phrase. When he had been asked this question in the past, Jamie had emphasized the importance of what inclusion proponents call a "print-rich environment." "Exposure to the printed word is like water to the desert," he said. "Only books could lead the way to gain understanding [of] how to say sounds."

At one point, Kieffer raised the issue of the infamous Autism Speaks fundraising pitch that I mentioned in the previous chapter; he even played a clip of the nearly satanic voice of ASD. Resisting our unequivocal denunciation of the ad (and others like it), he said, "These people mean well. What's wrong with wanting to fix autism?" While Jamie typed out his answer—"I hear Jamie clicking away on his keyboard," Kieffer remarked enthusiastically— Emily spoke about the conundrum of self-esteem in a world that conceives of the autist as regrettably broken: "Self-advocates have had to give themselves the confidence that they are worthy of being advocated for," she said. "There must be a way of advancing scientific agendas without demeaning people," I insisted. When Jamie was ready to speak aloud what he had typed, he dismissed the scary, Darth Vader–like voice: "It does not speak to the people of autism in my life. Fears are not supports but the destroyers of forward movement." They are a threat, he might have said, to "intelligent continuation." The audience couldn't have appreciated the full resonance of his statement. *I* didn't appreciate it at the time, but after reading *Ceremony* with Jamie and listening to the program again, I do now.

Carol Welch once commented, "Movement is a medicine for creating change in a person's physical, emotional, and mental states." It is also a way of uniting people. A recent study pointed to yet another benefit of auditory rhythmic cueing. It confirmed that, "having listened to a rhythmic beat, individuals' movements become more aligned to the frequency of that beat" and, even more important, that "when alignment to the rhythmic stimulus occurs in two interacting individuals, manifesting as increased motor coupling, their interpersonal attitudes toward one another become more positive." Here, we have the very basis of Native American community: the social bonding through ritual that neurologically knits people together.

In this context, prophecy is less an actual prediction than a holistic sense of how the body moves in the world. "There were transitions that had to be made in order to become whole again" (157), Betonie explains. We might think of these transitions as akin to the gaps or interstices in a complex motor task. Call what is required to navigate them *spiritual* priors. Tayo needs a sense of time that is at once productively spatial and linear. In touch with the spirit world, the former rejects the so-called ruin of Native history; the latter insists on pushing forward. The future will not be worth living if it cannot be remembered motorically.

A line from one of the poemlike chants that interrupts the novel proclaims, "I am walking back to belonging" (133), and Tayo himself is described as "want[ing] to walk until he recognized himself again" (143). At the end of the novel, as he moves ceremonially through the landscape with the woman who has drawn him out of traumatic remembrance, we are told, "Every step formed another word" (218). Movement is language, a fully embodied and embedded narrative of healing. There is simply no point in talking about Native recovery apart from the body or place of belonging. "The ear for the story and the eye for the patterns were theirs" (236), the novel declares. "The feeling was theirs: we came out of the land and we are hers" (236).

As we read *Ceremony* together, Jamie saw in Tayo's story his own story of coming to life through speech. "The ability to speak with voice curiously created many new patterns of access," he noted. "Before I had voice, I couldn't write because the letters were wavy." "The shapes," he continued, "were wading in waves. I could absolutely see the language, but when my voice moved forward, it formulated the form differently." "Now," he reported, "I am simply reading text when I see the words." Learning to speak also changed how Jamie retrieved language, and it gave his own language feeling. "When I lived in silence there wasn't emotion," he said, adding, "Keyboards carry no energy" and "Typing cannot return the emotion." Jamie is alluding, of course, to "emotional prosody," that crucial quality of the spoken word. Summing up his neuroplastic, sensorimotor journey and calling out experts who presume not only mental, but also social, incompetence in autism, he asserted, "I vitally correct the movement of much truth in the challenge of speaking."

It is more than a bit ironic that Western neuroscience has begun to embrace a notion of the integrated and holistic body that is similar to ancient Native notions—without, of course, the spiritual dimension, which Jamie relishes. The current concepts of embodied, embedded, and extended cognition depict human beings in a world of tangible affordances—one might even say, of undeclared assistive technologies. Disability reveals the fiction of the self-reliant individual by emphasizing the complex accommodative ecologies that make life possible for all of us. In this way, the idea of medicine as facilitating relationship, not correcting lamentable physiological flaws, is completely compatible with the concept of neurodiversity. Understanding his own progress as a mover in physical, mental, and spiritual terms, Jamie maintained, "We are just people on the transition, Ralph." "Harmony for me," he said, "is all structural realities and great worlds connecting with people and dimensions to create peace and calm and engagement of hearts and minds which then move in the dear success of lovely life."

· three ·

ANDYS AND AUTIES

Will robots inherit the earth? Yes, but they will be our children.
We owe our minds to the deaths and lives of all the creatures that
were ever engaged in the struggle called Evolution. Our job is to
see that all this work shall not end up in meaningless waste.
— MARVIN MINSKY

Toward the beginning of Philip K. Dick's jaunty sci-fi novel *Do Androids Dream of Electric Sheep?* the bounty-hunter hero, Rick Deckard, corners one of the rogue Nexus-6 androids in her dressing room at the opera. He has been tasked with "retiring" this group of ersatz humans who killed their overseers on Mars and have returned to the planet of their "birth," devastated though it is by the legacy of nuclear war. So advanced is the new model of humanoid robot that it may be able to defeat the only known method of distinguishing it from its organic counterpart: the Voigt-Kampff empathy test. Androids, though extraordinarily intelligent, are said to be incapable of feeling for other androids, let alone for animals or human beings.

Before confronting Luba Luft, Rick listened to her sing, "and he found himself surprised at the quality of her voice; it rated with that of the best, even that of notables in his collection of historic tapes. The Rosen Association built her well, he had to admit" (99). By this point in the novel, the bounty hunter has begun to founder in his fundamental convictions. Though driven by the money he will receive for each android he retires—he wants to buy his society's ultimate status symbol: a "real," as opposed to electric, animal—the killing bothers him. It bothers him precisely because the convenient label "android" doesn't effectively diminish—doesn't conceal—the dynamic life form that he has encountered and yet must eliminate.

In the sort of coruscating irony for which Dick is known, Rick experiences a full-blown identity crisis. As the term "android" loses its meaning, so, too, does the term "human." Empathy, that vaunted trait, becomes a kind of semantic quicksand, the "raging, mad wind" (93) of both the bounty hunter's .38 Magnum and of nuclear war—in short, one's own *retirement* party. If only the androids had "remained substandard, like the ancient q-40s made by Derain Associates" (99), there would be no need for such nastiness, Rick laments. But ever the man for the job, ever the man to fall morally to the occasion, he bucks up. "The better she functions," he tells himself in the opera house, "the better a singer she is, the more I am needed" (99), for the line between human and android must be preserved.

The scene in Luft's dressing room is extraordinary. Before Rick can legally kill her, he must administer the Voigt-Kampff empathy test, and she must fail it. Almost immediately, he begins to set up his equipment.

> "Do you think I'm an android? Is that it?" Her voice had faded almost to extinction. "I'm not an android. I haven't even been on Mars; I've never even seen an android!" ... "Do you have information that there's an android in the cast? I'd be glad to help you, and if I were an android would I be glad to help you?"
>
> "An android," [Rick] said, "doesn't care what happens to any other android. That's one of the indications we look for."
>
> "Then," Miss Luft said, "you must be an android."
>
> That stopped him; he stared at her. (101)

Luft's clever, yet frantic, maneuvering continues when she asks Rick if he's ever taken the test himself, and then proposes to take it but only after he does. "Wouldn't that be more fair?" she says. "Then I could be sure of you. I don't know; you seem so peculiar and hard and strange" (102). Although fairness is anything but a prevailing value in this society, Rick appears, in fact, to be more of an imposter than Luft. It's his first week as chief bounty hunter, and he's a bit edgy—his predecessor was shot by a Nexus-6. Who's to say that *Rick* isn't an android? Like some sort of haughty doctor, Deckard tells Luft she wouldn't be able to administer the test, as it requires "considerable experience" (102).

She then tries to pick at his questions, pretending not to understand certain words or taking them in wildly nonsensical directions. The questions are designed to elicit a physiological response. Desperate to escape, she manages to dislodge an electrode by pretending to scratch her cheek. After he retrieves it from the floor, Rick finds himself on the wrong end of a laser tube. Yet to his surprise—she ought to kill him—Luft calls the police, leading him to conclude mournfully, "She must think she's human" (106). In some Nexus-6 models a synthetic memory system has been laid down so as to deceive even the android herself. With this additional turn of the screw, Dick hopelessly confuses the distinction between the real and the fake, the caring and the uncaring. The latter has improved—has *evolved*. It is now indisputably, in Marvin Minsky's words, one of our children.

Rediscovering the novel—I was emptying a box of books after a move when it fell to the floor and opened to this scene—I decided instantly to use it in my project. Tito's allegorical reading of *Moby-Dick* had obviously primed me for any narrative involving a merciless hunt. But this one, because it hinged explicitly on the issue of empathy, seemed even more relevant to autism. Perhaps the most destructive and defining idea about autism spectrum disorders (ASD) to emerge from the scientific community is that autistics lack empathy. Despite research to the contrary, the notion persists, and it is very much responsible for the stereotype of unfeeling aloneness. Dick's ironic reversals—*Who* lacks empathy? *Who* is inhuman?—might resonate with an autistic reader who feels aggressively misunderstood.

So might the issue of testing and the power dynamics at its core. Luft's verbal sparring with Deckard reminded me of Rachel Rottenberg's now infamous, online scrap with Simon Baron-Cohen, who for years has promoted the theory of an empathy deficit in autism. With only the slingshot of reason and the meager pebbles of disability studies, the self-advocate David slayed the Goliath autism researcher. Ignoring her substantive points about testing procedures, he suggested that her feelings were hurt—she simply didn't like what the research found. Though careful to appear both sympathetic and respectful and "hop[ing] that dialogue between researchers and people with autism will lead to greater mutual understanding," he came off worse than Deckard, who at least admits to his prejudice: "A rough, cold android, hoping to undergo an experience from which, due to a deliberately built-in defect, it remained excluded" (185).

In *The Wounded Storyteller*, Arthur Frank likens medical and scientific subjects to colonized peoples: the former's bodies have been conquered and their indigenous, which is to say personal, experience of illness or disability has been disregarded. In its place an official narrative, in something like a foreign language, prevails, leaving them to feel both alienated and disempowered. Over the last thirty years, however, such subjects have begun to rebel. Not only has the subaltern learned to speak, but it has also learned to organize, as groups like the Autistic Self-Advocacy Network make clear. Insisting on the right to self-determination, ASAN has agitated for progress in a range of areas: from better education, employment, and housing opportunities to better, more respectful medical care and scientific research.

Here, too, I thought, might be a point of connection. While the novel doesn't give us much of the backstory on Mars, it more than hints at the idea of a slave rebellion: "Do androids dream? Rick asked himself. Evidently; that's why they occasionally kill their employers and flee here. A better life, without servitude. Like Luba Luft; singing *Don Giovanni* and *Le Nozze* instead of toiling across the face of a barren rock-strewn field. On a fundamentally uninhabitable colony world" (184). One of the androids, Roy Baty, is said to have "proposed the group escape attempt, underwriting it ideologically with a pretentious fiction as to the sacredness of so-called android 'life'" (185). We might label Baty's belief "silico-diversity" (and hear in our minds the often knee-jerk and snide dismissals of its neuro variety). As Arthur C. Clarke once wrote, "Whether we are based on carbon or on silicon makes no fundamental difference; we should each be treated with appropriate respect."

In choosing *Do Androids Dream of Electric Sheep?* I had a sense, a strong sense really, that autism and sci-fi went together. They were like two astronaut peas in a spaceship pod. Ray Bradbury's remark—"I have never listened to anyone who criticized my taste in space travel, sideshows or gorillas. When this occurs, I pack up my dinosaurs and leave the room"—had autism all over it. Or perhaps I should say, all *under* it. The attraction to space travel and to animals, the collection of toy dinosaurs, no doubt arranged meticulously according to genus and species—these were signs of an autistic sensibility.

I knew that Dawn Prince had published a well-regarded memoir of autism, *Songs of the Gorilla Nation*, which recounted her lifelong engagement with these primates who not only brought her out of her shell but also taught her how to relate to her fellow humans. Prince followed up that book with another one, *Circus of Souls*, in which she told the story of the first monkey in space, who cruelly suffocated, and of the physiologically distinctive people who had to parade themselves in front of late nineteenth- and early twentieth-century freak-show audiences.

Yet the link between science fiction and autism wasn't simply implicit or uncanny. The conceit of the autist-as-extraterrestrial runs through both the professional and the autobiographical literature. For example, the British psychiatrist John Wing compared autistic children to the offspring of earthling mothers and an alien force in the sci-fi novel *The Midwich Cuckoos*. His wife, Lorna Wing, would rediscover the work of Hans Asperger and coin the term "Asperger syndrome." In relating her struggle to understand complex social behavior, Temple Grandin told Oliver Sacks that she was akin to "an anthropologist on Mars": an alien stranded on an unfamiliar planet who must somehow learn its cryptic culture. (Matt Damon, by comparison, has it easy in *The Martian*.) Sacks, as I noted in the introduction, would later use the analogy as the title of both his *New Yorker* profile of Grandin and the book in which the profile appears.

In "Dating Data," a chapter from her 1995 memoir *Thinking in Pictures*, Grandin revealed that many autistics were "fans of the television show *Star Trek*." They loved the technology—all of those widgets and gizmos that allowed the crew to do futuristic things. They especially loved the animated objects. But for her, the series, with its emotionless Vulcan character, Mr. Spock, and its android character, Data, explained the fundamental difference between autistics and neurotypicals. Spock, of course, was repeatedly perplexed by illogical behavior, and Data failed miserably at love. "When he tried to be romantic," Grandin wrote, "he complimented his date by using scientific terminology." "Even very able adults with autism have such problems," she commented. As just such an adult herself, she had decided to remain celibate "because doing so helps me to avoid the many complicated social situations that are too difficult for me to handle."

Here, we can see the stereotype of autism that Grandin helped to crystallize: the socially inept and exceedingly logical sister-from-another-planet who prefers to be alone. It would take at least another decade for nonautistics to begin to acknowledge that they were just as ignorant of autistic behavior as autistics were of theirs. In an important article, the philosopher Ian Hacking argued that each group was simply a "form of life." Expecting either to be different was as absurd as expecting to see the ocean in Iowa. Other autistics objected to the stereotype itself, claiming on the one hand that they improve at conventional sociality—their brains are just as plastic as neuro-typical brains—and on the other that social intuition and performance are extremely variable in autism. The condition is heterogeneous, and from day to day (or even hour to hour), any given autistic person might succeed or fail in a particular situation.

Nothing was as static or as fixed as Grandin suggested. Whereas she be-lieved that "marriages work out best when two people with autism marry or when a person with autism marries a handicapped or eccentric spouse," other less prominent autistics believed just the opposite. The very show that highlighted stark differences between humans and nonhumans presented plots in which Kirk and Spock had to discover the limitations of their own cognitive processing and, as a result, began to appreciate the other. Their in-teraction, which leads to friendship, changes them. In a way, *Star Trek* was all about inclusion—both on the ship and off. As the *Enterprise* "boldly went where no man had gone before," it encountered other creatures and cultures in what can only be called a kind of galactic cosmopolitanism or, better, a galactic neurocosmopolitanism.

If I had any doubts about the autism–science fiction connection, they evaporated when I read Steve Silberman's *NeuroTribes*, the genesis of which was a 2001 article in *Wired* magazine titled "The Geek Syndrome." "Autism—and its milder cousin Asperger syndrome—is surging among the children of Silicon Valley," the subheading screamed. "Are math-and-tech-genes to blame?" Silberman would come to understand that autism was on the rise everywhere, but that in offering both a natural outlet for geeklike gifts and a more congenial and forgiving employment space, the high-tech industry had carved out an early neurodiverse refuge.

The same might be said of science fiction. According to Silberman, the emergence of sci-fi can be traced back to writers, editors, and fans who would likely have received an Asperger diagnosis had it been available at the time. "A genre of popular storytelling that blended hard science and specu-lative fiction, with a strong emphasis on gadgetry" almost seemed to require the kind of biocultural estrangement that is born of neurological difference and an inhospitable society.

One particular fan, Claude Degler, who was nearly sterilized in the East-ern Indiana Hospital for the Insane, appropriated the plot of a 1940 serial, in which genetically engineered humans are hunted by their typical peers, to make the point that Grandin would make some fifty years later. Like the char-acters in *Slan*, Degler and his fellow fen were "superintelligent, supersensitive, and profoundly misunderstood mutants struggling to survive in a world not built for them." Gary Westfahl, a historian of science fiction, put the matter of autistic otherworldliness and sci-fi like this: "To a teenager in the 1930s with Asperger syndrome, a story about an astronaut encountering aliens on Mars might have had an air of comforting familiarity, in contrast to stories set in the bizarre, inexplicable, and thoroughly socialized worlds of Andy Hardy and the Bobbsey Twins."

And yet it doesn't take autism to feel culturally alienated. As William Gibson explains, "One of the liberating effects of science fiction when I was a teenager was precisely its ability to tune me into all sorts of strange data and make me realize that I wasn't as totally isolated in perceiving the world as being monstrous and crazy." This overlap of the countercultural and neurodivergent also characterized cyberpunk, the subgenre for which Gibson became famous and which, despite its dystopic vision, still carried within it an oppositional politics, however jaded and ghostly. "Science fiction isn't just thinking about the world out there," wrote Samuel Delany. "It's also thinking about how that world might be—a particularly important exercise for those who are oppressed."

The fact that sci-fi was often marginalized as "genre fiction" seemed perversely appropriate, even symmetrical, because it reflected the social status of many of its readers. As important, it contributed to a sense of unacknowledged urgency: "Individual science fiction stories may seem as trivial as ever to the blinder critics and philosophers of today," warned Isaac Asimov, "but the core of science fiction—its essence—has become crucial to our salvation, if we are to be saved at all."

. . .

THE MORE I READ about the history of science fiction, the more convinced I was of the decision to include Dick's android novel in my project. But with whom would I discuss it?

I remembered a woman with a hip sci-fi name—Dora Raymaker—who had appeared in *Loving Lampposts, Living Autistic*, a documentary about the neurodiversity movement. With her kinky, red hair, she looked like a cross between Bernadette Peters and Nicole Kidman. I had been impressed by some of the things she had to say. For instance, when asked about functioning labels—experts like to speak of "low-" or "high-functioning" autism—she remarked, "Is functioning related to speech, to IQ, to scholastic achievement, to how well someone can appear nonautistic, to adaptive functioning?" Even if people could agree on what that term means, there would still be the problem, she said, of variability.

Another self-advocate, Kassiane Asasumasu, made the same point: "Functioning? Low-functioning? What are you measuring? Everybody bases it on two things: speaking and self-care skills. And that can fluctuate for those of us on the spectrum so much in the course of one day; I'm talking great now, but tomorrow? Who knows?"

In the documentary Dora did her talking with an augmentative communication device. Unlike Tito, who types with one finger, or Jamie, who types with two, she used all ten quite expertly. "I have difficulty with the motor planning involved in producing speech," she explained. "I also don't access words and put them together the way others do." She thought "in visual spatial landscapes and need[ed] to consciously translate [her] thinking into language." These landscapes weren't so much representational, I would later learn, as filled with complex, 3D shapes, at once abstract and extraordinarily colorful. Thought involved bringing these shapes together, fitting them according to a felt logic of synesthetic transformation. "I find the spot where it belongs. And then I plug it in and it goes purple," she would say. Both visual and auditory, this process "shimmered" and "swooshed." Call it pliant puzzling, where the pieces themselves, as if floating in the air in front of her, actively seek relation.

The transition from landscape to words depended, she would tell me, on "a lot of things":

> how much do I know about the topic, how interested I am in the topic, how "close" is it to the landscapes I have loaded into my thinking at the time, how often I have recited words about the topic in the past / told the same story, whether I've written about the topic, sensory load, who I'm speaking with and whether I can key off of / mimic their vocal patterns, how comfortable I am with their communication patterns, my general stress levels, my functional capacity that day.

Although Dora has a diagnosis of apraxia of speech, it "doesn't really cover the word-finding issues, which are sometimes more of a barrier than the speech production bit."

Of course, I knew plenty of people who danced on the page and yet stumbled in the mouth or brain. Why privilege speech? In *Wretches and Jabberers*, a documentary about autistics who type to communicate, the latter term wryly refers to those of us who can move our mouths but who sadly have little to say. And anyway, my book was all about how writers use printed words to paint evocative tableaus on the 3D canvas of our sensing bodies. While obviously a verbal medium, literature was akin to what the nonspeaking autistic artist Larry Bissonette calls "a muralistic, lettered view of life." It, too, begins, we might say, with "the movement of fingers on sopping, great malleable gobs of paint."

Dora's relationship to speech was complicated—as with any disability, it was more than just a matter of impaired physiology. She worried that her speech "sounded funny" and that, as a result, people thought she was "stupid." Her difficulties were not at the level of Tito's or Jamie's—on good days, when she was comfortable, she was as articulate as any of my silver-tongued colleagues in the English department. In our initial email exchange, she'd warn me about her changeable relationship to speech. "Sometimes I have needed to communicate by typing only; other times I mostly speak," she'd write, adding, "I can't speak for a few hours when I first wake up ever, but at this point in time I am in a phase where I 'remember' and 'warm up' and get quite fluent, particularly with people/topics that I'm familiar with."

In *Loving Lampposts*, she had made clear just how protean were all of her abilities: "There have been times in my adult life when I've had little problem getting up and getting dressed and going to a job and other times in my adult life when I have sat in a mostly catatonic state and been too confused to find the rooms in my own house." She was like a tree whose cycle of leafing was mysterious. It could be autumn one month and spring the next. The very idea of reliable seasons made little sense. The body deciduous—sometimes, when the leaves of cognition fell, they even fell upward.

Most experts don't have an adequate grasp of fluctuating performance in autism, and I think this failing affects their research. Imagine capturing a bad day and believing it constituted the norm. Nor do they fully appreciate the significance of support, accommodation, and routine, which can make someone appear much less disabled than they are. This, of course, is the fundamental insight of disability studies: provide an enabling environment, and impairment has a much better chance of becoming difference, not dysfunction.

Because people frequently "talked down to her" or found communication "so difficult that they g[o]t hostile," Dora preferred to use augmentative communication even when she felt she could speak—especially if she was communicating with strangers or in an alien environment. "Sometimes I turn off speech to conserve resources so I don't fully crash out," she would tell me. "Sometimes I turn off speech because it makes navigating the world easier, either by giving me more resources to manage other things, or because it plays into people's stereotypes of disability and enables them to accommodate me properly without a ton of explanation and hassle (e.g., when I travel I turn off speech because the airline people cope with interacting with my assistant much better if I appear completely nonverbal)."

The irony of appearing at times insufficiently disabled as to command basic accommodations was a common problem for Dora. Instead of trying to "pass" as neurotypical, she purposefully marked herself as "autistic." This struck me as interesting and certainly a departure from the plot of *Androids*. "Alternative and augmentative communication have changed the way others relate to me and for the better," she observed in *Loving Lampposts*.

While Tito, Jamie, and Dora obviously shared certain challenges with speech, the precise nature of those challenges was different—as different as the way their sensory systems worked or the way they thought. At the risk of repeating myself, let me say again (and again) that there's much diversity in autism. The concept of a spectrum, as Ian Hacking has argued, though of some value, is unfortunately linear and static. In a period of relative fluency in her thirties, Dora, I would learn, received an Asperger diagnosis; in a period of little to no speech, an autism one. (Before that, she was considered, among other things, "emotionally disturbed.") The point of a book like this, which engages in qualitative ethnographical research, was to capture distinction—across both people and time.

If her use of augmentative and alternative communication (AAC) had caught my attention, I was especially intrigued by the organization Dora had helped to found in 2006 with Christina Nicolaidis, a doctor and researcher whose son is autistic—Nicolaidis is also featured in the film. Called the Academic Autism Spectrum Partnership in Research and Education (or AASPIRE), the organization "brings together the academic community and the autistic community to develop ... research projects relevant to the needs of adults on the autism spectrum." A number of these projects, especially at the beginning, concerned access to quality healthcare. Consider, for example, that autistics are three times more likely to visit the emergency room than non-autistics. So alienating has been their interactions with doctors that they tend to seek help only when they absolutely have to. The idea was to forge informed solutions together, taking advantage of each other's experience. "Our partnership," Dora and Nicolaidis write on the organization's website, "adheres to the principles of Community Based Participatory Research (CBPR), whereby academics and community members serve as equal partners throughout the research process."

At the time I knew next to nothing about CBPR, yet I found myself fancying an equivalent partnership with Dick's androids! A kind of empathy corrective—not slick, professional paternalism, with pity at its core, but a genuine attempt at understanding. Alive for only a short time and constantly on the run, the andys, I thought to myself, must need both technological and psychological care. Of the humanoid robot named Pris, who hides in a dilapidated apartment building, the narrator tells us, "Fear made her seem ill; it distorted her body lines, made her appear as if someone had broken her and then, with malice, patched her together badly" (62). Who could live with such anxiety? The androids have no friends, no allies, and little hope of survival. The only character who sympathizes with them is John Isidore, a man rendered intellectually disabled by nuclear fallout.

The idea, ridiculous to be sure, of participatory research with robots presupposed the end of silico-eugenics. Access to better care, like the more egalitarian social science investigations that could yield it, was of a piece with recognizing and valuing difference. Although the novel doesn't develop the silico-diversity theme, the androids clearly want to define themselves—to break away from the damaging, because pejorative, notion of *artificial* intelligence. Whatever their humanlike features, they are distinctive organisms: creatures that not only have crossed some Turing threshold but also have undergone an inconceivable metamorphosis. They aren't so much caterpillars that have become butterflies as caterpillars that have become winged gazelles (with their cheetah predators behind them). "Beings of wonder," Dora would call them. "I don't like it when people take the magic out of something simply because it's technology," she'd say. "Just because it's made up of 1s and 0s doesn't mean it's stupid."

The morning I chanced upon Dick's novel, I had been reading an article about caterpillars in *Scientific American*—specifically, about how they become butterflies:

> First, the caterpillar digests itself, releasing enzymes to dissolve all of its tissues. If you were to cut open a cocoon or chrysalis at just the right time, caterpillar soup would ooze out. But the contents of the pupa are not entirely an amorphous mess. Certain highly organized groups of cells known as imaginal discs survive the digestive process. Before

hatching, when a caterpillar is still developing inside its egg, it grows an imaginal disc for each of the adult body parts it will need as a mature butterfly or moth—discs for its eyes, for its wings, its legs and so on.

Digesting the scene with Luba Luft, I pictured something like imaginal discs hidden in the android's software code. Instead of body parts, these discs gave rise to consciousness—to full-blown introspection. Literature, it occurred to me, was itself a kind of caterpillar soup, whereby the words become, in the reader's mind, something else entirely. "I wanted to crawl in between those black lines of print, the way you crawl through a fence, and go to sleep under that beautiful big green fig-tree," wrote Sylvia Plath in *The Bell Jar*.

I had conceived of my project as roughly akin to AASPIRE's: an effort, in a particular domain, by people of different neurotypes. As my collaborators and I chatted, we showed what they could contribute to discussions of literature. This, too, was a kind of research, though far from perfectly egalitarian or easily managed. My job was to be honest about the difficulties and, in particular, my own inadequacies. What Chris Martin has said of the poet Brandon Brown comes close to capturing my aim: "He is constantly (and humorously) articulating his own lapses in judgement, intelligence, foresight, etc., if only to end up demonstrating how much more labor and care we need to fully realize ourselves as ethical thinkers/writers. In that way, the lapses are what finally fill out the sketch of an ethical future and direct the reader toward it."

Dora would recount just such a lapse early in the life of AASPIRE, a lapse that has relevance for my project and that shows how genuine understanding among different peoples actually emerges. The autistic members, some of whom do not reside in Portland, Oregon, where the organization is based, requested that meetings take place via "text-based Internet chat"—essentially Skype, but with no speaking. "The autistic people were used to conversing with each other on-line," Dora would recall. "But the neurotypicals couldn't cope. They couldn't keep up. They didn't know any of the conventions for this kind of thing. Christina told me that for the first time in her life she knew what it was like to have a communication disability because all of a sudden we were communicating in a way that was comfortable for us and was very difficult for her."

With considerable irony, the team reported in an early paper:

We have learned to provide accommodations (e.g., telephone calls) for some of our non-autistic team members. Autistic partners have at times assisted non-autistic partners with learning how to use remote collaboration tools and become comfortable with basic "netiquette" (online rules for interaction). We have an e-mail list-serv for communication between meetings and for individuals who find real-time discussion insufficient for getting their ideas across. Given the team's diverse communication preferences, AASPIRE offers all partners—both autistic and non-autistic—the option to review and provide feedback to materials and contribute to decision making via e-mail, text-based chat, telephone, or, for those in Portland, in-person meetings.

The moral? For people with traditional advantages, whether physiological, economic, or cultural, goodwill only gets you so far. As in a winter storm, you must abandon your blithe reliance on your car, the smug simplicity of depressing the gas pedal. You must get out and traipse through heavy snow, often in darkness, for miles. The freeway—*your* freeway—must become impassable.

. . .

AS NEUROCOSMOPOLITAN AS Dora appeared, I nevertheless fretted about contacting her. For some self-advocates, the old disability rights adage "Nothing about us without us" had become starkly and unreservedly "Nothing about us." I understood this position and almost agreed with it. (After being relentlessly demonized and hunted, what android would want to hear about itself from a human?) So nervous was I about contacting Dora that I remembered an email a friend had forwarded about the horrors of cold-calling people—he was an investment guy who made his living that way: "I was cold calling today and an older woman picked up and I gave my introduction, followed by a bit of silence. Very politely she asks me if like carpet, I say, 'Yes,' which she promptly follows up with, 'Well then why don't you eat mine.' I am completely dumbfounded and say, 'Excuse me,' and she follows up with 'You heard me, you turd, eat it,' then the ubiquitous click."

To my great relief, when I sent an email describing the project and introducing myself, Dora said yes—in fact, she was thrilled to participate. I had proposed reading *Androids* and had mentioned that we could also watch *Blade Runner*, which is, of course, based on the novel. *Blade Runner*, it turns out, was her favorite movie. "I've seen it a zillion times," she replied. "I even use a *Blade Runner* light-up umbrella—and use it often because it rains almost as much in Portland as it does in the film. I am over-the-top excited by anyone who wants to discuss that movie with me. Wow." I had forgotten about those iconic umbrellas, which eerily illuminate the sinister rain-city of Ridley Scott's film.

That Dora was not only an aspiring cyberpunk writer—she had already completed a series of novels with a sleuthing, autistic heroine—but also a computer programmer with a background in robotics who was currently writing her doctoral dissertation at Portland State University seemed like the sort of coincidence that makes one buy a lottery ticket. Or believe in a scribbling god. The dissertation involved, as she put it, "applying the emancipatory promise of CBPR to critical systems thinking." Through the creation of an informational website and a healthcare toolkit for doctors and their autistic patients, it addressed power imbalances in the "learning organization concept," a term made famous by Peter Senge. In the last chapter of her dissertation, titled "Reflections of a Community Based Participatory Researcher from the Intersection of Disability Advocacy, Engineering, and the Academy," I would come across passages like this one about her early teenage years, prediagnosis, when she was enamored of her first computer and being bullied at school:

> Winter, 1986. It's Maine, so it's cold. The ground is so frozen they have to stash the dead in crypts until the spring thaw. . . . The Underground Railroad. Segregation in the 60s. I thread through the story of oppression and resistance as though it were my own. Which is ridiculous. I'm a white, Italian-American from a recently immigrated family; there's no reason for it to resonate. Yet in my bedroom a half-assembled robot and a Commodore 66 coexist with the Civil Rights movement. Cool mathematics and flaming social justice. Private rebellions and mental malfunctions.

And this one, about her graduate school years, postdiagnosis, when she was still very much interested in robots and working on her dissertation:

> Winter, 2014. It's Oregon, so it's raining. The ground is so wet it can steal your boot. I'm on the floor again, knees tucked under me as I try to extract the book I want without toppling the stack. *Power/Knowledge* (Foucault 1980). *Disability and the Internet* (Jaeger 2011). *Critical Systems Thinking* (Flood and Jackson 1991). Social justice stacked besides books on programming languages, dynamical systems, and fuzzy logic—plus a healthy collection of robot parts. My passion for narratives of oppression and resistance makes sense to me now.

"Coincidences are spiritual puns," wrote G. K. Chesterton: random occurrences *bent to me*. They are little, acoustic knots descending like helicopter seeds from the mouth of a maple tree. In "Esthetique du Mal," the poet Wallace Stevens casually declares, "At dawn / The paratroopers fall and as they fall / They mow the lawn." One after another, these soldiers, these seeds, would drop during the course of our discussions. As a child, Dora had lived in a house in Deer Isle, Maine, that was owned by a colleague from my high school teaching days. . . . The actress who played Pris in *Blade Runner*, Daryl Hannah, had been given an autism diagnosis as a young girl. . . .

And yet, while she was ecstatic about Scott's film, Dora was more than a bit hesitant about *Androids*. She devoured science fiction, she reported, and knew that Dick was important, but he remained "a huge gap in [her] reading." "There's something in his use of language that has kept his books largely inaccessible to me," she explained. "I've tried to read *Androids* so many times because of my great love for the film and failed. Maybe reading it with someone can get me through it." When we began our weekly discussions by Skype, she would speak of "personal struggles with language that are part of [her] disability." "This novel always hit them hard and fast from the start," she'd say. "It was never poetic enough for me just to gestalt it like a poem."

Her difficulties typically involved pronouns and what she called "filler words." "'Of,' 'around'—they have no meaning for me. I use them correctly in my own writing maybe 90% of the time, though I'm always missing a bunch of 'of's and 'the's. They're a sound that gets tacked on; they're part of the rhythm, but I don't have a picture for them in my head." Pronouns were similarly insubstantial, vacant, and for someone who had little concept of gender, even words like "he" and "she," which seem so basic, eluded *her*. She had learned how to use *them*, but pronouns had no natural claim on her attention. They were like substitute teachers in elementary school—hardly a cause for celebration, because she loved Mrs. Johnson who was, well, Mrs. Johnson, which is to say specific and unique.

Syntax sometimes presented challenges as well. In what was hardly an auspicious beginning to our partnership, the very first sentence of the novel stumped her. The sentence goes like this: "A merry little surge of electricity piped by the automatic alarm from the mood organ beside his bed awakened Rick Deckard" (3). "I see electricity," Dora wrote,

> then an alarm, then a piece of tech, then a bed, then a man, all jumbled and out-of-order, each new element forcing me to retrace the sentence and rebuild it, only to find that I still didn't get it right because more

jumble follows. And after getting the picture of the disparate elements glued together into a whole, I still need to figure out how the elements connect—is the mood organ sending current into Deckard's brain to wake him? I only come to that conclusion now as I analyze the sentence in this note. If only the sentence read something like: "Rick Deckard awoke when the mood organ's automatic alarm piped a merry little surge of electricity into him." Which is still awkward, but at least makes a coherent image.

Reading over Dora's notes before our initial Skype session, I thought, *Maybe I've chosen the wrong novel.* She complained that the writing "slows me down, pulls me out of the story, and makes me feel dumb."

She had a point about that sentence. The passive voice ("piped by the automatic alarm"), followed by the two prepositional phrases ("from the mood organ beside his bed"), interrupts the independent clause: "A merry little surge of electricity awakened Rick Deckard." Dora's solution was to make the bounty hunter the subject of a much simpler independent clause ("Rick awoke"), followed by a dependent clause beginning with the subordinate conjunction "when." This dependent clause had a clear subject ("alarm"), a verb ("piped"), and a direct object ("surge").

But the new sentence's clarity, I suggested, came at the expense of Dick's intention: namely, to invert customary notions of agency and animation. Here, the technological apparatus is active and animate; the human hero, passive and inanimate, despite his bounty-hunter bravado. In a novel so desperately conflicted about the effects of technology, including nuclear war and the rise of robots, we need something like an artificial or convoluted syntax. Before we can get to Rick in that first sentence, we must swim through an oil spill of technological mediation. Even his feelings aren't strictly organic.

In another Skype session, I would go so far as to propose that the narrator might be an android. The sentences are purposefully robotic, tonally off, withholding judgment as well as sympathy. Or, rather, they reflect the prejudicial stereotype of androids. The narrator in a sense gleefully mocks the human need to distinguish itself from the world it has made—to remain superior.

Dora, however, wasn't buying it, at least not at first. I had gone into flamboyant professor mode: words came out of me like water from a fire hose. ("Interpretation," quipped Susan Sontag, "is the revenge of the intellectual upon art.") We had agreed to speak at first and then move to typing if necessary. I remember Dora rhythmically bouncing in front of her computer—only later, when I visited her in Portland, did I see that she sits on a purple physio ball chair! From her office window, on a cloudless day, you can spot Mount St. Helens. Her head would regularly rise above it.

Yet, her objections to Dick's prose were also aesthetic. "Along with the jumbled sentences," she had written in her notes, "I find my inner editor babbling too much. Deleting unnecessary words, streamlining cumbersome prose and clunky dialogue. The characters all have the same voice so far, and none of it flows like human speech." "I am aware," she said, "that Dick is writing at a time when speculative fiction is dragging its way out of the soup of the pulp periodicals and into mainstream literature." She wanted me to understand that she could handle experimental prose; two of her favorite sci-fi authors were Jeff Noon and Harlan Ellison, who "fall over into poetry." "I do not read/hear words," she stressed. "I see the images and hear the sounds that the words symbolize, processing words-as-wholes into imaginary landscapes." Dick insufficiently rewarded "the way [her] brain processes text."

Her all-time favorite sci-fi author, William Gibson—we would later read his novel *Neuromancer* together—once remarked, "I can't do fiction unless I visualize what's going on. When I began to write science fiction, one of the things I found lacking in it was visual specificity. It seemed there was a lot of lazy imagining, a lot of shorthand." Whether or not he had Dick in mind, it seems a fair criticism of the novel, but visual specificity isn't Dick's strength. Ambiguity and irony are—wildly proliferating ambiguity and irony. He sows a kind of manic doubt, whose tonal strangeness flowers, you might say, only in winter—nuclear winter. He specializes in incommensurability: "It really seems to me that in the midst of great tragedy, there is always the possibility that something terribly funny will happen."

Again, Dora would have none of it. "One good thing about Dick's writing," she said, "is that it makes me feel like my prose is so much better by comparison. Someone's got to want to publish it someday! Usually when I read well-known fiction, I feel like I'll never be good enough." She had tagged the comment with a smiley face—☺—to let me know she was joking, but even if she'd been completely serious, I'd have loved it. She didn't care that I was an English professor; she had her opinions and she was going to voice them.

At Grinnell, my students sometimes fear disagreement. They don't want to stand out or "be mean." The seminar table becomes a Thanksgiving one: too accommodating and amenable. "Don't provoke Aunt Bertha!" Or it's like a hostage situation: as quiet as a gun yet to go off. Aristotle must have been especially irritated with his students when he said, "Criticism is something we can avoid ... by saying nothing, doing nothing, and being nothing."

Dora wanted "to put the characters on and become them," but the prose in the first four chapters made it difficult. Referring to Deckard; his wife, Iran; Isidore; and Inspector Bryant, Deckard's boss, she said, "I've had a hard time feeling for these characters because I'm so removed from them. I feel for the sheep most." After Rick is awakened by the mood organ, which allows people to "dial up" any feeling they want, he heads to work, though not before tending to his electric sheep—it "grazes" on the roof of his apartment building. With most of the Earth's animals dead from radioactive poisoning, people dream of owning an actual animal, the rarer the better, and, in a kind of keeping up with the Joneses, pretend they do.

As Rick "reached his sheep, ... it lay ruminating," we learn, "its alert eyes fixed on him in case he had brought any rolled oats. ... The alleged sheep contained an oat-tropic circuit; at the sight of such cereals it would scramble up convincingly and amble over" (9). But Rick is angered by imitation, however plausible it may be. "Owning and maintaining a fraud had a way of gradually demoralizing one" (9), the narrator tells us. "And yet from a social standpoint it had to be done, given the absence of the real article" (9). After all, people needed to demonstrate empathic abilities—their superior humanity depended on it.

So demoralized is Rick that he purposefully exposes the fraud to his neighbor: "[He] bent down, searching in the thick white wool—the fleece at least was genuine—until he found what he was looking for: the concealed control panel of the mechanism. ... After an interval Barbour said, 'You poor guy. Has it always been this way?'" (11). Later, spotting what he thinks is a real owl, Rick once again feels hatred for his sheep, "which he had to tend, had to care about, as if it lived. The tyranny of an object, he thought. It doesn't know I exist. Like the androids, it had no ability to appreciate the existence of another" (42). Rick, of course, has no ability to appreciate the existence of another. He is stuck in a binary: difference must be less.

In a remark that I didn't pay enough attention to at the time, Dora said, "I can make the sheep's perspective richer than what I've been given." She then added, "I want to rescue the electric sheep and cuddle it and love it and care for it, poor thing!" It wasn't just that she had an active imagination; she identified with the sheep, whom most readers wouldn't even accord the status of a minor character. "On a personal/emotional level," Dora reported, "I pretty much invariably identify with anything that can't fight back, so the electric sheep being the recipient of such abuse is pretty disturbing to me because it has no recourse. . . . That is baggage I come in with. I don't know whether other readers who haven't had similar experiences in their own lives would feel this way."

When at the end of our first session we began to talk about her life—invariably we would move to typing for such discussions because she found them so stressful—Dora related a string of humiliating events: the bullying from peers I previously mentioned (at times so scary she feared for her life), encounters with misogynistic doctors (one prescribed additional housework for her problems), running away from home with a friend (they made it all the way to Montana, after crossing into and out of Canada, before being caught); near institutionalization at seventeen (her mother struck a deal with her: she could live in an apartment in another town if she agreed to family therapy); dicey employment (for years she worked at night so as not to have to interact with people), sustained unemployment (homelessness seemed a real possibility). Struggles with speech and periods of decompensation only exacerbated her sense of powerlessness. While this account of the "baggage she comes with" helped to explain her fondness for the sheep, I wondered if something else was drawing her to the nonhuman.

. . .

PRIMED BY THE FILM, Dora also identified intensely with Rachael Rosen, the niece of the Rosen Association director, Eldon Rosen, to whom we're introduced at the beginning of chapter 5 and who at the end of the chapter discovers that she is an android. In the novel, as in *Blade Runner*, this "tyrannous object" serves as a foil to, and eventual love interest of, Deckard. Unlike the electric sheep, however, she learns to fight back—Dora would call the pair "twin tornadoes which tangle in each other"—but at this point Rachael is simply reeling from the news:

> "Don't be afraid of him," Eldon Rosen told her. "You're not an escaped android on Earth illegally; you're the property of the Rosen Association, used as a sales device for prospective emigrants." He walked to the girl, put his hand comfortingly on her shoulder; at the touch the girl flinched.
> "He's right," Rick said. "I'm not going to retire you, Miss Rosen." (60)

Here, too, Dora was appalled. She described the exchange, "so cold, so oblivious to its effect on Rachael," as "horrific." "More-so I think to me," she commented, "to anyone, who has had the experience of others saying heartless, dehumanizing things about them while they stand there knowing they have no power to make it stop." This included things people said about autism—both online and to her face.

Bryant had sent Deckard to Seattle to consult with Eldon Rosen about the continued viability of the Voigt-Kampff empathy test—if it couldn't detect the Nexus-6, they'd have big problems. The plan had been to run a controlled experiment using a mix of androids and a "carefully selected group of schizoid and schizophrenic human patients" (37) who show a "flattening of affect" (37) and who have always been vulnerable in the early stages of their disease, before they've been institutionalized, to misrecognition. "If you tested them in line with police work you'd assess them as humanoid robots" (38), Bryant had noted. "You'd be wrong, but by then they'd be dead" (38). Both groups suffer, according to scientists, from a "role-taking blockage" (38).

I had forgotten about these passages. I remember being flabbergasted as I encountered them again. The apparent lack of emotion, the failure to understand the intentions of another—Dick was talking about the adult version of autism! When he wrote *Androids* in 1966, it hadn't yet been differentiated from schizophrenia, except with respect to age of onset. This would only happen in 1971, after the publication of Israel Kolvin's seminal study, though not until 1980, with the appearance of the *Diagnostic and Statistical Manual of Mental Disorders III*, would the conditions be considered formally distinct. The connection between autistics and androids was thus *literal* in the novel—not my own allegorical imposition, as I had thought. The latter had developed to the point of a certain class of "deficient" human beings. According to the novel, the two groups were like ships passing in the night: one taking on water and about to go down, the other morphing quickly from wooden raft to schooner to stealthy nuclear sub.

Eager to protect their product, the Rosens had conspired to trap Rick by having him mistake Rachael for an android. If such a mistake ever got out, it would be a public relations disaster because the police can't be going around retiring "authentic humans" (54). When Rick measured her body's response to statements about the mistreatment or killing of animals, he had concluded that she was an android—she had been insufficiently disturbed by the prospect of eating oysters or spotting a mounted deer's head. (As Dora noted, it was apparently okay to mistreat electric animals.)

Rosen, according to plan, had informed him he was wrong—though understandably so. Rachael had spent fourteen of her eighteen years on a spaceship, "living off its tape library" (52), and possessed an inadequate grasp of culture and an underdeveloped sense of empathy. In effect, she was artificially schizoid. Because she'd been given these memories in production, she had believed the story about herself. Rick, they made clear, would have to tell Bryant that the Voigt-Kampff empathy test had failed. It was too perilous, both legally and morally, to retire androids. As a result, he wouldn't be getting his bounty-hunter bonuses.

But then, quickly recovering, he had asked a final question—about his briefcase, which he described as "one hundred percent genuine babyhide" (59). If this interstellar wild child, this corporate Caspar Hauser, didn't understand the cultural aversion to killing animals, surely she would understand the biological one to killing small children. "[Rick] saw the two dial indicators gyrate frantically," the narrator reports. "But only after a pause. The reaction had come, but too late" (59). He had been right after all: she wasn't human.

Although focused on the psychological injury to Rachael, Dora was impressed by Deckard's "slippery, sharp intelligence." "Babyhide? Babyhide? He comes up with babyhide? But, wow, oh-so clever," she said. Beginning to get into the novel, she called the duel between Deckard and Rosen "brilliant"— "icy and deadly and well-played on both ends." For the first time, Rick "had more than one dimension to him," she claimed.

We spent a great deal of time talking about the fact that the Nexus-6 androids cannot really be said to lack empathy. The text was clear: Rachael's body had produced the necessary response; it had just produced it at a slower rate. The issue of organic feeling might still obtain, but the novel makes it impossible to believe in the distinctions for which Rick fights. Toward the end, we are told that Isidore experienced a "momentary, strange hallucination; he saw briefly a frame of metal, a platform of pulleys and circuits and batteries and turrets and gears—and then the slovenly shape of [the android] Roy Baty faded back into view" (159). This outdated vision of artificial intelligence, however, cannot compete with the lived reality of robot life.

Described as remote and detached and extremely cerebral, "as if a peculiar and malign *abstractness* pervaded their mental processes" (156), the androids, like some autistics, may simply have trouble displaying emotion in a recognizable fashion. As Dora put it, "What if what's happening with the schizoid humans is the same thing that's happening with the androids? That empathy exists in the absence of display. What if there is no difference between the schizoid humans and the androids?" Put simply, the appearance of low affect is deeply misleading. After all, the androids experience fear. They are introspective and aspirational. When Isidore, who hasn't yet figured out that Pris is a robot, asks about Mars and she tells him that "all Mars is lonely. Much worse than this" (150), he says, "I understood that the androids helped" (150). To which she replies, "The androids . . . are lonely, too" (150). Affixed to the passage in Dora's notes appeared the pithy comment: "Saddest. Line. Ever."

The whole point of conducting the Voigt-Kampff was to move beneath outward manifestation to more ostensibly reliable neurobiological markers. This is precisely what R. J. R. Blair did in his study from 2005, which showed that empathy is not a "unitary system," but rather "a loose collection of partially dissociable . . . systems." Comparing and contrasting psychopaths with autistics, it found that psychopaths excelled at cognitive and motor empathy—the former is the ability to make abstract propositions about the mental states of others; the latter is the ability to perform an appropriate gesture with your body—but lacked emotional empathy or what Simone Shama-Tsoory terms "the capacity to experience affective reactions to the observed experiences of others." To be a psychopath, in other words, you must understand how people think and feel, you must be able to take their perspective and assume the posture of compassionate comprehension, but only so that you can manipulate them and later enjoy their pain.

In contrast, autistics struggled with cognitive and motor, but not emotional, empathy. This result was confirmed by a study from 2008, which found that subjects with Asperger syndrome had difficulty with cognitive empathy but did not "differ from controls in emotional empathy." The following year, the Scottish researcher Adam Smith went even further in overturning the scientific applecart by proposing the "Empathy Imbalance Hypothesis," which holds that autistics possess a "surfeit of emotional empathy," making them "susceptib[le] to empathic overarousal." Such overarousal has the effect of exacerbating difficulties with cognitive and motor empathy and of making the autist appear much less empathetic than he or she actually is. Describing autism as a difficulty attaching words to emotional states and motorically executing an expected response is very different from describing it as a lack of feeling for other people.

In our discussion of Rachael's empathy test, Dora made it clear just how pivotal are the motor and timing aspects of autism; everything that neurotypicals take for granted occurs more slowly: "There's the physical initiating of movements that must occur and the processing time of realizing what just happened. Sometimes it takes me a really long time to realize what happened. I'm always feeling a few steps—or days—behind. If you don't do things in the moment when you're interacting with people, you kind of miss the window." She then linked the issue of processing speed to the central challenge of AASPIRE: "getting the incredibly high-powered, senior researcher PI [principal investigator] people to slow down." "It makes the research always take substantially longer," she said," which is a problem because then you no longer fit your normal grant schedule."

Increasingly the central theme of Dick's novel appeared to be the tension between what people had been taught to believe about androids and what the androids were actually capable of. We're told that they lack sufficient warmth to care for animals, let alone for humans or for their own kind. Of Rachael, Rick says, "An android can't be appealed to; there's nothing in there to reach" (182). (Dora and I noted how much this remark sounded like what a number of prominent experts have casually said about autistics.) To Inspector Garland, who was just revealed to be a robot, he comments, "You androids don't exactly cover for each other in times of stress" (124). Baty himself makes this point when he, Pris, and his wife, Irmgard, are huddled together in Isidore's apartment building. The "chickenhead" has finally figured out that they are androids—"Actually you're not alive," he says. ". . . But what does it matter to me? I mean, I'm a special; they don't treat me very well either" (163)—and the group must decide whether to let him live. "If he were an android," Baty insists, "he'd turn us in about ten tomorrow" (164).

And yet, as Dora pointed out, "The androids are clearly helping each other; they're not turning each other in. They even have their own underground railroad going." When Luba Luft temporarily gets the best of him and Rick is taken to Garland's fake police station, the narrator reports, "Rick saw what the androids, working together, had achieved" (110). He must swim through the mud of his own thinking—of human ideology—to reach the shore of what he experientially knows. The androids and Isidore must do the same. "Isidore's told that he's stupid," Dora explained, "so he thinks he's stupid. Though he hasn't really done anything stupid. And I feel the same way about the androids. Because they've been told certain things, they believe them."

Dick doesn't entirely tip the scales in the androids' favor, however. His genius as a storyteller, as a lover of ambiguity, is to pit an inadequate understanding of android life against some credible evidence of lack, as in the scene where Pris and Roy sadistically torture a spider that Isidore has found. One by one, they cut off its legs, driving Isidore to great distress. Although the reader senses that the androids may be working out their own fear of being hunted, a stereotype is confirmed: they cannot care for animals. Even Isidore, who looks up to the androids and considers them superior, thinks, "Something ailed the . . . androids, something terrible" (211). Dick is mostly on their side, but he also seeks to capture the culture's anxiety about technology—in particular, the collapse of the real through proliferating forms of electronic mediation. And anyway, he's too fine a novelist to want to contain the Frankensteinian question he has birthed and, like Eldon Rosen, pushed into life.

Everything comes to a head when Rick, having found the androids and killed Pris, turns his gun on Irmgard: "'I'm sorry, Mrs. Baty,' Rick said, and shot her" (223). Her husband, the narrator tells us, "let out a cry of anguish" (223), which prompts the most remarkable admission from Deckard just before he kills Roy: "Okay, you loved her . . . and I loved Rachael. And the special loved the other Rachael" (223). (Though possessing distinct personalities and wearing different clothing, Pris and Rachael are the same android model.)

"There's a time bomb for every oppression," wrote Aniekee Tochukwu Ezekiel, and at this moment it goes off. Dora found Rick's remark "incredibly tragic yet perversely freeing." "On the one hand, Deckard's running the program, doing his job," she said, "though by this point, he doesn't agree with it. On the other, he plainly concedes that this sort of love exists. There's this weird hope and weird breakdown of social norms. An acknowledgment we're all the same. But then, kaboom!" In *The Fire Next Time*, James Baldwin skewers "the collection of myths to which white Americans cling: that their ancestors were all freedom-loving heroes, that they were born in the greatest country the world has ever seen, or that Americans are invincible in battle and wise in peace, that Americans have always dealt honorably with Mexicans and Indians and all other neighbors or inferiors." Rick, too, is a "slightly mad victim[] of [his] own brainwashing." As he discovers his love for Rachael, he discovers Roy's love for Irmgard: the androids are anything but emotionless ciphers.

It is precisely Deckard's brainwashing that Rachael fails to undo in a preceding chapter. She has been sent by her "uncle" to seduce Rick and thereby inhibit his willingness to retire androids. Eldon wants to save his product; Rachael, her fellow robots. The only weapon at her disposal, besides her trim girlish figure, is parody—what Rick mistakes as an android tendency to address "topic[s] of worldshaking importance . . . facetiously. . . . [with] no emotional awareness . . . of the actual meaning of what [is] said. Only the hollow, formal, intellectual definitions of the separate terms" (190). Think of Rachael's wit as a piece of malicious Halloween candy, but with the razor on the outside and a vulnerable, pining sweetness within.

"I'm not alive! You're not going to bed with a woman. Don't be disappointed; okay? Have you ever made love to an android before?" (194). Rachael asks him. When he says no, she responds, "I understand . . . it's convincing if you don't think too much about it. But if you think too much, if you reflect on what you're doing—then you can't go on. For ahem physiological reasons" (194). As he bends down to kiss her, she repeats the injunction: "Don't think about it, just do it. Don't pause and be philosophical, because from a philosophical standpoint it's dreary. For us both" (194). The android-human distinction, one of those "hollow, formal, intellectual definitions," threatens to forestall pleasure—whereas the mind will get stuck, the body doesn't care.

"Ooo I love how Rachael has played Deckard, how she has turned the knife of the sex-object the other way and landed it in his gut instead of her own," Dora said. "For a supposed not-alive, unempathic, intellectual android, and an exhausted stone-cold bounty hunter, the scene with Deckard and Rachael is on freakin' fire. Sexual, dangerous, passions on both sides, loud and complicated and messy. Everything promised by Rachael's portrayal so far. She is vibrant." After the sex concludes, Rachael says, with sublime irony, "I love you, Rick, if I entered a room and found a sofa covered in your hide, I'd score very high on the empathy test" (194). "I laughed and slapped the book when I read that," Dora exclaimed. By this point, she was really enjoying the novel: "It's gotten horrible and clever. Everything is so ugly and at the same time so sad. I love that duality. I want it to be ugly and petty, but it's so sad."

We spoke of Rachael as a kind of robot self-advocate and debated her feelings for Rick. She does seem, at least in part, to fall for him—or maybe that's just in the film. Their relationship prompted me to ask about Dora's own love life. She's been with the same nonautistic man, a theatrical lighting designer and set builder (whose email address cleverly reads "sparkenter . . ."), for over two decades. Before that she was with a woman. She said she is more attracted to women physically, but, again, she doesn't really understand gender. Her partner joked that they share an abiding fondness for "boobies." (Not a hundred yards from their house is a strip club shaped like a breast or, rather, a breastlike jug of rum. Scoffing at liberal, pandrogynous Portland, the club's sign reads, "Buns Packed with Gluten.")

Unlike Deckard, Jason is an especially thoughtful man: warm, imperturbable, comfortably in love with Dora. They're both able to laugh at themselves and, echoing Tim Burton, would likely say, tongue-in-silico-cheek, of their relationship, "We all know interspecies romance is weird."

. . .

ALTHOUGH I HAD PUBLISHED a scholarly article about the deep connection to nonhuman entities, including inanimate objects, in autism, I had not thought much about its implications for literature. The point of the article was to note a species bias, or privileging of the human, in neurotypical accounts of empathy. This bias shows up, interestingly enough, in research about the salutary effects of reading fiction on empathy's cognitive component.

A recent study by Italian researchers found that literary, but not science, fiction improved mentalizing abilities. Whereas the former genre involves "understanding characters," the latter, the authors claim, involves "imagining different realities." By "different realities" they mean, among other things, artificial intelligence or talking objects. "Perhaps for this reason," they propose, "science fiction . . . is preferred by individuals with autism, and does not affect social skills." One can object to all sorts of things in this statement: (1) the distinction between literary and science fiction, as if the latter can't be "literary"; (2) the claim that science fiction isn't character-based—Dora yelled, "What?????????" when I told her about the study; and (3) the very narrow conception of the social, as if the social were something that only humans did with each other.

The reference to autism is anything but gratuitous. As the authors note, "A more nuanced understanding of the effects of reading is necessary to inform potential rehabilitation treatments for disorders in which a deficit of empathy is central, such as Autism Spectrum Disorders (ASDs) and schizophrenia." Sadly, the article lacks a more nuanced understanding of literature itself, which resists reductive templates. Dick's novel cleverly exploits the confusion of the human and the robot, which is to say, that as the latter becomes more human to Deckard, the reader finds himself in an equivalent predicament. At first, Rick worries that he is sexually attracted to androids. It was "an odd sensation, knowing intellectually that they were machines but emotionally reacting anyhow" (95). Then he is plagued by moral concerns, feelings for his prey—what he calls "empathy toward an artificial construct" (141).

To treat Rachael as something other than an object whose "life" doesn't matter is akin to treating her as a complex character. Dick ensures that we do. It's an open question as to whether autistic readers would identify more with her than with Deckard, just as it is an open question as to whether neurotypical readers would identify more with Deckard than with her. But it seemed a possibility. Again and again, Dora commented, "Rachael remains the only character who feels alive." Of course, the business of identification is complicated. Which aspect of a reader's personhood customarily prevails? Maybe autistic men would identify with Rick. For Dora, gender itself was less decisive than the experience of belittlement and discrimination, which often come with being a woman. And yet something else appeared to be at play. Increasingly, what seemed an aesthetic judgment about Dick's authorial skill took on neurological significance.

In saying this, I'm not reducing Dora to her neurology; rather, I'm trying to account for the intensity of her feelings for Rachael. Sci-fi regularly relies on the human-robot inversion; autistic readers may be especially primed to embrace it. Consider, for example, the "weirdly poignant scene" in Stanley Kubrick's *2001: A Space Odyssey*. In Nicholas Carr's retelling, the astronaut Dave Bowman "calmly, coldly disconnect[s] the memory circuits that control [HAL's] brain." "Dave, stop. . . . My mind is going. I can feel it. I can feel it," the computer cries. According to Carr, "HAL's outpouring of feeling contrasts with the emotionlessness that characterizes the human figures in the film, who go about their business with an almost robot efficiency. In the world of *2001*, people have become so machinelike that the most human character turns out to be a machine."

When I interviewed Temple Grandin and asked her if literature or film had ever elicited a strong emotional response, she said that she had cried and cried while watching this scene, though not because she shared Carr's concern about the triumph of technology. She felt for HAL. In *Loving Lampposts*, an autistic woman calls an old General Electric refrigerator, whose cord she cut off, her "friend." "I want the whole world to know about my Rudy," she says. "We've been together for twenty-eight years now." She then remarks to the camera, "I met a real live steam locomotive. Union Pacific keeps him as a pet. He's very friendly. I bet if you tried to interview him, you could get him to talk."

The very title of the documentary suggests a fondness for the nonhuman—the director's autistic son exuberantly interacts with what the dictionary defines as a "tall pole with a light at the top" but what a writer might dub "evening's metallic sentinel." On the page, the writer, you might say, presents the inanimate world autistically or, put another way, through the figure of personification, he creates a momentary android. "I have named a broken cup at home as Prometheus. I have named a wooden frog on the windowsill as Mr. Voltaire,"

Tito comments in an interview. But for him the gesture is less a conceit than a vibrant reality. Or, rather, because he is a writer himself and can play with his own neurological proclivities, it is both—call it a living conceit.

Much anecdotal evidence points to a rich relationship with things in autism. They are alive and demand our care. Again, Tito: "There is a big sense of extreme connection I feel with a stone or perhaps with a pen on a tabletop or a tree." On the self-advocate website "Wrong Planet," the mother of an autistic child posted a message in which she sought guidance for her son's "obsessive empathy for inanimate objects." "If he drops a food wrapper he thinks the wrapper will be upset if he doesn't put it in the bin," she said. "If a chocolate chip falls off his biscuit then he will put it back with its 'friends.'" Responding to the mother, a number of people with autism and Asperger syndrome reported that they also treat objects in this manner. Dora, I learned, used to do the same. "I think I told you, that if I stubbed my toe, I would apologize to the furniture," she said. "And there were books I couldn't read because I got so upset when a character left mashed potatoes on her plate."

"We say *animism*," writes Dennis Silk. "Then we put it back on the shelf with the other relegated religions." "Maybe our flight from animism is our flight from madness," he says. "We're afraid of the life we're meagre enough to term inanimate." He reminds us that the poet Rainer Maria Rilke once had trouble leaving—one might even say breaking up with—a bar of hotel-room soap and that during the confession of the fifteenth-century child serial killer Gilles de Rais, the Bishop of Nantes shielded the wooden crucifix, which hung on a wall. "If a cross is a witness, why not a loaf of bread, or a shoe-tree, or a sugar-tongs or a piece of string?" Silk asks. "We should have an All Souls' Night for dead objects, and confer on them some hours of the life we deny them."

Of course, scientists have long known about—and frankly dismissed—such anthropomorphic tendencies. As one researcher writes, "Humans might project personality and character onto a car, based on the powerful mechanisms of social cognition involving . . . [the] attribution of intentionality and mental states, but the car itself remains a passive object, never initiating any interactions, any 'relationship' only exists in the mind of the human." In this view, anthropomorphism is simply "a side-effect of normal brain development," a "natural extension[] of the systems of the social brain to the inanimate world."

And yet there's more to anthropomorphism than previously thought—and more to think about with respect to auties and andys. Auties appear less to extend the systems of the social brain to nonhuman agents than to begin with these agents. As Grandin notes in *The Autistic Brain*, "Neuroimaging studies . . . have repeatedly indicated that the cortex of an autistic doesn't respond to faces as animatedly as it does to objects." Andys appear to constitute the perfect fulfillment of anthropomorphic desire: instead of a car, say, whose grill seems to smile, an actually smiling humanoid robot, but one that challenges our commitment to anthropocentrism and, in so doing, causes anxiety.

Researchers have found recently that autistic children "exhibit certain positive social behaviors while interacting with robots that are not observed while interacting with their peers, caregivers, and therapists," and yet they fear that this kind of therapy may be counterproductive. After all, the point is to shore up the "wise man" Homo sapiens, to protect his perch, to make him distinctively alluring. The normative drive won't allow an egalitarian diffusion of regard: "I attend to everything the same way with no discrimination, so that the caw of the crow in the tree is as clear and important as the voice of the person I'm walking with," explains autist Diana Krumins.

It's tempting here to speak of the "posthuman," of having moved beyond any stable sense of what the human is or what its values ought to be, but I prefer Erin Manning's much less linear concept of "the more than human," which makes room for a host of actors, including traditional human ones, and insists on a field of relation, an inclusive, antihierarchical ecology. In this context the concept has the added benefit of echoing the title of Theodore Sturgeon's 1953 sci-fi novel *More Than Human*. For Manning, the problem of what Graham Harvey calls the "old usage," which "constructed animists as people who did not or could not distinguish correctly between things and persons," fails to matter at the earliest stages of perception when the world hasn't yet resolved itself into agreed-upon categories.

Although anthropomorphism is thought to be universal, the degree of anthropomorphic engagement varies in the nonautistic population, according to a recent study. The study demonstrated "stable individual differences in anthropomorphism that predict[] . . . important consequences for everyday life." These consequences include "the degree of moral care and concern afforded to an agent, the amount of responsibility and trust placed on an agent, and the extent to which an agent serves as a social influence on the self." Anthropomorphism, in other words, isn't just a narcissistic projection, the tendency, as David Hume put it two hundred years ago, to "find human faces in the moon [or] armies in the clouds." It can be a measure of ecological care, an attentiveness to entities other than ourselves and, just as important, to historically demonized members of "extreme outgroups."

"Seeing human" when seeing a homeless person on the streets or a non-speaking child with autism in a group home seems to be correlated with a willingness—indeed an eagerness—to anthropomorphize nonhuman agents. The fact that "those who are socially connected are less likely than those who are lonely to anthropomorphize... [and] more likely to demonize other humans" should give us pause. It should also prompt us to consider the effect of weaker and stronger anthropomorphizing tendencies on readers of science fiction. What's at stake is precisely an openness to the genre's alternative sense of character and a rejection of its frequent disparagement by critics.

It's worth mentioning that scientists have documented a form of synesthesia in nonautistics that incorporates especially vigorous anthropomorphism. A study from 2007 focused on a woman "for whom inanimate objects... are experienced as having rich and detailed personalities" and for whom letters and numbers are experienced as "highly consistent and specific sensory experiences of color," a condition referred to as "grapheme-color synesthesia." As the researchers report, "Synesthesia can involve complex semantic personifications, which can influence visual attention"—their subject's personifying propensities were so vigorous as to be "indiscriminately activated by almost every object." Previous research had documented a more modest version of the phenomenon called "ordinal linguistic personification" in which individuals "attribute animate-like qualities such as personality and gender to sequential linguistic units (e.g. letters, numerals, days, months)."

The authors of the 2007 study refer to "a personification network... [which is] strongly activated by objects that for normal individuals either do not activate, or weakly activate, this network," and they propose that "object-personality pairings" are "likely due to a greater number of neural connections in the network or reduced inhibition of normally occurring connections." Such connections probably take place in the parietal and frontal regions, in areas associated with "personification and the self" and with "shifts of covert and overt attention." Parietal regions, they note, have been associated with "disengaging attention from objects." The intensity of this sort of anthropomorphism may thus result, in part, from becoming perceptually glued to things that a person would otherwise deem, in a typical "topology of salience," to be unworthy of sustained attention. If you look long enough at a chair or a light fixture or a lamppost, how can it not appear to be a social partner? ("Mother fork, grandmother fork, ex-father fork...")

While "object-personality pairings" may constitute "an extreme end-point of a normal mechanism"—that is, a version of anthropomorphic inclinations in nonsynesthetes—they may also be something else entirely, something that disappears through a process of neural pruning as the typical child develops. "When we are born, we are born with everything wired to everything else. There's a gene [that causes] trimming, and if that gene mutates, then you get deficient trimming," explains V. S. Ramachandran. The former view, however, deemphasizes the cross-activation of "far-flung brain areas," holding that synesthesia is "closely related to normal sensory integration going on in everyone below the level of consciousness." Personifying synesthetes may retain a "heightened awareness" of lower-level input before it has been subjected to—you might even say suppressed by—higher-order categorical analysis. Think, for example, of the motion-detection system in humans, which initially doesn't distinguish between kinds of movement. If only for a hundredth of a second, there is no difference between the wind-blown limbs of a tree and a person waving her arms.

Although we don't know if this model can account for extraordinary anthropomorphism in autism, we do know that autistics are three times more likely to be synesthetic than nonautistics—Dora experiences synesthesia—and that autistics possess privileged access to precategorical sensory information. Recall my discussion in chapter 1 of Laurent Mottron's theory of enhanced perceptual functioning in autism. A penchant for detail and a resistance to abstraction delay the emergence of the ordinary world, which for nonautistics arrives each moment, by comparison, predictably arranged and assembled.

For Dora, the distinction between animate and inanimate entities didn't exist until high school—it still doesn't entirely exist. "The lines between things are fuzzy," she explained. "The lines between figure and ground are fuzzy; the lines between foreground and background are fuzzy. All of these things have to get threaded out and sorted." People present particular challenges in that they are especially animated—and often in unpredictable ways. "It's a lot to take in and process," Dora said. For this reason, she prefers a book or a movie to "real life" because "the artist who has created it has pulled out the relevant bits." Just as Tito rendered metrical poetry an unlikely accommodation by using it to calm his anxiety, so Dora rendered fiction an unlikely accommodation by using it to quell the mass of random detail that regularly confronts her. Art's shapeliness, its intention, acts as a kind of filter—like breadcrumbs in the forest or blinders at the racetrack.

At one point the narrator of *Do Androids Dream of Electric Sheep?* says, "In .45 of a second an android . . . could assume any one of fourteen basic reaction postures" (30). The remark occurs in the context of a discussion of how deceptively realistic are the android's movements—deceptive enough to require an empathy test to determine its status and yet insufficiently flexible and varied when compared to a human being's more robust motoric repertoire. Pursuing Dora's sense of art's accommodative function and dismissing any and all value judgments about artificial intelligence, we might think of science fiction itself as a Nexus-6 android. What Samuel Taylor Coleridge said of the writer generally may, with some modification, be said of the science fiction writer specifically: he must "transfer from [his] inward nature a [more than] human interest and a [purposeful simplification of sensory] truth sufficient to procure for these shadows of [reality] that willing suspension of disbelief [and ontological preeminence]." By teaching us to see beyond ourselves, by helping us to forge a new "topology of salience," science fiction can function as an accommodation for neurotypicals as well.

. . .

HOW MUCH DID Dora believe in this account of her attachment to Rachael? Not as much as I did. Again and again, she reminded her ethnographer that she was more complicated than any hypothesis I might have about her. She pointed out that her love of androids also derived from the "seamless integration of technology into [her] activities of daily life." Though all of us are what Donna Haraway termed cyborgs, "fabricated hybrids of machine and organism," Dora, like many autistics, was a giga-cyborg, for want of a better term. "Technology has been the other piece of my brain my whole life," she said. "Whatever's missing I have a device that does it for me. Very early PDA user, gadgets—I'm always reaching for a technology first." Her study in Portland looked like a cross between a 1980s punk-rock stage and the bridge of *Battlestar Galactica*. Futuristic lights, music, and furniture—all of it pulsating, all of it carving its syncopated signature on the brain. "OMG. The tech is delightful," she said when encountering Deckard's "nondirectional Penfield wave transmitter" (88). "In reality, I am a 15-year-old boy who can't get enough of this stuff."

She told me that she had spent a lot of time thinking about assistive technology and "how it blurs human/machine lines." "I don't believe that these dichotomies exist," she remarked. "What is AI? Whatever computers can't do yet. We keep moving the line on what we call AI every time computers do something new." Perhaps the "fuzziness" of perceptual distinctions allowed her to see fully the contrivance of philosophical ones and to embrace a robot who, through its own assistive technology, seemed "more human than any of the other humans."

In her sci-fi novels, assistive technology figures prominently. After we finished with *Androids*, I read and commented on *Hoshi and the Red City Circuit*. "The premise of the world I write in is that only 1% of the population is capable of operating quantum computers due to a genetic condition," Dora explained—a genetic condition that conspicuously resembled autism even if it didn't go by that name. "The condition enhances sensory-associative thinking at the expense of verbal-sequential thinking," she said. "The reason why only 1 percent of the population can program is because the ability to produce complex synesthetic landscapes is restricted to just that group. The whole idea is they have an idioglossia, a language only one person knows, because it's the only way to do encryption once computers reach a certain level of sophistication." The link to Dora's cognitive style, those complex synesthetic landscapes, was unmistakable—in fact, she later joked about this aspect of her novels, "Everybody thinks it's fiction!"

Implanted beneath the skin of the forehead, the quantum computers function as assistive technology "because verbal-sequential reasoning can be programmed into them."

> However, they also serve as a mark of caste and shame, and have led to a society in which visible displays of technology and the use of (most) implanted tech are taboo. Like Rachel's short delay before exhibiting a response to the babyhide probe, the results of programmed cognition—speech, physical movement, emotive expressions, actions—never come across as "natural" to normals. A short delay, in fact, is often present while complex programming signals through the nervous system and engages the body.

Dora had pushed the lived reality of assistive technology as far as she could and created a world, not unlike our own, in which neurological difference is begrudgingly, if narrowly, appreciated and yet consistently demonized.

Listen to Hoshi, the novel's "defective detective," describe the process by which she thinks:

> Between my mind and my machine, information churned as the programs I'd started last night ran, using the meat of my brain as swap and

storage. No matter how advanced material technology gets, nothing compares to the brain for sheer memory capacity. I'd erected a partition between my consciousness and the programs, but the parts of me that think through the system were going a bit sloggy with so many extra processes running in the background. I rely on my navis' hardware just as much as it relies on my wet-memory. Symbiosis, in a sense.

Each aspect of Hoshi's brain plays a role, a blended one, in thought.

The "Operators" in Dora's novel access a space called the "Mem." Like the "digital natives" from Silicon Valley whom Steve Silberman writes about in *NeuroTribes*, these autistic-like beings serve as the "architects of our future." Hoshi says,

> The blank blackness of my mental workspace contained only the window [of my apartment], the crackling blue spark of a channel out, and a vague sense of up and down. The window is where I access my memory, both meat and machine. The spark is the link between my hardware and the city's micro and radio networks; through it I access the Mem, informationspace. Not a "virtual" reality, but an actual reality, one made of electromagnetic signal, information encoding, and the occasional degradation of noise. A reality made by centuries of my people's thoughts.

The Mem is an extraordinary, multidimensional realm, the imaginary creation of an extraordinary "spatial visualizer." The novel finds a way of narrating the different realms or threads of thought as Hoshi occupies the Mem. But in this world, no two Operators, no two spatial visualizers, are the same.

When I suggested a link to Daniel Tammet, an autistic savant who thinks in synesthetic landscapes and who once recited, from memory, twenty-two thousand digits of Pi, Dora told me about her dyscalculia. While she can do complex math and while she can code, simple arithmetic remains elusive because numbers mean nothing to her. They are like windblown seeds that can find no purchase, no foothold, on the rocky cliffs of her brain. When Tammet looks at a numeric sequence, his "head begins to fill with colors, shapes and textures that knit together spontaneously to form visual landscapes." "To recall each digit, I simply retrace the different shapes and textures and read the numbers out of them," he says. He is also aided by ordinal linguistic personification: "Numbers are my friends, and they are always around me. Each one is unique and has its own personality. 11 is friendly and 5 is loud, whereas 4 is both shy and quiet."

If Tammet "see[s] numbers as shapes, colors, textures and motions," then Dora sees computer symbols as shapes, colors, texture, and motions, though she doesn't have his memory. Like many a synesthete, she discovered rather late how uniquely she "apprehend[s] the world," and it was only at work one day, after being interrupted while programming, that she learned just how uniquely she "writes" code. She was complaining about the interruption to her fellow programmers: "I've got my shapes; I've got my landscape all set up. It's really hard to hold the contents of a hash inside your head. It's so complex. I've got that going there, and I'm trying to move this around. And they're all like what the fuck are you talking about? And I was like, you know the shapes, the code landscape. . . . They didn't have one." "I like the landscapes," she said, "but people don't seem to understand them. They back away slowly when I talk about how I code."

Dora had built into her novel the notion of type—autistics tend to possess considerable visuospatial skills—and yet at the same time she had insisted on particularity. Here is Hoshi once again:

> Every Operator sees these things differently but we all see them: personal memory, transmission flow, data pools, trace wakes—the underlying architecture of the Mem. Ultimately it's just information flowing through the airwaves or jammed into memory matrices. We create programs in our own unique idioglossias. Then we encode the programs of our idio with a lingua franca, a bridge language, so others can understand them. . . . I don't know how Martin, or Luzzie, or any other Operator experiences true-code. We only share the franca.

After retiring the six rogue androids and discovering that Rachael has killed his goat, which he bought with the bounty-hunting bonuses, Deckard retreats to the uninhabited wasteland of Oregon, where he stumbles upon a toad. Out of his mind with grief and self-loathing, he once again thinks that an animal will save him. When he brings home this creature thought long extinct, he sees that it is artificial. "It doesn't matter. The electric things have their lives, too" (241), Rick says to his wife, before adding, "Paltry as those lives are" (241). Deckard has traveled a great distance, in thought and feeling, with respect to the inorganic, but he hasn't traveled far enough.

"It would be unrealistic for someone like him to be pro-android," Dora commented. "When people's paradigms are changing, there are a lot of qualifiers along the road to that paradigm change. They say something that's in the new paradigm, and then they have to go reframe it somehow within the context of their old paradigm." The "structure of scientific revolutions," Thomas Kuhn called it. We talked about the current revolution in autism, about analogously weak and strong versions of neurodiversity, and about how our culture seems at last to have embraced the idea of lives for autistics: still "paltry lives," for the most part, but lives all the same.

Looking back on his work during the 1960s and 1970s, Dick recognized that he, too, had been stuck in a paradigm shift: "There are 'androids' or 'the mantis' among us which appear human but only *simulate* humans. . . . Here is where I went wrong: the simulation is . . . not evil (as I thought) and it is not *less* than what it simulates (as I thought) but more; not clever simulacra-reflex machines, but angelic." The comedian Stephen Wright once quipped, "When I die, I'm leaving my body to science fiction." In a sense, that's what Dora has been doing: leaving her atypical body to collaborative medicine and to an art form that celebrates differences both general and specific. "Write me a creature that thinks as well as a man or better than a man, but not like a man," implored John W. Campbell Jr., a prominent writer and editor during the golden age of science fiction.

· four ·

FINDING HER FEET

There is only a queer divine dissatisfaction, a blessed unrest....
— MARTHA GRAHAM

It could almost be a joke, like the one I told my mother when I was ten: "What do a Buddhist and a man at a hot-dog stand have in common?"

"I don't know."

"What do a Buddhist and a man at a hot-dog stand have in common? Think!"

"I don't know."

"They both say, 'Make me one with everything!'" Loud groan from my mother, very loud. I was ten and had discovered puns—what Alfred Hitchcock called "the highest form of literature." I couldn't get over how such disparate things could be brought together, could be made to intermix, and then, with their boundaries softened, to lose themselves in one another.

Years later, after scribbling in my notebook, "What do autism and ballet have in common?" I remembered it. The answer to this question, which is anything but humorous, can be found in their exclusionary histories. Each, as the dance scholar Jennifer Fisher has described ballet, constituted a "kingdom of the pale," barring the barre, as it were, or diagnosis to nonwhite populations. "The ballet's aristocratic origins, intense scrutiny of the body, and emphasis on aesthetic uniformity have left the African American in the wings," writes Jenna Sullivan. Even the Russian choreographer George Balanchine, who pioneered the inclusion of many aspects of African American music in classical ballet, balked at dissolving traditional distinctions and categories: "I don't want to see two Japanese girls in my *Swan Lake*. It's just not right. It's not done for them," he said. "It's like making an American blonde into a geisha. It's a question of certain arts being things unto themselves."

Similarly, experts used to believe that autism was an upper-middle-class disorder, one affecting the progeny of highly educated, Caucasian people. Hans Asperger called his patients "little professors" for their ability to discourse precociously on their intellectual interests. Stereotypes, along with brute economic facts, which prevented minorities from seeking treatment for their children, wildly overdetermined the portrait of autism that emerged—and that continues to this day. As one commentator argues, "The autism world prides itself on honoring neurodiversity, but it has been less successful at recognizing racial and ethnic diversity." In 2014, a white child was 30 percent more likely to receive an autism diagnosis than a black child and 50 percent more likely than a Latino one, and when the latter groups did receive a diagnosis it came much later than it did for the former group.

Things unto themselves: hot dogs and baseball, white people and ballet. Not black people or Asian people or deaf people or autistic people and ballet—that would be too much like a *relishing Buddha* or *loving ketchup*, a two-ply (two-plie!) concept functioning as an invigorated, if not entirely unified, third term.

. . .

THE SUBJECT OF THIS chapter—she has asked to be called Eugenie—is a multiracial, Jewish, Deaf woman with Asperger syndrome who was trained as a classical ballerina and who now works as a choreographer for competitive figure skaters. Married to a Jewish man named Jacob, she is also the mother of an autistic child. If Dora has elected to mark herself as conspicuously autistic, then Eugenie has elected, in some settings, to pass, but it's no ordinary passing, bearing as she does the signs of multiple forms of Otherness. In her chosen profession, disclosure has met with discrimination, and so she cannot afford the associations that autism calls forth—in particular, the idea that autistics are at once emotionless and physically clumsy. The old ballet joke—"What do ballerinas run on? Batterie power"—evokes the specter of roboticism. (A "batterie," the dictionary explains, is "the action of beating or crossing the feet or calves together during a leap or jump.")

For Eugenie, feeling is paramount: she thinks in feelings, moves with them when dancing, like a ribbon in the wind or like the words in a line of beautifully modulated pentameter, the emotion all the more powerful for the pressure the line is under to follow certain dictates. But perhaps my analogy misleads. Her difficulties as someone on the spectrum lie in the translation of feelings into language—into immediately deployable social scripts—though to speak of her difficulties is to miss just how naturally she functions as a social actor. Her difficulties as a ballerina lie in the "transfer of visual and verbal information into motor action." Eugenie has termed such difficulties "motion dyslexia": confusing left and right, transposing steps in complex combinations.

"Dancers," notes Bettina Bläsing, "modify movements with respect to direction in space, speed, rhythm, and amplitude, and express them precisely as observed from the choreographer's demonstration or in a modified form, depending on the choreographer's wishes." Call it the here-and-now urgency of action perception. At the highest levels of ballet, there's little room for struggles with spatial reasoning or the multimodal integration of sensory input. Determined to be a ballerina, Eugenie, who has nearly perfect recall for visual detail (like Grandin, she can be considered an "object visualizer"), overcame her challenges through sheer will—at least until she had to compete for parts with other professionals and semiprofessionals. Of course, ballet is so demanding as to humble everyone; there is nothing easy about it. She simply had to work harder to power through, and around, her impairment.

But lest you think the end result would be mechanical, a feat of memorization or mime, I must report that it wasn't. She was like a singer who can't read music and yet whose voice and phrasing are sublime. By the time you hear her sing on stage, even her accompanist has forgotten the process of trial and error that got her there. Eugenie could "read" complicated choreography, but she couldn't put it all together expeditiously. And just as she spent extra hours rehearsing steps and sequences, so she spent extra hours rehearsing social ones. Not in a Temple Grandin sort of way, where, in the absence of feeling, she must use stored experiences to reason out what motivates people. Just the opposite: Eugenie needed help rendering emotion cognitive, giving it a usable meaning and doing so in real time.

"I'm not deciphering other people's feelings," she said. "I'm feeling them. I feel everything someone else feels." She, too, used stored experiences but only to make the music stop, as it were, to take off her slippers—to find her frontal lobes. (Picture someone fishing their medial prefrontal cortex from the bottom of a drain—or, in this case, her toes.) "The ballet needs to tell its own story in such a way it can be received without having to be translated into language," Twyla Tharp said famously. Balanchine echoed this point: "A complicated story is impossible to tell.... We can't dance synonyms." Narrative complexity has been displaced onto the body; it becomes a matter of how the dancers dynamically inhabit the air. In everyday life, Eugenie required a more traditional, more self-consciously verbal, frame.

And yet she took from ballet the need to be graceful—the need to be graceful and a commitment to perfection. She would carry herself convincingly; she would look the part. She was like a Nexus-6 with superior feelings! A pirouetting Luba Luft! "I study and see everything," Eugenie said. "Everything. I've studied social life so much that my database is huge. The only thing that will throw me off is a disingenuous person." While visiting her in Chicago, I remarked, "If Grandin is an anthropologist of neurotypical behavior, then you're something else entirely. You've gone native!" Later, reflecting on my remark, I recognized its thoughtless irony. What could "native" possibly mean for someone so multiracial, -ethnic, and -disabled?

I met Eugenie through a friend. I knew that I wanted to explore what scholars in the humanities and social sciences call "intersectionality": the idea that different identities overlap or intersect in a given person. No one is just a woman or a Jew or a Democrat or Hispanic or autistic or gay or black or middle-class. They are many things simultaneously, and whatever the particular combination, these things are mutually and fluidly constitutive. Of course, some identities are more salient than others; indeed, some overwhelm, to the point of eclipsing, others.

When I say that Eugenie "looks predominantly black and Asian," I appear to be offering a neutral observation, but I am in fact revealing how a monoracial writer has been taught to view a multiracial subject—both reductively and gradably. When I say that being multiracial *and* disabled is a bit like wearing orange during hunting season, my wit belies the privilege of being inconspicuous when I long to be—unavailable to stigmatizing eyes.

I wanted to understand how these identity categories, which many people think of as distinct, intersected with autism, and I wanted to see what difference such intersectionality made in reading a novel. I was especially interested in the relationship of autism to deafness, both of which have been conceived, at least by some, as a difference to be celebrated, not bemoaned. I chose *The Heart Is a Lonely Hunter* by Carson McCullers because the novel features a Deaf protagonist, John Singer, who was taught to speak but who prefers to use sign language. "It was painful for him to try to talk with his mouth," the narrator tells us, "but his hands were always ready to shape the words he wished to say" (11).

Eugenie is herself fluent in sign, and she speaks—in fact, she speaks perfectly well. Born with bilateral sensorineural hearing loss, which went undetected as a child, she contracted the chicken pox in high school and experienced additional hearing loss. Over time, that loss progressed, and like her maternal grandmother who had been born hard of hearing, she went deaf. She was "severely to profoundly deaf" for six years before getting a single cochlear implant (CI) at the age of twenty-two—back then, doctors wouldn't give you two implants at once. The implant, however, didn't work, at least initially. Everything sounded the same to her. "Music was actually the first identifiable thing," she reported. Years of listening to books on tape while reading them in her lap allowed her to relearn the alphabet. By the time she turned twenty-seven— she is now forty—her CI outcome was rated "highly successful."

Almost from the beginning of her hearing loss, Eugenie immersed herself in the Deaf community, and she became quite interested in the disability rights movement. Her second son, Meir, was born during the period of adapting to her implant; his subsequent diagnosis of autism (and later her own) would be perceived through a progressive lens. Beneath Eugenie's Skype moniker—we would both use the sidebar to type our comments when discussing the novel—appears the well-known disability rights adage "Nothing about us without us." To her, deafness, like autism, was a political and cultural identity as much as it was a medical impairment.

For this reason, she would find some of the language and depictions in the novel offensive. At first glance, such criticism would seem merely an enlargement or broadening of a customary point—what conservatives like to dismiss as political correctness. Because she was both deaf and multiracial, she could lay claim to additional prejudice—additional forms of roughly the same phenomenon. But, as we will see, she was just as dismayed by identity enclaves, which to her were no less oppressive and inhospitable.

Published in 1940, the novel constitutes an early attempt at thinking intersectionally. It does so primarily at a collective, not an individual, level. The characters, which include a drunken labor activist, Jake Blount; a proud African American doctor, Benedict Mady Copeland; a gender-bending café owner, Biff Brannon; and a musically talented, lower-class tomboy, Mick Kelly, all struggle to free themselves from the cage of narrow, socially imposed identities. All turn to Singer as an antidote to despair, believing that he understands their innermost desires. By not using speech, he takes on almost mystical powers.

On the one hand, the novel presents the clearly delineated groupings of race, gender, class, and disability; on the other, it relates them in a surprising, even tantalizing, manner: through a spatial trope that positions disability, long relegated to the margin of social life, at the center. "Each person addressed his words mainly to the mute" (211), the narrator says. "Their thoughts seemed to converge in him as the spokes of a wheel lead to the . . . hub" (211). Deafness becomes the fantastical solution to existential misunderstanding. The tragic plot of the novel—Singer commits suicide when his deaf friend and love interest, Anton, dies—concerns precisely the foreclosure of a less categorical sense of identity and a more hopeful commitment to communication and boundary crossing.

By the end of *The Heart Is a Lonely Hunter*, Blount has been run out of town—labor is less organized; Copeland has lost his house, is in failing health, and has all but abandoned the dream of racial uplift; Mick has given up music, taken a low-wage job, and become a conventional woman; and Biff, despite greater freedom to play with gender roles after the death of his wife— at one point he rubs her perfume on his armpits—clings to a traditional performance of masculinity in public. (Early in the novel, impotent, unwilling to wash his genital region because he doesn't want to touch himself, he notices "the new, tender nipples beginning to come out on [Mick's] breast" [29]; later, he says that "by nature all people are of both sexes. So that marriage and the bed is not all by any means" [132].) The heart is a lonely hunter because it wants that most elusive of hides—understanding—and because it only shoots blanks, which is to say *words*.

The novel's attack on language, a staple of modernist literature, seemed especially fitting for a reader whose chosen art form is profoundly nonlinguistic. It seemed fitting as well for someone who struggles not with the mechanics of speech but with finding the right words—as if the right words could ever be found. "There is something wrong with the 'wiring' in my brain," Eugenie claimed. "Something happens when I am listening and then thinking and then speaking. Something gets broken down and I am not smooth." She could manage generally, but she could "rarely show brilliance or refinement," and she resented that. "Most people wouldn't notice it unless I'm stressed or overstimulated," she said. "Oh, and I have the same 'wiring' issues when I sign. I struggle just like when I am speaking."

In the course of our conversations, she would admit that she is "extremely fluent in what [she] wants to say" when typing. This has to do with being able to control the pace and stress of communication. She would also admit that "motion dyslexia" can affect her signing—as can anxiety. Once, in her early twenties, when she worked at a school for the deaf, her hands had a meltdown while communicating with the mother of a student. "She was very nice, but she was loud and had a BIG personality," Eugenie explained. "It had been a looooong day at the school with lots of family events going on. I was sooooo overstimulated."

> The mom came up and asked me something and I started to respond, but it looked like my signs were having a seizure and they made NO SENSE AT ALL. I was just moving and darting my hands, arms, and fingers while having a mini-panic attack. She looked at me like I had turned into a giant alien with 8 heads and then turned around and walked away. She neither talked to me nor took me seriously again.

The encounter shows just how hard it is to be Deaf *and* autistic—let alone Deaf *and* autistic *and* black *and* white *and* Mongolian *and* Japanese *and* Indonesian *and* Cherokee *and* Jewish, as Eugenie is.

Even her mother, Shanna, from whom she'd learned much about multiraciality, couldn't embrace autism. "While she values my uniqueness, that's about all of the difference she can accept in me," Eugenie said. For complicated reasons, her mother couldn't add neurological difference to the mix. Her husband, from whom she was estranged, was likely on the spectrum—both he and Eugenie thought so. To Shanna, autism was the straw that broke the camel's identity. (Not one to worry about excess, Jerry Garcia, that champion of street party music and psychedelic neurodiversity, once proclaimed, "Too much of a good thing is just about right.")

Discussing the novel with Eugenie, I would discover that she had had many experiences like the one at the school for the deaf. Whatever the enclave, it couldn't make room for multiple forms of difference. In response, she had decided to be herself—her multiple, slippery self, as I termed it. "Yes, I am quite slippery," she would say.

> I have always been irked by people boxing me into what they want me to be. I want to be who I truly am, not who someone thinks I should be. And if this offends someone white who really needs me to be black, then too bad. And if this offends someone black who really

needs me to be black, then too bad. . . . I have to move out of old patterns of thinking about race.

One can hear in this remark considerable struggle and pain—but also a kind of triumph. Emily Dickinson wrote, "I pull a flower from the woods,—/ A monster with a glass / Computes the stamens in a breath, / And has her in a class." Taking up the same theme, William James mused, "Probably a crab would be filled with a sense of personal outrage if it could hear us class it without ado or apology as a crustacean, and thus dispose of it. 'I am no such thing,' it would say; 'I am MYSELF, MYSELF alone.'"

As Eugenie well understood, the "categorization 'rules' used by perceivers" of multiraciality rarely match those used by multiracial individuals. Social science research has documented the harm that reductive, monoracial perceptions and frameworks can do. As one researcher puts it, "Instances of identity constraint are associated with tension, decreased motivation, and damaged self-esteem." But multiraciality can also lead to more "flexible . . . strategies in dealing with . . . [one's] social environments."

A dip into this research revealed an uncanny parallel: just as autistics, with their detail-oriented vision, put pressure on the generally labeled thing, so multiracial people, with their complex genetic and cultural inheritances, put pressure on the generally labeled person. While the terms we deploy can't possibly accommodate the fullness of the individual example, the minds we have—we neurotypicals, that is—aren't inclined to see it anyway. "Due to the widely recognized limits and biases in our perceptual systems," writes one diversity scientist, "going beyond simple categorization may be relatively rare because it can be quite effortful."

Speed of processing is valued above all else, and yet here again it becomes a problem. Multiraciality is said to produce in monoracial perceivers "dysfluency in categorization," which causes them to assign multiracial people to "devalued social categories, with subsequently biased evaluations and behavior." As we have seen, my autistic collaborators make a virtue of dysfluency. They not only disregard established distinctions but also disrespect established hierarchies. Think of Tito on the masthead of speech, failing to make phonemes and identifying with a whale; or Jamie, who follows Silko into the Laguna-Pueblo landscape, a space of spirit-time and itself a kind of character; or Dora, who values the "more than human" of so-called artificial intelligence. The very notion of social "ingroups" and "outgroups" ends up reconfigured. We might borrow Tito's phrase and speak of a "world as fluid as the sea."

In this way, the precategorical proclivities of autism line up with the anti-categorical proclivities of multiraciality. As Eugenie and I got going with our discussions, she would seem to be the ideal reader for—indeed, the perfect antidote to—*The Heart Is a Lonely Hunter*. Because she was a ballerina, I couldn't help but map onto the characters' intersectional troubles a kind of failed choreography and an inability to dance in a manner that might save them. Whatever her own difficulties as a dancer, whatever the checkered history of ballet—it, too, was a category that needed to be broken down—Eugenie moved at just the right speed and with just the right fluency. The feeling world of her feet, as opposed to the thinking world of her head, became an advantage, leading me to ask: "In exactly whom does a social disability lie?"

. . .

WE DECIDED TO MEET virtually on Wednesday afternoons for about an hour and a half. Eugenie's older boys, ages sixteen and eleven, would be at school, and her toddler, almost three, would be taking a nap. The toddler, she would later tell me, was supposed to be a girl, her ballerina, someone with whom she could share her passion for dancing. On more than one occasion, she'd refer to ballet as—wink, wink—her "restricted interest," yet the demands of motherhood, marriage, and coaching made that sort of narrow focus impossible.

The plan was to discuss three chapters a week. Like all of my other collaborators, Eugenie would send me notes in advance. About her educational background or experience with literature, I knew little. Although she had a bachelor of arts in speech and hearing science and had worked for a time as a licensed speech-language pathology assistant, she was "an avid lover of books." "I've been a lifelong reader," she would tell me. "I love how I can connect with the characters on my terms (and how the characters will always be my friends no matter what). I know the characters personally. I can see into their lives. And there they are, steady as ever, page after page."

Once again, a collaborator would point to how literature can serve as an accommodation: a way of managing the messiness, unpredictability, and meanness of social life. Novels allowed her to confront this maelstrom, to be intimate and introspective, on "her terms"—as slowly, that is, and as calmly as she wanted.

After greeting Eugenie online, I typed a bit about the author, including the fact that McCullers had written *The Heart Is a Lonely Hunter* at twenty-three;

that she was Bohemian and polyamorous (she once had a crush on a ballerina); and that she had experienced considerable disability in her life: she suffered a stroke at thirty-one, which paralyzed the left side of her body, and died at fifty of a brain hemorrhage. I then mapped out the emerging structure of the book. McCullers, who had studied at Juilliard and who had dreamed of becoming a concert pianist, described it as "contrapuntal" and akin to "a fugue." In a fugue, "a short melody or phrase (the subject) is introduced by one [voice] part and successively taken up by others" and then developed "in a continuous interweaving of the voice parts." Think of "the subject," I proposed, as the problem of identity and the "voice parts" as the different characters.

The opening chapter introduces the first two such parts: Singer and his deaf friend Antonapoulos, who live together. The latter's "face was round and oily, with half-closed eyelids and lips that curved in a gentle, stupid smile. The other mute was tall. His eyes had a quick, intelligent expression. He was always immaculate and very soberly dressed" (3). After reacting negatively to the word "mute," Eugenie remarked,

> I understand the term "stupid smile" or "stupid grin," but I am curious why a deaf character's smile is stupid. Is this character going to be fleshed out in just the same way as a hearing character would be—and he just happens to have a stupid grin, the same stupid grin he might have if he were hearing? Or will the character be involved in a lot of folly? Lastly, is he unintelligent, and so therefore wears a stupid grin? In a nutshell, is this character going to be a stereotype?

Conceding that the two men are "opposites, which should make for good storytelling," Eugenie nevertheless worried about the negative meaning that had attached itself to disability.

I agreed but sought to complicate this notion. McCullers traffics in the grotesque, which can operate as an extreme version of stereotype, yet which can also carry within it flickers of critique. The word "grotesque" means "strange . . . fantastic . . . incongruous, unpleasant, or disgusting and [it] is . . . often used to describe weird shapes and distorted forms such as Halloween masks." Like pickled punks preserved in jars of formaldehyde, it purports to be containable. A threat disguised as pleasure, it stirs the womb of embodied possibilities. It's sudden quicksand for the normal.

"In art . . . , *grotesque* may also refer to something that simultaneously invokes in an audience a feeling of uncomfortable bizarreness as well as sympathetic pity." The grotesque moves the viewer in multiple ways at once, and even in literature, that other visual medium, it presupposes a kind of effortless gawking. It takes advantage of the subject's propensity to stare and, much more subtly, of the object's commitment, in the words of Kenny Fries, to "stare back," to put pressure on the given or agreed upon. Figuring the novelist's pen as an aquarist's hose, Edward Abbey points to the curious pageant of representation in Marcel Proust. In the giant tank of the Frenchman's work, "fish drift[] with languid fins through a subaqueous medium of pale violet polluted ink."

Both Singer and Antonapoulos function as grotesques—Antonapoulos more obviously. The "big Greek" "loved food" (5), we are told, and after a meal, while Singer did the dishes, he "would lie back on his sofa and slowly lick over each one of his teeth with his tongue" (5). The man's corpulence suggests a balloon about to burst; his gluttony, an ungovernable force. We never see him actively signing to Singer, and after he has been taken to an insane asylum for belligerent behavior, we learn that he cannot read. He is a figure at once scary and pathetic. Yet Singer, who is pathetic in his own way, pathetic and sublime, writes to him letter after letter. "The way I need you is a loneliness I can't bear" (217), he says in one.

When he later visits Anton at the asylum, he beholds what many would call a spectacle but what he takes in through the refracting prism of love:

> He wore a scarlet dressing-gown and green silk pajamas and a turquoise ring. . . . He was knitting. His fat fingers worked with the long ivory needles. . . . The splendor of his friend's raiment startled him. On various occasions he had sent him each article of the outfit, but he had not imagined how they would look when all combined. Antonapoulos was more enormous than he had remembered. The great pulpy folds of his abdomen showed beneath his silk pajamas. (219–20)

Encountering this passage, Eugenie would comment, "I'm envisioning Anton in bed looking like Liberace." There would be nothing derogatory about the comparison; she'd simply be responding in a way that McCullers intended.

Yet even in our first few meetings, before Anton's character was fully developed, Eugenie revealed her impatience. "I could hold with Singer quite a conversation I could," she said. Her sense of the man's loneliness was profound. She could relate to it intensely—relate to it, moreover, in his native hand. (At one point in the novel, she'd favorably tag a description of Singer's signing: "His hands worked nervously as though they were pulling things unseen from the air and binding them together" [210–11].) At the same time, her comment resembled an affectionate scolding—something like, "You can do better, John. Anton doesn't treat you very well." Indeed, Anton seems to be using Singer, indulging, yet also thwarting, the man's homosexual desire in order to benefit materially. Not halfway into the novel, she'd complain, "Out of Singer's entire life experience, and in comparison to what he is and does for others, how can he be desperate for the attention of such an unlikeable person?"

Eugenie's great ability as a reader was to hop inside the tank and to move fishlike, with her own languid fins, through McCullers's "violet polluted ink." "It's like I can become these characters and people," she would tell me. "I know how all of this feels. When I read things, I relate via emotions. Everything is about connecting with emotions for me." She'd then add, having just commented on my stubbornly intellectual approach—I stood on the outside of the tank looking in—"So this is a great exercise: putting big words to characters and their actions and what drives them."

I was doing what I do in class: advancing analytical propositions, ignoring the reader's experience. Repeatedly, she'd exclaim, "My brain is about to break—your questions are getting much harder as we go along, lol" and "I adore how you are stretching my brain. Let me think on your words more as they settle in." Toward the end of our time with the novel, after reading a critical article about it, she'd type, "The dreaminess floats away. This is where I struggled with you at times with *Heart*. I just wanted to feel it, but you wanted more dissection and opinion."

Chapter 2 gives us the third and fourth "voice parts": namely, Biff Brannon, proprietor of the New York Café; and Jake Blount, communist labor organizer. For twelve days, Blount, who is penniless, has been eating and drinking on credit. Biff justifies serving him by saying, "I like freaks" (14). To which, his wife barks, "I reckon you do . . . being as you're one yourself" (14).

Alice, Biff contends, has no "real kindness" (15). When he tells her, "Not but one woman I've ever known had this real kindness I'm talking about," she replies, "I've known you to do things no man in the world would be proud of. I've known you to—" (15). Biff cuts her off: "Or maybe it's curiosity I mean. You don't ever see or notice anything important that goes on. You never watch and think and try to figure anything out" (15). McCullers thus establishes Biff as a sympathetic observer of human affairs, someone whose own perplexing, though largely concealed, difference connects him to others. Said differently, like Singer (and really all of the characters), Biff is "pulling things unseen from the air and trying to bind them together." Or, like Anton, he's fashioning a new identity ensemble, a kind of all-things-and-colors-at-once "raiment."

At first, Eugenie was "sooooooooo confused by what was shared about Biff"—the unwillingness to wash his genital region; his interest in the androgynous Mick. "But I was also intrigued," she said, "and happy that he was so in touch with his sexuality." Here, the refusal to observe a gender norm is analogous, McCullers implies, to having a distinctive body—to being exceedingly corpulent or deaf.

We then move backward in time and hear about Blount's first night in the New York Café. The man who was short with "heavy shoulders like beams" (16) was "talking some queer kind of politics" (17). The other patrons were laughing at him because he directed his drunken harangue at Singer without knowing he was deaf. "The mute's eyes were cold and gentle as a cat's and all his body seemed to listen" (23), the narrator states ironically. "You're the only one in town who catches what I mean" (23), Blount says.

The labor organizer thus inaugurates the peculiar habit of attributing to Singer a kind of supernatural comprehension. Of Singer, the narrator observes, "His eyes made a person think he heard things nobody else had ever heard, that he knew things no one had ever guessed before. He did not seem quite human" (25). That last line worried Eugenie a great deal. "It would be offensive," she said, "if something fantastic isn't done with Singer's character. The book began with two Deaf men. I am curious to see where things go."

In subsequent weeks she would understandably harp on this point. "I am in hopes that Singer is not a prop," she would say, and still later, "I pray that things develop with Singer. I'm beginning to tire of him being a silent sounding board for others. I imagine the author is taking us somewhere special." As noted previously, each of the characters forges an imaginary bond with Singer. By the end, Eugenie would call him a "doll that can be bent and turned any which way to a person's liking. He doesn't talk back and he always listens." When I picked up on her conceit and spoke of the novel's "ragdoll fantasy," she typed, "Yes, yes, yes. Singer the ragdoll, lol! Tell it!"

How to make sense of this contradiction—the desire, on the one hand, to exclude people with disabilities from meaningful pursuits and, on the other, to imbue disability and its communicative accommodations with transcendent meaning? "The disabled body," writes Emily Russell, "is . . .

so thoroughly subject to repression that in its very exclusion from modern life it produces insight and knowledge." Singer's "nonverbal communication preserves [the] belief in interpersonal connection beyond the limits of conventional social discourse."

I call this phenomenon the "ET effect." In the blockbuster film by Steven Spielberg, ten-year-old Elliot develops a connection with an alien, one far superior to any he might have with his fellow humans. For such a connection to take hold, the creature, in this fantasy, must not be from here—an institution or group home is about as far from the public square as another galaxy—and it must not look like a member of your own species. The fascination with sign language or a text-to-voice synthesizer reflects despair about ordinary communication, but it's a selfish delusion, as Eugenie pointed out: "Why don't any of the characters bother to learn ASL [American Sign Language] or at least scribble notes to Singer?" she asked. Why, for that matter, must ET learn English?

The grotesque, of course, has limits as critique. It's never entirely clear if McCullers is making fun of her characters. How can she not be mocking Blount, whom Eugenie thought detestable? "Looks like Singer has found himself another Anton," she commented, "a motormouth one anyway." Upon finishing the novel, she would type, "I could do without ever running into large doses of the boorish Blount again."

And yet, his politics, the narrator tells us, are "queer": a word that has come to suggest, in contemporary critical circles, a more explicit and unambiguous opposition to the norm. The novel deploys the word "queer" at least twenty-five times—and in a number of different contexts. Scholars, as Eugenie and I discussed, have made much of this fact, connecting it to another word, "freak," previously encountered. According to Rachel Adams, "As McCullers uses these terms, their function depends not upon their correspondence to any fixed identity but upon their opposition to normative behaviors and social distinctions." In this way, Blount's politics can be considered "queer," and he can be a "freak" without being gay, trans, fat, or deaf.

On that first night in the New York Café, he was accompanied by "a tall Negro man" (22). When another patron chastises Blount, "Don't you know you can't bring no nigger in a place where white men drink"? (22) he yells, "'I'm part nigger myself. . . . I'm part nigger and wop and bohunk and chink. All of those.' . . . 'And I'm Dutch and Turkish and Japanese and American'" (22). Parroting the communist party's universalist understanding of class oppression, Blount provocatively refuses the traditional divisions of race, ethnicity, and nationality. He also echoes the opening lines of an essay that Eugenie wrote for an autism organization: "White. Japanese. Mongolian. Black. Cherokee. Indonesian. Multiracial. American. Autistic. Married. Parent of an autistic child. Deaf. Bilingual. Jewish. Female. As a person of color, I face a multitude of . . . challenges as I strive to define my unique experiences and to have my voice heard."

To be queer is to be anticategorical, to wander the country of identity like a hobo on a train—to plow right through the periods that mark off, and ostensibly distinguish, the identities above. (As seen through the slats of a boxcar, the landscape of "I" is one long blur.) Yet, again, in the novel, queerness never loses its grotesque aura. It's like a valley cloaked in mist, a valley where the sun never fully rises.

For Biff, disability is so central to the concept of queerness that he can't help looking for it in the labor organizer. As he "regarded Blount steadily with half-closed eyes," the narrator says, "Blount was not a freak, although when you first saw him he gave you that impression. It was like something was deformed about him—but when you looked at him closely each part of him was normal and as it ought to be" (21). Because he can't be contained by the gender binary, Biff conceives of a more capacious grouping of alternative identities, a kind of loose confederacy perhaps best symbolized by disability though not restricted to it.

If, as Isadora Duncan suggests, "the dancer's body is simply the luminous manifestation of the soul," then disability is simply the luminous manifestation of queerness: a strangely positive, scarlet "Q." Scholars have taken up this prescient idea with great enthusiasm. Think, for example, of the work of Robert McRuer, whose book *Crip Theory* makes it impossible to investigate LGBTQ issues without investigating disability ones. Together, he argues, the fields of disability studies and queer theory can fully dismantle "compulsory" understandings of embodiment.

How queer, how disabled, can dance be? Quite, as the activist/scholar/dancer Petra Kuppers has demonstrated. But ballet may be another cup of tea altogether. While acknowledging its discriminatory past, Eugenie resisted overtly queering her beloved art form, even as she embraced a malleable sense of racial, ethnic, and disabled identity. She wanted to defend both its merciless standards and its willingness to include her. "My hair looked the same in a bun as everyone else's," she explained. And she wanted, as we will see, to move beyond the very notion of conspicuous identity markers:

"I am standing in a queue at a train that is heading for the future," she stated emphatically.

Biff, however, isn't headed anywhere. He can't imagine coming out of the closet—can't imagine claiming his role as a freak. At the novel's conclusion, we are told that he stood at the counter in his café and "felt a warning, a shaft of terror" (359). The narrator says, "Between two worlds he was suspended" (359). When I asked Eugenie about that "shaft of terror," she joked, "You mean the one he never washes?" "Biff is forever stuck," she typed. "He's incapable of full expression. It's the realization that there's no way out of a cave or a labyrinth and that there's also no food or water. The coming to terms with how long one can survive—that's very scary."

Full expression—within or across (or against) available categories. In Mick, McCullers adds a sixth voice part (and the character whom Eugenie most appreciated) to her loose confederacy of freaks. A boisterous tomboy who climbs onto the roof of an unfinished, upper-class house and then scribbles a "very bad word—pussy" (37) on a wall in the front room, Mick seeks refuge from poverty in the plastic nature of art and the equally plastic nature of her own sensory impressions. Her very body, in its adolescence, and her very mind, in its synesthetic predilections, suggest a reprimand to the deterministic force and unyielding expectations of class and gender.

"I want to jump through the book and offer to pay for music lessons," Eugenie exclaimed upon first encountering Mick's interest in music. She was quite sensitive to the issue of cultivating talent in young people. Her notes for that week included this sentence: "I read a teensy bit of the next chapter. Yay, Mick finally has access to a piano at school!"

For Mick, as for Eugenie, all the time—"no matter what she was doing" (35)—there was music. She especially liked Mozart, whom she referred to as a "fellow . . . who had lived in some country in Europe a good while ago" (37). "Sometimes . . . [his music] was like little colored pieces of crystal candy, and other times it was the softest, saddest thing she had ever imagined about" (35). She described a few of his compositions as "quick and tinkling" (38); one was akin to "that smell in the springtime after a rain" (38). When Mick's "hands hunted out . . . beautiful new sounds, it was," we are told, "the best feeling she had ever known" (161). "She could see the shapes of the sounds very clear and she would not forget them" (119).

McCullers deploys the conceit of synesthesia, along with Mick's characterization as both male and female—"she was at an age when she looked as much like an overgrown boy as a girl" (132)—to underscore the ineluctably blended nature of life. To see or to smell while hearing is akin, McCullers intimates, to not just feeling masculine while being feminine (or feeling feminine while being masculine) but actually being so. Just as, according to one theory of synesthesia, synesthetes intuit the low-level integration of sensory input that makes multisensory experience possible and that otherwise lurks beneath our conscious understanding of discrete modalities—sight, touch, hearing, taste, and smell—so trans people, McCullers proposes, intuit the hidden, integrated life of hormones that exists beneath our narrow understanding of gender. Speaking reductively of sight or touch, as if they were distinct, is like speaking reductively of "men" and "women." Categories, in short, betray.

When focalized through Mick, the narration thus becomes pointedly analogical. It disrespects what the dictionary teaches us. It moves like a swollen river beyond the banks of denotation—soaking everything, dislodging everything, allowing the fixed to float. Beginning with words (literature), notes (music), or positions (ballet), art, to use another metaphor, behaves like a fondue fountain (an edible pirouette!). We're mesmerized by the tension between what is solid and stationary and what is fragile and flowing. In this way, art itself is inherently queer.

After Mick is forced by her family to take a menial job and to comport herself like a meek young woman, both the music and synesthesia fittingly stop. By the end, even her body, no longer in an obviously transitional state, appears to cooperate with the triumph of categories, but as the narrator, focalized through Biff, insists, there is nothing stable about gender: "Often old men's voices grow high and reedy and they take on a mincing walk. And old women sometimes grow fat and their voices get rough and deep and they grow dark little moustaches" (132).

· · ·

OVER THE LAST DECADE, a number of autistics—I'm thinking, for example, of Nick Walker, Ibby Grace, Athena Lynn Michaels-Dillon, Melanie Yergeau, and Lydia Brown, among others—have laid claim to the luminous scarlet "Q," though not simply as an accepted signifier for deconstructive thinking (the kind that autism seems especially to make possible). Many autistics, as they point out, are actually gay, lesbian, bisexual, trans, questioning, intersex, asexual (or aromantic), among other things! Or, rather, many refuse such labels and allow them, as Amy Grant said of the passing years, "to fold like an accordion over each other." These activists have coined terms such as "neuroqueer" and "gendervague" to articulate an explicitly intersectional understanding of autism, gender, and sexuality, an understanding whose implications, at the same time, go beyond these spheres.

Listen to Lydia Brown, who, in a blogpost titled "Gendervague: At the Intersection of Autistic and Trans Experiences," writes,

> Growing up, everyone around me assumed I was a girl based on the genitals I was born with, but I always felt deeply uncomfortable with being labeled a "girl" or "woman." I don't feel like a woman, but I know I'm not a man either. I now identify as genderqueer or non-binary. It wasn't until partway through college, though, before I began to question what gender might mean to me, my explorations largely kindled by developing important relationships with many openly trans autistic people through my activism.

According to Brown, "gendervague" "refer[s] to a specifically neurodivergent experience of trans/gender identity." "For many of us," she says, echoing Dora, "gender mostly impacts our lives when projected onto us through other people's assumptions, but holds little intrinsic meaning."

This is not the case with Eugenie. "I am very feminine," she told me. "I love things like make-up and fashion. And I enjoy that part of myself. There is something about female energy and female gender norms that I love to fulfill. I truly love it. And it was never forced upon me." As if reaching through the Skype chatbox and telepathically observing the quizzical look on my face (we didn't use the video function), she typed, "I take pleasure in doing things associated with that same old tired female identity. Except it's not 'tired' to me at all. I could easily have been Cleopatra in another life—the good parts only."

Obviously ballet had something to do with her attitude toward gender— ballet and modeling (both print and runway), which Eugenie had done from her early teens until her early twenties. Just as she believed that autism had prevented a career in ballet, so she believed that it had prevented a career in modeling, though clearly not before she had absorbed what these stereotypical endeavors had to teach her about being a woman. And yet the effort required to pull off such performances, the effort and self-consciousness, which again reminded me of the androids in Dick's novel, distinguished her relationship to this identity category. "Even though I had the 'complete package,'" Eugenie explained,

I couldn't master the nuances of how models should act—down to the degree of how much an eye should be open or shut, or exactly how a mouth should be held to show different emotions. It was too early for me to understand these things. So I was nice and pretty and had a good body, but my print work never looked quite right. I am too robotic in my expressions, and a camera can see that immediately. It could see that I was an imitator and not a natural. On the runway, I had a hard time being sexy. Ballerinas are not supposed to be overtly sexy.

She had a hard time *appearing* sexy as a model, she stressed, not *being* that way as a woman or wife. "It seems that sexuality is a language I can speak," she reported. "It's not elusive to me. Sexuality is about feelings. And I know feelings very well. I speak feelings very well."

In ballet, she also had the "complete package"—"all of the physical qualities desired in a ballerina (qualities you must have in order to dance for a professional company)," including the "exact look needed"—but the "inside of [her] head, which couldn't be seen, wasn't suited," she said, to the art form. By implication, that internal ballerina, the body's brainy counterpart, was at once ill-shaped and uncoordinated. Eugenie's skin color hadn't been a problem, despite what I assumed. "Yes, I am brown," she typed, "but a light brown. An 'acceptable' brown, if you will." (The scare quotes reflected considerable contempt for colorism.) She did admit to feeling, as an adult, a "teensy self-conscious" about her "derriere and thighs," which she said were "a smidge too big for elite levels."

When I pressed her on the apparent contradiction between embracing conventional notions of gender but rejecting conventional notions of race and disability, she replied, "I suppose that I've never been hurt or offended by being pegged as a female or woman. It's a compliment to me. I hope I look like a female as hard as I try to be one. (Kidding! I'm being sassy.)" I came to think of Eugenie's approach to identity as akin to solving an elaborate mathematical equation. If she could assign a fixed value to at least one of the variables, in this case gender, then maybe a solution could be found. Even for the multiracial person herself, there was a limit, it seemed, to how underdetermined—how queer—identity math could be.

The gender part of Eugenie was *readable*, immediately so, while the other parts of her were not. The other parts, especially her racial and ethnic heritage, confounded people. It made them work to label her; it revealed the inadequacy of prevailing categories and, in so doing, prompted anger.

Imagine serving as a frequent, unwitting provocation. Her multiraciality was like a juggler juggling hieroglyphs—too many of them. Each was a knife or flaming torch that landed in the crowd. Or it was like boxing. ("Everyone has a plan," Joe Louis once joked, "until they get hit.") Or, better yet, like *mixed* martial arts, if you'll pardon the pun. "So there I was," Eugenie recounted, "a person who had to walk with a sign over my head that read: 'Yep, I am part black and part white and part other things. I am here to make you uncomfortable. I am here to question how you feel about race. Now, throw out whatever ugly thoughts you have—right at me, right into my face. Go ahead.'"

She spoke of being rejected by white people but also by black people. "Matter of fact, I've been rejected by all kinds, including family members." She had cousins, she said, who "considered themselves 100% black who were not 100% black." They had been raised in predominantly African American communities and insisted that she identify as African American. When she "tried to credit" all aspects of her personhood, "they made fun of [her] for being part-white." They wouldn't fully accept her.

Compounding the sense of alienation, Deaf acquaintances sometimes dwelled on her racial makeup; others, on the fact that she wasn't Christian. One Deaf person who was "born again" actually asked if she had horns. When she participated in a statewide Ms. Deaf competition and advanced to the final round, she was instructed, in a particularly humiliating way, to change her outfit because she "showed." She had informed the organizers of her pregnancy. (It was her first child; she was twenty-two and hadn't yet married Jacob.) Needless to say, *Miss* Eugenie did not win.

Listening to such anecdotes, I marveled at her resolve. How to feel comfortable in a narrow, identity-based group? A group that can't abide complication, that doesn't conceive of the ostensible glitch—praise the pregnant beauty queen!—as a sort of Socratic overture? *You must think more deeply. You must question your assumptions.* Eugenie had been primed to resist reductive thinking and perhaps, when alienated, to feel more aggrieved. Multiraciality, like bisexuality, wasn't a dodge or a form of cowardice. In the words of the poet and feminist June Jordan, it simply "invalidates . . . either/or analysis."

With the persistence of a district attorney, Eugenie noted the novel's repellant representations of African Americans—because they offended her. Exhibit A: "Of course Portia's house would have a colored smell. And of course the kids would be eating nigger toes (pecans or whatever) on X-mas."

Exhibit B: "Glad to know Willie's hands are dark." Exhibit C: "I wonder why the mulatto has to be 'loose-limbed'?" Exhibit D: "O, those malodorous negroes—give us something new!" Exhibit E: "And now the negroes are shivering in their overalls, loitering, too. Well, I suppose I did ask for something new." When McCullers kept returning to the olfactory motif, Eugenie threw up her hands, unselfconsciously using a Yiddish expression: "Every time with the 'negro smell,' oy vey!"

Her parents had taught her to think of herself as "mixed"—and *this* most certainly showed. "I was not raised to identify with just one race," she said. "My home was like a museum with lots of different art pieces that reflected the rich background of our identities." Her mother, who had grown up in the South and who despite being mixed herself was forced to identify as black, came to loathe the way that people were defined by race and ethnicity. "When she moved to the Midwest, she did not carry herself as a black woman from Texas who was waiting for the next racial incident. She didn't play that game. She dealt with people on a person-to-person basis. A name-to-name basis."

Eugenie deeply admired her mother's insistence on individuality, her refusal to be subsumed by any category or generalization, whether negative or positive. She could be all sorts of things, including black, but not if these things hardened like cement, ceased being relational, provisional, fluidly intersectional. In a word (though it was not her word), *queer*. "My mother is like an entity with no form," Eugenie said. "She's a ball of energy that can somehow be seen. She does not dwell in the world of needing to classify others or herself. She is just Shanna."

Although her mother couldn't make room for autism—an irony, to be sure, since, at the most basic sensory level, autism insists on irreducible particularity—Eugenie had absorbed something of the formless, ball-of-energy approach to who she was. Or at least the wish to elude being pegged by a "monster with a glass." If behaving like the comic book superhero E-Man wasn't possible, she could always aim for the complicated passing of Reep Daggle, that shapeshifter from the planet Durla.

In the aforementioned essay for an autistic organization, Eugenie commented on the paradoxical upside of being mixed: as people sought to reduce her to one race or ethnicity, she could be things she wasn't. ("When one has no form," declared Bruce Lee, "one can be all forms.") "In my travels around the world, I have often been pleasantly mistaken as a native . . . ," she writes. "In Israel, I was Israeli. In Palestine, I was Palestinian. In Italy, I was Italian. And in Mexico, I was Mexican."

Eugenie continues,

A dear friend of mine is Vietnamese. When we're together, I tend to be pleasantly labeled as also being Vietnamese. The same thing happens when I'm with a friend who is Filipina. I am transported to all these great worlds and experiences simply because I effortlessly blend in with other people of color. This is the most beautiful part of being mixed, as sometimes there are . . . no barriers to break.

It's as if, I want to say, she were a Smith's dwarf chameleon, which can adjust its colors "in accordance with the vision of the specific predator species (bird or snake) by which [it is] being threatened." Yet, here, in the first quotation, she's talking about the pleasure of being casually assigned to the majority and not, as she often is in the United States, to a denigrated outgroup. And in the second, she's talking about subverting the process of "identity constraint" in order to affirm an already existing bond—a bond in which she operates as an individual.

All of this was "queer." Even Eugenie's hearing impairment—or, rather, her response to it—was a mixed (or queer) bag. When I asked if she planned to get another implant, she replied, "I do not want another CI because I enjoy pairing what I hear with my CI with the natural hearing that I have in my other ear." While she greatly appreciated her CI, with respect to music it was like "eating Chinese food at the mall"—not even close to the genuine delicacy. Her "natural" hearing was amplified, as I've said, by a hearing aid.

Like the disabled cyborgs in Dora's fiction, Eugenie used multiple forms of assistive technology at the same time—which produced, you might say, auricular intersectionality, an auditory version of Anton's "raiment." Sometimes, she used none: "I love being deaf. I love having a CI and a hearing aid because I can choose what I want to hear. There is so much beauty in silence. There is so much beauty in sound."

It's difficult to fathom such fluidity. When I commented on it, Eugenie remarked, "I'm glad to know that my sense of identity is perceived as fluid by at least one person." Largely for this reason, the novel's final voice part, Dr. Benedict Mady Copeland, aggravated her to no end, though in a way that was different from Blount.

Blount she could dismiss out of hand; with Copeland she seemed eager to avoid being misunderstood—eager to distinguish her frustration with him as a character who represents certain ideas of race from something truly damning: evidence that she just might be uncomfortable with blackness. Just might be someone who, protestations to the contrary, doesn't like African Americans or is embarrassed by them. While Eugenie trusted me, she knew how fraught the subject of race was. Both whiteness and monoraciality could distort the judgment of even the most sensitive of ethnographers. She'd seen me make mistakes, misinterpret things, and, sadly, no matter how hard I tried, be less than sensitive.

About Dr. Copeland, Eugenie said, "He is a lonely man. An ashamed man. A nearly outdone man. A very sad and angry man. Hope you like big nutshells." While she acknowledged the horrors of the Jim Crow South—in McCullers's depiction, it was indeed a *land* in which African Americans could at best try to *cope*—she found the doctor to be unbearably grotesque. If he were a dancer, he could not twirl, he could not leap, he could not kick, he could not *lift*. He was simply dressed in a leotard.

An unwitting parody of the "talented tenth," the idea, promulgated by W. E. B. Du Bois, that with a classical education "exceptional [black] men" could rise and lead their race, Copeland studies the work of Benedict Spinoza but cannot understand it. Philosophy, that dance of ideas, takes place on a faraway stage. It is a show for which he will never have a ticket. Eugenie refused the picture of defective longing—the belief that not only social obstacles, but also racial inadequacy, prevent African Americans from succeeding at a refined pursuit like philosophy or ballet.

While pointing out the impediments to genuine opportunity, McCullers sews into Copeland's character a number of fatal weaknesses, which render him pitiable. In addition to his intellectual limitations, he is almost entirely alienated from his family: his wife has left and he has no relationship with his sons, whom he repeatedly prodded to better themselves. Principle means more to him than people; in fact, he seems to feel contempt for the very masses he would save. As Eugenie, who prizes family and good parenting, put it, "Copeland is surrounded by hostility and racism. And he is also surrounded by his own folly."

One of the doctor's sons, Willie, the cook at the New York Café, is arrested while fighting over a woman and is sentenced to nine months in prison. Sadistic guards lock him in an ice-cold shed where for three days he is hung by his feet, which swell beyond recognition. When gangrene sets in, they have to be amputated. The novel revels in the shocking spectacle of Willie's lost feet. Yet another character has become a freak, though one who mourns his disfigurement and who is baffled by its haunting aftermath. Willie says, "I feel like my feets is still hurting. I got this terrible misery down in my toes.... It a hard thing to understand. My feets hurt me so bad all the time and I don't know where they is. They never given them back to me. They s-somewhere more than a hundred m-miles from here" (289). Like broken shards of pottery, picked up and dispersed by a social tornado, the characters are all "more than a hundred miles" from each other and themselves. In the absence of collective integrity, there is only the phantom reminder, the phantom pain, of what could be.

And yet something invidious intrudes on the portrait of tragedy, a kind of merciless condescension, and Eugenie sensed it. She was appalled by the violence done to Willie but couldn't abide its depiction. She needed to get beyond the trauma of race, which casts people of color as perpetual victims. This wasn't the "beyond" of Chief Justice Roberts, who, in a case about voluntary school desegregation, said famously, "The way to stop discrimination on the basis of race is to stop making discriminations on the basis of race." Her "beyond" recognized the need for social, economic, and political remedies, but it also understood the violence of categories, and it wanted to turn that violence away from people and toward the kind of thinking that made it possible.

When Copeland judges an essay competition for African American youth and selects as the winner a boy whose eleven-year-old sister was raped by a white man and who initially, after reading about the Scottsboro boys, tried in fear to emasculate himself but who now aspires to be a lawyer "who will only take cases of coloured people against white people" (183), Eugenie all but cried, "Enough!" The boy, who ends up being killed during a race riot, responds to the prompt—"My Ambition: How I Can Better the Position of the Negro Race in Society"—by writing, "I hate the whole white race and will work always so that the coloured race can achieve revenge for all their sufferings" (183). "There isn't a single well-adjusted Black person in the entire novel," she remarked.

In the end, Eugenie's predicament as a reader was less a matter of finding particular characters unlikeable or offensive than of bringing a keen sensitivity—one might even say, a ferocious reactivity—to the book's intersectional struggle, its failure to meaningfully relate the various identity positions. In contemporary parlance, Dr. Copeland "triggered" feelings of profound frustration with "old patterns of thinking about race." Like bumper cars at a carnival, the categories collide but remain unchanged, as isolated as they were before. Eugenie brought home to me just how distinctive was her response to the book. A monoracial reader, to say nothing of a nondisabled one, wouldn't have been as invested in the drama of integration.

With glaring irony, Copeland tells Blount, "The most fatal thing a man can do is try to stand alone" (302). Yet standing alone as a narrowly defined group presents its own problems. If being multiracial, -ethnic, and -disabled was like having to play the part of Humpty Dumpty, then Eugenie refused to fall, no matter how much people might try to push her. Or if she had fallen, she had put herself back together. Moved not like the doctor by inflexible ideas but by the feeling of gliding across invisible boundaries, she had found her own feet by dancing.

. . .

AFTER EUGENIE AND I finished *The Heart Is a Lonely Hunter* and then read a book about ballet, I made plans to fly to Chicago. As with the other subjects of this ethnography, I wanted to see her in her home environment. I wanted to meet her partner and kids, I wanted to watch her coach her skaters, and I wanted to attend a ballet. Because it was just a few weeks before Christmas, the ballet would have to be *The Nutcracker*, which Eugenie had danced in many times herself and which she genuinely loved, despite its status as a money-making cliché.

The Nutcracker had been her first ballet; her mother and grandmother had taken her to see it when she was three. "I was bitten. Possessed. Whatever you want to call it. And when I stepped on stage to perform my first *Nutcracker*, I knew that a HUGE part of my soul was at home." While fearing that her response was "teenagerish," she refused to apologize for its intensity, recalling with great fondness the ritualistic pleasure of those Christmas performances:

> Every second was magic. Even waiting backstage. I LOOOOOOVED IT. I couldn't get enough. I wanted to sleep there. I never wanted to leave. Other girls complained, and there I was unable to get enough. I loved everything from where we parked, to where we walked to enter the building, to where my costume and changing area was, to the theatre seats, to the stage, to the fuzz on the stage, to the things sold out in front to the audience.

I could relate: my own high-level tennis, when I was a boy and then a young man, had come wrapped, like grip tape around the racket handle, in such agreeable details.

In preparation for the trip, I began to read up on the emerging field of diversity science, especially as it pertained to multiraciality. I was intrigued by the seemingly built-in problem of racism as a function of our category-making minds: the way that thinking abstractly about a group of people saves us from having to think sensuously about them as individuals—saves us, that is, considerable effort and time but at the expense of a just society. However consciously or unconsciously, we read people as belonging to "ingroups" or "outgroups" and behave accordingly. Multiracial individuals, as I have suggested, act as a wrench in the system, slowing it down and causing frustration. Studies have confirmed that monoracial perceivers "make fewer multiracial categorizations of multiracials and that these categorizations . . . take longer than monoracial categorizations." Shoved into one or the other denigrated outgroup, multiracial people experience two forms of oppression.

So central is the notion of categories to the field that experts interested in ameliorating bias speak of "shaping social categorization outcomes." Even when the aim is ultimately to disrupt categorization, they invariably *begin* with categories and try either to complicate them by adding other categories (or subcategories) or to "recast [them] as overlapping or continuous in recognition of the many individuals whose identities lie within the intersections of . . . conventional[] binary distinctions (e.g., multiracial and transgender persons)." Autistics, I kept thinking to myself, generally *end* with categories or something like them, and they refuse to sacrifice or subordinate distinguishing details. What difference might this make with respect to multiraciality?

I found a number of fascinating studies. In a study of the facial recognition abilities of Asian, white, and biracial Asian/white subjects in which Asian, white, and biracial Asian/white faces were labeled as either "Asian" or "white," monoracial subjects "relied on the provided labels and had better memory for ingroup faces." In contrast, multiracial subjects "*disregarded the labels* and demonstrated better memory overall, regardless of face type" (my italics). If the multiracial subject did not hold essentialist views of race, the "effect was particularly pronounced." As Michael Stipe, the lead singer of REM, once proclaimed, "I think labels are for food. Canned food." To the best of my knowledge, autistics have never been tested on ingroup/outgroup perception, but I'd bet the farm on different results for monoracial autistics.

Another study showed that with monoracial perceivers you could change the definition of "ingroup" and thereby affect categorization outcomes. As the researchers put it, "Who constitutes the ingroup was entirely flexible."

"Testing memory for faces categorized according to race or university affiliation," they once again found better memory for racial ingroup faces but only when race was emphasized. As soon as university affiliation was emphasized, they found better memory for university ingroup faces, regardless of race. A study involving people with disabilities asked the following question: "How many shared ingroup identities would an able-bodied perceiver need . . . to override the initial perception of the target as a devalued outgroup member?" The answer? Without explicit instruction or emphasis, it generally "takes two shared ingroups to overcome the influence of one dimension of differentiation." Someone like Eugenie might, by this logic, need at least a dozen points of similarity.

Researchers stress that "multiple categorization is associated with decategorization, a move toward more individuated processing of a target." With individuation comes "increased liking, a reduction in evaluative bias, and more accurate perceptions in general." Yet, there are other, less deliberative pathways to individuation. In a recent study of racial prejudice, "participants were asked to detect near-threshold tactile stimuli delivered to their own face while viewing either an ingroup or an outgroup face receiving a similar stimulation." Researchers found that "individuals' tactile accuracy when viewing an outgroup face . . . was negatively correlated to their implicit racial bias." In other words, the more prejudiced a subject, the less likely he was to correctly identify an inappreciable sensation on his own face.

The study relied on the principle of sensorimotor resonance, the process by which "we come to understand other people's physical and mental states by mapping their bodily states on to our sensorimotor system." Automatic and unconscious, this process acts as a kind of lower-level foundation for higher-order social cognition, such as empathetic perspective taking, but it is quite susceptible to prejudice. So much so that when we observe an outgroup member in pain, "sensorimotor resonance vanishes." It is also susceptible, it turns out, to manipulation. When researchers increased perceived physical similarity through "interpersonal multisensory stimulation" (sight plus more conspicuous touch, IMS), tactile accuracy for outgroup faces improved significantly in high-prejudiced subjects. Whereas vision had previously divided them from racial or ethnic others, touch—the *feeling* of similarity—now united them. By itself, the former's data had readily supported a noxious idea.

As important, the difference in the "visual remapping of touch effect" between observing your own face and that of someone else disappeared, suggesting a conflation or confusion of self and other—even when, to repeat, the self was white and the other was from a different racial or ethnic group. Scientists call this phenomenon the "enfacement illusion." High-prejudiced subjects, we might say, discovered themselves in people whom they implicitly disdained. The study's authors speculate that the "gradual incorporation of the other's facial features into the mental representation of one's own face, occurring during the synchronous IMS, might induce the outgroup face to be processed at an individual-, rather than at a categorical-level." We all think of ourselves as singular and, after such an intervention, high-prejudiced subjects may have accorded this status to racial and ethnic others. Here, engaging with an outgroup member in a sensuous, bottom-up (as opposed to an abstract, top-down) manner made all the difference, a fact that has significant implications for diversity training.

This sort of approach to prejudice intervenes, I must emphasize, at a precategorical or perceptual level. Autistics, according to Laurent Mottron's theory of enhanced perceptual functioning, have privileged access to such input. It's not only more readily available to consciousness, but it's also more "autonom[ous] . . . with respect to top-down processes." In other words, the frontal lobes don't immediately subordinate sensory information to pre-ferred higher-order constructs, such as racial or ethnic categories. The result is perhaps too much individuation. Neurotypicals, or at least many of them, suffer from generating too little. Because they possess unisensory representa-tions of the Other, they need something like a multisensory booster shot to overcome their own natural processing proclivity.

Reflecting on this account of autism, whereby autistics show "*increased* activation of cortical areas associated with visual perception" and "*reduced* frontal cortex activity" (my italics)—or, said another way, local overcon-nectivity and global (or long-range) underconnectivity—I discovered an irony. The neurotypical brain, which scientists think of as properly con-nected, produces a social sphere that, at least with respect to embodied differences, is anything but. Divided, tense, embittered, and sometimes vio-lent, this sphere boasts relatively little long-range, and too much short-range, communication. Even its historical remedy—identity politics—looks, in this conceit, like the stereotype of autism. And autism, with its distrust of general-izations, looks like some optimal norm.

Yes, I'm playing with language—that's what writers do—but when experts speak of social deficits in autism they can neither imagine accompanying benefits nor critically examine their own neurologies. How about a new slo-gan? *Feel globally. Perceive locally.*

Eugenie understood many of her challenges—with movement, with communication, and with certain aspects of sociality—in terms of faulty connectivity. "My brain is not holding hands with my emotions. Nothing in my body is holding hands with each other except for my heart and my ears that hear music. Those two are in love," she said memorably.

Autism, however, was never just bad or good—it was "mixed," you might say, even "queer." Her feeling-based approach to ballet allowed her to "easily connect with characters she might be dancing or portraying." It also allowed her to live inside of the music—that "fluid architecture," as Joni Mitchell once described it. "I can feel . . . what the music wants me to do," Eugenie said. "Now if only my body would keep up." Yet even as she lamented the body piece—the speed and ease with which she translated verbal commands or visual demonstrations into precise action—she acknowledged the focus that autism brought: "Perhaps I might not have been as dedicated to the training and the life of the trainee without autism."

The body piece had to be learned, as I've already suggested, through will and repetition—much the same way that the cognitive and linguistic aspects of the social piece had to be learned through will and repetition. To this day, she painstakingly writes out what she wants to say to her older boys when they have to have a serious talk. If the mind were an orchard and words were apples, then she'd need a ladder to pick them. But if the orchard had music and the ladder could move. . . . I was struck, watching Eugenie work with her skaters, watching her help them to implement dance elements into their routines, at how effortlessly she performed her role as coach. If you watched my son, DJ, walk, you'd notice how uncoordinated he seems, but if you watched him jump on a trampoline, you'd think he was an acrobat. Additional proprioceptive input and the rhythmic entrainment of music-enhanced bouncing completely transform him. Maybe something like this was at play with Eugenie.

With pupils ranging in age from seven to eighteen—a fifty-year-old woman popped into the studio above the ice rink for ballet instruction about half-way through the Saturday I observed her—Eugenie easily adjusted her pedagogy and demeanor. She was tough with the lazy students and overtly supportive with the fragile ones. "Ballet fingers. Pull in your core. Be ready. Be ready. Arms up," Eugenie shouted to a girl I later learned came from a badly dysfunctional family and who looked like she was skating on a pond in mid-April! Her face was that clenched. Another student appeared perfectly proficient but lifeless, mechanical. "Shoot your arms up. You're telling your story. Up and over like a waterfall. Get into it and make it pretty. Give me chills. Emote. Emote."

In the studio, Eugenie had no trouble with words—hers were frequently metaphorical—and if anyone seemed autistic, stereotypically so, it was her pupils, who often couldn't connect with the music, who seemed, in fact, distant and awkward. They were like people who had gone camping but who didn't know how to set up their tent, how to really live among the trees. With what flare and grace, what captivating immediacy, did Eugenie model a relationship between movement, sound, and space! An evolving relationship, at once precise and flowing. "All that is important is this one moment in movement. Make the moment important, vital, and worth living. Do not let it slip away unnoticed and unused," urged Martha Graham.

Eugenie took great pride in coaching, just as she took great pride in parenting. She would give her children what they needed: instruction, of course, but also warm, full-hearted affirmation. "I put a lot of pressure on myself to be the best mother that I can be to all of my children because that is one of my most important jobs here on earth and I take it very seriously," she told me. She was, she said, a better parent to her middle son, who received an autism diagnosis at the age of two and who didn't start speaking until he was three, for being on the spectrum. "It has been one of the greatest gifts because I can spot things and sense things and explain them to my son and others before anything even has a chance to become a problem."

She related an anecdote about dropping Meir off at the bus stop and watching him stand "way too close to another cool looking kid," then fumble with the zipper on his backpack while bumping the cool kid with it. "Needless to say, I had a private heart attack," Eugenie said.

I had to think quick. That kind of thing can end a kid in middle school. I pulled over and called my son back to the car telling him I had something else for him. When he came I said something along the lines of, "Meir, you're standing way too close to that other kid. Give him some room. Remember personal space? If someone's not a family member or a friend, we don't stand that close. I'm not saying this to be mean, I just want to make sure you have all of the info necessary before you make a decision. If you want to stand close to him, knock yourself out, little man. But you must know that he might not like it, and he might also think you're immature or weird. Got it?"

No one had offered her such coaching when she was young—people would later attribute her own behavioral oddities to deafness—and she was determined to help Meir. "I spent so much of my life confused, not knowing what to do. And I hated it," she said.

And yet mother and son didn't perseverate on autism. They talked about it, they accommodated it, but they preferred, for the most part, to let difference be: "He just has a zest for life and wants to live and do. It's not his thing to sit back and constantly think about autism (like I did). And why should I make him?" I could detect a tension between accepting the label and being proud of it and moving past labels, indeed reductive social identities, altogether. Of course, once it has been reclaimed, the autistic (or neurodivergent) label helps to make possible a certain kind of politics, and Eugenie had eagerly made use of it—it and a host of others that pertained to race, ethnicity, and deafness—but they also made her uncomfortable, as I have noted repeatedly.

Upon returning from the ice rink, I learned about Eugenie's own diagnosis, and about how she had met her husband, Jacob. She said that she never suspected she was autistic because her only reference had been *Rain Man*, but she sensed she was different from other people by age three. "I knew that my hearing loss was not what was weird about me because Deaf people thought I was weird too," she explained. "It's funny and pathetic all in one. . . . And I knew that being multiracial was not what made me weird. I knew that I was weird because I acted differently and responded differently to things in comparison to both my peers and people in general." For Eugenie, receiving a diagnosis came as a great relief: "I let out a breath I had been holding since I was three. . . . I finally had a reason. It was like never being adopted and then finally being adopted."

Her husband, she reported, was "extremely accepting" of the diagnosis. They had met when she was sixteen, as she was beginning to lose her hearing. He was five years older. Although they shared a common religion, many obstacles to a relationship lay before them: age, race, ethnicity, and disability. Or at least to outsiders it seemed so; to Jacob and Eugenie, however, they had each found a soul mate. Unlike the characters in *Heart*, Jacob devoted himself to learning ASL—"At the beginning, I just wanted to talk to her," he said. He became so proficient at ASL that he later went on to teach at the American Sign Language and Secondary School in lower Manhattan. He now works as a middle-school science teacher in a gifted program; the weekend I visited, he and Meir were preparing for a statewide engineering competition.

As a result of the traffic in Chicago, I ended up wearing Jacob's shirt and blazer to the ballet. I had planned to drive back to my hotel in order to change, but after a full day of coaching and more conversation, that seemed unwise—from their street we could see the cars backed up on the highway. I felt more than a bit foolish having to borrow fancy attire, especially since I recalled what Eugenie had written in one of our Skype sessions: "There's something very exciting about dressing up to attend a ballet at a theatre. You just know you're in for a treat." As a person (and an ethnographer), I can sometimes be clueless: the day before, I had brought a poinsettia to the house as a gift. "They're Jewish!" I later chastised myself.

Whatever the spell that ballet had cast on Eugenie, it didn't stop her from critiquing the expressivity—and even the technique—of some of the dancers we saw that night. We both admired the two leads, Clara and the Sugar Plum Fairy, who, interestingly enough, were from China. So much for "certain arts being things unto themselves"! Yes, we were watching *The Nutcracker* in a major American city, but attitudes have clearly changed since the time of Balanchine. Through globalization and other forces, the world has become a large salad bowl (*not* a melting pot!). The United States continues to experience a significant demographic shift toward multiraciality. The first decade of the twenty-first century witnessed, for example, a 50 percent increase in multiracial children—from 2.8 million to 4.2 million in 2010. In 2013, 10 percent of all children born in the United States were multiracial. With more multiracial people, the cognitive habits of monoracial people will have to adapt accordingly.

On the drive home, Eugenie and I talked about the concept of intersectionality. Though she wasn't an academic and, thus, didn't regularly chew on jargon, she possessed a keen sense of how the concept was typically applied. While an improvement upon single-identity frameworks, it was still too rigid, we agreed, still too primitively triangular (or trilateral), to capture the myriad, morphing permutations of complex personhood—permutations in which certain aspects of identity, ever evolving in relation to one another, become more apparent at particular moments and in particular places. It's as if, with intersectionality, we're trying to use a GPS to locate who we are. ("Turn left on Callahan Rd. The multiracial, Deaf, autistic woman sits at the intersection of Callahan and Pointer St.") Or maybe the concept of intersectionality is like a fondue machine on low or barely moving. The magic act collapses when our account of it fails to be equivalently dynamic.

Comparing the sort of abstract theorizing found in scholarly work to the more bodily theorizing found in dance, I recalled another ballet joke: "Position, heal thyself." Positions, of course, are the beginning and ending points for elaborate sequences in ballet, and they refer to the placement of one's feet on the floor. Alluding to a proverb mentioned in the Gospel of Luke, the malapropism makes hilarious fun of the art form's foundational difficulty. (Just as Jesus expects to be confronted by people who demand to see more miracles, so the prima ballerina expects to be confronted by an audience that demands to see more perfection.)

While these positions can be "healed" through the refinement of technique, the joke suggests in this context the need for a more robust intersectionality—and a larger project of repair. As with Jamie's own movement journey, the social world itself must be healed: of its many histories of discrimination but also of the Left's own fixed and confining responses to these histories. We would all do well, Eugenie reminds us, to remember the queer instability of categories.

· five ·

TAKE FOR GRANDIN

In all affairs, it's a healthy thing now and then to hang
a question mark on the things you have long taken for granted.
— BERTRAND RUSSELL

In the penultimate stanza of John Keats's "Ode on a Grecian Urn," the speaker
of the poem addresses a priest who is depicted in one of the urn's scenes:

Who are these coming to the sacrifice?
　　To what green altar, O mysterious priest,
Lead'st thou that heifer lowing at the skies,
　　And all her silken flanks with garlands drest?

Not until I was conversing with Temple Grandin for the first time and she
recalled reading the poem in college did I pay any attention to that heifer. But
there, as the ode moves toward its ambiguous conclusion—"Beauty is truth,
truth beauty,—that is all / Ye know on earth, and all ye need to know"—is
indeed a cow, a decorated one whose slaughter is ceremonially enacted.

Sometimes encountering a familiar literary work, you are shocked to discover what it contains. It's a bit like pulling a tie out of your cereal box, draping
it around your neck, and going to work. I couldn't believe that I was talking
to the grand dame of autism and livestock handling about the British Romantic poet John Keats! And that she had brought him up! *This is uncanny*, I

thought to myself, *an immediate link between literature and cattle.* As I sat in my hotel room in Bochum, Germany—I was there for a conference—the words of Alice Walker came to mind: "Expect nothing. Live frugally / on surprise."

To be clear, *I* was the one who noticed the heifer, having looked up the poem on my computer as we spoke. This wasn't a case of autistic perseveration, where the person can only talk about her "restricted interests" or can only like something if it is somehow related to them. No, Temple remembered her professor's enthusiasm for the theme: the relation of immutable art to mutable life. A beautifully painted burial urn can offer solace in the face of death, the poet tells us, but it remains frustratingly aloof from the ravages of time. The eternity it advertises is frozen, out of reach—like the sky for wingless creatures.

It's a good thing we didn't talk about the heifer, I later realized, because the depiction is inaccurate. As Thomas Bayne remarked in 1905, citing other critics, "The poet . . . makes the animal raise its head unnaturally high, and thereby destroys the effect of his picture." Bayne called Keats "a townsman unfamiliar with the ways of cattle." I had read that Temple had been especially worried about the details of the livestock handling equipment and breed of cattle in the HBO film about her life: "We can't have a silly thing like that *City Slickers* movie, where they had Holstein cattle out there," she said. "If you know anything about cattle, you'd know that was stupid."

. . .

A FEW MONTHS before this extended conversation with Temple, the first of two that I would have, I had written to her assistant, a very nice woman named Cheryl Miller, about the possibility of reading some short stories by Skype. Right from the beginning, I had sought to "control" for Temple's well-known sequencing difficulties (I talk about them in the introduction) by purposefully choosing shorter works whose plots weren't especially complicated. I also suspected that she wouldn't be able to devote months and months to weekly discussions of a novel. I wanted to give myself the best shot at her participation and to give her the best shot at showing what she could do.

I decided to include Temple in this book because, on the face of it, she seemed the last person with autism to be receptive to literature. Oliver Sacks had made that clear in his *New Yorker* profile of her, "An Anthropologist on Mars," and she herself had contributed to the image of an obdurately rational alien who is stumped by social nuance and feeling. In the book that made her famous, *Thinking in Pictures*, she had said, "My emotions are simpler than those of most people. . . . I only understand . . . fear, anger, happiness, and sadness." She "relate[d] better," she claimed, "to scientists and engineers" because her thinking, like theirs, at least professionally, "was governed by logic instead of emotion." On the Web she is reported to have said, "The part of other people that has emotional relationships is not part of me."

Can literature be strictly logical? Can narrative conflict exist without complicated human relationships? Feeling, of course, is the colorful playground of stories and poems. We climb on feelings, swing from them, and through a writer's artistry, we become immediate acrobats, responsive Olympians. Even if Temple could fathom a short story intellectually, she likely couldn't feel it, the conventional wisdom held, and if she couldn't feel it, she couldn't truly appreciate it. But was this reasoning correct, and did it actually matter? Why pooh-pooh intellectual understanding when, as a teacher of literature, I ask my students to analyze the texts I give them? I want them to love literature, but I expect that love, that pleasure, to be disciplined by sophisticated understanding.

I knew that when most Americans thought of autism, they thought of Temple, and my argument would invariably be measured against what she has said about the condition. It almost didn't matter that she was increasingly emphasizing variation in autism or that my other collaborators in this book are so plainly different from her and from each other. It didn't matter that Temple often contradicts herself, especially with respect to emotional understanding. The stereotype prevails; that's what stereotypes do. To use a political metaphor, if my readers were the president of the United States, then Temple was their chief of staff: to get to them, I'd have to go through her first.

I also wanted a crack—the ultimate one—at proving the conventional wisdom wrong. It had not only been useless with respect to my son but also damaging. In my darkest moments, I tend to think of the narrow medical view of autism in the way Victor Hugo thought of small-town life: "There are many mouths that talk, and very few heads which think." And, anyway, I wasn't the least bit scared of a reader who fails to "swoon" in the face of literature. (Eugenie, from the previous chapter, might level that charge at brainy old me.) Put simply, I was used to people protesting, "I'm bored by literature. It does nothing for me." That, after all, is what students are for! Each semester some of them sit in the back of the class and proclaim, with their yawning, "I'd rather be having lunch!" My job as a teacher, to borrow Temple's own words from one of our conversations, is "to make it interesting." Maybe I could do that with her.

But there was another important reason for including Temple in the book. Any logic-emotion dichotomy that places engineers, scientists, and autistics on one side of the cognitive canyon and artists and musicians on the other, with nary a bridge to join them, is just too rigid to be true. Moreover, it belies the conspicuously poetic way she thinks. However logical its final form, thought for Temple begins as a game of visual free association. As she says in a video on her website, "My brain is visually indexed. . . . Everything in my mind works like a search engine set to the image function. You type in a key word and I get pictures. And it comes up in an associational sort of way." For example, "If I think about Great Danes, the first memory that pops into my head is Dansk, the Great Dane owned by the headmaster at my school. The next Great Dane I visualize is Helga, who was Dansk's replacement. The next is my aunt's dog in Arizona, and my final image comes from an advertisement for Fitwell seat covers that featured that kind of dog." It may be a stretch to compare this rather orderly flow of images to what happens in a poem or in a novel that employs stream of consciousness, but Temple makes clear how the process can go awry, which is to say, become *creative*.

Consider the following sentence from a *Time* magazine article about Olympic figure skating: "All of the elements are in place—the spotlights, the swelling waltzes and jazz tunes, the sequined sprites taking to the air." "In my imagination," Temple remarks, "I see the skating rink and skaters. However, if I ponder too long on the word 'elements,' I will make the inappropriate association of a periodic table on the wall of my high school chemistry classroom. Pausing on the word 'sprite' triggers an image of a Sprite can in my refrigerator instead of a pretty young skater." Temple views this sort of associational proclivity as an impediment to learning. "Teachers who work with autistic children need to understand associative thought patterns," she says rather dryly.

Yet in another context, the literature or creative-writing classroom, it's a potential strength, and Temple could be taught to exploit it. *When I open the fridge, a Sprite can does a double toe loop and falls on the floor. What a fizzy, sequined mess!* Literature, I tell my students, visualizes inappropriately. At its most inappropriate, it veers toward surrealism. It also visualizes specifically, which is to say concretely. "My thinking pattern always starts with specifics and works toward generalization," Temple tells us. She might have added that it never actually arrives at generalization. As she says of Great Danes, for her "there is no generalized, generic Great Dane." Rather, she fashions something like a loose composite or amalgam of sensuous particulars.

It's an affiliation strong enough to suggest relation but not so strong as to collapse into singular abstraction.

This is how literature works; its fidelity is to Dansk or to Helga, not to the concept of Great Dane. It's about *this* dog with *these* markings. It provides a fully emergent account of life, not a top-down, preformulated one in which the particulars don't matter because they get in the way of the idea. Literature's vaunted universality comes precisely from our belief in the individual, idiosyncratic instance. It moves toward the general, we might say, while strangely eschewing it.

Here, too, an autistic proclivity can serve as an advantage—less so perhaps when the student is asked in a literature course to present a thesis (or generalization) about a work and to adduce specific examples to support it. (I say "perhaps" because I've seen autistic students shine at this task.) It's a rare young person who can think equally well in both directions. My brightest neurotypical students often struggle in creative-writing courses until they decide, like Odysseus, to lash themselves to the mast of bottom-up specificity and thereby resist the siren call of abstraction. In contrast, my brightest autistic students often walk the deck entirely unaffected. "The truth of the story lies in the details," says Paul Auster. "Tiny details, imperceptible to us, decide everything," W. G. Sebald insists.

It's a great irony that Temple now stands in for autism. This bottom-up, detail-driven visualizer has become—perversely—a generalization, a way of doing quick, top-down thinking about the "disorder." She is no longer one of many Great Danes, as it were. If autism is a condition characterized by global underconnectivity and local overconnectivity, then there are myriad ways to be under- and overconnected. There might be too much, or too little, feeling, for instance. By having Temple come last in the book, I am trying to unsettle a pernicious habit. I am trying to be faithful to the process of thinking that she describes.

When I wrote to Cheryl, she said she would forward my email to Temple but warned me about how busy she was. Temple had blurbed my memoir *Reasonable People* and had mentioned my son, DJ, in one of her books, so I wasn't a complete stranger to her. She also had a habit of accommodating the research requests of fellow academics. A professor of animal science at Colorado State University, she had cheerfully climbed into all manner of imaging machines to further the science of autism. In fact, she felt a duty to do so. Might she climb into a couple of short stories with me?

One night, awaiting her reply, I had a dream in which I sought to make an appointment with a doctor. The doctor, it became increasingly clear, was John Dolittle of Dr. Dolittle fame. His secretary kept saying, "I'm sorry. He doesn't see human patients, and you don't speak the language of animals." I remember waking with a start: *She's not going to read fiction with me.* But, then, a week later, an email popped up in my inbox:

Dear Ralph—

I would be happy to do an interview and I would prefer to talk by phone and you can record our conversation. I am constantly traveling and the regular phone is easier for me.

Temple

I was ecstatic.

In choosing which stories to send to Temple, I fell back on the principle that had guided me from the beginning: pick something of likely interest to my collaborator. Still under the sway of that Dolittle dream, I settled on two stories from a recent anthology, *Among Animals: The Lives of Animals and Humans in Contemporary Short Fiction.* In one, called "Meat," a man is appalled by the horrors of commercial livestock production and decides to humanely raise and slaughter the animals that his family eats. In the other, called "The Ecstatic Cry," a female biologist devotes her life to saving endangered penguins. In both stories, of course, complications arise. The family becomes attached to "Meat"—the name they give to their first pig in order to remind themselves of its fate. The biologist, who has grown to abhor her own species, longs in her Antarctic solitude for companionship and sex.

With the first story, I wanted to see if Temple would respond emotionally to material that in life sometimes reduced her to tears. In his *New Yorker* profile, Sacks reported that she "wept and wept" at the slaughter of pigs that were the basis of her doctoral dissertation. "I was very attached," she told him. "I was so attached I couldn't kill them." In *Thinking in Pictures,* we learn that touching cattle as a teenager had awakened a sense of subjectivity: "I was able to remain the neutral scientist," she wrote, "until I placed my hands on them at the Swift Plant and feedlots in 1974."

Might a story about an animal activate the sort of affective processes that literary fiction activates generally in typical readers? Might it take what psychologists call the "emotionally avoidant" person, one who doesn't read much literary fiction, by surprise? Does subject matter matter, in other words, when it comes to assessing the readerly abilities of some people with autism? We saw that it mattered a great deal in the chapter on Dora, though not for the reasons many would imagine. I also wanted to see how Temple would respond to fiction as a mode of expression: its images, its ironies, its figures of speech—all of that marvelous indirection.

With the second story, I wanted to see if she would identify with the biologist and, further, if the story would elicit from her a reflection on her own life choices. This, after all, is one of the great pleasures of literature: the way it enables self-discovery and growth. Temple has been very public about her decision to be celibate, which she viewed as a natural response to difficulties comprehending emotion. Might the story encourage her to revisit this fundamental belief and, at the same time, offer practice in that other, crucial form of exploration: namely, coming to understand other people's joys and sorrows?

Increasingly, research has demonstrated that reading literary (as opposed to popular) fiction can improve theory-of-mind (or mentalizing) abilities and empathy. In the words of Raymond Mar and Keith Oatley, "Engaging in the simulative experiences of fiction . . . can facilitate the understanding of others who are different from ourselves and can augment our capacity for . . . social inference." While the claim may sound to some like classic humanist—if you'll forgive me—*hog*wash, we now have some hard evidence to support it. Literary fiction also provides an opportunity to better understand one's own self. In short, it changes people, which, as Oatley and Maja Djikic, put it, "is impressive, given the stability of the personality system."

In one study, reading literary fiction for just a few minutes resulted in temporarily enhanced emotional perception. In another, "individuals who were habitually avoidant in their attachment style, and who usually reported diminished emotionality," felt more emotion when they read a story by Anton Chekhov than when they read a "version of the story in which nothing was changed but its formal artistic properties." Might literary fiction, as the latter study's authors maintain, "provide a method for circumventing a person's natural defenses and . . . a useful tool for studying those with affective disorders (e.g., alexithymia)"?

I want to be careful with the appeal to bibliotherapy, as I don't subscribe to the idea that autistic people are broken and need to be fixed. In the end, my aim with Temple was to do what literature does: complicate simple propositions, render them ambiguous—instructively so. We agreed to have two conversations by phone: one for each story. "Gratitude," Joseph Stalin infamously remarked, "is a sickness suffered by dogs." While I would have preferred to have multiple conversations, I was all too happy to bark!

. . .

WHEN I CALLED her from Germany, Temple was waiting to catch a flight back to Colorado Springs—she had just given one of her many professional talks. I began by asking about her experience reading literature, and I was surprised to discover her familiarity with the liberal arts. Somehow I had assumed that she possessed a strictly vocational education, what with her professional focus on livestock, but, no, she had graduated in 1970 from Franklin Pierce College in New Hampshire with a bachelor of arts degree in psychology, and she had taken courses in history, French, philosophy, and English, among other disciplines.

One of those courses, "Western Civilization," which she described as "classical humanities," had clearly had a lasting impact on her because she remembered not only the name of her professor—Mr. De Simone—but also some of the works they discussed, including "Ode on a Grecian Urn" and *The Inferno* by Dante Alighieri. "We had one of those big fat books," she said, "like a hundred pieces of great literature, which really made you think." She enjoyed how the professor helped to explain what the author was trying to say. Perhaps this process resonated with her own need to interpret the actions and words of neurotypicals, but figurative language in and of itself was not an impediment to understanding. If you've read Temple's many books, you know that she uses metaphors, novel metaphors, a lot.

You also know that she has an existential bent. There's a chapter in *Thinking in Pictures* called "Stairway to Heaven: Religion and Belief." In it she writes, "I had never given much thought to what happens after death, but then I started working with cattle in the Arizona feedlots. Did the animals just turn into beef or did something else happen?" (In the HBO movie *Temple Grandin*, the actress Claire Danes looks down at a dead cow and says, much too loudly and awkwardly, "Where does it go?") Temple is instinctively drawn to big questions, though in our conversations she was quick to point out that her thinking had changed:

When I was young, I used to search for the magical meaning of life, but now that I'm in my sixties, my meaning has become a whole lot simpler. If the things I do make the world better in some concrete way, like I just had a rancher tell me how they had built some systems I designed and no longer screamed at their cattle or I had someone else tell me that their kid, who has autism, went to college because she read one of my books, well, that's doing something valuable.

When I asked to what she attributed this change, she replied, with an exaggerated twang, "Gettin' older, gettin' older. As I got older, my meaning of life became a whole lot simpler."

Still, being drawn to big philosophical and ethical questions must have served her well in her "Western Civilization" course, which "[she] was certain she was gonna hate" but which "turned out to be [her] favorite class." *You gotta be kidding me*, I thought to myself. "With all of the things that have been written about you, how is it possible that we don't know this fact?" I said. "Well, no one has ever asked me about literature," she replied. When I seemed too stupefied to speak, she repeated herself: "No one has ever asked me about literature, but the class I was certain I was gonna hate was actually one of my favorite classes." She had softened the claim, but nevertheless I was stunned. I wanted to take out an ad on the National Autism Society website. I wanted to live *extravagantly* on surprise, or at least this surprise. (Alice Walker be damned!)

I had just been given a lesson on the importance of asking the right question. How many times has an autistic person dutifully submitted to the research agenda of someone who has preconceived ideas about autism? Too much of the work being done today is driven by the consensus we call stereotype. Autistics can't do theory of mind, so let's study whether they can catch another person's yawn. As we saw in the chapter about Dora, the research we have is only as good as the questions we ask. Including autistics as our research partners will only improve these questions.

Sadly, I, too, had fallen prey to narrow expectations: for Temple I had selected stories about animals, not, for example, a tricky story about race, such as "Recitatif" by Toni Morrison. Why was it so hard to think of Temple Grandin and John Keats or Temple Grandin and Dante Alighieri together? Why, for that matter, hadn't I asked her what *she* wanted to read?

What Temple had affirmed, of course, was the very premise of the liberal arts: introducing young people to subjects they know nothing about and are convinced they will loathe. With this sort of education increasingly under assault, I wondered about the invisible role it had played in her highly specialized professional life. Certainly, learning how to write and to think well had been a boon for the author—to say nothing of the person—she would become. I wondered as well about the strange parallel between rigid, unimaginative notions of autistic interests (and the subsequent educational tracking that results) and the business of compelling young people to decide on a career trajectory early in their first year of college or university. How can we know in advance what someone might love or be good at?

"But you have to make it interesting," Temple emphasized, jolting me from my thoughts. "Mr. De Simone made it so interesting. I mean he tried to explain the emotional point the author was trying to get across." She then added, "I think he had personal problems because he cut quite a few classes." She remembered being "really disappointed," as she "wanted to hear what he had to say about the next thing [they] were reading in [their] anthology." Temple has written about the importance of mentorship, citing William Carlock, a science teacher at Mountain Country School in Rindge, New Hampshire, as having played a crucial role in her development as a scientist. (He figures prominently in the HBO movie about her life.) But here we can see the more limited, though enduring, influence of her humanities professor. She was talking, after all, about a class she had taken in 1966!

After hearing about this class, I was eager to turn to the story "Meat." A week before our conversation, I received Temple's written response:

> The short story clearly illustrates the mixed emotions about raising an animal that you love and then eating it. Many students in both FFA [Future Farmers of America] and 4-H are sad when their animal is processed, but then they get another animal the following year.
>
> A living animal is not a thing like a car or a house. It must be given a life worth living. The animal would never be born unless we bred it. While it is alive, we must give it a good life.

The summary, in the first paragraph, is commendably concise; the account of the theme or moral, in the second, echoes statements that Temple has made about the obligation to treat commercial livestock ethically.

Yet a literary work is so much more than its paraphrase, as the New Critics would say. "Much of the distempers of criticism come about," wrote Cleanth Brooks, "from yielding to the temptation to take certain remarks which we make *about* the poem—statements about what it says or about what truth it gives or about what formulations it illustrates—for the essential core of the poem itself." In "20–200 on 747," Heather McHugh wittily confronts this problem. When a passenger on a plane asks, "What / are your poems about?" she replies,

> They're about
> their business, and their father's business, and their
> monkey's uncle, they're about
>
> how nothing is about, they're not
> about about.

Temple seemed to understand that literature resides, as W. H. Auden said of poetry, in "the valley of its saying." Its indirection didn't bother her; to the contrary, she enjoyed it, and she appreciated how a skilled teacher, like a mountain guide, could lead you down into its verdant meanings.

So was her paraphrase just a paraphrase, or did it reflect a less than exemplary appreciation of the story's subtleties? I glanced at the questions I had prepared: *What do you make of the fact that "Meat" is narrated by a seven-year-old girl? Why did the author, C. S. Malerich, choose such a narrator? What do you make of the story's tone?* The girl says things like:

> Dad always said we should think about Meat's feelings and give her a nice life. (61)

> [Dad] wanted to find someone committed to a respectful, clean death, even if it meant driving fifty miles. (62)

> "Well, you've saved me from a life of vegetarianism," said Dad, half-joking. "Really I can eat meat again with a clear conscience." (65)

It was probably too much to expect Temple to remember the trope of dramatic irony. In "Meat," the narrator's innocence ensures that her words say more—much more—to the reader than she knows. But what is that meaning, and can it be reduced to the propositions that are espoused in Temple's second paragraph? Put another way, does the story really condone the slaughter of animals? Is the father's conversion to the "home-raised . . . movement" (56) morally sufficient?

The story is by no means a one-trick pony—or pig—however. It balances irony with genuine pathos and then complicates that admixture with something like a ghoulish paradox. Over the course of the narrative, Meat becomes as much a cherished pet as a future meal. The girl does everything with her, including taking a bath, which makes the preordained slaughter that much harder to accept. Here's how she describes Meat's death:

> Mom told me to hug Meat. I did. . . . When I pulled away, she was confused. And then the butcher came up behind her with his stun gun, and his big hand was on her shoulder. She was still looking at me, and there was no more curiosity and no more confusion. Meat was scared.
>
> . . . It was all over in less than two minutes. [The butcher] stunned her, lifted her, and hung her by one of the hooks above us. Then he cut her throat. Blood came pouring out of her on each side of her head. I wondered if it wasn't too late, if they couldn't stop it and fix her. . . . I'd always thought about [death] like a light switch you flicked off. But here was Meat, not on or off. (64–65)

The girl felt "as if the butcher had stunned [her], too" (65). "Everything I heard seemed to come from very far away, and every move I made seemed like it was someone else making it" (65), she reports. As she was ushered out of the room, she looked back at her mother, who had opposed the idea of raising their own livestock. "Isn't it enough we spend twice as much on organic?" (56), she had groused to her husband. Her mother was holding Meat, "like the way sometimes she still held me even though I was too big for it" (65), the girl notes, adding, "Meat was definitely too big for it" (65).

This sort of matter-of-fact naïveté turns macabre as she is fully initiated into the regime of humane slaughter. "It was a few weeks before I was over [Meat's death]" (67), she tells us. "I got a little better after we ate her. . . . With the tender flesh practically melting on my tongue, I thought Dad was right—something you raise yourself always tastes better" (67). Here, the ethical imperative produces an unexpected (and, to the reader, ghastly) boon: gustatory pleasure. The story refuses to collapse, like a portable chair, into platitude: even if it believes in humane slaughter as a practical necessity, its primary allegiance is to what Brooks called the "recognition of incongruities." There's no easy way to reconcile caring and killing. In a closing gesture, the girl relates that she didn't fully recover from the loss of Meat until her eighth birthday: "That's when we got Drumstick" (68), she says.

As I was asking my first question, Temple interrupted me: "I couldn't figure out what kind of animal it was. It's gotta be a pig, but it doesn't say so." I had noticed this omission myself, yet it didn't bother me the way it seemed to bother her.

"Do you think that's because the narrator's a child?" I inquired.

"I don't know, but I kept waiting for her to say it was a pig. I wanted more detail about the animal." Of course she did. *How could I have been so stupid? I thought to myself. Choosing a story about an animal in which the animal is vague?* A sense of panic ballooned inside me.

"Why did the author pick the girl, and not the father, for instance, to be the narrator?"

"Well, she reminded me of 4-H and FFA kids I've met," Temple replied.

"Okay, but what does hearing about this familiar topic from the point of view of a child accomplish? What does it add to the debate, with the PETA [People for the Ethical Treatment of Animals] folks on one side and the ranchers on another?"

"It makes it personal," she said, which was certainly true. I was trying to get her to analyze the story itself, not the topic it engages. I often have this problem with beginning students, and I need to show them how to look for meaning in the context of aesthetic form—to see it emerging from form, like smoke from a fire. Because Temple hadn't been in a humanities classroom for half a century, her tendency to make statements *about* the story was understandable.

"But what is literature?" I pressed.

"It's a way of expressing complicated things in an accessible manner," she said, pausing to offer an example from Dante's *Inferno*: "When I took that literature class in college, a long time ago—I think my mother still has the book somewhere—the professor explained why the middle of hell is cold." The image had stayed with her over the years, and she returned to it a number of times in our conversations. (Having discussed the spiritual landscape of Silko's novel with Jamie, I recalled suddenly how spatial Dante's poem is, what with the circles, rings, ditches, and rounds laid out, as if by some surveyor, within the earth.)

In the poem, Satan flaps his wings, and the wind they generate turns water in the lowest circle of hell to ice. The more he tries to escape, the more he becomes immured. "It's a paradox," Temple claimed, and though she didn't directly tie the idea of paradox to the story "Meat," I sensed that that's what she was trying to say about killing livestock. The image of Satan half-encased in ice, literally precipitating the terms of his own misery, conveys a complex psychological truth. This paragon of fiery rage is entirely removed from the warmth of God.

Before I could make the link to "Meat" explicit, she launched into a discussion of ambiguity, and she used a recent film, *Eye in the Sky*, to make her point. Temple travels so much that she ends up seeing lots of movies. In fact, on a recent flight to Australia, she saw four in a row.

The film explores the notion of collateral damage in the "War on Terror" by presenting a scenario in which British and American intelligence officers have a chance to take out a terrorist they've been hunting for years. The calculations about collateral damage fall within acceptable limits and, the drone operators, some five thousand miles away, are about to pull the trigger. But then a girl wanders into the picture and sets up a bread stand close to the terrorist's house, which attracts customers. Unwilling to let the terrorist enact his plan, one of the officers pressures the man who is responsible for predicting collateral damage to lessen his assessment. The missile is fired and the girl at the bread stand is killed.

Temple relished *Eye in the Sky*. She was "blown away by the ethical issues it raises—how complex they are"—and she was sensitive to the predicament of the drone operators who must live with the consequences of their all-too-remote actions. In the film they are quite disturbed by the death of the girl. When I later watched the movie, it reminded me of a line by John Updike: "It is in middles that extremes clash, where ambiguity restlessly rules." And another by F. Scott Fitzgerald: "The test of a first-rate intelligence is the ability to hold two opposed ideas in the mind at the same time, and still retain the ability to function."

Although she clearly evinced a sophisticated understanding of ambiguity, Temple once again failed to tie the literary device she was speaking about to "Meat." Her mind was as associative as she claimed, and it did "wander off the subject." Not too far off, mind you, because she had simply moved from ambiguity in one arena to ambiguity in another. As with a connect-the-dots puzzle, she seemed to be inviting me to draw a line between these two provocative points, to view the killing of livestock as akin to the killing of human beings with drones. Both present terribly vexing quandaries. Both demand an ability to function. And yet clearly there are differences between these things as well—big differences.

In *Thinking in Pictures* she had written, "People with more severe autism have difficulty stopping endless associations. . . . When I find my mind wandering too far away from a design problem I am trying to solve, I just tell myself to get back to the problem." I could have pushed Temple to be more focused, to make the link between the film and the story apparent, but it was our first conversation, and I really wanted to see where her thoughts would take her. Besides, she'd encouraged me to ponder the eternal punishments of intelligence officials—and perhaps even industrial butchers. But was she indicting herself, or was she critiquing the strict code of justice in the *Inferno*? The leap from cows to Dante and from Dante to suicide bombers seemed to have something to do with complicating a conventional moral calculus.

. . .

OF COURSE, TEMPLE had explicitly addressed the paradox of caring and killing in her writings. Her first encounter with a meatpacking plant in Arizona triggered a dream in which the white walls of the six-story building appeared to be a "sacred altar." After she killed her first cow, she came to terms with the inevitable fact of death, which allowed her, she said, to appreciate life more fully. Later, when she designed a new cattle ramp and conveyor restraining system, which she named "the Stairway to Heaven," she remembered driving around the plant and "look[ing] upon it as if it were Vatican City." These descriptions carry some of the strange, earnest glee of the narrator's comments in "Meat." I say "strange" because, viewed from another perspective, Temple's Vatican City resembles a concentration camp for cattle.

Animal sacrifice and its close relative ritual slaughter have been practiced for millennia in cultures around the world. The conundrum of killing domesticated livestock with whom one has a caring relationship is resolved—or at least managed—through the notion of God-fearing respect. Recall the scene depicted on the urn in Keats's poem. Temple would gladly impose such a framework on the slaughter and processing of animals. "I believe that the place where an animal dies is a sacred one," she has written. "There is a need to bring ritual into the conventional slaughter plants, and to use it as a means to shape people's behavior. It would help to prevent them from becoming numbed . . . or cruel."

What makes this attitude so striking in Temple is her ability to preserve the particularity of the animals on a grand scale. (Here, she parts company with those conducting the "War on Terror": for them, "violent jihadists" dissolve into an undifferentiated mass.) Visually, in the plant, it's as if she had a relationship with each cow, as if she were working on a small farm or, like the girl in "Meat," engaged in a modest suburban experiment. This is perhaps what annoyed her about the story: the animal should have been described in more detail, and by naming it "Meat," the family was working at cross-purposes: it insisted on respect but, at the same time, it denied the pig its individuality. It settled for "abstractification" (one of Temple's favorite neologisms), as if all caring and truthful roads led there. The animal was finally its use value.

Stalin—yes, I'm quoting that monster again—said, "If one man dies of hunger, that is a tragedy. If millions die, that's only statistics." Cognitively callous, "the cockroach," as Korney Chukovsky and Osip Mandelstam referred to him, reveals in the extreme the problem with neurotypical thinking. Animal activists, no matter how noble their intentions, rail against the meat industry *in general*. "They attack[] things," Temple complains, "they don't . . . know anything about." By "know" she means, experience sensorially, particularly, in the way that a cow with its much smaller frontal lobes experiences its handling. Whereas she digs like a mole beneath the idea of slaughter, working to prevent pain and fear, her activist counterpart ambles above it, heralding horror. To the latter, the ground of death appears undisturbed; to the former, a packed church of detail, to which her ethics belong, sings below.

Compassionate slaughter requires, Temple contends, a bottom-up approach: "To design a good restrainer system . . . you have to imagine what it would be like if you were the animal entering it." Adopting what she calls a "cow's eye view," she deploys her "visual skills to simulate what an animal would see and hear in a given situation." Is that shadow, for instance, spooking it? How about that rattling gate? Temple "credit[s] autism for enabling [her] to understand cattle"—in particular, the long-range underconnectivity that frees "raw [sensory] data" from frontal lobe homogenization and abstraction. During sensory simulations there are "no words in [her] head at all, just pictures. . . . Words come in . . . *after* [she's] finished thinking [a problem through]."

Abidingly practical, she values those "who produce tangible results." And what could be more tangible than a happy cow or, conversely, a gleaming, shrink-wrapped package of ground beef? If Temple were a Christian (and not simply someone with spiritual yearnings), she would favor the "works" side of the great "faith vs. works" debate. Fifty percent of the cattle entering slaughter plants in this country move through center-track restrainer systems that she designed. Like those intelligence officers in *Eye in the Sky*, she is also a realist, and we may label her approach to the caring-and-killing dilemma "sensory pragmatism." Because carnivores, as Jesus might have said, will always be with us, for her "the question is: what should a humane feedlot and slaughterhouse be like?"

In this way, people are understandably confused by what she does. From one perspective, she resembles the most abominable killer (she's the Pol Pot of chuck and loin); from another, a saint (say, Mother Teresa or Francis of Assisi). "The strongest feeling I have today is one of intense calm and serenity as I handle cattle and feel them relax under my care," she has said. Except in a religious context, we're unaccustomed to finding love and death so inextricably bound. It's like a knotty piece of maple: no matter how sharp the ax, it can't be neatly split.

But what about emotion? Does it inform her sense of paradox? Temple has plenty of "sensory empathy"—her term for adopting a cow's eye view—yet she says she is steadfastly logical. So reluctant is she to conceive of herself as a feeling creature that she invents an entirely different form of empathy, one neither cognitive nor emotional. Was she disturbed by Meat's slaughter? Or, if not disturbed, affected by its ambiguous depiction? It was time to inquire about this bugaboo.

"Did the story move you?" I asked.

"Well, I don't get overly emotional," she replied. "But the words created images in my head, and they moved me." With that we were off to the races. It was like being on a giant water slide. She cried, she told me, at the end of *Titanic*, when Jack and Rose don't get to be together. She cried as well listening to "The Widow Maker," a song about a man named Billy Mack who steers his rig off the road to save a stalled pickup filled with kids—like Rose, his lover, Wanda Anne, is left alone. Contrary to what many think, Temple has an acute sense of tragedy. "I can't even think about that song without getting upset," she remarked. From "The Widow Maker," her mind leapt to a truck she had seen on the highway. A sign said, "We Ship Anything Anywhere." "You wanna make a bet," Temple laughed. "I'll make you a load you won't ship again because it's gonna be gross!" And then she was telling me about a time she laughed so hard on a plane while watching a movie that everyone turned around and stared at her.

In *Thinking in Pictures* she had written, "Modulating emotions is difficult for me. . . . My emotion is either turned on or all turned off." A good deal of the time it's the latter, and she was eager to point out the hidden advantage. "I find in science—and I am just horrified at this—that I can review a journal article by somebody I don't like and be totally objective. With other people, they can't seem to separate hating the person from reviewing their research. I can separate the two things." She found the common investment in partisan politics equally horrifying: "It blows my mind how irrational normal people are.... With certain subjects, certain hot-button social issues, which I will not discuss—I save that for the voting booth—their brains completely shut down."

When I asked Temple to account for such irrationality, she replied, "It's normal human behavior and to me it's scary." She explained that her own "emotions aren't hooked up quite tight." But she has also said that her emotions are "reduced and simplified in some areas"; they are "more like the emotions of a child than an adult." She has even said they are more like those of cattle. Subtle social-emotional cues elude her. In *Animals in Translation*, she notably remarked, "Autism made . . . social life hard, but it made animals easy."

How to make sense of these patchwork comments? Temple is decidedly logical, yet music and animals seem to trigger her emotions. For one thing, music appears to remove the barriers that some autistics report to feeling, recognizing, and labeling emotions. A study from 2014 found no difference between the way autistics and nonautistics process the emotional aspects of music. In contrast, considerable research has demonstrated significant variation in ordinary social cognition. Thus, Temple's response to "The Widow Maker" or "My Heart Will Go On" could be quite different from her response, say, to a dispute between colleagues in her department. Interestingly, a study from 2015 found that when words are sung as opposed to spoken, autistic processing of language matches that of nonautistic processing. Music may have an integrative force that consciously stitches emotion and higher-order thought together.

The fact that *touching* cattle allowed her to feel what nonautistics feel isn't that surprising. Temple encounters the world primarily through her senses, yet her senses are neither typically integrated nor typically connected to other systems in the brain. It's as if she were two different people: a visually rational one and a tactile, feeling one. While her eyes solve engineering problems, her hands solve ethical problems. In *The Autistic Brain*, after discovering the difference between object- and spatial-visualizers and labeling herself the former, she comments, "I *see* like an artist, . . . but I don't *feel* like one."

Yet that's not quite right because the visual for her is linked to anxiety. To take in the kind of detail that she takes in produces hypervigilance, a state of constant arousal. In our conversations she referred to visual thinkers as "real panic monsters" and noted that many of them take Prozac, which has "kept them out of the gutter and straightened out their lives." She herself has been on Prozac since 1980, and while she admits that it has "attenuated many of [her] emotions," she can't function without it. "Imagine if we closed up all of the doors in an auditorium," she said to me, "and then put in the most poisonous snakes in the world and turned off the lights. Well, that's the way I was all of the time until I took antidepressant medication."

Neuroimaging of Temple's brain appears to confirm her struggles with anxiety. Her amygdalae, which play a central role in processing emotion, especially fear, are 22 percent larger than the average person's. "My amygdalae are telling me I have everything to fear, including fear itself," she has written. In the aforementioned study of emotionally avoidant readers, the authors pointed out that "increased sympathetic nervous system reactivity" often lurks behind an aloof or inexpressive demeanor: "Avoidantly attached people tend to avoid the experience of emotions, especially negative emotions, and this gives rise to what appears to be a paradox—a subjective self-report of reduced emotionality accompanied by physiological measures that imply increased emotionality." This statement seemed, when I read it, to fit Temple to a t.

When as a teenager she noticed that cattle relaxed in their squeeze chutes, she famously built one for herself; she was desperate for the panic attacks to stop. In addition to teaching her empathy for animals, the machine gave her "feelings of kindness and gentleness toward other people—social feelings." In *Thinking in Pictures* she wrote, "To have feelings of gentleness, one must experience gentle bodily comfort. As my nervous system learned to tolerate the soothing pressure from my squeeze machine, I discovered that the comforting feeling made me a kinder and gentler person." In the HBO movie, Danes explains, "It feels like a wire gets reconnected."

And so through touch Temple received glimpses of ordinary feeling and sociality, but mostly she relied on what experts have termed "hacking": a more labor-intensive, "cognitively mediated processing of social information." To me, the metaphor initially evoked an image of crude, as opposed to surgical, cutting: someone inelegantly accessing the organs of the social body. Now it has a digital resonance. Temple was like some console cowboy or WikiLeaks activist stealing the files of basic human interaction. She deliberately thought her way into the world, using her talent for visual imagery to compensate for the absence of intuitive emotional processing.

Her commitment to the cognitive deepened when she discovered that it could help tame anxiety. As a young woman, she survived the emergency landing and evacuation of a plane she was traveling in, which subsequently rendered her a white-knuckle flier. The only way she could get over the fright was "to make aircraft interesting." "In order not to be afraid, I have to be interested," she told me, and to be interested is to learn everything there is to know about a topic. Such a coping strategy proved to be a boon in academia—especially the sciences, where she found a congenially rational atmosphere.

A different brain whose visual proclivities generate anxiety thus turns to medication, cognitive mastery, and a career that rewards logical thought. Each of these things then acts as a reinforcer for the others in an endless biocultural loop, with the result being that conscious emotion becomes a kind of foundling, appearing on this doorstep and that but never joining, as it were, the family.

A good deal of the time, her feelings seemed to be locked in some sort of basement, fully alive there but unable to communicate with the people living above. Or they were like a scuba diver who fails to return to the surface, floating with an endless supply of oxygen in a watery limbo. Temple, of course, didn't think of herself this way—no, she blamed autism and autism alone for truncating, if not eliminating, emotion. Her vision of herself was narrowly neurological. Indeed, she has compared herself to patients for whom a stroke has spared everything else but emotion.

Attracted to the study of avoidantly attached readers, yet not entirely certain that it applied to Temple, I had wondered whether reading literary fiction might ameliorate this problem. According to some researchers, even those with "intact behavioral ability" in autism reveal electro-physiological differences in how they process social information, leading some to worry that "interventions . . . focus[ing] on cognitive appraisals of emotional information may fail to address the core deficit underlying emotion recognition impairment in this population." Literature, of course, is not only sensory-driven, and as such designed to simulate experience, but also drenched in feeling. While poetry more clearly approximates the condition of music, fiction is hardly just a cognitive appraisal of human sociality—there's nothing "hacked" about it.

Ironically, Temple has pointed to literature to illustrate what she cannot feel. Despite having deployed the idiom of "mixed emotions" in her written response to "Meat," this sort of blending, she insists, escapes her:

As far as I can figure out, complex emotion occurs when a person feels two opposite emotions at once. Samuel Clemens, the author of *Tom Sawyer*, wrote that "the secret source of humor is not joy but sorrow," and Virginia Woolf wrote, "The beauty of the world has two edges, one of laughter, and one of anguish, cutting the heart asunder." I understand these ideas, but I don't experience emotion in this way.

Although she claims to have "replaced emotional complexity with visual and intellectual complexity," she may be selling herself short. After all, she once confessed in print, "It is a sobering experience to be a caring person, yet to design a device to kill large numbers of animals. When I complete a project I am left with a feeling of great satisfaction, but I usually cry all the way to the airport."

Is this not emotional complexity? In J. D. Salinger's *Franny and Zooey*, the narrator laments, "I can't be running back and forth forever between grief and high delight." Clearly Temple grasps this sort of mental messenger service: as in the days of old, runners, homing pigeons, and riders on horseback deliver to us our inconstant, psychological response to life. Maybe her emotions weren't mixed at the time, but the reflection tries to account for them simultaneously. What Robert Penn Warren said of the poet may also be said of this livestock equipment designer: she "wishes to indicate that [her] vision . . . can survive reference to the complexities and contradictions of experience." I'm certain she would agree with Martha Nussbaum who speaks of "an ineliminable residue of tragedy in the relationships between humans and animals."

But did the story itself elicit emotion? Could I feel this sense of tragedy in Temple's comments about "Meat"? Our discussion yielded no real evidence of greater emotionality—or at least what might pass as such. She hadn't mentioned crying or feeling sad. Her response, while associative, was conspicuously intellectual—even when I asked her to report on the feelings that the story may have aroused. I say "conspicuously intellectual," but I could just as easily have said "*passionately* intellectual," for she was animated in the way that a good teacher is animated. She was happy to be talking about the story's ideas—or, rather, talking about the story's ideas made her happy—but its pathos (or negative emotions) seemed to be cordoned off like a crime scene. (In my mind I could almost see the yellow tape.)

At one point, she mentioned wanting to teach the story in a class. In fact, she spoke of assigning pieces from all points of view, including those of ranchers. I quickly joined the discussion, excited by the prospect. Here, we were like a double scull or coxless pair, plowing through the waters of course design. "You gotta make kids think," she said. "Nothing is simple."

And then somehow we were back to poetry and that class from 1966: she remembered a line, which she recited, from William Wordsworth's poem "Intimations of Immortality from Recollections of Early Childhood": "Shades of the prison-house begin to close / Upon the growing Boy." "When he was young," Temple said, "he was open to all kinds of experience and then, you know, experience gets ossified." I was amazed—most students couldn't remember a line of poetry from last semester! Was Temple talking about the girl in the story, the girl who, like this boy, "daily farther from the east / must travel"? When we leave her, the narrator of "Meat" is already thinking as a monarch from the throne of her head rather than as a commoner from the soil of her feet. I don't know, and I didn't ask because Temple had to board her plane. "Gotta go," she said.

When I hung up, I thought more about the Wordsworth poem—specifically its concluding lines:

Thanks to the human heart by which we live,
Thanks to its tenderness, its joys and fears,
To the meanest flower that blows can give
Thoughts that do often lie too deep for tears.

I wondered if these lines couldn't serve as a rejoinder to any simple thought-emotion dichotomy or to any spatial mapping that necessarily places the latter below the former. The speaker, who has lost the "visionary gleam" of childhood, the sense of an immanent god in nature, and who finds strength "in the faith that looks through death, / in years that bring the philosophic mind," imagines an alternative to immediate, visible emotion. Temple, I want to say, could feel such thoughts—or think such feelings.

. . .

OUR SECOND CONVERSATION, three weeks later, was much more leisurely. I caught her at her home in Fort Collins, Colorado, on a Wednesday evening. I was in Columbia, Maryland, at an autism conference. "So, let's just start with the simple question: Did you enjoy 'The Ecstatic Cry'?"

"Well, it wasn't something I was familiar with," Temple answered. "I got a lot of pictures of what, you know, would be going on in Antarctica in my mind 'cause I think visually."

"Any other reactions?"

"It definitely brought up the whole idea of ambivalence. I mean, the guy jumping in and drowning?"

She was referring to the story's climax. After an excursion to an island, a passenger on a tour boat fails to return—he plans to commit suicide when the boat departs. His wife, we later find out, left him; they were supposed to take an anniversary trip together. The narrator, a misanthropic marine biologist whose research is funded by the tour boat company—she studies gentoo penguins—hears splashing in the frigid bay and rescues the man. To fend off hypothermia, they remove their clothing and physically warm one another. Though each of them feels conflicted, sex ensues. In the morning, when the narrator awakens, the man is gone. He's later found dead in the water.

I had chosen this story by Midge Raymond because I thought Temple might identify with a character who had renounced intimate relationships for an animal-centered career, but then suddenly, and almost involuntarily, reconsidered. I wanted not so much for her to talk about her celibacy as to see if the story would tap into that decision and, by tapping into it, generate insights about her life. Yet not only about her life—about the story itself, in a continuing process.

The literary critic David Miall, in "Emotions and the Structuring of Narrative Responses," writes about "the integrative capacity of feeling." Literature, he argues, triggers "evocations, boundary-crossings, and modification." The first are simply emotion-laden memories of personal experience; the second are tentative connections between these memories and what happens in the text; and the third is a reconsideration of the original emotion. For Miall, literature constitutes an "effective vehicle[] for calling up feelings and modifying their significance."

Following the work of Damasio and others, Miall assumes the "primacy of emotion." He sees emotion as "initiating and directing" the reader's cognitive understanding, and he nicely sketches the role of the amygdala, which is ever alert to harm or threat, in processing the trope of ambiguity. An evolutionary inheritance designed to keep us alive finds itself responding to a textual version of what Richard Davison calls "underdetermined contingencies, such as novel, 'surprising' or 'ambiguous' stimuli." It's as if the lion that chased our forbearers had moved onto the page. (Did you see that yellow flash of metaphor?)

Because the amygdala is also involved in the formation of autobiographical memories, especially ones "derived from emotionally arousing events," it's the perfect engine for readerly engagement, and, at the start, the frontal lobes need not know it's even running. Think of reading literature as akin to riding in a Mercedes, where the tony craftsmanship conceals everything but the sound of your own thoughts and the songs on the radio. Emotion, to be clear, propels the reader; it's less a response to something than a condition for thinking. As Miall writes,

> If textual indeterminacy, whether arising from description, character, or action, is a particular force for the elicitation of a reader's feelings (and associated cognitions), it provides a more congenial framework for the enactive . . . rather than reactive understanding of emotion. . . . In this perspective, literary reading seems likely to provide a continuously renewed array of affordances: each point of ambiguity represents a nexus of affective possibilities.

Each point of ambiguity provides a chance to reevaluate both story and self.

But is this true in autism, specifically in Temple's form of autism? I'd already witnessed how unemotional she could be with a story about ritual slaughter, but perhaps that story's subject was too familiar, and perhaps its familiarity made it even easier to remain in cognitive mode. She seemed genuinely surprised by "The Ecstatic Cry"; I could hear it in her voice when she mentioned the suicidal tourist. If the amygdalae play a crucial role in literary reading, what does it mean that hers are so large and overactive? Furthermore, what does it mean that she takes medication to dampen their effects?

Reader-response criticism, of which cognitive literary studies is an offshoot, asks us to take seriously what individual readers bring to literature: their experiences, their age, their gender, their race, their class, and so forth. *See It Feelingly* may be thought of as adding a person's neurology to the list, though not necessarily as a factor that trumps all others. And not as some kind of monolith that affects people in exactly the same way. Nor as something that forecloses typical responses.

If my description of reader-response criticism seems a little dry, then I encourage you to conceive of it as sometimes akin to introducing Mentos Mints to a jug of Diet Coke. As any fan of YouTube knows, the eruption can be quite impressive. When my son, DJ, read about Harriet Tubman, his feelings, if you recall, shot up some fifteen feet into the air. How would Temple the animal scientist and Temple the celibate woman and Temple the autist who struggles with emotion interact with "The Ecstatic Cry"?

"Please describe the narrator," I said, expecting, though not explicitly asking for, a psychological portrait.

"She wants to get rid of all the people, and that's not gonna work. If they don't get money from those tour boats, they're probably not gonna be funded. You need the fees from the tourists to pay for the research." Although she had begun by talking about a psychological concern, the drowned man's "ambivalence," Temple moved quickly to a matter of practical importance.

Early in the story the narrator complains:

Because we're in one of the last pristine environments in the world, we go to great lengths to protect the animals from anything foreign. Visitors sterilize their boots before setting foot on the island, and again when they depart.... I've seen tourists drop used tissues and gum wrappers, not knowing or caring enough to pick them up. I want to chase after them, . . . to tell them how much the fate of the penguins has changed as more and more tourists pass through these islands. (89–90)

When a tourist slips on the ice and hits his head, the narrator cares not a whit about his welfare: "His blood is an unwelcome sight," she states, "bright and thin amid the ubiquitous dark-pink guano of the penguins, and replete with new bacteria, which could be deadly for the birds" (88). She even makes fun of the man for being overweight.

After I read these passages aloud, Temple commented, "If you look at things in Africa, I mean if elephants are just horrible creatures that destroy your crops, you're not gonna want to save them. You gotta make it so people in Africa want to protect the elephants."

She was ignoring the story as story. Couldn't she see how defensive the narrator was? How her commitment to the environment was infused with a deep aversion to human intimacy? Was Temple being emotionally avoidant or stereotypically autistic—or both? I couldn't tell. *So much for identification*, I thought to myself.

But what precisely did I mean by identification? And what sort of feeling did I think powered it? "In sympathy," writes Mar and colleagues,

we feel bad for a character whose goals are not being met, but we do not need to model these goals . . . in order to do so. In identification, we take on these goals and plans as our own, and see ourselves as the character feeling what he or she feels. In empathy, we understand a character's goals through our model of his or her mind, and feel something similar to what the character feels, but we do not see ourselves as that character and identify these emotions as our own rather than as the character's.

With sympathy, in other words, the reader is more of a spectator; with empathy, a kind of fellow traveler. Recent research stresses the importance of "emotional transportation" for positive changes in empathy. The reader, in short, must lose herself in the narrative. While Temple's visual cortex had clearly traveled to Antarctica, her feelings seemed to have stayed at home.

"I'm a very logical person," she continued, "so I focus on policy. You won't have money for research if you don't have tour boats, but you gotta do it in a way that protects the wildlife 'cause I know with chimpanzees, for example, and gorillas, you have to make sure they don't get people diseases."

I was thinking about sex, my wife would later joke, while she was thinking about how to solve intractable environmental problems. (In the HBO movie, to drive home Temple's failure to understand romance, Danes is pictured watching TV. She passes over a program in which two lovers passionately kiss for one in which a lion rips apart its prey.)

"Okay, I get that," I said, "but why does the author present a character who is at once deeply critical of her own species and yet so forlorn?" In the story, when her married research partner, Thom, accompanies the tourist who fell to the nearest medical facility, the narrator reports, "I feel a sudden, sharp loneliness, like an intake of cold air" (91). She describes herself as "comfortably isolated" (91) in Antarctica, and yet she aches for human companionship. Of Dennis, the man she saved, she says, "I watch his fingers on my arm, and I am reminded of the night before, when only Thom and I were here, and Thom had helped me wash my hair. The feel of his hands on my scalp, on my neck, had run through my entire body, tightening into a coil of desire that never fully vanished" (100).

"I don't know why she's forlorn," Temple replied. "I've interacted with a lot of people who become really interested in wildlife, and some of them are loners." The story has Dennis use this very word to describe the narrator. When the biologist pulls him out of the water, she yells, "What are you doing here? What the hell happened?" (95–96). She doesn't know that he was trying to kill himself. Later, after they've talked a bit, he turns the question back on her: "What are *you* doing here?" (98) he asks, adding, "You'd have to be a real loner to enjoy being [in Antarctica]" (98). "I'm just not a people person, that's all" (100), she responds nervously. Pitting the instinct to mate against a woman's commitment to her career, the story introduces the wild card of an individual psyche, one that hides behind environmental logic.

Here, I thought initially, I was coming up against an autistic wall: the standard account of imaginative and empathetic deficits, which seemed, in this case, not so much to be true as to be not entirely false. For the life of her, Temple couldn't detect the drama behind the narrator's words. I wanted her to get inside of the conflict, to move around as in an unlit attic or crawl-space under a house. (Reading a novel or story is like living in a time before electricity.) But at every turn, she balked, remaining on the front porch and simply looking in through a window.

Yet maybe "balk" isn't the right descriptor? She said that she *focuses* on policy—it's what she's good at—what, for a host of reasons, comes naturally. And anyway why would she identify with someone who wasn't a pragmatist, whose environmental views, in fact, were mercilessly extreme? Temple didn't want to get rid of human beings; nor did she want them to stop eating meat. Why, for that matter, would she identify with a human character instead of an animal one?

I took another stab at a sense of interiority. "What did you make of the story's conclusion—that final image of animal grief?"

As she leaves her research post, the narrator spots an emperor penguin, the only species in which the male cares for the egg and the female "travel[s] a hundred miles across the frozen ocean . . . to forage for food" (93). By the time the female "is fat and ready to feed her chick" (93), the male is typically near death. "Still hopeful about marriage and grandkids" (93), the narrator's mother says her daughter thinks like an emperor: she "expect[s] a man to sit tight and wait patiently while [she] disappear[s] across the ice" (93). Believing she's lost her chance at love, the narrator pictures the ecstatic cry: that ritual in which, heads bobbing, beaks raised, the emperor couple reunites. But the penguin she sees has waited too long to return: the male has left, the chick is dead, and the female has assumed "the hunched posture of sorrow" (106).

"Well," Temple responded, "there are stories about a dog that would go down to a Japanese railway station every day at four o'clock when his master returned from work. After the master died, the dog kept going down to the train station—every afternoon for months and months, but the master never came."

It couldn't be clearer: she wasn't going to slop through the mud and mouse droppings beneath our fictional home. She didn't relate to the marine biologist.

(She didn't seem to relate to relating.) She certainly didn't conceive of herself as a loner. Traveling as much as she does, she meets with more people in a month than most of us do in a year. I remember jotting down in my notebook: *Her mind is like an airline hub from which she randomly catches flights in all directions.*

. . .

AT THIS POINT, I must stop the narrative and cry foul—against myself. I must admit that I was so intent on proving literature could move Temple that I lost sight of the spectacle I was precipitating: a disability studies scholar and proponent of neurodiversity straining to recover a norm—a norm of neurology and reading! Why, you might reasonably ask, must she be emotional? Why must she identify with anyone, let alone a character who has sex with a distraught stranger? Why can't she just be different?

For one thing, I couldn't accede to a strictly neurological account of her personhood. Surely culture had played some role in shaping her. For another, I couldn't accept a static—and potentially cynical—idea of neurodiversity. In such a version of the concept, we are called upon as parents, physicians, or educators "to be realistic" about impairment, "to face facts," to stop dreaming. "We were able to move forward and accommodate our son," writes Mark Osteen, the editor of *Autism and Representation*, "only after we realized that our high expectations for him were unfair, even damaging. Presuming competence was often exactly what hindered us all the most." Don't, in other words, expect a rhinoceros to fly. Don't even expect it to play with the other rhinos. "Learn[] to see and accept your loved one as he or she is, rather than trying to normalize or change the person."

Let us stipulate, at least for the sake of argument, that Osteen is right about his son, yet when we know so little about autism and when we've frequently been wrong in our pronouncements, there is enormous peril in accepting anything. And, anyway, autistic brains, like neurotypical ones, are plastic. In letting Grandin be Grandin we may be *taking her for Grandin*, as Bertrand Russell might say. Can we presume competence without striving for normalcy? I think so, but in my quest to uncover emotion, I was certainly muddying the waters.

When I thought more about Temple's response to that final image of animal grief, I, of course, recognized how appropriate it was. Her "cow's eye view" had become a penguin's waddle: *she was identifying with the animal,* not erasing it with metaphor, as the narrator does. Yes, the woman in the story prefers penguins to humans and, yes, she rightly attributes feeling to them, but in the end, the animal drama is merely an occasion to reflect on herself. Temple was doing, in her own way, what Dora had done with those persecuted androids in Dick's novel. (Let's not forget that Temple cried when HAL in *2001: A Space Odyssey* was taken apart.) She was vigorously relating to "the more than human," and she was doing it, as my friend Gillian Silverman proposed, by telling another story, by flying, as it were, supersonically from Antarctica to Japan. If Temple's mind is like an airline hub, then the flights she catches are so quick she doesn't even have to pack a bag or pass through security! It's more like *Star Trek*: "Beam me up, Scottie."

The two stories (about the penguin and the dog) occupied the same space—they lay side by side like beds in a room—but they didn't interact in an expected manner. They were cautious, you might say, respectful. They didn't reject communication so much as imply a strong preference for company, for proximity—the way that an autistic child might want to be in a room with his family but not conventionally interact. "Let's just be together," the stories said.

Temple's reaction to "The Ecstatic Cry," was, in Gillian's words, a rejection of the "neurotypical propensity toward becoming a character," a rejection of "the kind of empathy that resembles possession—an entering into and knowing the Other." It may even reveal a problem with empathy itself—with the interiority it assumes. Reminded of Temple's comment about making sure that chimpanzees and gorillas don't get "people diseases," Gillian mused, "Maybe neurotypical empathy is a 'people disease.'" What would be contagious and sometimes lethal in this scenario is not raw, boundary-less emotion, but the unwarranted conviction that we know how to properly engage with, know wisely what's best for and what rightly to expect from, the Other. In a flash, I became that dreaded tourist who drops his ethnographical tissues and gum wrappers all over the place.

And yet, even now, as I accept this critique, I still hold out for a psychological Grandin—or at least a neuropsychological Grandin. Make that a neuropsychological and historically contingent Grandin! Why can't she be avoidantly attached *and* exquisitely different?

Watching her flail at my line of questioning, I began, I remember, to feel bad. Had I really expected her to be moved by the narrator's sudden change of heart—or loins? In my eagerness to put pressure on the assumption that autistic people can't handle, or don't want, romantic relationships, I had assumed that a life without romance and sex was necessarily lacking. I had envisioned—cue the orchestra; dim the lights—a nearly operatic admission of regret. Recovering yet another norm, I had pitied her, which is no venial sin when it comes to disability.

Worse, I had borrowed the story's saturnine landscape and reinstantiated the most pernicious of clichés: the autist as person alone. "A more inhospitable place could scarcely be imagined," wrote a member of Ernest Shackleton's disastrous Imperial Trans-Antarctic Expedition. Of that other pole, the explorer Frederick Albert Cook once exclaimed, "We were the only pulsating creatures in a dead world of ice." While no one believes anymore in refrigerator mothers, all sorts of people believe in freezer autistics. I had wanted Temple to disrupt the cliché, but when she didn't . . . ? (As I write this paragraph, my mind drifts to the southernmost region of Hell where Satan, as though autistic himself, flaps his rime-covered wings.)

If you Google "interviews with Temple Grandin," you will see how often she is asked about this supposed lacuna in her humanity. In one interview, she does, in fact, express regret about having never found love, but she says she has an "exciting career." And who could argue with that? When I waded into these waters—"Do you feel the, I mean do you feel the same way about yourself and romantic love as you once did?"—she graciously threw me a life preserver: "You know when I am the happiest: when I'm trying to problem-solve. Or when I'm teaching. I wanna get my students into careers they're gonna like, jobs where they're gonna do some good in the world."

She spoke about students who had "trashed their careers because of breakin' up with boyfriends and romance." "So much psycho-drama, ugh!" she said. The career-minded Temple seemed to have taken the dais—her voice was now confident, even upbeat—and I remembered an interesting detail from the study of avoidantly attached readers. In the control condition, where the Chekhov story had been robbed of its artistic elements, the "self-reported happiness of High Avoidance participants increased while that of Low Avoidance participants decreased."

The authors reasoned that the "complex attachment issues presented in the documentary text functioned as an argument—'close personal relationships are trouble and bad for you'"—thus confirming the strongly held view of this group. In contrast, "Low Avoidance" participants were disappointed by the documentary text. If Temple were somehow translating the story into argument, if aided by autism and years of emotionally avoidant behavior, she could, like some sort of antiliterary superhero, block the story's mysterious effects, then she would be anything but "defenseless against art," in the authors' phrase.

But then, as if right on cue, which is to say when all hope of an emotional response seemed to be lost, a rather straightforward point about the need for women to focus on their own professional fulfillment suddenly became more urgent. "The thing that is beyond my imagination," Temple remarked, "is how a woman can stay with a guy that's abusing her. The only reason I can think to do that is economic necessity. I'd be gettin' money and buryin' it in the garden in a jar." Was she referring to one of her students, or to something more personal? Were we finally seeing, as Miall would say, "evocations" and "boundary crossings"? The feeling in her voice was unmistakable. "I've seen so many bad marriages," she added. "I haven't seen a single marriage that I could imagine being in."

I was stunned: the neurological explanation for her disavowal of romantic love, which she had so frequently put forward, was giving way to the sort of explanation that is common to literature: namely, lived experience. It's not that autism hadn't played a role in her decision to be celibate. But maybe it had played a role that was different from what we had been taught to believe. Maybe it had rendered the ordinary conviction of a young person who swears off marriage that much more resolute. For someone who doesn't engage with the world abstractly, marriage only exists in the specific instances she has encountered. Marriage, we might say, is like a Great Dane. How could she have envisioned anything better?

Whether Temple knew it or not—and it wasn't clear that she did—she was offering a different, much less rigidly deterministic account of herself. This account brought to mind other experiences that must have shaped her psychologically, such as the rampant sexism in the cattle industry. Of the period in the 1970s when there were no women working in feedlots, she has written, "Back then I didn't know which was a greater handicap, being a woman or having autism. . . . What people call harassment today is nothing compared to what I went through." Imagine, after a long day at work, returning to your car, as she did, and finding it adorned with bulls' testicles.

Ludwig Wittgenstein once wrote, "There can *never* be surprises in logic." Of course, he hadn't met Temple Grandin. From the mouth of this living proof came something even more unexpected than her criticism of marriage or vague allusions to spousal abuse: "My aunt, you know, out at the ranch—her husband was a mean drunk. God, when he got drunk he was like Jekyll & Hyde. It was horrible." If you picture the moment in the first *Alien* movie when the creature erupts from the sleeping astronaut's stomach, you'll understand how shocking this seemed to me. Through the phone, my ears could see Temple shudder.

She was referring, of course, to the summer she had spent at her aunt's ranch in Arizona when she was fifteen. It was there that her passion for cattle was born. Nowhere in print had she ever mentioned this man's violent behavior or spoken negatively of marriage—you can't find either in the HBO movie. If a good day back then was filled with snakes in a dark auditorium, what was a bad day like? With her amygdalae shouting, as through a bullhorn, "Fear! Fear! Fear!" it must have been terrifying to witness such outbursts. The revelation may seem run-of-the-mill by the standards of contemporary confessional culture, yet it was extraordinary for Temple—as much the revelation itself as the feeling that accompanied it.

What to make of her disclosure? According to Mar, reading can generate either "fresh emotions," which depend "on our perception of a protagonist or character and his or her goals and mental state (i.e., emotions of sympathy, identification, empathy)," or "remembered emotions," where "the text has produced a particular resonance with a piece of personal autobiography, so that the reader relives emotions associated with it." Grandin was obviously experiencing the latter. While it may be tempting to label the first a sophisticated response and the second an unsophisticated one, the two often take up with each other, and, anyway, the point isn't necessarily to give birth to more literary critics or English majors.

In a separate study of undergraduates, which used the same story by Chekhov, Djikic and Oatley found that emotion elicited during reading drove "transformation of . . . personality," but they "stress[ed] that participants did not show a collective change in the same direction":

> Not all of them became more extraverted, or open, or conscientious, for example. In other words, they were not persuaded by a moral embedded in a story. Rather, each reader experienced a fluctuation in a unique direction in their entire personality profile. Reading Chekhov induced changes in their sense of self—perhaps temporary—such that they experienced themselves not as different in some way prescribed by the story, but as different in a direction toward discovering their own selves.

Miall, as I indicated, calls such discovery "modification," and he understands it as "a process that may serve to reconceptualize a recognized situation"— in this case, Grandin's decision to be celibate.

Whereas Miall stresses the importance of ambiguity as a triggering agent, Oatley and Djikic stress literature's indirection. Miall, though, is especially sensitive to the hidden life of feeling—in all of us, not just those with alexithymia or autism or both.

> Since, at any given stage of life, the self almost certainly pursues conflicting concerns, the feelings associated with these concerns will often also conflict: one feeling will reconfigure, modify, or cancel another. Possibly this process occurs continually, with little sense of its significance reaching conscious awareness. As the novelist [Georges] Bernanos puts it, "The simplest emotions are born and grow in impenetrable darkness, attracting and repelling each other like thunderclouds, in accordance with secret affinities." For the reader a literary text provides a framework for such conflicting processes of feeling, causing them to be felt consciously and, at times, their significance realized.

However inchoately, Grandin seemed to be "experienc[ing herself] not as different in some way prescribed by ["The Ecstatic Cry"], but as different in a direction toward discovering [her] own sel[f]."

What I like about the conclusion of the Djikic and Oatley study is just how capacious it is. The process may be general, but its direction and effects are particular. Various. And although we're still clearly in a human-centered framework, one that presupposes normative notions of identification and transformation, there's room for Grandin's animal affinity and sometimes wild associations. What is more, the process appears to work immediately. Characterizing the study of first-year undergraduates, Mar writes, "It shows that reading literary art can have an effect even on non-avid-readers, that you don't have to be a booklover for reading to transform you."

Toward the end of our second conversation, Grandin admitted to warding off loneliness by remaining extraordinarily busy, and at one point, with a sigh, she said of romantic love, "It's just not part of my life." By connecting the Japanese dog to the story's male penguin, by presenting another image of doleful waiting, she may have been trying to tell me something about herself: she had moved on. She was no longer returning each day at 4:00 to the train station. Instead of anthropomorphizing these animals, however, she had allowed *them*—and not the human narrator—to lead her into ambivalent self-understanding. Put another way, the squeeze machine of the short story may have provided the necessary animal frame in which this autistic scientist could unlock her feelings—unlock her feelings and reflect, as a woman in her sixties, on her past.

Now, you might think that she had simply traded one narrative of avoidant attachment (autism makes romantic relationships impossible) for another (I was exposed to scary men), but the latter rendered celibacy a choice, an overdetermined one to be sure but not inevitable. It also embraced the idea of historical contingency—what we might term, with Grandin's livestock achievements in mind, the crap*chute* of life—while simultaneously honoring the difference an individual can make in carving out a particular course. I still marvel at the coincidence of Grandin discovering cattle at the moment she discovered abusive men. Hers was just one path through an alternative neurology.

Finally, the latter narrative moved her closer to the "fresh emotions" of sympathy, empathy, and identification. The story doesn't tell us why the marine biologist is so conflicted about romantic love—it just plops us down in troubled Antarctica—but with her stubborn aversion to "psycho-drama" disarmed and some of her own life experiences present in her mind, Grandin was in a much better position to infer the reason or reasons. With practice, who knows? Maybe she'd more regularly feel the wind and ice: that landscape of the self-reproaching heart. Maybe she'd even assume the "hunched posture of sorrow," at once in imitation of the narrator and yet completely herself—though not because she is tragically single or autistic.

Or maybe she'd just stick to animals—to animals and her own form of relating to stories and people. Again, I don't see why we have to choose between notions of respectful yet static, or disrespectful yet evolving, neurological difference. A legitimate critique of normativity should neither stand in the way of "rehabilitative" efforts nor fetishize alterity, especially when doing so can end up being just another, covert sort of pity. Better to assume that we are *all* changing all of the time—that each of us, whatever our neurotype and individual differences, needs some kind of rehabilitation or accommodation. Grandin can learn to be more, and we can learn to be less, conventionally emotional. She can learn to empathize with human characters, and we can learn to empathize with more than human ones—without any loss of what might be called "natural" predilection. It's a fluid, neurocosmopolitan world, I like to say.

More than once in our conversations, Grandin remarked, "What you're doing with literature and autistic people is really interesting," but she considered it opposed to what the profession of literary studies was doing with literature generally. "I went to a session at a conference on empathy," she recalled, "and it was nothing but weird rhetorical crap. There's a certain tendency in the humanities where they dissect stories in journal jargon, and I don't even know what they're talking about. The thing I liked about Mr. De Simone's class is that he explained in common sense terms what the author was trying to convey. . . . I think deconstructing literature is just rubbish."

Who knew? Temple Grandin, conservative literary critic! If we had had more time, I would have pointed out that the "theory" she despised can lay bare the cultural biases that frame the romance-career tension as inevitably a matter of loss. This is not to say that some women don't feel impossibly divided; rather, it's to point out that men have not been taught to understand the bind in this way. Thom, for example, blithely manages to juggle a career in Antarctica with a wife and family. I would have also pointed out that the concept of neurodiversity—"I am different . . . not less," Grandin has said— depends on a deep understanding of the historical impulse to pathologize people unlike ourselves. I might even have tried to show her that autistic sensing works like deconstruction. If Tito is a "Derridean of sound" for the way he preserves precategorical auditory information, then she is a "Derridean of sight" for the way she preserves precategorical visual information.

In J. M. Coetzee's *Life and Times of Michael K*, the doctor complains, "There is no home left for universal souls, except perhaps in Antarctica or on the high seas." By this logic, we must retreat nostalgically to a space of crushing naturalism, we must feel infinitesimally small and incalculably imperiled, to slough off unimportant things like race, class, gender, and national identity. Only then will we be able to recall what unites us as a species. In an age as superficially attentive to difference, which is to say as in love with social categories, as our own, autistics, I remember thinking, can teach us how to be constructively universal. We need better, tentative generalizations, which, by safeguarding detail (and thus distinction), do not march across the earth like a vanquishing army. "The human," like "the Great Dane," doesn't exist; only humans and Great Danes exist, highly particular ones.

In this way, I admit to being perversely heartened by Grandin's objection to "theory." She still believed in the old-fashioned idea of "great" literature— in its ability to tell us something important about our lives. She still believed in a medium that demanded reflection and rewarded the instruction of a skilled teacher. (When her plane landed after our first conversation, she left a message on my phone: she'd remembered other satisfying things about

Mr. De Simone's course.) The fact that she sounded like a generation of literary scholars long retired—or like many scientists in the academy today who are baffled by what we do in the humanities—only made her appear less stereotypically autistic. In the context of medical claims about neurological deficits, on the one hand, and the current fetish of the "posthuman," on the other, her appeal to our common humanity seemed the sort of irony worthy of stories and poems.

It's a Sunday in March; spring has come early to Iowa. The warm temperatures and pristine skies are like a false promise: winter, conman winter, hides behind them.

My regular Skype session with Tito begins the way it always does: with a greeting—"Hi"—and a question—"How are you?" "I am fine," he types, "but a little concerned about the shooting down of Indians." He is referring to the murder of Srinivas Kuchibhotla, a thirty-two-year-old computer engineer, in a crowded Kansas bar. Another Indian man and a white man who tried to intervene were seriously injured. Apparently mistaking the Indian men for Iranians, the attacker yelled, "Get out of my country!"

A month before, Tito seemed relatively unconcerned about our new president, Donald Trump, quipping, "He will succumb to his own expansion." But that expansion turned lethal, and he hardly needed another reason for people to stare at or, god forbid, attack him. It's a short walk from virulent xenophobia to brutalizing anyone who doesn't fit some vaunted norm. Unwilling to complain, at least overtly, Tito allowed a sense of unease to puncture his customary stoicism, which made it all the more crushing.

Of what use is literature in the face of such barbarism? For one thing, it can think differently. For another, it can arrive at its ideas in a different fashion. It's not enough *to have* different ideas—better ones, say, like affirmative notions of identity. They must be reached in a different way—by unicycle, let us imagine, or hang glider or even pogo stick. As I hope the chapter on Eugenie makes clear, the burgeoning field of diversity science offers a warning about categorical thinking. It's what we humans do, it's what we do quickly and well, but it comes at a terrible cost. The generalizing force of language—its conceptual nature—reduces experience, including the experience of encountering people different from ourselves, to a set of convenient propositions.

Racism, sexism, homophobia, and ableism are thus the understandable—*sadly* understandable—by-products of a categorizing mind.

In his book *Playing by Ear and the Tip of the Tongue*, Reuven Tsur argues for literature, in particular poetry, as an essential corrective. "We are flooded by a *'pandemonium'* of precategorical sensory information, day by day, moment by moment, which we categorize into a relatively small number of more easily handled categories for efficient use, which constitute 'ordinary consciousness,'" he writes. Although made of words (which "refer to concepts, not to unique experiences") and hence "ill-suited to convey" what it wishes to convey, literature, through its plastic approach to sound and sense, nevertheless recovers "rich precategorical information." It "brings us nearer to the unique, individual experience, with all of the disquieting elements implied." Literature, according to Tsur, "has something of the unpredictability, of the feeling of trembling on the brink of chaos." In this way, both the cognitive study of literature and the cognitive study of diversity insist on individuation—individuation borne of significant bottom-up processing.

Could it be that what Temple Grandin found so interesting in Mr. De Simone's class was, on the one hand, the engagement with precategorical sensory information and, on the other, the instruction of New Criticism, which by modeling how to move from narrow detail to holistic idea offered her a way of being abstract—*palpably* abstract? Temple's complaint about contemporary literary studies might be understood less as an attack on professional jargon than as a plea for the appreciation of literature as a more hospitable mode of thought.

To be clear, I'm not advancing an antitheory argument—far from it. I'm simply suggesting that we rebalance our approach to literature. After nearly sixty years of critiquing it, we have perhaps lost sight (and smell and touch . . .) of its distinctiveness, which has more to do with breaking or bending categories than with denouncing things categorically. The former teaches us how to think in a new way, to outfox our own cognitive architecture; the latter reinscribes the problem. (Yes, I'm overstating things; I'm generalizing.) Both, of course, engage with politics.

Literature has more value, more utility, than many people recognize. If poetry can calm an autistic listener's anxiety or help him to tie his shoes; if novels can help to suppress the social "noise" in everyday life through steady, detail-selective character depictions; if short stories can help to elicit and shape unreachable emotion, then it's time to think of literature as a reasonable accommodation and, more generally, as a kind of social medicine. By that I mean, following Jamie's reading of *Ceremony*, a way of treating *both* the individual and her community—a way of restoring relation. After all, the individual can only be said to be "broken" when the community is.

If, in turn, literature can help to improve theory of mind and to promote prosocial behavior in the nonautistic person; if it can disrupt categorizing tendencies through sensory identification, making it more difficult to place someone in a social out-group; if it can alter attentional habits, allowing nonhuman entities to play a role in our planetary drama; then, again, it's time to think of literature as a reasonable accommodation and, more generally, as a kind of social medicine. Each group needs help to live fully in the world.

Some part of me wants to shout: "So much for the idea that literature has nothing to contribute to American life—nothing practical, that is." We still have no idea what literature can do. Like a dog, it needs to be let out of its cage and taken for a walk. It needs to "get busy." As anyone familiar with guide dogs knows, that's the phrase you use to get your dog to pee or poop. Harness off, moving in ecstatic, olfactory circles, it has a job to do but also a wondrous world to take in. Think of reading literature as a service dog at work and a service dog at play.

One of the anonymous reviewers of this book, who was otherwise very helpful, urged me "to stop picking on the frontal lobes." At the same time, he or she urged me to avoid making generalizations about autism. But how to do the latter without doing the former? Wasn't there some fundamental tension between the natural habits of the typical brain and the nearly political rights of details, between the need for usable knowledge and the insistence on particularity? The advice seemed a bit like the mischievous wisdom of Mark Twain: "Good judgment is the result of experience and experience the result of bad judgment." Then again, if anyone should appreciate such wisdom it is an English professor. As the Danish physicist Niels Bohr once remarked, "How wonderful that we have met with a paradox. Now we have some hope of making progress."

As I stated in the introduction, there's no literature—no linguistic categories to bend—without the frontal lobes. I simply offer a corrective: generalizations arrived at much more slowly and tentatively through the singular (though by no means single) example, as in novels and, yes, autism. Think of the chapters in this book as halfway between the kind of hyperfocusing that Tito talks about and the photographs that his mother takes to help him understand what he has seen—to understand it from a more neurotypical perspective. (The camera operates like ordinary language, received wisdom.) Think of patient, humble ethnography as an autistic version of science. Qualitative particularity matters. We may not be able to extrapolate from it easily—"Autistics make wonderful readers of literature"—but nor can we just dismiss it by clinging to the standard, deficit-based generalization: "Autistics can't do literature." I'm with Marcel Proust when he says, "The real voyage of discovery consists not in seeking new landscapes, but in having new eyes." New eyes, you might say, for difference, for possibility.

In six weeks, my son, DJ, will graduate from Oberlin College with a degree in anthropology and creative writing—he has a 3.9 GPA. He lives in the dorm with an aide—my wife lives in town and helps him to coordinate his support services. Soon they will both come back to Iowa. Tito continues with his routine in Austin, Texas—he spends time at an adult daycare facility and at a construction site while his mother works; at night and on the weekends they read literature and philosophy. He's presently finishing a new book, his sixth, on autistic perception. Jamie remains in Syracuse, New York; he keeps busy with numerous activities, including advocacy work and art making, but he'd like a satisfying job. Dora just won a National Science Foundation grant as the principal investigator; she was recently promoted at Portland State University from research associate to assistant research professor. Eugenie continues to raise her children, to dance, and to coach competitive skaters—if I learned anything from her, it's that my mind needs to move as fluidly as her mind and body do. Temple is traveling and lecturing as much as she always has.

So much diversity in neurodiversity. So much promise waiting to be fulfilled. And yet so many threats as well. It's as if, in Trump, the category as belligerent force has returned. Some commentators called his election victory "whitelash"—it certainly felt like a social car accident (my neck hasn't quite recovered)—but I think of it a bit differently. The billionaire Tom Sawyer has talked his friends into whitewashing Aunt Polly's fence, his penalty for skipping school. They've offered him their small treasures for the privilege of doing this work. Yet the fence has gotten bigger—they may never finish. They may have to fork over more treasures.

Even Robert Frost, no paragon of liberal politics, understood the problem with walls: "Before I built a wall I'd ask to know / What I was walling in or walling out, / And to whom I was like to give offense." Offense, of course, is the point. In addition to the current immigration fiasco, we're looking at a budget that, among other things, cuts funding for medical research and eliminates the National Endowments for the Arts and Humanities. What is more, Trump's Supreme Court pick, Neil Gorsuch, authored a decision affirming a less than rigorous education for those with disabilities—the case involved an autistic student. And recently, Betsy DeVos, the secretary of education, cited historically black colleges as an example of school choice. As if the segregation and discrimination that engendered them were a boon! (I suppose if Ben Carson, the secretary of housing and urban development, can refer to slaves as "immigrants," then DeVos can refer to undercutting public education as saving poor children.)

How to protect the recent gains of the neurodiversity movement? How, in this climate, to extend them? "You must blow against the walls of every power that exists the small trumpet of your defiance," exclaimed Norman Mailer. But on that small trumpet you must also play a tune of joy. Beyond what I learned about these novels, beyond what I learned about autism (and my own neurotypicality), beyond the claims I might make about the value of literature, there was the simple joy of reading a book and discussing it with another equally invested reader.

Jane Austen once remarked—she could have been talking about someone like Trump—"The person, be it gentleman or lady, who has not pleasure in a good novel, must be intolerably stupid." Writing in a different time and in a different context, Azar Nafisi, an Iranian professor who secretly discussed Nabokov's *Lolita*, among other novels, with her female university students, insisted on pleasure: whatever the ancillary benefits of literature, they flow from the way it engages our senses. "We read," she said, "for the pure, sensual, and unadulterated pleasure of reading. . . . Our reward is the discovery of the many hidden layers within these works that do not merely reflect reality but reveal a spectrum of truths, thus intrinsically going against the grain of totalitarian mindsets." A spectrum of truths indeed, but one stretched and amplified, in the case of this book, by a spectrum of readerly minds.

· notes ·

INTRODUCTION

I have cited only autism-related books and articles, cognitive literary studies–related books and articles, and literary criticism. The first mentions of the primary novels and short stories appear in the endnotes; after those first mentions, I use in-text citations within parentheses. All other quotations come from the conversations that I had with my collaborators, or from other writers and thinkers, which I've treated, the way a memoirist would, as little, uncited flares of wisdom or humor.

1 Simon Baron-Cohen, chief purveyor of the ToM hypothesis . . . Simon Baron-Cohen, *Mindblindness: An Essay on Autism and Theory of Mind* (Cambridge, MA: MIT Press, 1995), 5. For a trenchant critique of ToM claims in autism, see Melanie Yergeau, "Clinically Significant Disturbance: On Theorists Who Theorize Theory of Mind," *Disability Studies Quarterly* 33, no. 4 (2013), http://dsq-sds.org/article/view/3876/3405.

2 Consider, for example, the passage . . . Oliver Sacks, *An Anthropologist on Mars: Seven Paradoxical Tales* (New York: Vintage, 1996), 259.

2 Not half a page . . . Sacks, *Anthropologist on Mars*, 261.

3 "Her inability to respond deeply . . ." Sacks, *Anthropologist on Mars*, 86.

3 "There is a similar poverty . . ." Sacks, *Anthropologist on Mars*, 86.

3 While in some ways Grandin . . . Sacks, *Anthropologist on Mars*, xx.

3 Because he is such a fine writer . . . Sacks, *Anthropologist on Mars*, xvi.

4 But my point isn't simply . . . In line with the thinking of many self-advocates, I prefer the term "autistic" (or "autist"), as a noun, over "person with autism." As Jim Sinclair notes, "Saying 'person with autism' suggests that the autism can be separated from the person." If autism isn't understood pejoratively, as something that needs to be eliminated, but rather is celebrated, as a form of neurological difference, then the linguistic problem disappears. See Jim Sinclair, "Why I Dislike 'Person-First' Language," http://autismmythbusters.com/general-public/autistic-vs-people-with-autism/jim

-sinclair-why-i-dislike-person-first-language/. However, in the interest of style and variation, I sometimes use the phrase "person with autism."

4   "The thing is I don't . . ." Quoted in Verlyn Klinkenborg, "What Do Animals Think?," *Discover* (May 1, 2005), http://discovermagazine.com/2005/may/what-do-animals-think.

4   If, as studies have demonstrated . . . See, for example, Hideya Koshino et al., "Functional Connectivity in an fMRI Working Memory Task in High-Functioning Autism," *NeuroImage* 24, no. 3 (2005): 810–21. This study asked subjects to remember individual letters presented to them on a screen. Whereas the control group "used the expected verbal strategy . . . to facilitate memory . . . the autism group processed the letter stimuli as nonverbal, visualgraphical codes" (818). The study spoke of autistics as engaging in "lower level visuospatial feature analysis," and it cited the attachment to such analysis as confirmation of a 2004 study's claim of underconnectivity in autistic brains. Literate autistics, the theory goes, ought to suppress such basic sensory information in favor of frontal lobe abstractions; instead, they really looked at the letters! According to the study, autistic cognition is "shifted toward the right hemisphere as well as toward the posterior part of the brain" (819).

4   Neurotypicals, Grandin believes, are . . . Temple Grandin and Catherine Johnson, *Animals in Translation: Using the Mysteries of Autism to Decode Animal Behavior* (New York: Mariner Books, 2006), 30. Neurotypicals miss much of the actual world—both with respect to *what* they attend to and *how* they attend to it. As Olga Bogdashina explains, "With maturation, there is a strategy to suppress ['raw sensory information']. The maturing mind becomes increasingly aware only of concepts to the exclusion of the details that comprise these concepts." And to the exclusion, we might say, of the things themselves. See Olga Bogdashina, *Autism and the Edges of the Known World: Sensitivities, Language, and Constructed Reality* (London: Jessica Kingsley, 2010), 84.

4   "Animals don't see their ideas . . ." Grandin and Johnson, *Animals*.

4   Using a remarkable poetic analogy . . . Klinkenborg, "What Do Animals Think?"

4   "Everything else is shut off . . ." Klinkenborg, "What Do Animals Think?"

4   Neurotypical brains, by contrast . . . Klinkenborg, "What Do Animals Think?"

5   To explain the distinction . . . Laura Otis reminds us that generalizations can only take us so far and often occlude significant differences in the ways that individual minds engage in the production of sensuous mental imagery. Here, in my own ethnographical project, I want to be particularly sensitive to this point. On the one hand, there do indeed appear to be

conspicuous differences between autistic and nonautistic processing; on the other hand, no two autistic or nonautistic people think in exactly the same way. See Laura Otis, *Rethinking Thought: Inside the Minds of Creative Scientists and Artists* (New York: Oxford University Press, 2015).

5   **While the blind may lack images . . .** See, for example, Helder Bertolo, "Visual Imagery without Visual Perception?," *Psicologica* 26, no. 1 (2005): 173–88. For years, debate reigned about the relationship between visual perception and the generation of visual mental imagery. Was the latter actually a kind of seeing? Did it rely on the same brain regions as the former? Stephen Kosslyn's work showed that in general it did, but the degree to which it activated these regions varied from person to person. As Otis explains, "When . . . Martha Farah asked participants to form visual images in response to verbal cues, she noticed that in some people the activity reached farther back into the occipital cortex than it did in others. In people with visually rich mental lives, imagery was not *like* vision; it *was* vision, relying on the same neural structures that made vision possible" (*Rethinking Thought*, 67). And yet, to conflate visual perception with visual imagery would be a mistake, for it would then follow that the blind cannot produce mental imagery, which is not the case. Indeed, some blind people use mental images more effectively than sighted people.

5   **My son, for example, carries . . .** I have chosen not to update the book's biographical elements; rather, I let them develop as the book develops. My son graduated from Oberlin in May 2017—with High Honors in anthropology and election into Phi Beta Kappa.

6   **My fellowship project tried . . .** Ilona Roth, "Imagination and the Awareness of Self in Autistic Spectrum Poets," in *Autism and Representation*, ed. Mark Osteen (London: Routledge, 2008), 145–65, quote on 150. See Ralph James Savarese, "What Some Autistics Can Teach Us about Poetry: A Neurocosmopolitan Approach," in *The Oxford Handbook of Cognitive Literary Studies*, ed. Lisa Zunshine (Oxford: Oxford University Press, 2015), 393–417.

6   **As Roth explains, "Prose and . . ."** Roth, "Imagination," 146.

8   **For instance, reading Mark Twain's . . .** Mark Twain, *The Adventures of Huckleberry Finn* (New York: Harper & Brothers, 1896).

9   **When I discussed Herman Melville's . . .** Herman Melville, *Moby-Dick: A Longman Critical Edition*, ed. John Bryant and Haskell Springer (New York: Longman, 2006).

9   **For example, I knew that Jamie . . .** Leslie Marmon Silko, *Ceremony* (New York: Penguin, 2007).

9   **More and more, scientists are viewing autism . . .** See, for example, the work of Laurent Mottron at the University of Montreal—in particular,

Laurent Mottron et al., "Enhanced Perceptual Functioning in Autism: An Update, and Eight Principles of Autistic Perception," *Journal of Autism and Developmental Disorders* 36, no. 1 (2006): 27–43. See, as well, Maria Brincker and Elizabeth B. Torres, "Noise from the Periphery in Autism," in *Autism: The Movement Perspective*, ed. Elizabeth B. Torres and Anne M. Donnellan (Frontiers, 2015), eBook, http://journal.frontiersin.org/researchtopic/801/autism-the-movement-perspective.

10   We had both appeared in an . . . *Loving Lampposts, Living Autistic*, dir. Todd Drezner, Cinema Libre Studio (2011).

10   Dora was apparently interested in . . . Philip K. Dick, *Do Androids Dream of Electric Sheep?* (New York: Del Rey, 1996).

10   All too frequently, autism . . . A wonderful new anthology has rectified this problem. See *All the Weight of Our Dreams: On Living Racialized Autism*, ed. Lydia X. Z. Brown, E. Ashkenazy, and Morénike Giwa Onaiwu (Lincoln, NE: DragonBee Press, 2017).

10   With Eugenie, I chose to read . . . Carson McCullers, *The Heart Is a Lonely Hunter* (New York: Mariner Books, 2000).

11   In an effort to be sensitive . . . John Yunker, ed., *Among Animals: The Lives of Animals and Humans in Contemporary Short Fiction* (Ashland, OR: Ashland Creek Press, 2014).

12   She related that her aunt . . . After Temple's mother got divorced, she married a man whose sister was married to a rancher. At this man's ranch, she was introduced to cattle.

13   A few years back, I wrote to the authors . . . Rinat Gold and Miriam Faust, "Right Hemisphere Dysfunction and Metaphor Comprehension in Young Adults with Asperger Syndrome," *Journal of Autism and Developmental Disorders* 40, no. 7 (2010): 800–811.

13   Lisa Zunshine has pointed out . . . Ralph James Savarese and Lisa Zunshine, "The Critic as Neurocosmopolite; Or, What Cognitive Approaches to Literature Can Learn from Disability Studies," *Narrative* 22, no. 1 (2014): 17–44, quote on 28.

PROLOGUE

15   Having been abandoned by his birth mother . . . For a narrative of DJ's early years, see Ralph James Savarese, *Reasonable People: A Memoir of Autism and Adoption* (New York: Other Press, 2007).

15   In the case of Tubman . . . Savarese, *Reasonable People*, 417, 418. To be clear, I am not disparaging intellectually disabled people; nor am I uncritically venerating intelligence. Rather, I am resisting—strenuously—the equation between outward appearance and inward inability, and I am doing so in the context of a historical underappreciation of autistic talent.

16   In the chapter he wrote for . . . Savarese, *Reasonable People*, 442.

16   The great United States of America . . . Savarese, *Reasonable People*, 417.

17   It's as if DJ had condensed . . . Savarese, *Reasonable People*. This sentence
     and the one before it appear in *Reasonable People.*

17   In that chapter he includes . . . Savarese, *Reasonable People*, 434.

17   "You ignored the resentment . . ." Savarese, *Reasonable People*, 435.

17   "As long as I treat people resentfully . . ." Savarese, *Reasonable People*, 434.

17   "Respect for others," he concedes . . . Savarese, *Reasonable People*, 434.

17   At the end of the chapter . . . Savarese, *Reasonable People*, 435.

18   Stephen Shore, for example, speaks of . . . Stephen Shore, "What We
     Have to Tell You: A Roundtable with Self-Advocates from AutCom," ed.
     Emily Thornton Savarese, *Disability Studies Quarterly* 30, no. 1 (2010),
     http://dsq-sds.org/article/view/1073/1239.

19   Rita Rubin has told me . . . *Autism Is a World*, dir. Gerardine Wurzburg,
     State of the Art Inc. (2005).

21   "I resent these very hurtful conversations . . ." Savarese, *Reasonable
     People*, 433.

21   How could I not recall . . . Savarese, *Reasonable People*, 433.

ONE. FROM A WORLD AS FLUID AS THE SEA

23   Tito struggles with perseverative behavior . . . A hallmark of autism,
     according to the fifth edition of the *Diagnostic and Statistical Manual of
     Mental Disorders*, is repetitive behavior, which experts sometimes refer
     to as "perseveration." The autistic person *perseveres too long* in flicking his
     fingers or manipulating an object or making a sound. Whereas experts con-
     sider these actions to be disruptive and pointless, autistics consider them to
     be unavoidable and soothing.

23   The writing table, we learned . . . Melville dedicated *Pierre*, his seventh
     novel, to Mount Greylock: "To Greylock's Most Excellent Majesty," the
     dedication reads. W. D. Wetherell has called it a "brave and poignant
     thing to dedicate a novel to a mountain. Brave to match up an imperfect,
     man-made creation against one of nature's masterpieces; poignant to be so
     disenchanted with your fellow humans that a hillside seems your one and
     only friend." By this point, Melville's career as a writer was in great decline.
     Moby-Dick was a popular failure, and *Pierre*, a strange novel with incestuous
     undertones, would only make things worse. It's as if, in Greylock, Melville
     imagined the ideal reader. Tito and I would talk much about the disap-
     pointments that mark a writer's life, and he would be especially moved
     by Melville's loneliness and determination. See W. D. Wetherell, "Where
     Melville Paid Homage to a Mountain," *New York Times* (June 7, 1998).

25   "Why can't I just be . . ." Critics often read Melville's 1853 short story "Bartleby, the Scrivener" as an allegory for the writer's despair: he would "prefer not to" write the kind of fiction that sold in the commercial marketplace; he would also "prefer not to" have a job that took time from his writing.

25   I was interviewing him . . . See "Autism and the Concept of Neurodiversity," ed. Ralph James Savarese and Emily Thornton Savarese, *Disability Studies Quarterly* 30, no. 1 (2010), http://dsq-sds.org/issue/view/43.

26   At age twelve . . . Tito Rajarshi Mukhopadhyay, *Beyond the Silence: My Life, the World and Autism* (London: National Autistic Society, 2000).

26   In its American publication . . . Tito Rajarshi Mukhopadhyay, *The Mind Tree: A Miraculous Child Breaks the Silence of Autism* (New York: Arcade, 2003).

26   "I have been gifted this mind . . ." Mukhopadhyay, *Mind Tree*, 169.

26   Clearly a figure for the nonspeaking . . . Mukhopadhyay, *Mind Tree*, 169.

26   Tower of London . . . Mukhopadhyay, *Mind Tree*, 211.

27   "Tito is for real" . . . Quoted in Sarah Blakeslee, "A Boy, a Mother, and a Rare Map of Autism," *New York Times* (November 19, 2002).

27   "I've seen Tito sit in front . . ." Blakeslee, "A Boy."

28   In *The Mind Tree*, Tito . . . Mukhopadhyay, *Mind Tree*, 90.

28   He would later recount . . . Tito Rajarshi Mukhopadhyay, *How Can I Talk If My Lips Don't Move? Inside My Autistic Mind* (New York: Arcade, 2008), 176.

28   When they at last extricated themselves . . . In *How Can I Talk If My Lips Don't Move?* Tito reports that CAN "policed our every move, prevented opportunities for interviews, and signed away rights to our story on our behalf, without even having the courtesy of consulting us" (176–77). He is alluding, of course, to the publication of Portia Iverson's own memoir of autism, *Strange Son*, which depicts him in a terribly unfavorable manner. Iverson sold these rights to a production company for a huge sum. "The book *Strange Son* felt like a slap on my face from someone who Mother and I trusted most," Tito writes in his Amazon.com review of the book. "Overstimulation and [the] puberty stage can be difficult for many like me. But getting recorded . . . like that hurts more than my autism." At the end of his review, he tells Iverson's readers that his new book, *How Can I Talk*, will soon be published, and it will "describe my sensory conditions, in detail, so that other authors may be more equipped before writing about them as observers if they watch the show." He also notes that his review "got deleted again" from the Amazon website, sarcastically exclaiming, "Strange deletion!" And he warns that if anyone deletes his review again—say, Iverson or her agent or publisher—he will "put it back." See

http://www.amazon.com/Strange-Son-Portia-Iversen/dp/1573223115/ref
=sr_1_1?ie=UTF8&s=books&qid=1260669715&sr=1-1.

28   With a sort of heartbreaking pragmatism . . . Tito would later savagely
     satirize this period of his life. See Tito Rajarshi Mukhopadhyay, *Plankton
     Dreams: What I Learned in Special-Ed* (London: Open Humanities Press,
     2015).

28   The fact that DJ had in effect . . . The tagline for the documentary about
     his life, a documentary that DJ wrote and coproduced, reads, "Inclusion
     shouldn't be a lottery." See *Deej*, dir. Robert Rooy, Rooy Media and ITVS
     (2017).

29   In response to an interviewer's question . . . Quoted in Douglas Biklen,
     Autism and the Myth of the Person Alone (New York: New York University
     Press, 2005), 135.

29   I remembered one as we conversed . . . Mukhopadhyay, *Mind Tree*,
     158–59.

30   About his relationship with Soma . . . Quoted in Biklen, *Autism*, 128.

30   Soma had a reputation . . . Tito has described his mother like this: "And
     she became my teacher. A very firm teacher who would not give me the
     next meal unless I used the pencil in the proper way. And because I was
     constantly dropping the pencil down she tied it to my hands with a rubber
     band. And when I was not completing the questions which she had given
     me after reading a chapter, I was tied down to the chair till I finished it."
     Biklen, *Autism*, 128.

30   He would write books . . . Tito: "[Mother] has one demand. Become a
     somebody. And she means it." Biklen, *Autism*, 129.

30   When DJ would start thinking . . . And this is exactly what my wife, Emily,
     and I did: live apart for five years while DJ attended Oberlin. Emily lived
     in the town, and DJ lived in the dorm with an aide. She coordinated DJ's
     many support services and served as an additional aide for studying and
     socializing. Schools are only required to provide—that is, pay for—an aide
     while the student is in class. As economically advantaged as we were, we
     couldn't possibly afford round-the-clock support. An inclusion specialist,
     Emily also helped to ensure that DJ received the accommodations he needed.

31   *Apollo II on a horse* . . . Temple Grandin and Richard Panek, *The Autistic
     Brain: Thinking across the Spectrum* (Boston: Houghton Mifflin Harcourt,
     2013), 79.

31   Tito's thinking self had lost out . . . Grandin and Panek, *Autistic Brain*.

32   Grandin explains, "Auditory . . ." Temple Grandin, "My Mind Is a Web
     Browser: How People with Autism Think," *Cerebrum* 2, no. 1 (2000):
     14–22, quote on 16.

34   **When I pressed him . . .** "I knew that the doors of education would always remain closed for me through a school or through a college because [in India] Autism is another word for madness," Tito told Professor Biklen. "Why, it is not even allowed for a mad person to become a voter. So when one school said 'sorry' and the next school referred me to a school for the mentally retarded, mother did not even try to ask a third" (Biklen, *Autism*, 128). Tito's view of education has been deeply influenced by the early experience of rejection in India.

34   **Melville, too, was denied . . .** Though born into a prosperous family, Melville abandoned the dream of a proper education when his father's importing business went bankrupt and he later died, leaving his wife to support eight children. Melville was just thirteen at the time, and from this point forward he worked to supplement the family's income. At age twenty, he served as a cabin boy on a merchant ship bound for Liverpool, and at twenty-one he began his career as a whaler aboard the whaleship *Acushnet*.

36   **Tito did some more book-sniffing . . .** For an excellent discussion of the way some autistics alternatively engage with books, see Gillian Silverman, "Neurodiversity and the Revision of Book History," *PMLA* 131, no. 2 (2016): 307–23.

37   **In a new environment, he can't readily . . .** One of the prevailing theories of autism is called "weak central coherence" (WCC). First advanced by Uta Frith, it holds that autistics excel at perceiving details but struggle with perceiving wholes. Much has been made of this cognitive proclivity. Indeed, it has been marshaled to explain the traditional "triad of impairments"—in communication, imagination, and social interaction. It has also been presented as lamentably fixed, immune to intervention. The research on WCC is, however, anything but clear. Some scientists have found "local bias" but typical "global" ability, which means that autistics gravitate toward details but when asked about wholes they respond appropriately. In the case of Tito, fragmented perception initially impeded his ability to take in Arrowhead but it in no way prevented the kind of rich, global processing that literary tourism demands. For him, writing is not a record of what he saw and felt; rather, it is the means by which raw perceptual data become what neurotypicals commonly refer to as experience.

37   **According to the theory, in autism . . .** Laurent Mottron and Jacob Burak, "Sensory, Motor and Attentional Characteristics of Autistic Children," in *Encyclopedia on Early Childhood Development (2012–15)*, http://www.child-encyclopedia.com/sites/default/files/textes-experts/en/572/sensory-motor-and-attention-characteristics-of-autistic-children.pdf.

37   **A relative lack of "top-down processing . . ."** Mottron and colleagues write, "According to the EPF model, superiority of perceptual flow of information

in comparison to higher-order operations led to an atypical relationship between high and low order cognitive processes in autism, by making perceptual processes more difficult to control and more disruptive to the development of other behaviors and abilities" (28). See Laurent Mottron et al., "Enhanced Perceptual Functioning in Autism: An Update, and Eight Principles of Autistic Perception," *Journal of Autism and Developmental Disorders* 36, no. 1 (2006): 27–43.

38   "Hyperfocusing makes the world seem . . ." Mukhopadhyay, *Plankton Dreams*, 37.

38   "Visual imagery," write Vittorio . . . Hannah Wojciehowski and Vittorio Gallese, "How Stories Make Us Feel: Toward an Embodied Narratology," *California Italian Studies* 2, no. 1 (2011), http://old.unipr.it/arpa/mirror /pubs/pdffiles/Gallese/2011/california_italian_studies_2011.pdf.

38   Call it the upside of . . . Donna Williams, *Autism and Sensing: The Unlost Instinct* (London: Jessica Kingsley, 1998), 17.

38   For example, "The number . . ." Rajesh K. Kana et al., "Sentence Comprehension in Autism: Thinking in Pictures with Decreased Functional Connectivity," *Brain* 129, no. 9 (2006): 2484–93, quote on 2484.

39   In the low-imagery setting . . . Kana et al., "Sentence Comprehension," 2488–89.

39   For neurotypicals, a wealth of . . . Frida Martensson et al., "Modeling the Meaning of Words: Neural Correlates of Abstract and Concrete Noun Processing," *ACTA Neurobiologiae Experimentalis* 71, no. 4 (2011): 455–78, quote on 456.

39   As one literary critic has argued . . . Quoted in Alan Richardson, "Imagination: Literary and Cognitive Intersections," in *The Oxford Handbook of Cognitive Literary Studies*, ed. Lisa Zunshine (Oxford: Oxford University Press, 2015), 225–45, quote on 227.

40   Literature is our linguistic lifeline . . . Michel Serres, *The Five Senses: A Philosophy of Mingled Bodies* (London: Continuum, 2009), 128.

40   Even figures of speech . . . Simon Lacey, Randall Stilla, and K. Sathian, "Metaphorically Feeling: Comprehending Textural Metaphors Activates Somatosensory Cortex," *Brain and Language* 120, no. 3 (2012): 416–21. In an interview, one of the authors appealed to Aristotle to explain his team's results: "It's an old idea . . . that we understand complex things, abstract concepts, by reference to simpler things, concrete concepts." See Steven Cherry, "This Is Your Brain on Metaphor," *IEEE Spectrum* (2012), http://spectrum.ieee.org/podcast/biomedical/imaging/this-is-your-brain -on-metaphor. In fact, the study purports to confirm a central premise of conceptual metaphor theory: "that knowledge is structured around metaphorical mappings derived from physical experience."

40   If, in the words of . . . Julian Jaynes, *The Origin of Consciousness in the Breakdown of the Bicameral Mind* (Boston: Houghton Mifflin, 1976), 51.

40   "Abstract words," writes Jaynes . . . Jaynes, *Origin of Consciousness*. The metaphor of worn coins comes from Nietzsche's "On Truth and Lie in an Extra-Moral Sense."

40   Indeed, studies from 2012, 2013, and 2014 . . . In her seminal article "Understanding Minds and Metaphors: Insights from the Study of Figurative Language in Autism," Francesca Happé established the problem of metaphoric comprehension in autism, connecting it to impaired theory of mind (ToM). See Happé, "Understanding Minds and Metaphors: Insights from the Study of Figurative Language in Autism," *Metaphor and Symbol* 10, no. 4 (1995): 275–95. By comparing autistic children and children with language impairments, a study from 2005, however, disputed this thesis. It concluded that autism per se did not inhibit metaphor comprehension. As the author writes, "These analyses showed that only children with language impairment, with or without concurrent autistic features, were impaired on the metaphor task. . . . Semantic ability was a stronger predictor of performance on the metaphor task." See Courtenay Frazier Norbury, "The Relationship between Theory of Mind and Metaphor: Evidence from Children with Language Impairment and Autistic Spectrum Disorder," *British Journal of Developmental Psychology* 23, no. 3 (2005): 383–99, quote on 383. For evidence of autistic amenability to figurative language instruction, see Angela Persicke et al., "Establishing Metaphorical Reasoning in Children with Autism," *Research in Autism Spectrum Disorders* 6, no. 2 (2012): 913–20. In this study, "multiple exemplar training" not only increased metaphoric understanding but also enabled "generalization to untrained metaphors" (913). See also Jennifer Ranick et al., "Teaching Children with Autism to Detect and Respond to Deceptive Statements," *Research in Autism Spectrum Disorders* 7, no. 4 (2013): 503–8. Addressing the characteristic inability to lie and to perceive the lying of others in autism, researchers in this study used "multiple exemplar training, including rules, modeling, role-play, and immediate feedback" (503) to teach these abilities. The intervention was not only effective but "generalization was demonstrated to novel, untrained lies and to same-age peer confederates who were not involved in training" (503). The study's authors commented, "The results are promising for a behavioral approach to teaching nonliteral language comprehension and other forms of cognition to individuals with ASD" (503). Finally, see Sergio Melogno and Maria Antonietta Pinto, "Enhancing Metaphor and Metonymy Comprehension in Children with High-Functioning Autism Spectrum Disorder," *Psychology* 5, no. 11 (2014): 1375–83.

40   In my creative-writing courses at Grinnell . . . It's important to recognize that nonautistic people often need tutoring in metaphor comprehension.

Indeed, this is one of my primary responsibilities in introductory literature courses. In creative-writing courses, where the challenge is to produce
effective novel metaphors, I often have to show my nonautistic students
how to be less cognitive—less top-down and more bottom-up in their
thinking. While they can make sense of complex metaphors by professional
poets, they cannot generate such metaphors themselves. When your natural
inclination is to think in a bottom-up manner, as in autism, you follow
your eyes or nose or fingers or tongue and, as a result, make provocative
and potentially fruitful connections. Put simply, you organically disrespect
convention, while grounding insight in the body. In calling for "the system-
atic derangement of the senses" in art, Arthur Rimbaud wanted the balloon
of perception to be freed from its customary tether.

41   A researcher once tested . . . Beate Hermelin, *Bright Splinters of the Mind:
      A Personal Story of Research with Autistic Savants* (London: Jessica Kingsley,
      2001), 47. Hermelin writes, "Some psychologists investigating 'creativity' have
      suggested that such 'field independent' and 'diverse thinking' (i.e. forming
      unusual and unexpected associations) shows the workings of an original
      mind. Asperger would have agreed with this and would probably have
      taken such a far-fetched association as a piece of ravioli on a bed for a sign
      of what he called 'spontaneous thought,' not restricted by conventional and
      contextual boundaries" (47–48).

41   One almost wants to side with . . . Quoted in Gillian Silverman, *Bodies
      and Books* (Philadelphia: University of Pennsylvania Press, 2012), 89. The
      reviewer, George Washington Peck, was referring to *Pierre*, but he could
      just as easily have been talking about *Moby-Dick*. Silverman writes, "Peck
      was even more discomfited by Melville's use of 'word-combinations,' his
      tendency to pair language that 'we cannot, by any mental process hitherto
      discovered, induce our reasoning faculties to accept'" (89).

42   The aforementioned study involving . . . Hideya Koshino et al., "Functional
      Connectivity in an fMRI Working Memory Task in High-Functioning Au-
      tism," *NeuroImage* 24, no. 3 (2005): 810–21, quote on 818–19.

42   The control group "coded each stimulus letter verbally . . ." Koshino et al.,
      "Functional Connectivity," 818.

43   This evidence led researchers to postulate . . . Koshino et al., "Functional
      Connectivity," 819.

43   "Designs can be visual . . ." See Ralph James Savarese, "More Than a Thing
      to Ignore: An Interview with Tito Rajarshi Mukhopadhyay," *Disability Stud-
      ies Quarterly* 30, no. 1 (2010), http://dsq-sds.org/article/view/1056/1235.

43   The pattern . . . Savarese, "More Than a Thing to Ignore."

43   Although he obviously learned . . . Savarese, "More Than a Thing to
      Ignore."

43   He has even compared . . . Savarese, "More Than a Thing to Ignore."

43   A study from 2008 found . . . Anna Järvinen-Pasley et al., "Enhanced Perceptual Processing of Speech in Autism," *Developmental Science* 11, no. 1 (2008): 109–21, quote on 109.

43   As Reuven Tsur notes . . . Reuven Tsur, "The Poetic Mode of Speech Perception Revisited: What Our Ear Tells Our Mind," lecture (2010), http://www.tau.ac.il/~tsurxx/Poetic_Mode_Revisited.pdf.

43   "We hear a unitary phoneme . . ." Tsur, "Poetic Mode."

43–44   In the process . . . Tsur, "Poetic Mode."

44   In contrast to the generalizing talent . . . Tuulia Lepisto, "Cortical Processing of Speech and Non-speech Sounds in Autism and Asperger Syndrome" (PhD dissertation, University of Helsinki, 2008), 40.

44   In addition, autistics do not appear to have . . . Järvinen-Pasley et al., "Enhanced," 117.

44   As the authors of another study comment . . . A. Klin et al., "The Enactive Mind, or from Actions to Cognition: Lessons from Autism," *Philosophical Transactions of the Royal Society of London B: Biological Sciences* 358, no. 1430 (2003): 345–60, quote on 349.

44–45   Instructed to listen to a book . . . Mukhopadhyay, *How Can I Talk*, 200–201.

45   When the researcher asked . . . Mukhopadhyay, *How Can I Talk*, 201.

45   Diane Sawyer, the former host . . . Diane Sawyer, *Good Morning, America* (June 10, 2008).

46   While the sensory frequently . . . Williams, *Autism and Sensing*, 15.

46   For her this sort of . . . Williams, *Autism and Sensing*, 15.

47   "What is my contribution . . ." Mukhopadhyay, *How Can I Talk*, 216.

47   "With my physical . . ." Mukhopadhyay, *How Can I Talk*, 216.

47   But then his words . . . Mukhopadhyay, *How Can I Talk*, 216.

48   In a letter to Nathaniel Hawthorne . . . Letter to Hawthorne, June 1851, http://www.melville.org/letter3.htm.

48   Built in 1841 . . . For information about the *Morgan*, see "Charles W. Morgan: The Last Wooden Whaleship in the World," Mystic Seaport, http://www.mysticseaport.org/visit/explore/morgan/. See also "The Ship," Mystic Seaport, http://www.mysticseaport.org/voyage/ship/.

49   "When the line is darting out . . ." Ishmael also compares being seated in the boat to men juggling snakes: "Thus the whale-line folds the whole boat in its complicated coils, twisting and writhing around in almost every

direction. All the oarsmen are involved in its perilous contortions; so that to the timid eye of the landsman, they seem as Indian Jugglers, with the deadliest snakes sportively festooning their limbs." Herman Melville, *Moby-Dick: A Longman Critical Edition*, ed. John Bryant and Haskell Springer (New York: Longman, 2006), 252.

49   In preparing for our trip . . . See "Whales and Hunting," New Bedford Whaling Museum, https://www.whalingmuseum.org/learn/research -topics/overview-of-north-american-whaling/whales-hunting.

50   "I am autism," a particularly . . . "Horrific Autism Speaks 'I Am Autism' Ad Transcript," ASAN, http://autisticadvocacy.org/2009/09/horrific -autism-speaks-i-am-autism-ad-transcript/.

50   In 2015 alone . . . See "2016 Day of Mourning Vigils," ASAN (January 15, 2016), http://autisticadvocacy.org/2016/01/2016-day-of-mourning -vigils/.

52   In this way, it required . . . The social construction of normalcy affects not only humans but also animals insofar as *any* departure from the cognitive norm of neurotypical Homo sapiens is frequently viewed as "lack." It shouldn't be surprising that autistic environmentalists seek to link issues of biodiversity with those of human neurodiversity. Increasingly the fields of disability studies and animal studies are cross-fertilizing one another.

53   Admittedly, it is something of a cottage industry . . . I can't think of another author who was as interested as Melville in the many different kinds of minds that populated the nineteenth century before the medicalization of cognitive difference. These minds were especially prevalent on whaling vessels. The prominent autism researcher Simon Baron-Cohen has suggested that Caspar Hauser, a famous eighteenth-century "wild child" who grew up imprisoned in a dark, underground cell, is "the first well-documented case of autism in literature, or even in history." See "The Best Books on Autism and Asperger Syndrome Recommended by Simon Baron-Cohen," interview by Cal Flyn, 2010, http://fivebooks .com/interview/simon-baron-cohen-on-autism-and-asperger-syndrome/. Melville, interestingly enough, makes key allusions to Hauser in *Pierre*, *The Confidence Man*, and *Billy Budd*. Each of these novels takes up the issue of cognitive disability. For an analysis of these allusions and Melville's treatment of cognitive disability, see Ralph James Savarese, "Neurocosmopolitan Melville," *Leviathan: A Journal of Melville Studies* 15, no. 2 (2013): 7–19. I had never paid attention to the character of the carpenter until Tito pointed him out; when he did, he said that the carpenter reminded him of Temple Grandin.

53   The portrait is indeed highly suggestive . . . Quoted in Oliver Sacks, *An Anthropologist on Mars: Seven Paradoxical Tales* (New York: Vintage, 1996), 252–53.

55   In a letter . . . Herman Melville, *The Writings of Herman Melville: Correspondence*, ed. Lynn Horth (Evanston, IL: Northwestern University Press, 1993), 173.

TWO. THE HEAVENS OF THE BRAIN

57   He dreamt of lunch . . . Quoted in Douglas Biklen, *Autism and the Myth of the Person Alone* (New York: New York University Press, 2005), 250.

57   Lunch should be "a time . . ." Biklen, *Autism*, 250.

57   "My ears hear colossally well . . ." Biklen, *Autism*, 250. Jamie once explained to a writer from *People Magazine* why the TV bothered him: "The TV drove me crazy because I heard every molecule of energy moving within the nucleus of sound." See Thomas Fields-Meyer, "Autism: Breaking the Silence," *People* (April 11, 2005).

57   It arrived, the burly . . . Quoted in Biklen, *Autism*, 252.

57   He believed his "cells . . ." Biklen, *Autism*, 252.

57   "Sensory integration has been like . . ." Biklen, *Autism*, 252.

57–58   "It wraps up the stingers . . ." Biklen, *Autism*, 252.

58   For instance, Jamie used . . . Jamie Burke, "The Power of Communication and Collaboration: When Partnership Supports the Potential," presentation, "Making Communication Happen" conference, Burlington, VT (2010).

58   According to Jamie . . . Quoted in Biklen, *Autism*, 251.

58   Suddenly, Jamie could hear . . . Biklen, *Autism*, 251.

58   "Before," he commented . . . Biklen, *Autism*, 251.

58   These therapies, Jamie contended . . . Burke, "Power of Communication."

58   "In elementary school, beanbag . . ." Burke, "Power of Communication."

58   To make lunch bearable . . . Burke, "Power of Communication."

59   He, too, had his quirks . . . See, for example, Robert M. Thorson, "Thoreau and Asperger Syndrome?," *Thoreau Society Bulletin*, no. 262 (2008), https://archive.org/stream/thoreausociety2008262unse /thoreausociety2008262unse_djvu.txt. Or see John Mahoney, "A Psychologist Looks Thoreau in the Eye: Did He Meet Criteria for Asperger Disorder?," *Thoreau Society Bulletin*, no. 267 (2009), https://archive.org/stream /thoreausociety2009267unse/thoreausociety2009267unse_djvu.txt.

59   "Really, I think my stims . . ." Burke, "Power of Communication." By "stims," Jamie means perseverative behavior.

59   "I feel stronger when . . ." Burke, "Power of Communication."

59   Jamie much preferred a . . . Burke, "Power of Communication."

59   "Certainly students like me . . ." Burke, "Power of Communication."

59   "I have been truly fortunate . . ." Burke, "Power of Communication."

60   He was especially appreciative . . . Burke, "Power of Communication."

60   "I am not planning a . . ." Burke, "Power of Communication." That support extends to friendship. And yet Jamie doesn't want simply to be "helped." He doesn't want support to come at the expense of his independence or autonomy. "In friendships," he writes, "it is important to be as a tiger, camouflaged in the background. For I do need the support, but I do not want to have that in full view. It is a dance of steps that takes much rehearsing to accomplish the success, but it is vital."

60   Speaking directly to educators . . . Burke, "Power of Communication."

60   "I am greatly perplexed when . . ." Burke, "Power of Communication."

60   The summer before my son, DJ . . . This exchange can be seen in *Deej*, the documentary about my son. *Deej*, dir. Rob Rooy, Rob Rooy Media and ITVS (2017).

60   For him autism was . . . Burke, "Power of Communication."

60   But lest you hear too much resignation . . . The previously cited article from *People* recounts Jamie's breakthrough. As he began to speak, he typed, "A new era is coming."

60   As a small child, he had been taught . . . See my book *Reasonable People: A Memoir of Autism and Adoption* (New York: Other Press, 2007) for a discussion of this technique and the controversy that swirls around it. In Jamie's case that controversy is irrelevant because he types independently— that is, without facilitation.

60   "I decided to take a risk . . ." Biklen, *Autism*, 251.

60   "I know my voice . . ." Biklen, *Autism*, 251.

60   "When I was growing up . . ." Biklen, *Autism*, 250–51.

61   "This is the journey I am on" . . . Burke, "Power of Communication."

61   "It has taken many, many people . . ." Burke, "Power of Communication."

61   "I was a little boy . . ." Burke, "Power of Communication."

62   At the end of the book, he . . . Thomas Irmer, "An Interview with Leslie Marmon Silko," *Write Stuff*, http://www.altx.com/interviews/silko.html.

62   As the Western writer . . . Larry McMurtry, "Introduction," in Leslie Marmon Silko, *Ceremony* (New York: Penguin, 2007), xxi.

62   The Native writer . . . McMurtry, "Introduction," xxii.

62   In every sense, my son, DJ . . . When DJ was admitted to Oberlin, Jamie sent him this note:

dearest dj

I hear that the news is very lovely to your ears and heart about oberlin college and the next beginning. this is the next strong power of
movement, communicating the call of truth. love us who seemingly,
boldly, simply-directed our lives to these moments of processing the
power of potential. you are certainly my friend and journeyman dj.

your friend in life, Jamie

62   I knew that, having now graduated . . . It's worth pausing to stress once
again the achievement of a college degree. As he awaited graduation, Jamie
sent this note to friends and family:

my dearest friends of the spirit,

today my letter arrived that will send me to another portion of my
journey. this is emotional for engaging the review of memories of the
good and the difficult. reasoning this as an educational experience
fundamentally required a larger lens of possibility than i formulated
on many times in this journey. i love that you hold both my true
abilities and my true identity in your minds. this is highly exciting to
me attempting to reform the ideas of the power of challenge.

your friend in the journey, and with love, Jamie

63   As he pointed out, his hometown . . . As in the chapter about Tito,
remarks without citation occurred in the course of our Skype
conversations.

63   I have uprooted the Great White Pine Tree . . . For more information
about the Great Law of Peace, see the "History" page of the Onondaga
Nation website, http://www.onondaganation.org/history/.

63   The Onondaga welcomed them . . . For more about the 1613 treaty with
the Dutch, see "Two Row Wampum—Guswenta," Onondaga Nation,
http://www.onondaganation.org/culture/wampum/two-row-wampum
-belt-guswenta/.

63   The discovery of salty . . . For more on the history of salt production on
Lake Onondaga, see Valerie Jackson Bell, "The Onondaga New York Salt
Works (1654–1926)," *Science Tribune*, October 1998, http://www.tribunes
.com/tribune/sel/bell.htm.

64   It was as if Skyholder . . . For a concise history of Lake Onondaga, see the
Wikipedia entry at https://en.wikipedia.org/wiki/Onondaga_Lake. For
a more detailed history, see the documentary *Beneath the Surface: The Storied History of Lake Onondaga*, Onondaga Historical Association (2017).

64   In English we speak . . . Ancient Roman soldiers were often paid with
salt. The word *salary* comes from the Latin word *salarium*, which meant a
soldier's allowance to buy salt.

64   **She also exposed him to . . .** Only recently have autism professionals begun to encourage "restricted interests" as a way of communicating with autistic people and drawing them into more typical sociality. The assumption had always been that such interests were at best meaningless and at worst detrimental. The obvious irony is that the notion of "restricted interests" could easily be applied to all sorts of neurotypical behavior—from Facebook to TV watching to shopping. In this case, Jamie's "obsession" with Native American culture seems a fitting corrective to Anglo-American neglect and conquest.

64   **As one website puts it . . .** See Interactive Autism Network, "Restricted Interests, Obsessions, 'Special Topics,' and Attention Deficits" (April 2, 2007), https://iancommunity.org/cs/challenging_behavior/challenging_behavior_restricted_interests.

65   **Imagine a philosophy so organically accepting . . .** How people react to my son and the other autistics I know has taught me much about the limits of a "diversity" model, which often begrudgingly makes room for difference while refusing to relinquish the idea of a racial, ethnic, gender, class, or cognitive norm.

65   **When I asked him how . . .** I met a number of the therapists who worked with Jamie, and I found their approaches to the many challenges of classical autism to be deeply humane and often ingenious. Two people deserve special mention: Maureen Brady, an occupational therapist, and Mark Fohs, a psychologist.

66   **Jamie's understanding of traumatic recovery . . .** It took me years as the father of a traumatized child to see that vanquishing fear was not only impossible but also counterproductive. Such fear, Jamie teaches us, is a sign of one's fundamental "connection to life." This vitality must be preserved as the person works through an overwhelming sense of danger.

66   **Rather, by identifying with him . . .** Jamie called this phenomenon "the Native belief that all exists in the same time representation."

68   **"What I called a . . ."** Temple Grandin and Richard Panek, *The Autistic Brain: Thinking across the Spectrum* (Boston: Houghton Mifflin Harcourt, 2013), 155, emphasis original.

68   **As Grandin notes, "People . . ."** Grandin and Panek, *Autistic Brain*, 156.

68   **In the 1980s, a mathematician . . .** Quoted in Grandin and Panek, *Autistic Brain*, 153.

70   **Just as Grandin learned . . .** When Grandin was tested using high-definition fiber tracking, her visual track was shown to be 400 percent of a control subject's; in contrast, the "say what you see" connection, which links vision with language, was 1 percent of a control subject's. She attributes her ability to draw complex, 3D cattle-processing designs to the

enhanced visuospatial, and reduced linguistic, skills of autism. See Grandin and Panek, *Autistic Brain*, 44–45.

70 When Jamie reported that he "really enjoys . . ." Chapter 3 of Laura Otis's *Rethinking Thought: Inside the Minds of Creative Scientists and Artists* (New York: Oxford University Press, 2015) is bracingly titled "The Vast Range of Visual Worlds." It bears repeating that generalizations can only take us so far. I provisionally deploy such generalizations in order to make literature seem more hospitable to autism than it has traditionally been thought to be. That said, there is as much variety in the autistic population as there is in the nonautistic population. Even as Grandin has complicated her initial, reductive dichotomy—visual *or* verbal—she has continued to posit other dichotomies: object *or* spatial visualizers. As Otis points out, "Visual thinking may be articulable into more than two styles" (113). Indeed, visual thinking may involve, as in Jamie's case, a mix of two or more styles.

71 "I think in pictures . . ." Temple Grandin, *Thinking in Pictures*, expanded ed. (New York: Vintage, 2006), 3.

72 With this kind of seeing . . . Here, the implications of autistic perception for the environmental movement seem profound: when you perceive the natural world in "the process of creation," you are perhaps more inclined to care for it.

72 "Delayed decoding," to borrow another scholar's . . . The phrase is Ian Watt's. See Melba Cuddy-Keane, "Narration, Navigation, and Nonconscious Thought: Neuroscientific and Literary Approaches to the Thinking Body," *University of Toronto Quarterly* 79, no. 2 (2010): 680–701.

72 The researcher Tim Langdell . . . Quoted in Grandin and Panek, *Autistic Brain*, 121.

72 As Grandin writes, "The . . ." Grandin and Panek, *Autistic Brain*, 131.

72 Hans Asperger, the doctor . . . Steve Silberman, "Was Dr. Asperger a Nazi? The Question Still Haunts Autism," National Public Radio (January 20, 2016), http://www.npr.org/sections/health-shots/2016/01/20/463603652/was-dr-asperger-a-nazi-the-question-still-haunts-autism. A forthcoming book by Edith Sheffer, *Asperger's Children: The Origins of Autism in Nazi Vienna*, paints a very different picture of Asperger. I have not read it, but in a recent editorial, Sheffer writes, "Asperger was long seen as a resistor of the Third Reich, yet his work was, in fact, inextricably linked with the rise of Nazism and its deadly programs." See Edith Sheffer, "The Nazi History behind 'Asperger,'" *New York Times*, March 31, 2018.

74 Neurobiological accounts of trauma . . . See, for example, Bessel van der Kolk, "Clinical Implications of Neuroscience Research in PTSD," *Annals of the New York Academy of Sciences* 1071, no. 1 (2006): 277–93. See also van der Kolk, "Psychobiology of Post-traumatic Stress Disorder," in *Textbook*

of Biological Psychiatry, ed. Jaak Panksepp (Hoboken, NJ: Wiley & Sons, 2004), 319–44. Finally, see "Yoga and Post-traumatic Stress Disorder: An Interview with Bessel van der Kolk, MD," http://www.traumacenter.org /clients/maginside.su09.p12-13.pdf. Van der Kolk has championed the importance of body-based therapies for trauma because trauma lodges at the level of the sensory or perceptual—beneath consciousness. The talking cure, while clearly still important, is too cognitive to fundamentally change how the body itself is afraid, how the person's sensory system has been hijacked by fear and hypervigilance.

75   Robertson, who was vice president . . . Scott Michael Robertson, "Neuro-diversity, Quality of Life, and Autistic Adults: Shifting Research and Professional Focuses onto Real-Life Challenges," *Disability Studies Quarterly* 30, no. 1 (2010), http://dsq-sds.org/article/view/1069/1234.

75   "I must send forward my bold appreciation . . ." See Emily Thornton Savarese, "'The Superior Half of Speaking': An Introduction," *Disability Studies Quarterly* 30, no. 1 (2010), http://dsq-sds.org/article/view/1062/1230.

76   The social psychologist Carol Gilligan . . . Carol Gilligan, *In a Different Voice: Psychological Theory and Women's Development* (Cambridge, MA: Harvard University Press, 1993), xvi.

76   After all, "listening," as . . . Dawn Prince, "The Silence Between: An Autoethnographic Examination of the Language Prejudice and Its Impact on the Assessment of Autistic and Animal Intelligence," *Disability Studies Quarterly* 30, no. 1 (2010), http://dsq-sds.org/article/view/1055/1242.

76   That view had emerged when . . . A less modular view of the brain allows us to see autism as a complex condition in which sensorimotor challenges can have profound effects on high-order thought and sociality. It also allows for the possibility of innovative treatments and accommodations that intervene in ways previously thought irrelevant to the core "deficits" in autism.

76   In fact, Gerald Edelman . . . Gerald M. Edelman, *Second Nature: Brain Science and Human Knowledge* (New Haven, CT: Yale University Press, 2007), 61.

76   Language, argued Marcel . . . Quoted in Iain McGilchrist, *The Master and His Emissary: The Divided Brain and the Making of the Western World* (New Haven, CT: Yale University Press, 2012), 111.

76   It evolved from "utterances . . ." McGilchrist, *Master*, 111.

76–77   Or as Iain McGilchrist put it . . . McGilchrist, *Master*, 119.

77   Over the last five or six years . . . Quoted in Ralph James Savarese, "Moving the Field: The Sensorimotor Perspective on Autism," *Frontiers in Integrative Neuroscience* 7, no. 6 (2013), http://journal.frontiersin.org/article /10.3389/fnint.2013.00006/full.

77   This study went so far as . . . Savarese, "Moving the Field."

77   If we remember the pithy . . . Quoted in Pat Amos, "Rhythm and Timing in Autism," in *Autism: The Movement Perspective*, ed. Elizabeth B. Torres and Anne M. Donnellan (Frontiers, 2015), eBook, 141, http://journal.frontiersin.org/researchtopic/801/autism-the-movement-perspective.

77   We might also be less tempted . . . Maria Brincker and Elizabeth B. Torres, "Noise from the Periphery of Autism," in Torres and Donnellan, *Autism*, 175, http://journal.frontiersin.org/researchtopic/801/autism-the-movement-perspective.

77   This last bit is researcher-speak . . . Amos nicely evokes the idea of "downstream effects" when she references early video research on the atypical movements of autistic infants and toddlers: "Watching the subtle struggles embodied in these videos, viewers are reminded of the ways typically developing children proceed to capture their bodies' spontaneous movements in increasingly intentional and goal-directed ways . . . , and of the profound ways that a lack of predictable movements and reflexes would alter that dynamic, creating a developmental cascade that flows with increasing velocity toward an autism diagnosis" (Amos, "Rhythm," 142).

77   I quote Elizabeth . . . Elizabeth Torres and Anne Donnellan, "Introduction," in Torres and Donnellan, *Autism*, 2, http://journal.frontiersin.org/researchtopic/801/autism-the-movement-perspective.

78   Analyzing the movements of . . . Quoted in Maria Brincker, "Navigating beyond 'Here and Now' Affordances—On Sensorimotor Maturation and 'False Belief' Performance," *Frontiers in Psychology* 5 (2014), http://www.ncbi.nlm.nih.gov/pmc/articles/PMC4266020/.

78   These toddlers haven't yet assimilated . . . Brincker and Torres, "Noise," 175.

78   Brincker views "'sensorimotor priors.' . . ." Brincker, "Navigating."

78   In contrast, autistics must . . . Brincker, "Navigating."

78   I am unaware of anyone . . . Reviewing this manuscript for publication, I came across a study that does exactly this: propose a link between movement difficulties in autism and perceptual predilections—what the authors describe as "either a reduced drive to extract overall meaning, termed Weak Central Coherence . . . or an increased dependence on local detail, termed Enhanced Perceptual Functioning." The authors write, "An alternative [explanation for movement difficulties] is that autistic individuals are able to plan individual aspects of their actions (how to grasp the bar) but are less good at organizing the temporal detail of the action in the chaining tasks. Thus, autistic individuals may plan and execute each component of the action separately and the degree to which they separate action sub-goals may depend on whether they are low or high functioning. . . . Both [weak central

coherence and enhanced perceptual functioning] emphasize that individuals with autism are good at processing details and small components but less good at integrating these into a global percept. Further study of the relationship between perceptual integration and motor integration could be used to test this possibility." See Emma Gowen and Antonia Hamilton, "Motor Abilities in Autism: A Review Using a Computational Context," *Journal of Autism and Developmental Disorders* 43, no. 2 (2013): 323–44, http://www.antoniahamilton.com/GowenHamilton_JADD_2012.pdf.

79   For this reason, another researcher . . . Amos, "Rhythm," 146.

79   Amos concludes, "If these . . ." Amos, "Rhythm," 146.

79   As the authors of yet another . . . Michael W. Hardy and A. Blythe Lagasse, "Rhythm, Movement and Autism: Using Rhythmic Rehabilitation Research as a Model for Autism," in Torres and Donnellan, *Autism*, 90.

79   Research has demonstrated that auditory . . . Hardy and Lagasse, "Rhythm," 93.

79   It affects both "the . . ." Hardy and Lagasse, "Rhythm," 90.

79–80   By "influencing motor . . ." Hardy and Lagasse, "Rhythm," 93.

80   As the authors note, the cerebellum . . . Hardy and Lagasse, "Rhythm," 90.

80   It "predicts the timing . . ." Hardy and Lagasse, "Rhythm," 92.

80   "So many things were hard . . ." Biklen, *Autism*, 251.

80   About that latter milestone, which . . . Biklen, *Autism*, 251.

80   "Like saying letters, mostly there . . ." Biklen, *Autism*, 251.

80   The authors of the aforementioned . . . Hardy and Lagasse, "Rhythm," 93.

80   If we should no longer think . . . Currently under assault as impractical, if not worthless, the humanities need a revival that tries to convert its opponents less by means of extolling the value of ideological critique or cultural refinement than by revealing the forgotten or undiscovered uses of art as they relate to the body and human functioning. In this way, I am perplexed by the categorical resistance of many humanities scholars to the burgeoning field of neurohumanities—really, to any use of science in the humanities. This is not to say that I dismiss the need for ideological critique or that I fail to recognize the privileged enthrallment of reading great books. Indeed, what motivates this book is precisely a desire to render such enthrallment less privileged and to critique the prevailing stereotypes of autism. At the same time, I wish to broaden the way that we traditionally conceive of the importance of humanistic inquiry.

80–81   They are not simply effete refinement . . . In *How the Mind Works*, Pinker completely dismisses the adaptive value of music. "It confers no survival advantage," he writes. It is simply "an exquisite confection crafted to tickle the sensitive spots of . . . our mental faculties." See Steven Pinker, *How the Mind Works* (New York: W. W. Norton, 1997), 534.

81   "The predictability of musical . . ." Hardy and Lagasse, "Rhythm," 94.

81   "It gives me a secured feeling . . ." See Ralph James Savarese, "More Than a Thing to Ignore: An Interview with Tito Rajarshi Mukhopadhyay," *Disability Studies Quarterly* 30, no. 1 (2010), http://dsq-sds.org/article/view/1056/1235.

81   When I pressed Tito on this notion . . . Savarese, "More Than a Thing to Ignore." At least one study has shown that metrical poetry recitation—specifically, hexameter verse—"exerts a strong influence on [respiratory sinus arrhythmia, or RSA]," which is low in autism and other conditions marked by anxiety, through cardiorespiratory synchronization. RSA is the natural, coordinated, and indeed rhythmic variation in heartbeat as it relates to breathing. Interestingly, the benefits of hexameter recitation exceeded those of controlled breathing exercises without such recitation. Formal poetry, as Tito implies, may bring not only the cortical and subcortical minds but also the heart and lungs into better relation. It may honor, in short, the whole organism—the linguistic *animal*. See Dirk Cysarz et al., "Oscillations of Heart Rate and Respiration Synchronize during Poetry Recitation," *American Journal of Heart and Circulatory Physiology* 287, no. 2 (2004), http://www.waldorfresearchinstitute.org/pdf/RCSpeechRes.pdf.

81   Delving into the matter . . . Christian Obermeier et al., "Aesthetic and Emotional Effects of Meter and Rhyme in Poetry," *Frontiers in Psychology* 4 (2013): 10, http://journal.frontiersin.org/article/10.3389/fpsyg.2013.00010/full.

81   There was even evidence that . . . Obermeier et al., "Aesthetic."

81   It may also aid in what . . . Fredrick Turner and Ernst Pöppel, "The Neural Lyre: Poetic Meter, the Brain, and Time," *Poetry* (August 1983): 24, http://munnecke.com/papers/Turner-Neural-Lyre.pdf.

81   "By ruling out certain rhythmic . . ." Turner and Pöppel, "Neural Lyre."

81   That need, as I have shown . . . Without controlled novelty, the autistic person must resort to habit as a way of managing anxiety. As Tito explains, "Habit can accomplish what reasoning cannot. People don't understand why there is such an urge for an autistic person like me to scribble on my hand with a ballpoint pen, almost giving it a Queequeg-like look. The habit of making marks, the habit of looking at these marks, the habit of fondly rediscovering them, and the habit of looking at them even more when my visual surroundings become complicated and drown my eyes—habit provides a modicum of comfort." "Habit is parented," Tito goes on, mischievously making a habit of using that word. "Habit is watered and

sunned. Habit fruits. Habit seeds. I am the father of my habit. I am ready to grandfather it." "One can never have enough hand-flapping, back-rocking, finger-flipping, string-twirling or pen-marking," he says. "Habit thrives in the nerves of autism." By providing some means of controlled novelty, the need for habit can loosen.

82   **Rarely do parents or clinicians . . . I can't** underscore this point enough. These key stakeholders are frequently dismissed and patronized. Yes, I say this as a (defensive) parent, but if you simply take the measure of where the scientific community currently stands on autism, you will miss all sorts of developments—both with respect to what autism, in all of its heterogeneity, is and with respect to the innovative supports and accommodations that allow autistic people to flourish.

82   **With Sheree sitting quietly beside him . . .** You can listen to the program on the Iowa Public Radio website: "Autism As Diversity" (August 10, 2012), http://iowapublicradio.org/post/autism-diversity#stream/0.

82   **"It's seeing and hearing . . ."** Alicia A. Broderick and Christi Kasa-Hendrickson, "'Say Just One Word at First': The Emergence of Reliable Speech in a Student Labeled with Autism," *Journal of the Association for Persons with Severe Handicaps* 26, no. 1 (2001): 13–24, quote on 21.

83   **A recent study revealed . . .** Josef Rauschecker et al., "Differentially Recruited Brain Areas for Familiar and Unfamiliar Segments of a Progressively Presented Musical Sequence," presentation, Neuroscience conference, New Orleans, LA (2012).

83   **"Exposure to the printed word . . ."** Broderick and Kasa-Hendrickson, "'Say Just One Word,'" 22.

84   **A recent study . . .** Martin Lang et al., "Lost in the Rhythm: Effects of Rhythm on Subsequent Interpersonal Coordination," *Cognitive Science* 40, no. 7 (2015): 1797–815, https://www.researchgate.net/publication /282709256_Lost_in_the_Rhythm_Effects_of_Rhythm_on_Subsequent _Interpersonal_Coordination (pp. 1–19).

84   **It confirmed that, "having . . ."** Lang et al., "Lost in the Rhythm," 1, 11.

84   **Here we have the very basis . . .** Neural coupling appears to characterize all sorts of pleasurable social behavior. A study from 2010 found that in successful verbal communication "the speaker's activity is spatially and temporally coupled with the listener's activity" (14425). It also noted that such "coupling vanishes when participants fail to communicate" (14425). No one has tested whether rhythm can amplify verbal coupling, but I suspect it can. See Greg J. Stephens, Lauren J. Silbert, and Uri Hasson, "Speaker-Listener Neural Coupling Underlies Successful Communication," *Proceedings of the National Academy of Sciences* 107, no. 32 (2010): 14425–30.

84   The future will not be worth living . . . "A pattern moved into my brain, giving direction to my hands," Jamie has said of learning to tie his shoes "after much practice" (Biklen, *Autism*, 250). Just as our motor systems can "listen" in the absence of sound, so our auditory system can move in the absence of movement—both foster "intelligent continuation," as I have suggested. A spiritual understanding of these neurological workarounds—"a pattern moved into my brain"—allows us to see a way forward for Native American people, a way that remembers the future by rediscovering the past. At the very end of the novel, Silko writes, "[Tayo] had arrived at a convergence of patterns; he could see them clearly now. The stars had always been with them, existing beyond memory. . . . Under these same stars the people had come down from White House in the North" (235).

85   The current concepts of embodied, embedded . . . For more on these different types of cognition and their relation to disability, see Ralph James Savarese, "Cognition," in *Keywords for Disability Studies*, ed. Rachel Adams, Benjamin Reiss, and David Serlin (New York: New York University Press, 2015), 40–42.

85   In this way, the idea of medicine . . . Traditionally, the field of disability studies has been deeply critical and suspicious of the medical and scientific fields, which it rightly sees as purveyors of pathology and dehumanizing rehabilitation schemes. But disability studies often goes too far in rejecting medicine and science. As Jamie's case makes clear, when broadly and humanely construed, healing practices restore the community of which an individual is a part as much as it does the individual himself. Indeed, healing doesn't take place *in* the individual; it takes place in the field of relation. For decades autistics have been depicted as inexorably alone, and so any therapy that facilitates greater inclusion and self-determination, while insisting on the work that nonautistic people must do to transform society, should be embraced.

THREE. ANDYS AND AUTIES

88   Luft's verbal sparring with . . . See Rachel Cohen-Rottenberg, "Deconstructing Autism as an Empathy Disorder," http://www.disabilityandrepresentation.com/deconstructing-autism-as-an-empathy-disorder-a-literature-review/. See also Rachel Cohen-Rottenberg, "Unwarranted Conclusions and the Potential for Harm: My Reply to Simon Baron-Cohen," https://autismandempathyblog.wordpress.com/unwarranted-conclusions-and-the-potential-for-harm-my-reply-to-simon-baron-cohen/.

88   Though careful to appear both . . . Cohen-Rottenberg, "Unwarranted Conclusions."

89   In *The Wounded Storyteller*, Arthur . . . Arthur W. Frank, *The Wounded Storyteller: Body, Illness, and Ethics* (Chicago: University of Chicago Press,

1995). See my own Frank-inspired article, "Toward a Postcolonial Neurology: Autism, Tito Mukhopadhyay, and a New Geo-poetics of the Body," *Journal of Literary and Cultural Disability Studies* 4, no. 3 (2010): 273–90.

89   I knew that Dawn Prince had . . . See Dawn Prince-Hughes, *Songs of the Gorilla Nation: My Journey through Autism* (New York: Broadway, 2005).

89   Prince followed up that book . . . Dawn Prince, *Circus of Souls: How I Discovered We Are All Freaks Passing for Normal* (Seattle: CreateSpace, 2013).

90   For example, the British psychiatrist . . . See William R. Albury, "From Changelings to Extraterrestrials: Depictions of Autism in Popular Culture," *Hektoen International: A Journal of Medical Humanities* 3, no. 3 (2011), http://hekint.org/from-changelings-to-extraterrestrials-depictions-of-autism-in-popular-culture/.

90   In "Dating Data," a chapter . . . Temple Grandin, *Thinking in Pictures*, expanded ed. (New York: Vintage, 2006), 152. All subsequent citations in this chapter refer to this edition.

90   "When he tried to be romantic" . . . Grandin, *Thinking*, 154.

90   "Even very able adults with autism . . ." Grandin, *Thinking*, 154.

90   As just such an adult . . . Grandin, *Thinking*, 154.

90   In an important article, the philosopher . . . Ian Hacking, "Autistic Autobiography," *Philosophical Transactions of the Royal Society of London B: Biological Sciences* 364, no. 1522: 1467–73.

91   Whereas she believed that . . . Grandin, *Thinking*, 154.

91   As the *Enterprise* "boldly . . ." Nick Walker and I independently coined the term "neurocosmopolitanism." See Savarese, "Toward a Postcolonial Neurology"; Ralph James Savarese and Lisa Zunshine, "The Critic as Neurocosmopolite; Or, What Cognitive Approaches to Literature Can Learn from Disability Studies," *Narrative* 22, no. 1 (2014): 17–44; Ralph James Savarese, "What Some Autistics Can Teach Us about Poetry: A Neurocosmopolitan Approach," in *The Oxford Handbook of Cognitive Literary Studies*, ed. Lisa Zunshine (Oxford: Oxford University Press, 2015); Ralph James Savarese, "Neurocosmopolitan Melville," *Leviathan: A Journal of Melville Studies* 15, no. 2 (2013): 7–19. See Nick Walker, *Neurocosmopolitanism*, neurocosmopolitanism.com.

91   "Autism—and its milder cousin . . ." Steve Silberman, "The Geek Syndrome," *Wired* 9 (2001): 174–83, https://www.wired.com/2001/12/aspergers/.

91   "A genre of popular storytelling . . ." Steve Silberman, *NeuroTribes: The Legacy of Autism and the Future of Neurodiversity* (New York: Penguin Random House, 2015), 230.

91   Like the characters in *Slan* . . . Silberman, *NeuroTribes*, 236.

92   "To a teenager in the 1930s . . ." Silberman, *NeuroTribes*, 239.

92   The more I read about the history . . . In 1964, four years before the publication of *Do Androids Dream of Electric Sheep?*, Dick published a novel that explicitly features autism, *The Martian Time-Slip*. While I could have chosen it for this project, I wanted to foreground the topics of empathy and artificial intelligence.

92   For instance, when asked about . . . *Loving Lampposts, Living Autistic*, dir. Todd Drezner, Cinema Libre Studio (2011).

93   Another self-advocate, Kassiane . . . *Loving Lampposts*.

93   Unlike Tito, who types with one . . . *Loving Lampposts*.

93   "I also don't access words . . ." *Loving Lampposts*.

93   She thought "in visual . . ." Skype conversation. Unless otherwise noted, Dora's remarks occurred during our weekly conversations.

93   In *Wretches and Jabberers* . . . *Wretches and Jabberers*, dir. Gerardine Wurzburg, State of the Art Inc. (2011).

94   While obviously a verbal medium . . . *My Classic Life as an Artist: A Portrait of Larry Bissonnette*, dir. Douglass Biklen and Zach Rossetti, Syracuse University (2005).

94   It, too, begins, we . . . *My Classic Life as an Artist*.

95   The concept of a spectrum . . . See Ian Hacking, "Humans, Aliens and Autism," *Daedalus* 138, no. 3 (2009): 44–59. Hacking writes, "Spectra are linear and autism isn't. The metaphor suggests that you can arrange autistic people on a line, from more to less" (47).

95   Called the Academic Autism . . . See https://aaspire.org/?p=home.

95   A number of these projects . . . In existence for over a decade, AASPIRE currently pursues multiple paths of research in healthcare, employment, and violence. As Dora explained the nature of what they do, it is basically "social services research for autistic adults."

95   Consider, for example, that . . . Dora elaborates: "For some it may be alienation, but for others it is not understanding the healthcare system, not being able to access it, having insufficient support, or, more generally, a failure within the healthcare system to meet needs. The ER-use stat in particular is a key indicator of the failure of the healthcare system to meet patient needs."

95   "Our partnership," Dora and . . . See https://aaspire.org/?p=home.

96   The morning I chanced upon . . . Ferris Jabr, "How Does a Caterpillar Turn into a Butterfly?," *Scientific American* (August 10, 2012), https://www.scientificamerican.com/article/caterpillar-butterfly-metamorphosis-explainer/.

97   What Chris Martin has said . . . Personal correspondence.

97   With considerable irony, the team . . . Christina Nicolaidis et al., "Collaboration Strategies in Nontraditional, Community-Based Participatory Research Partnerships: Lessons from an Academic–Community Partnership with Autistic Self-Advocates," *Progress in Community Health Partnerships: Research, Education, and Action* 5, no. 2 (2011): 143–50, https://www.ncbi.nlm.nih.gov/pmc/articles/PMC3319698/.

99   The dissertation involved . . . Dora Raymaker, "Intersections of Critical Systems Thinking and Community Based Participatory Research in Developing a Web Site for Autistic Adults" (PhD dissertation, Portland State University, 2015).

99   In the last chapter . . . titled . . . Raymaker, "Intersections," 117.

99   And this one, about her . . . Raymaker, "Intersections," 119.

102   Her all-time favorite sci-fi author . . . Harvey Blume, "Q&A with William Gibson," *Boston Globe* (August 19, 2007), http://archive.boston.com/news/globe/ideas/articles/2007/08/19/qa_with_william_gibson/.

105   This would only happen . . . Israel Kolvin, "Studies in the Childhood Psychoses: Diagnostic Criteria and Classification," *British Journal of Psychiatry* 118, no. 545 (1971): 381–84.

106   If this interstellar wild child, this corporate . . . Simon Baron-Cohen considers Hauser to be the first documented case of autism. See my article about Herman Melville and Caspar Hauser, "Neurocosmopolitan Melville."

107   This is precisely what R. J. R. Blair . . . R. J. R. Blair, "Responding to the Emotions of Others: Dissociating Forms of Empathy through the Study of Typical and Psychiatric Populations," *Consciousness and Cognition* 14, no. 4 (2005): 698–718, quote on 698.

107   Comparing and contrasting psychopaths with . . . Simone G. Shamay-Tsoory, "The Neural Bases for Empathy," *Neuroscientist* 17, no. 1 (2011): 18–24, quote on 18.

107   This result was confirmed by . . . Isabel Dziobek et al., "Dissociation of Cognitive and Emotional Empathy in Adults with Asperger Syndrome Using the Multifaceted Empathy Test (MET)," *Journal of Autism and Developmental Disorders* 38, no. 3 (2007): 464–73, quote on 464.

107   The following year, the Scottish . . . Adam Smith, "The Empathy Imbalance Hypothesis of Autism: A Theoretical Approach to Cognitive and Emotional Empathy in Autistic Development," *Psychological Record* 59, no. 2 (2009): 489–510, quote on 489.

111   Although I had published . . . See Ralph Savarese, "I Object: Autism, Empathy, and the Trope of Personification," in *Rethinking Empathy*, ed. Sue Kim and Meghan Marie Hammond (New York: Routledge, 2014), 74–92.

111   Whereas the former genre . . . Maria Chiara Pino and Monica Mazza, "The Use of 'Literary Fiction' to Promote Mentalizing Ability," *PLOS ONE* 11, no. 8 (2016), http://journals.plos.org/plosone/article?id=10.1371/journal.pone.0160254.

111   "Perhaps for this reason" . . . Pino and Mazza, "Use of 'Literary Fiction.'"

111   As the authors note, "A more . . ." Pino and Mazza, "Use of 'Literary Fiction.'"

112   Consider, for example, the "weirdly poignant . . ." Nicholas Carr, "Is Google Making Us Stupid? What the Internet Is Doing to Our Brains," *Atlantic* (July/August 2008), https://www.theatlantic.com/magazine/archive/2008/07/is-google-making-us-stupid/306868/.

112   In Nicholas Carr's retelling . . . Carr, "Is Google Making Us Stupid?"

112   "Dave, stop. . . . My mind . . ." Carr, "Is Google Making Us Stupid?"

112   According to Carr . . . Carr, "Is Google Making Us Stupid?"

112   "I have named a broken cup . . ." Ralph James Savarese, "More Than a Thing to Ignore: An Interview with Tito Rajarshi Mukhopadhyay," *Disability Studies Quarterly* 30, no. 1 (2010), http://dsq-sds.org/article/view/1056/1235.

113   Again, Tito . . . Savarese, "More Than a Thing to Ignore."

113   On the self-advocate website . . . "Obsessive Empathy for Inanimate Objects," *Wrong Planet*, ed. Alex Plank (March 21, 2006), http://wrongplanet.net/forums/viewtopic.php?t=12187.

113   "If he drops a food wrapper . . ." "Obsessive Empathy."

113   "We say *animism*" . . . Dennis Silk, "The Marionette Theatre," in *The Next American Essay*, ed. John D'Agata (Minneapolis, MN: Graywolf, 2003), 170, emphasis original.

113   "We're afraid of the life we're . . ." Silk, "Marionette Theatre," 171.

113   "If a cross is a witness . . ." Silk, "Marionette Theatre," 171.

113   As one researcher writes . . . Kerstin Dautenhahn, "Roles and Functions of Robots in Human Society: Implications from Research in Autism Therapy," *Robotica* 21, no. 4 (2003): 443–52, quote on 443.

113   In this view, anthropomorphism . . . Stephen Farmer, "The Neurobiological Origins of Primitive Religion: Implications for Comparative Mythology," in *New Perspectives on Myth: Proceedings of the Second Annual Conference of the International Association for Comparative Mythology*, ed. Wim M. J. van Binsbergen and Eric Venbrux (Haarlem: Shikanda, 2010), 285, 305–6.

114   As Grandin notes in . . . Temple Grandin and Richard Panek, *The Autistic Brain: Thinking across the Spectrum* (Boston: Houghton Mifflin Harcourt, 2013), 23.

114   Researchers have found recently . . . Daniel J. Ricks and Mark B. Colton, "Trends and Considerations in Robot-Assisted Autism Therapy," Robotics and Automation (ICRA), IEEE International Conference (2010), 1.

114   The normative drive won't allow . . . Quoted in Erin Manning, *Always More Than One: Individuation's Dance* (Durham, NC: Duke University Press, 2013), 150.

114   It is tempting here to speak . . . Manning, *Always More Than One*, xx.

114   In this context, the concept . . . Dora called Sturgeon's novel "one of my all-time favorites. . . . It's an exploration of neurodiversity in many ways, as well as humanity, and so many things . . . plus, a rare instance where I get some characters I can identify with." Theodore Sturgeon, *More Than Human* (1953; New York: Vintage, 1998).

114   For Manning, the problem . . . Graham Harvey, *Animism: Respecting the Living World* (New York: Columbia University Press, 2005), xiv.

114   The study demonstrated "stable . . ." Adam Waytz, John Cacioppo, and Nicholas Epley, "Who Sees Human? The Stability and Importance of Individual Differences in Anthropomorphism," *Perspectives on Psychological Science* 5, no. 3 (2014): 219–32, https://www.ncbi.nlm.nih.gov/pmc/articles/PMC4021380/.

114   These consequences include . . . Waytz, Cacioppo, and Epley, "Who Sees Human?"

115   "Seeing human" when seeing . . . Debate continues about the neurological underpinnings of anthropomorphism—specifically, the extent to which it reflects a genuine regard for objects. A study titled "The Brooms in Fantasia" found that anthropomorphism does not appear to activate the medial prefrontal cortex (MPFC), a brain region considered central to social cognition. See Lasana T. Harris and Susan T. Fiske, "The Brooms in Fantasia: Neural Correlates of Anthropomorphizing Objects," *Social Cognition* 26, no. 2 (2008): 210–23. Harris and Fiske note with respect to the Disney cartoon that their study references, "One can imagine an army of brooms without thinking about their minds as humanly complex" (221). Deploying the insights of their previous neuroimaging work on the perception of "extreme outgroups," such as homeless people and drug addicts, Harris and Fiske hypothesized that objects, unlike people in "extreme outgroups," do not profit from the individuation that familiarity occasions. Whereas simply wondering what a particular homeless person had for lunch can bring the MPFC online, an object, despite its apparent humanization in anthropomorphism, remains resolutely nonhuman. It remains, that is, like members of an "extreme outgroup" who have been conceived in strictly categorical terms. Other researchers, however, suggest that the MPFC might be activated: "Although there are very few neuroimaging

studies of personification, the available evidence implicates a *personification network* that includes five critical areas," including the medial frontal cortex. See Daniel Smilek et al., "When '3' Is a Jerk and 'E' Is a King: Personifying Inanimate Objects in Synesthesia," *Journal of Cognitive Neuroscience* 19, no. 6 (2007): 981–92, quote on 989.

115   The fact that "those . . ." Waytz, Cacioppo, and Epley, "Who Sees Human?"

115   A study from 2007 focused . . . Smilek et al., "When '3' Is a Jerk," 981.

115   As the researchers report . . . Smilek et al., "When '3' Is a Jerk," 989.

115   Previous research had documented . . . J. Simner and E. M. Hubbard, "Variants of Synesthesia Interact in Cognitive Tasks: Evidence for Implicit Associations and Late Connectivity in Cross-Talk Theories," *Neuroscience* 143, no. 3 (2006): 805–14, quote on 806. Grapheme-color synesthesia and ordinal linguistic personification "tend to co-occur and share characteristics . . . with other variants of synesthesia" (806).

115   The authors of the 2007 study . . . Smilek et al., "When '3' Is a Jerk," 990.

115   Such connections probably take place . . . Smilek et al., "When '3' Is a Jerk," 990.

115   Parietal regions, they note . . . Smilek et al., "When '3' Is a Jerk," 990.

115   The intensity of this sort of anthropomorphism . . . I hope that it is unnecessary to defend the repeated appeal to neurology. I am in no way reducing the complexity of life to mechanistic functioning. As the study by Waytz and colleagues ("Who Sees Human?") makes clear, neurological predispositions interact with specific features of social life to produce "individual differences in anthropomorphism." Even the neurological predispositions themselves are variable from person to person.

115   "Mother fork, grandmother fork . . ." Silk, "Marionette Theatre," 173.

116   While "object-personality pairings . . ." Jamie Ward and Michael J. Bannisy, "Explaining Mirror-Touch Synesthesia," *Cognitive Neuroscience* 6, no. 2–3 (2015): 118–33, quote on 119.

116   "When we are born, we . . ." V. S. Ramachandran, "Ted Talk: Ramachandran on Your Mind" (November 25, 2010), https://brainchemist.wordpress.com/2010/11/25/ted-talk-ramachandran-on-your-mind/.

116   The former view, however . . . Ramachandran, "Ted Talk"; Farmer, "Neurobiological Origins," 26.

116   Personifying synesthetes may . . . Farmer, "Neurobiological Origins," 17.

116   Although we don't know if . . . See Simon Baron-Cohen et al., "Is Synaesthesia More Common in Autism?," *Molecular Autism* 4, no. 1 (2013): 40.

117   Though all of us are . . . Donna Haraway, "A Cyborg Manifesto: Science, Technology, and Socialist-Feminism in the Late Twentieth Century," in *Simians, Cyborgs, and Women: The Reinvention of Nature* (New York: Routledge, 1991), 149.

118   Listen to Hoshi, the novel's . . . For a discussion of the term "defective detective," see *The Defective Detective in the Pulps*, ed. Gary Hoppenstand, Garyn G. Roberts, and Ray B. Browne (Bowling Green, OH: Bowling Green University Popular Press, 1983).

119   Like the "digital natives" . . . Silberman, *NeuroTribes*, 3.

119   When Tammet looks at . . . Daniel Tammet, *Born on a Blue Day: Inside the Extraordinary Mind of an Autistic Savant* (New York: Free Press, 2006), 177.

119   "To recall each digit . . ." Tammet, *Born on a Blue Day*.

119   He is also aided by . . . Tammet, *Born on a Blue Day*, 2.

120   If Tammet "see[s] numbers . . ." Tammet, *Born on a Blue Day*, 2.

121   The "structure of scientific revolutions" . . . Thomas Kuhn, *The Structure of Scientific Revolutions*, 3rd ed. (Chicago: University of Chicago Press, 1996).

121   Looking back on his work . . . See Philip K. Dick, *The Exegesis of Philip K. Dick*, ed. Pamela Renee Jackson and Jonathan Lethem (Boston: Houghton Mifflin Harcourt, 2011), 257. After revising this chapter, I came across an essay titled "How Am I Not Myself? Philip K. Dick, the Autism Connection." Jasun Horsley suggests that Dick himself may have been autistic but that he was an "autist-author in denial of his own autism." He writes, "Ironically—and tellingly—it is the film version and not Dick's original book that turns a sympathetic eye toward the autist-androids, showing, in very clear terms, that empathy, as a lost human trait, has now moved into the realm of the machine." While the claim may be largely true, it undervalues the novel's raging ambiguity: the part of Dick, whether autistic or not, that very much sides with the androids. See https://auticulture .wordpress.com/2013/10/28/philip-k-dick-autistic-time-slip/.

FOUR. FINDING HER FEET

122   Each, as the dance scholar . . . Jennifer Fisher, "Ballet and Whiteness: Will Ballet Forever Be the Kingdom of the Pale?," in *The Oxford Handbook of Dance and Ethnicity*, ed. Anthony Shay and Barbara Sellers-Young (Oxford: Oxford University Press, 2016), 585–97.

122   "The ballet's aristocratic origins . . ." Jenna Sullivan, "Saving the Black Swan: Responses to Racial Disparity in Classical Ballet," Rhodes Institute for Regional Studies, unpublished (2012), 1.

123   Even the Russian choreographer . . . Quoted in Sullivan, "Saving the Black Swan." When reading this chapter, Eugenie stuck a digital note to this

remark: "Funny how Balanchine was so adamant about color in ballet. Yet he married an Osage Indian (Maria Tallchief) and told her that he felt as if he were one of her people."

123   As one commentator argues . . . Carrie Arnold, "Autism's Race Problem," *Pacific Standard* (May 26, 2016), https://psmag.com/news/autisms-race -problem.

123   In 2014, a white child . . . Arnold, "Autism's Race Problem."

123   The subject of this chapter . . . I follow the common practice of capital-izing the word "Deaf" when it refers not to audiological status but to membership in the Deaf community.

123   If Dora has elected to mark . . . The issue of passing, of choosing not to disclose one's disability, is not only complicated but also contentious. As I note, Eugenie chooses this strategy in some settings but not in others, and she is careful to avoid making any general recommendations about when and if to pass. This is *her* solution to the problem of discrimination in the highly particular context of *her* coaching life. With regard to disguising her identity in this book, she well understands that some readers will know immediately who "Eugenie" is, but she seeks to protect the privacy of her mother, husband, and autistic son.

124   Her difficulties as a ballerina . . . Bettina Bläsing et al., "Neurocognitive Control in Dance Perception and Performance," *Acta Psychologica* 139, no. 2 (2012): 300–308, quote on 301.

124   "Dancers," notes Bettina . . . Bläsing et al., "Neurocognitive Control," 301.

125   When I say that Eugenie . . . Eugenie kindly but firmly pointed out the problematic nature of such statements. In the spirit of this book—and in the interest of dramatizing the difficult labor of progressive anthropology—I have not tried to clean up my own shortcomings.

126   To her, deafness, like autism . . . In using the term "impairment," I follow the accepted distinction in the field of disability studies. An "impairment" only becomes disabling when a society refuses to accommodate it. Of course, many Deaf people reject the notion of impairment, insisting that it preserves a hearing norm.

129   As Eugenie well understood . . . Sonia K. Kang and Galen V. Bodenhausen, "Multiple Identities in Social Perception and Action: Challenges and Oppor-tunities," *Annual Review of Psychology* 66, no. 1 (2015): 547–74, quote on 560.

129   As one researcher puts it . . . Kang and Bodenhausen, "Multiple Identi-ties," 560.

129   But multiraciality can also lead . . . Sarah E. Gaither, "'Mixed' Results: Multiracial Research and Identity Explorations," *Current Directions in Psychological Science* 24, no. 2 (2015): 114–19, quote on 114.

129   "Due to the widely recognized . . ." Kang and Bodenhausen, "Multiple Identities," 565.

129   Multiraciality is said to produce . . . Kang and Bodenhausen, "Multiple Identities," 554.

131   The word "grotesque" means . . . Wikipedia, "Grotesque," https://en .wikipedia.org/wiki/Grotesque.

131   "In art . . . , *grotesque* . . ." Wikipedia, "Grotesque."

132   It takes advantage of . . . Kenny Fries, ed., *Staring Back: The Disability Experience from the Inside Out* (New York: Plume, 1997).

134   "The disabled body," writes . . . Emily Russell, *Reading Embodied Citizenship: Disability, Narrative, and the Body Politic* (New Brunswick, NJ: Rutgers University Press, 2011), 76.

135   Singer's "nonverbal communication . . ." Russell, *Reading Embodied Citizenship*, 76.

135   According to Rachel Adams . . . Rachel Adams, "A Mixture of Delicious and Freak: The Queer Fiction of Carson McCullers," *American Literature* 71, no. 3 (1999): 551–83, quote on 552.

136   He also echoes . . . At Eugenie's request, I am withholding the citation.

136   Because he can't be contained . . . Biff's enthusiasm for disability is astonishing, and it's hard not to read it as a half-repressed wish to mark his own body as different, even disfigured. He longs, it would seem, to be able to corporeally express a trans sensibility. "What he had said to Alice was true—[Biff] did like freaks. He had a special feeling for sick people and cripples. . . . There was one fellow who had had his peter . . . blown off in a boiler explosion, and whenever he came to town there was a free pint waiting for him." See Carson McCullers, *The Heart Is a Lonely Hunter* (1940; New York: Mariner Books, 2000), 22.

136   Think, for example, of . . . Robert McRuer, *Crip Theory: Cultural Signs of Queerness and Disability* (New York: New York University Press, 2006).

136   Quite, as the activist/scholar . . . Petra Kuppers, *Disability Culture and Community Performance: Find a Strange and Twisted Shape* (Basingstoke, UK: Palgrave Macmillan, 2011).

138   Just as, according to one theory . . . I am not equating hormones with gender, which is socially constructed. Rather, I am noting how McCullers views stable notions of gender as a gross betrayal of the fluid, changing, and varied nature of human bodies.

139   Listen to Lydia Brown . . . Lydia X. Z. Brown, "Gendervague: At the Intersection of Autistic and Trans Experience," *The Blog* (web log) (June 22,

2016), https://thetaskforceblog.org/2016/06/22/gendervague-at-the
-intersection-of-autistic-and-trans-experiences/.

139   According to Brown . . . Brown, "Gendervague."

139   "For many of us," she . . . Brown, "Gendervague."

139   This is not the case with Eugenie . . . This book has been seven years in the making. Were I to commence writing it today, I would most certainly include a neurodivergent trans reader. Some of the most important writing today is coming from this group of diverse autistics.

141   With the persistence of . . . Eugenie didn't entirely dismiss the novel's treatment of race. She recognized how, in some ways, it could be considered progressive for the period and place in which it was written. Perhaps Richard Wright was engaged in this sort of mental gymnastics when he remarked, in a blurb, "The most impressive aspect of [McCullers's work] is the astonishing humanity that enables a white writer, for the first time in Southern fiction, to handle Negro characters with as much ease and justice as those of her own race."

141   Exhibit A . . . Eugenie objected to the way that McCullers's black characters never move beyond stereotype—never show a richness or dynamism within, and in spite of, the oppression to which they are subjected.

142   If behaving like the comic . . . According to Wikipedia, "E-man is a sentient packet of energy thrown off by a nova." See Wikipedia, "E-Man," https://en.wikipedia.org/wiki/E-Man. For more about Reep Daggle, see Wikipedia, "Reep Daggle," https://en.wikipedia.org/wiki/Reep_Daggle.

145   This wasn't the "beyond" of . . . See Wikipedia, *Parents Involved in Community Schools v. Seattle School District No. 1*," https://en.wikipedia
.org/wiki/Parents_Involved_in_Community_Schools_v._Seattle_School
_District_No._1.

147   Studies have confirmed that . . . Jacqueline M. Chen and David L. Hamilton, "Natural Ambiguities: Racial Categorization of Multiracial Individuals," *Journal of Experimental Social Psychology* 48, no. 1 (2012): 152–64, quote on 152.

147   So central is the notion . . . Kang and Bodenhausen, "Multiple Identities," 552.

147   Even when the aim is ultimately . . . Kang and Bodenhausen, "Multiple Identities," 548.

147   In a study of the facial . . . Kang and Bodenhausen, "Multiple Identities," 552.

147   In contrast, multiracial subjects . . . Kang and Bodenhausen, "Multiple Identities," 552.

147   If the multiracial subject did not . . . Kang and Bodenhausen, "Multiple Identities," 552.

147   To the best of my knowledge . . . I recognize that prosopognosia (or face-blindness), which is fairly common in autism, would make it difficult to test my hypothesis.

147   As the researchers put it . . . Kang and Bodenhausen, "Multiple Identities," 556.

148   "Testing memory for faces categorized . . ." Kang and Bodenhausen, "Multiple Identities," 556.

148   A study involving people with . . . Kang and Bodenhausen, "Multiple Identities," 555.

148   Without explicit instruction or . . . Kang and Bodenhausen, "Multiple Identities," 555.

148   Researchers stress that "multiple . . ." Kang and Bodenhausen, "Multiple Identities," 554.

148   With individuation comes . . . Kang and Bodenhausen, "Multiple Identities," 554.

148   In a recent study of racial . . . Chiara Fini et al., "Embodying an Outgroup: The Role of Racial Bias and the Effect of Multisensory Processing in Somatosensory Remapping," *Frontiers in Behavioral Neuroscience* 7 (November 2013), https://www.frontiersin.org/articles/10.3389/fnbeh.2013.00165/full.

148   Researchers found that "individuals' . . ." Fini et al., "Embodying an Outgroup."

148   The study relied on the principle . . . Fini et al., "Embodying an Outgroup."

148   So much so that when . . . Fini et al., "Embodying an Outgroup."

148   When researchers increased . . . Fini et al., "Embodying an Outgroup."

148   As important, the difference in the . . . Fini et al., "Embodying an Outgroup."

149   Scientists call this phenomenon . . . Fini et al., "Embodying an Outgroup."

149   The study's authors speculate . . . Fini et al., "Embodying an Outgroup."

149   Here, engaging with an outgroup . . . Literature, I've been intimating, might work partly in this way. It offers a multisensory representation of the other, and it insists that characters be "processed at an individual-, rather than at a categorical-level."

149   Autistics, according to Laurent . . . Laurent Mottron et al., "Veridical Mapping in the Development of Exceptional Autistic Abilities," *Neuroscience and Biobehavioral Reviews* 37, no. 2 (2013): 209–28, quote on 210.

149   Because they possess unisensory . . . Exclusively visual apprehensions of the Other lend themselves to abstract categorization.

149   Reflecting on this account of autism . . . Mottron et al., "Veridical Mapping," 213.

152   No one had offered her . . . Being deaf likely didn't delay Eugenie's Asperger diagnosis, though this isn't the case for deaf autistics generally. According to a 2008 study, deaf children receive an autism diagnosis almost two years later than their hearing counterparts. See Michelle Leach, "Deafness with Autism: A School Age Communication Perspective," *Audiology Online* (November 17, 2014), http://www.audiologyonline.com/articles/deafness-with-autism-school-age-13001.

152   Of course, once it has been reclaimed . . . As an activist, Eugenie understood the appeal of identity claims—how they organize, empower, and provide solace—but, as a multiracial person, she worried about their divisive, self-perpetuating trap. Her goal, in the words of aforementioned scientists, was "decategorization"—utterly "natural [which is to say unremarkable] ambiguity."

153   The first decade of . . . Susan Saulny, "Census Data Present Rise in Multiracial Population of Youth," *New York Times* (March 24, 2011), http://www.nytimes.com/2011/03/25/us/25race.html.

153   In 2013, 10 percent . . . Saulny, "Census Data."

FIVE. TAKE FOR GRANDIN

I dedicate this chapter to Lisa Zunshine, who once used Temple Grandin to show the importance of theory of mind (ToM) to reading fiction. Autism, she argued, prevented Grandin from following, or being interested in, the purposeful convolutions of social inference. At the 2011 meeting of the Modern Language Association, I challenged this view. Two years later, at the same conference, Zunshine delivered a paper titled "Real Mindblindness, or, I Was Wrong," leading Michael Bérubé to joke that it "may have been the first paper in the history of the MLA since 1884 to bear that subtitle" (Bérubé, *The Secret Life of Stories: From Don Quixote to Harry Potter, How Understanding Intellectual Disability Transforms the Way We Read* [New York: New York University, 2016], 170). See Lisa Zunshine, *Why We Read Fiction: Theory of Mind and the Novel* (Columbus: Ohio State University Press, 2006). See also Lisa Zunshine, "Theory of Mind and Experimental Representations of Fictional Consciousness," in *Introduction to Cognitive Cultural Studies*, ed. Lisa Zunshine (Baltimore, MD: Johns Hopkins University Press, 2010), 193–213. I very much admire Lisa's willingness to change her mind. Over the last half decade, she has worked diligently to incorporate nonnormative notions of Otherness into the burgeoning field of cognitive literary studies. For her, the assertion of "loose universals" is entirely compatible with cultural, historical, neurological, sexual, class, and gender differences. In 2014, we published an article together. See Ralph James Savarese and Lisa Zunshine, "The Critic as Neurocosmopolite; Or, What Cognitive Approaches to Literature Can Learn from Disability Studies," *Narrative* 22, no. 1 (2014): 17–44.

156   As Thomas Bayne remarked . . . Quoted in William White, *Notes and Queries* (Oxford: Oxford University Press, 1905), 464.

156   Bayne called Keats . . . White, *Notes and Queries*, 464.

156   I had read that . . . *Temple Grandin*, dir. Mick Jackson, HBO (2010); quoted in Rick Lyman, "No More Crushes; This Is Serious," *New York Times* (January 29, 2010).

156   In the book that made her famous . . . Temple Grandin, *Thinking in Pictures*, expanded ed. (New York: Vintage, 2006), 91. All subsequent citations in this chapter refer to this edition.

157   "She relate[d] better," she . . . Grandin, *Thinking*, 93, 222.

157   On the Web she is . . . Wikipedia, "Temple Grandin," https://en .wikipedia.org/wiki/Temple_Grandin.

158   As she says in a video on . . . See the Temple Grandin website, http:// www.templegrandin.com.

158   For example, "If I . . ." Grandin, *Thinking*, 12.

158   Consider the following sentence . . . Grandin, *Thinking*, 15.

158   "In my imagination," Temple . . . Grandin, *Thinking*, 15.

158   "Teachers who work with . . ." Grandin, *Thinking*, 16.

158   "My thinking pattern always . . ." Grandin, *Thinking*, 16.

158   As she says of Great Danes . . . Grandin, *Thinking*, 12.

160   His secretary kept saying . . . Grandin herself adopts this conceit in *Animals in Translation*: "Autism is a kind of way station on the road from animals to humans, which puts autistic people like me in a perfect position to translate 'animal talk' into English." Temple Grandin and Catherine Johnson, *Animals in Translation: Using the Mysteries of Autism to Decode Animal Behavior* (New York: Mariner Books, 2006), 6–7.

160   In one, called "Meat," . . . C. S. Malerich, "Meat," in *Among Animals: The Lives of Animals and Humans in Contemporary Short Fiction*, ed. John Yunker (Ashland, OR: Ashland Creek Press, 2014), 55–68.

160   In the other, called . . . Midge Raymond, "The Ecstatic Cry," in Yunker, *Among Animals*, 87–106.

160   In his *New Yorker* profile . . . Oliver Sacks, *An Anthropologist on Mars: Seven Paradoxical Tales* (New York: Vintage, 1996), 261.

160   "I was very attached" . . . Sacks, *Anthropologist*, 261.

160   In *Thinking in Pictures*, we . . . Grandin, *Thinking*, 85.

161   Increasingly, research has demonstrated . . . A study from 2013 offers a nice summary of previous efforts to understand the prosocial effects

of reading fiction: "Familiarity with fiction, self-reported empathy, and performance on an advanced affective ToM test have been correlated . . . , and limited experimental evidence suggests that reading fiction increases self-reported empathy. . . . Fiction also seems to expand our knowledge of others' lives, helping us to recognize our similarity to them." See David Comer Kidd and Emanuele Castano, "Reading Literary Fiction Improves Theory of Mind," *Science* 342, no. 6156 (October 18, 2013): 377–80, quote on 377. Two things make this study distinctive: (1) it distinguishes between popular fiction, literary fiction, and nonfiction, finding that only the second "temporarily enhances ToM" (377), and (2) it uses empirical tests, instead of self-reports, to measure a subject's ability to infer the thoughts and emotions of other people. In this study, reading literary fiction before taking the "Reading the Mind in the Eyes" test improved participants' scores. The authors believe that literary fiction "uniquely engages the psychological processes needed to gain access to characters' subjective experiences" (378).

A study from 2016, which I previously critiqued for its sweeping claim that "the pleasure in reading science fiction . . . comes from imagining different realities than from understanding characters," thus making it the "preferred genre [of] individuals with autism," also found that reading literary fiction improves mentalizing abilities. See Maria Chiara Pino and Monica Mazza, "The Use of 'Literary Fiction' to Promote Mentalizing Ability," *PLOS ONE* 11, no. 8 (2016), doi:10.1371/journal.pone.0160254. While the authors of these studies do admit to the problem of precisely defining "literariness," they lean quite hard on old-fashioned distinctions of genre and authorial reputation, which seem far from reliable. A study from 2012 found genre to be less important than perceived "artistic merit" in driving changes in a reader's personality, perhaps suggesting that the former is not especially, or at least entirely, decisive. See Maja Djikic, Keith Oatley, and Matthew Carland, "Genre or Artistic Merit? The Effect of Literature on Personality," *Scientific Study of Literature* 2, no. 1 (2012): 25–36. The field is obviously in its infancy, and much more research needs to be conducted, but the aforementioned studies appear to capture something important about what Kidd and Castano, quoting Roland Barthes, call "writerly" (as opposed to "readerly") texts. Such texts "unsettle readers' expectations" ("Reading Literary Fiction," 377) by "trigger[ing] presupposition (a focus on implicit meanings)" (378).

161   In the words of Raymond Mar . . . Raymond A. Mar and Keith Oatley, "The Function of Fiction Is the Abstraction and Simulation of Social Experience," *Perspectives on Psychological Science* 3, no. 3 (2008): 173–92, quote on 173. "We have recently shown," write Mar and Oatley, "that individuals who have been exposed to more fictional literature tend to exhibit better empathic abilities . . . , and that this relation cannot be explained by individual differences in personality. . . . Further research

from our group indicates that reading appears to invoke a social-processing mode in readers, priming them for the understanding of social relations" (182). Although genre may not be decisive, some studies have connected reading fiction with social inclusion and support. See Raymond A. Mar et al., "Bookworms versus Nerds: Exposure to Fiction versus Non-fiction, Divergent Associations with Social Ability, and the Simulation of Fictional Social Worlds," *Journal of Research in Personality* 40, no. 5 (2006): 694–712. See also Raymond A. Mar, "Simulation-Based Theories of Narrative Comprehension: Evidence and Implications" (PhD dissertation, University of Toronto, 2007). Confirming and extending the results of their 2006 study, Mar and his colleagues found that "fiction was positively correlated to social support" whereas "exposure to nonfiction . . . was associated with loneliness, and negatively related to social support" (407). They write, "The myth that avid fiction readers are socially isolated is untrue; their social networks were found to be better than those of people who read less fiction" (499). See Raymond A. Mar, Keith Oatley, and Jordan B. Peterson, "Exploring the Link between Reading Fiction and Empathy: Ruling Out Individual Differences and Examining Outcomes," *Communications* 34, no. 4 (2009): 407–28. This finding, while needing additional investigation, may be relevant to some autistics who, through a combination of neurological difference and societal neglect, if not antipathy, struggle with "comorbid" conditions such as depression.

161   In short, it changes people . . . A study from 2009 by Maja Djikic and colleagues found that literary fiction "can cause significant changes in the experience of one's own personality traits under laboratory conditions." See Djikic et al., "On Being Moved by Art: How Reading Fiction Transforms the Self," *Creativity Research Journal* 21, no. 1 (2009): 24–29, quote on 24. One hundred sixty-six first-year undergraduates participated, with some reading Chekhov's short story "The Lady and the Dog" and others reading a "comparison text that had the same content as the story, but was documentary in form" (25). In other words, all literary or stylistic aspects had been removed. The results, the authors contend, were "due to the difference in the artistic form between the experimental and control conditions, rather than the difference in interest level or story content" (25). Conceiving of the act of reading literary fiction as "cognitive and emotional simulation," they believe it invites a "re-schematization of categories, including those relating to oneself" (25). (Here, the term "re-schematization of categories" should resonate with the term "decategorization" from the last chapter: literary fiction, like multiraciality, can move us beyond established ways of understanding experience.) In addition to its various stylistic features (rhythm, syntax, sound effects, tone, and figurative language), literary fiction depends on open-endedness and indirection—what Emily Dickinson famously called a "slanted" approach to the truth. Djikic and Oatley

comment, "A striking feature of self-change through literature is that the effects are not direct, as occurs with persuasion, where the author intends the reader to think, feel, or to be disposed to act, in a way she desires. The art in fiction is a social influence, but one that helps people to understand and feel, and even change their selfhood, in their own ways." See Maja Djikic and Keith Oatley, "The Art in Fiction: From Indirect Communication to Changes in the Self," *Psychology of Aesthetics, Creativity, and the Arts* 8, no. 4 (2014): 498–505, quote on 498.

161   In one study . . . Kidd and Castano, "Reading Literary Fiction."

161   In another, "individuals . . ." The quotation appears in Raymond A. Mar et al., "Emotion and Narrative Fiction: Interactive Influences before, during, and after Reading," *Cognition and Emotion* 25, no. 5 (2011): 818–33, quote on 830. It describes a finding of a previous study. See Maja Djikic et al., "Defenseless against Art? Impact of Reading Fiction on Emotion in Avoidantly Attached Individuals," *Journal of Research in Personality* 43, no. 1 (2009): 14–17. This study used the same story by Chekhov and the same setup ("art" versus "non-art" conditions) to show that reading literary fiction can "subvert habitual emotional disengagement of avoidantly attached individuals" (14). "Some aspects of art," write the authors, "such as form or structure, cannot be defended against. How does one defend against a structure or rhythm of a short story? How does one defend against a juxtaposition of images or thoughts? So, while it is conceivable that one can potentially distance oneself from the content of a short story or a novel—by not engaging fully, or by discounting what is going on as merely a story and therefore unimportant—to defend against the form of a piece would be difficult, not least because it cannot be easily isolated or located" (15). Their hypothesis—that avoidantly attached people in the "art" condition would experience greater emotional change than "less defensive individuals"—proved correct. As in the study of undergraduates, the story did not "promote change of emotion in any prescribed way" (16).

161   . . . when they read a story by Anton Chekhov . . . Djikic et al., "Defenseless," 5.

161   Might literary fiction . . . Mar et al., "Emotion," 830.

161   I want to be careful . . . Can the notion of neurodiversity be squared with therapeutic intervention? CNN's Dr. Sanjay Gupta once interviewed my son, DJ, asking him, "Should autism be treated?" "Yes," DJ replied, "treated with respect." This witty retort nicely undermines the stark (and misleading) binary—difference or disorder—by insisting that respect ought to motivate *both* conceptions of autism. One can help Jamie with his movement or Tito with his anxiety or Temple with her emotions without subscribing to the idea that autistics are broken. Let us not forget that autism often brings considerable talents, thus blurring the ability/disability divide. Autism is

either an enabling disability or a disabling ability—just like so-called neu-rotypicality. (My son, for example, helps me with my memory and sense of direction.) See the final endnote of chapter 2. See Emily T. Savarese and Ralph J. Savarese, "'The Superior Half of Speaking': An Introduction," *Disability Studies Quarterly* 30, no. 1 (2010), http://dsq-sds.org/article/view /1062/1230.

161   In the end, my aim . . . As the reader will see, particularly in the third section of the chapter, I actively root for an emotional response to "The Ecstatic Cry." I do so less because I am invested in a fundamental norm than because I loathe autistic stereotypes and because Grandin has come to represent the condition as a whole. Complicating what we think we know about her will encourage us, in the words of Anne Donnellan, to practice "the least dangerous assumption" and to make room for many different kinds of autism and autistic emotion. As the previous chapters should make clear, while I frequently refer to scientific studies, I completely acknowledge the normative impulse that tends to drive them. Anne M. Donnellan, "The Criterion of the Least Dangerous Assumption," *Behavioral Disorders* 9, no. 2 (1984): 141–50.

162   In it she writes, "I had . . ." Grandin, *Thinking*, 226.

164   "Much of the distempers of criticism . . ." Cleanth Brooks, *The Well Wrought Urn: Studies in the Structure of Poetry* (New York: Harcourt, 1970), 199.

166   The story refuses to collapse . . . Brooks, *Well Wrought Urn*, 209.

167   A sense of panic ballooned . . . My student Merlin Mathews suggested that the author purposefully fails to tell us what kind of animal "Meat" is so as to make it seem more human.

167   "It's a way of expressing . . ." Dante Alighieri, *The Inferno of Dante: A New Verse Translation*, trans. Robert Pinsky (New York: Farrar, Straus and Giroux, 1997). "The emperor of the realm of grief protruded / From mid-breast up above the surrounding ice" (367).

168   Before I could make the link . . . *Eye in the Sky*, dir. Gavin Hood, Entertainment One, 2015.

168   Her mind was as associative . . . Grandin, *Thinking*, 9.

168   In *Thinking in Pictures* she . . . Grandin, *Thinking*, 9.

169   But was she indicting herself . . . That code depends on the notion of *contrapasso* (or counterpenalty), whereby sinners receive a punishment that mirrors the crime. As with a boomerang, their actions come back unerringly to clobber them.

169   Her first encounter with . . . Grandin, *Thinking*, 227.

169   Later, when she designed . . . Grandin, *Thinking*, 230.

169   "I believe that the place where an animal . . ." Grandin, *Thinking*, 239.

170   It settled for "abstractification" . . . Grandin and Johnson, *Animals*, 27.

170   "They attack[] things" . . . Quoted in Nathanael Johnson, "Temple Grandin Digs in on the Practical Side of What Animals Want," *Grist* (July 22, 2015), http://grist.org/food/temple-grandin-digs-in-on-the-practical-side-of-what-animals-want/.

170   Compassionate slaughter requires . . . Temple Grandin and Mark Deesing, *Humane Livestock Handling* (Pownal, VT: Storey Publishing, 2008), 207.

170   Adopting what she calls . . . Grandin, *Thinking*, 167, 168. When she does this, she is not, she says, a person in a bovine costume. Grandin thus disagrees with the philosopher Thomas Nagel, who argued that we cannot know what it is like to be a bat because we do not possess a bat's perceptual experience. We can only "imagine what it would be like for [us] to behave as a bat behaves" (439). A person engaging in such a *thought* experiment would, according to Nagel, be precisely a bat *man* in, yes, a bat costume. See Thomas Nagel, "What Is It Like to Be a Bat?," *Philosophical Review* 83, no. 4 (1974): 435–50.

170   Temple "credit[s] autism . . ." Grandin, *Thinking*, 111.

170   . . . in particular, the long-range . . . Grandin and Johnson, *Animals*, 65.

170   During sensory simulations there are . . . Grandin and Johnson, *Animals*, 17. Grandin writes, "My final judgment comes out in words, but not the process that led up to the judgment. If you think about a judge and a jury, all my deliberations are in pictures, and only my final verdict is in words" (17). Ironically, the "final verdict" functions in a top-down manner. Although she champions sensuous particularity, her books present one long stream of generalizations, and I wonder if Grandin the writer isn't at odds with Grandin the livestock handler—if with the latter's translation into language, something fundamental isn't lost. Imagine if she could write creatively.

170   Abidingly practical, she values . . . Grandin, *Thinking*, 160.

171   Because carnivores, as . . . Grandin and Johnson, *Animals*, 180.

171   "The strongest feeling I have . . ." Grandin, *Thinking*, 91.

171   Temple has plenty of . . . Grandin, *Thinking*, 94.

171   So reluctant is she . . . Grandin doesn't seem to fit the research showing that autistics, on average, struggle not with emotional empathy, that bottom-up feeling system, but with cognitive empathy, that top-down thinking system. As she says of her sensory simulations, she "tune[s] into what the actual sensations are like . . . rather than having the idea of death rile up [her] emotions" (*Thinking*, 94). Part of what the chapter explores

is the tension between purposeful avoidance of emotion, diminution of emotional response as a side effect of anxiety medication, and alexithymia, an actual condition in which people cannot feel, express, or describe their emotions.

171   In *Thinking in Pictures* she had . . . Grandin, *Thinking*, 164.

172   But she has also said that her . . . Grandin, *Thinking*, 93, 89.

172   In *Animals in Translation*, she . . . Grandin and Johnson, *Animals*, 1.

172   A study from 2014 . . . Line Gebauer et al., "Intact Brain Processing of Musical Emotions in Autism Spectrum Disorders, but More Cognitive Load and Arousal in Happy vs. Sad Music," *Frontiers in Neuroscience* 8 (2014), https://www.frontiersin.org/articles/10.3389/fnins.2014.00192/full.

172   Interestingly, a study from . . . Megha Sharda et al., "Fronto-temporal Connectivity Is Preserved during Sung but Not Spoken Word Listening, across the Autism Spectrum," *Autism Research* 8, no. 2 (2015): 174–86. Another study from 2015 found that "sung directives . . . may enhance socio-communicative responsiveness." See Paul Arkoprovo et al., "The Effect of Sung Speech on Socio-communicative Responsiveness in Children with Autism Spectrum Disorders," *Frontiers in Human Neuroscience* 9 (October 29, 2015), https://www.frontiersin.org/articles/10.3389/fnhum.2015.00555/full.

172   In *The Autistic Brain*, after . . . Temple Grandin and Richard Panek, *The Autistic Brain: Thinking across the Spectrum* (Boston: Houghton Mifflin Harcourt, 2013), 168.

173   She herself has been on Prozac . . . Grandin, *Thinking*, 91.

173   "My amygdalae are telling . . ." Grandin and Panek, *Autistic Brain*, 32.

173   In the aforementioned study of . . . Djikic et al., "Defenseless," 14, 16.

173   In addition to teaching her . . . Grandin and Johnson, *Animals*, 114.

173   In *Thinking in Pictures* she wrote . . . Grandin, *Thinking*, 84.

173   And so through touch Temple . . . For more on the hacking hypothesis, see Uta Frith, Francesca Happé, and Frances Siddons, "Autism and Theory of Mind in Everyday Life," *Social Development* 3, no. 2 (1994): 108–24. Elinor Ochs and Olga Solomon explain, "'Hacking' implies that the children work through stored algorithms to decipher the encrypted logic of messages conveyed in social situations." See Ochs and Solomon, "Practical Logic and Autism," in *A Companion to Psychological Anthropology: Modernity and Psychocultural Change*, ed. Conerly Casey and Robert B. Edgerton (Hoboken, NJ: John Wiley and Sons, 2005), 140–67, quote on 151.

173   She deliberately thought her way . . . In her book *Authoring Autism: On Rhetoric and Neurological Queerness* (Durham, NC: Duke University

Press, 2018), Melanie Yergeau aggressively pushes back against the "hacking hypothesis": "Reason, topoi, tropes, narrative arcs, diplomacy—these will only ever be attempts or, as Frith and Happé call them, 'hacks' toward a normative embodiment, 'hacks' toward a normative rhetoric. Appearing to know myself or others is merely appearing to know myself or others. I can appear, but I can never know. I have symptoms, and they have rhetoric." Yergeau reminds us of just how normative the thinking of many scientists is; they can't imagine another way of doing something. Nor can they imagine, in a different context, the potential advantages of what they pejoratively label a "hack." (There is nothing "hacked" about Grandin's interactions with animals.) I invoke the "hacking hypothesis" because Grandin alludes to it, in one way or another, to explain her own social development.

174   **Such a coping strategy . . .** A study from 2006, compellingly titled "The Bitter-Sweet Labor of Emoting: The Linguistic Comparison of Writers and Physicists," predictably found that the former use many more feeling words, "in particular more negative-emotion words, including the greater use of anger-related, anxiety-related, and depression or sadness-related words" to describe what they do. The authors of the study attribute this tendency to the fact that "the writers' work is *suffused* with these emotions," and they speculate that "some individuals might choose artistic rather than scientific endeavor because artistic vocation provides a culturally sanctioned means of remaining preoccupied with one's emotional life." See Maja Djikic, Keith Oatley, and Jordan B. Peterson, "The Bitter-Sweet Labor of Emoting: The Linguistic Comparison of Writers and Physicists," *Creativity Research Journal* 18, no. 2 (2006): 195–201, quotes on 195, 200. The obverse could also be true and may, in part, explain Grandin's own choice of career.

174   **Indeed, she has compared herself . . .** The scientist Antonio Damasio demonstrated that such people often make catastrophic financial decisions because what they took to be a rational process actually depends on feeling. "I can handle situations where stroke patients may fail because I never relied on emotional cues in the first place," Grandin says. Yet the very stark comparison belies her own clear, if uneven, emotional abilities. See Temple Grandin, "An Inside View of Autism," in *High-Functioning Individuals with Autism*, ed. Eric Schopler and Gary B. Mesibov (New York: Plenum Press, 1992), available at https://www.iidc.indiana.edu/pages/An-Inside-View-of-Autism.

174   **According to some researchers, even . . .** Matthew D. Lerner, James C. McPartland, and James P. Morris, "Multimodal Emotion Processing in Autism Spectrum Disorders: An Event-Related Potential Study," *Developmental Cognitive Neuroscience* 3 (2013): 11–21, quote on 20. Obviously this study subscribes to the "hacking hypothesis."

174　Literature, of course, is not only sensory-driven . . . Building on previous neuroimaging studies of single-word reading, which showed that "readers' representations of word meaning are grounded in visual and motor representations," a study from 2009 had subjects read four short narratives in a scanner. The authors found that "regions involved in processing goal-directed human activity, navigating spatial environments, and manually manipulating objects in the real world increased in activation at points when those specific aspects of the narrated situation were changing. . . . These results suggest that readers use perceptual and motor representations in the process of comprehending narrated activity, and these representations are dynamically updated at points where relevant aspects of the situation are changing." See Nicole K. Speer et al., "Reading Stories Activates Neural Representations of Visual and Motor Experiences," *Psychological Science* 20, no. 8 (2009): 989–99, quotes on 989, 998. A neuroimaging study from 2015, however, found that readers "differ in their engagement with fiction: some people are mostly drawn into a story by mentalizing about the thoughts and beliefs of others, whereas others engage in literature by simulating more concrete events such as actions." See Annabel D. Nijhof and Roel M. Willems, "Simulating Fiction: Individual Differences in Literature Comprehension Revealed with fMRI," *PLOS ONE* 10, no. 2 (2015), http://journals.plos.org/plosone/article?id=10.1371/journal.pone.0116492. The very title of the study affirms the central point of this chapter: that generalizations about anything occlude important differences.

174　While poetry more clearly . . . A study from 2013, which sought "to identify the regional brain activations associated with the special qualities of literary language use" (133), found that, in both poetry and prose, "the emotional charge of literary texts is mediated by similar brain structures to the emotional charge of music" (151). Stylistically evocative fiction may thus be suited to the therapeutic needs of some autistic readers. See Adam Zeman et al., "By Heart: An fMRI Study of Brain Activation by Poetry and Prose," *Journal of Consciousness Studies* 20, no. 9–10 (2013): 132–58.

174　Despite having deployed the idiom . . . Grandin, *Thinking*, 91–92.

175　Although she claims to have . . . Grandin, *Thinking*, 199.

175　After all, she once confessed . . . Temple Grandin, "A 'Hog Slaughter' Commentary," http://www.grandin.com/welfare/hog.slaughter.commentary.html.

175　What Robert Penn Warren said . . . Quoted in Brooks, *Well Wrought Urn*, 212. With her squeeze machine in mind, we might imagine Grandin borrowing the words of Wallace Stevens, who, describing how he went about writing poems, once remarked, "I don't feel that I have touched the thing until I touch it in ambiguous form." Quoted in James Longenbach, *Wallace Stevens: The Plain Sense of Things* (Oxford: Oxford University Press, 1991), 148.

175   I'm certain she would agree . . . Martha Nussbaum, *Frontiers of Justice: Disability, Nationality, Species Membership* (Cambridge, MA: Harvard University Press, 2006), 404.

177   The literary critic David Miall . . . David S. Miall, "Emotions and the Structuring of Narrative Responses," *Poetics Today* 32, no. 2 (2011): 323–48, quote on 339.

177   Literature, he argues, triggers . . . Miall, "Emotions," 340.

177   For Miall, literature constitutes . . . Miall, "Emotions," 341.

177   Following the work of . . . Miall, "Emotions," 325.

177   He sees emotion as . . . Miall, "Emotions," 330.

177   An evolutionary inheritance designed . . . Quoted in Miall, "Emotions," 331.

177   Because the amygdala is also . . . Miall, "Emotions," 330.

178   As Miall writes . . . Miall, "Emotions," 334.

179   "In sympathy," writes Mar . . . Mar et al., "Emotion," 824.

180   Recent research stresses the importance . . . A study from 2014 by John Stansfield and Louise Bunce helped to clarify the effects of reading fiction on empathy. Confirming previous studies that had linked "transportation," or "how vividly a person imagines scenes and characters in a particular episode of story-reading," with increased affective empathy and prosocial behavior, they demonstrated that significant exposure to fiction is associated with better mentalizing abilities (or cognitive empathy) but not necessarily with increased affective empathy and altruistic action. For the latter, transportation appears to be key. See Stansfield and Bunce, "The Relationship between Empathy and Reading Fiction: Separate Roles for Cognitive and Affective Components," *Journal of European Psychology Students* 5, no. 3 (2014): 9–18, quote on 14. See also Dan R. Johnson, "Transportation into a Story Increases Empathy, Prosocial Behavior, and Perceptual Bias toward Fearful Expressions," *Personality and Individual Differences* 52, no. 2 (2012): 150–55. In this study, subjects who reported greater transportation while reading were more likely to pick up pens that had been "accidentally" dropped by the experimenter. Finally, see Dan R. Johnson et al., "Potentiating Empathic Growth: Generating Imagery while Reading Fiction Increases Empathy and Prosocial Behavior," *Psychology of Aesthetics, Creativity, and the Arts* 7, no. 3 (2013): 306–12. In this study, instructions to generate mental imagery while reading resulted in greater transportation, affective empathy, and helping tendencies.

182   "We were able to move forward . . ." Mark Osteen, participant, "Neurodiversity and Caregiving: A Roundtable with Parents and Siblings of Children with Autism," *Disability Studies Quarterly* 30, no. 1 (2010), http://dx.doi.org/10.18061/dsq.v30i1.1061.

182   "Learn[] to see and accept . . ." Osteen, "Neurodiversity."

183   She was vigorously relating to . . . Gillian Silverman, personal correspondence.

183   Temple's reaction to "The Ecstatic Cry" . . . Silverman, personal correspondence.

183   Reminded of Temple's comment . . . Silverman, personal correspondence.

183   Why can't she be avoidantly attached . . . My aim is less to diagnose Grandin or to insist on some sort of emotional or relationship norm than to rescue her from neurological fatalism. By substituting a psychological reading, I risk reducing her difference, and yet by not insisting on a psychological reading, I risk consigning her to unfeeling Otherness.

183   In my eagerness to put pressure . . . For a discussion of "queering" autistic sexuality, see Rachael Groner, "Sex as 'Spock': Autism, Sexuality, and Autobiographical Narrative," in *Sex and Disability*, ed. Robert McRuer and Anna Mollow (Durham, NC: Duke University Press, 2012), 263–84. Groner critiques the many implications of heteronormativity as they pertain to the lifestyle choices of autistic people.

184   Recovering yet another norm . . . Pity, of course, is an insidious, self-congratulatory response to physiological and behavioral distinctiveness. Much has been written about this subject. See, for example, Joseph P. Shapiro's seminal book, *No Pity: People with Disabilities Forging a New Civil Rights Movement* (New York: Crown, 1993).

184   In one interview . . . Tom Leonard, "Temple Grandin: My Autism Made Me a Cowgirl Superstar," *Telegraph* (September 27, 2010), http://www .telegraph.co.uk/news/health/8023603/Temple-Grandin-My-autism-made -me-a-cowgirl-superstar.html.

184   In the control condition, where . . . Djikic et al., "Defenseless," 17.

184   The authors reasoned that . . . Djikic et al., "Defenseless," 17.

185   Of the period in the 1970s . . . Grandin, *Thinking*, 115.

186   According to Mar . . . Mar et al., "Emotion," 827.

186   In a separate study of undergraduates . . . Djikic et al., "Moved by Art," 25.

186   . . . but they "stress[ed] that participants . . ." Raymond A. Mar, Maja Djikic, and Keith Oatley, "Effect of Reading on Knowledge, Social Ability, and Selfhood," in *Directions in Empirical Literary Studies*, ed. Sonia Zyngier et al. (Philadelphia: John Benjamins, 2008), 135.

186   Not all of them . . . Mar et al., "Effect of Reading."

186   Miall, as I indicated . . . Miall, "Emotions," 341.

187   Miall, though, is especially sensitive . . . Miall, "Emotions," 341.

187   Characterizing the study of first-year . . . Mar et al., "Effect of Reading," 135.

187   Put another way, the squeeze machine . . . The poet Chris Martin, who teaches poetry writing to autistic people, once said to me that a poem's formal elements and/or organizational structures work like a squeeze machine: with the right amount of pressure, a kind of musical, thought-feeling amalgam occurs. I have adapted this insight for fiction. In *Thinking in Pictures*, Grandin actually speaks of a "language of pressure": "In developing many varied, complex ways to operate the squeeze machine on myself, I keep discovering that slight changes in the way I manipulate the control lever affect how I feel. When I slowly increase the pressure, I make small changes in the rate and timing of the increase. It is like a language of pressure. . . . For me this is the tactile equivalent of a complex emotion and [it] has helped me to understand the complexity of feeling" (92). The very idea of embodied cognition presupposes a tight link between lower-level sensory input and higher-level thought. Sensory equivalents, *integrated* sensory equivalents, are precisely what literature has to offer. As Grandin has said of this machine, so with additional experience she might say of fiction or poetry, "[It] made me feel *social*." See Grandin and Johnson, *Animals*, 114.

188   I still marvel at the coincidence . . . In an interview in *Arizona Agriculture*, Grandin remarks, "If I hadn't gone to my aunt's ranch I wouldn't have gone into the beef industry. It's that simple. If I had not been exposed to cattle, I would not have gotten interested in them." See Julie Murphree, "Arizona Agriculture Shares the Full Conversation We Had with Temple Grandin," *Arizona Farm Bureau* (March 25, 2015), https://www.azfb.org/Article/Arizona-Agriculture-Shares-the-Full-Conversation-We-Had-with-Temple-Grandin.

189   I would have pointed out . . . Temple Grandin, *Different . . . Not Less* (Arlington, VA: Future Horizons, 2012).

189   If Tito is a "Derridean of sound" . . . Although they may end up in the same place, it's worth distinguishing between top-down and bottom-up deconstruction. The former unmakes the world in a deliberate, abstract way; the latter constructs it slowly and concretely.

190   In the context of medical claims . . . Describing animal studies and disability studies as "two of the most philosophically ambitious and ethically challenging" fields "to have emerged over the past decade," Cary Wolfe criticizes the latter for not properly adhering to the dictates of posthumanism, that "'after' [in which] new lines of empathy, affinity, and respect between different forms of life, both human and non-human, may be realized in ways not accountable . . . by the basic coordinates of liberal humanism." See Cary Wolfe, "Learning from Temple Grandin, or, Animal Studies, Dis-

ability Studies, and Who Comes after the Subject?," *New Formations* 64 (Summer 2008): 110–23, quotes on 110. According to Wolfe, the problem with liberal humanism "is not so much what it wants, as the price it pays for what it wants: that in its very attempt to recognize the unique difference and specific ethical value of the other, it reinstates the very normative model of subjectivity that it insists is the problem in the first place" (118). No doubt Wolfe, who tellingly refers to Dawn Prince as a "sufferer" (111) of autism, would level this charge at me. But just as women and African Americans resisted the smug announcement of the "death of the subject" in the 1970s and 1980s, so many people with disabilities resist it now. They can't afford Wolfe's poststructuralist acrobatics—there is too much left to fight for. Grandin's appeal to our common humanity is thus quite different from a privileged person's. And even if we accept Wolfe's critique, the recuperation of universals isn't necessarily as regressive as he thinks. Rough and hesitant—barely functional—autistic universals preserve distinction and reconfigure value.

EPILOGUE

191   Apparently mistaking the Indian men . . . Audra D. S. Burch, "He Became a Hate Crime Victim. She Became a Widow," *New York Times* (July 8, 2017), https://www.nytimes.com/2017/07/08/us/he-became-a-hate-crime -victim-she-became-a-widow.html.

192   "We are flooded by a . . ." Reuven Tsur, *Playing by Ear and the Tip of the Tongue: Precategorical Information in Poetry* (Amsterdam: John Benjamins, 2012), 1.

192   Although made of words . . . Tsur, *Playing by Ear*, 3.

192   It "brings us nearer . . ." Tsur, *Playing by Ear*, 3.

192   Literature, according to Tsur . . . Tsur, *Playing by Ear*, 9.

194   Dora just won a National . . . What is more, Dora's novel just found a publisher. *Hoshi and the Red City Circuit* will appear in 2018 from Argawarga Press, which is the sci-fi/fantasy imprint of the autistic-run Autonomous Press.

· bibliography ·

Adams, Rachel. "A Mixture of Delicious and Freak: The Queer Fiction of Carson McCullers." *American Literature* 71, no. 3 (1999): 551–83.

Albury, William R. "From Changelings to Extraterrestrials: Depictions of Autism in Popular Culture." *Hektoen International: A Journal of Medical Humanities* 3, no. 3 (2011). http://hekint.org/from-changelings-to-extraterrestrials-depictions-of-autism-in-popular-culture/.

Alighieri, Dante. *The Inferno of Dante: A New Verse Translation*. Translated by Robert Pinsky. New York: Farrar, Straus and Giroux, 1997.

Amos, Pat. "Rhythm and Timing in Autism." In *Autism: The Movement Perspective*, edited by Elizabeth Torres and Anne Donnellan. 2015. http://journal.frontiersin.org/researchtopic/801/autism-the-movement-perspective.

Arkoprovo, Paul, Megha Sharda, Soumini Menon, Iti Agora, Nayantara Kansal, Caveat Arora, and Nandini C. Singh. "The Effect of Sung Speech on Socio-communicative Responsiveness in Children with Autism Spectrum Disorders." *Frontiers in Human Neuroscience* 9 (October 29, 2015). doi:10.3389/fnhum.2015.00555.

Arnold, Carrie. "Autism's Race Problem." *Pacific Standard*, May 26, 2016. https://psmag.com/news/autisms-race-problem.

Autism Is a World. Directed by Gerardine Wurzburg. State of the Art Inc., 2005. DVD.

Baron-Cohen, Simon. *Mindblindness: An Essay on Autism and Theory of Mind*. Cambridge, MA: MIT Press, 1995.

Baron-Cohen, Simon, Donielle Johnson, Julian Asher, Sally Wheelwright, Simon E. Fisher, Peter K. Gregersen, and Carrie Allison. "Is Synaesthesia More Common in Autism?" *Molecular Autism* 4, no. 1 (2013): 40. doi:10.1186/2040-2392-4-40.

Bell, Valerie Jackson. "The Onondaga New York Salt Works (1654–1926)." *Science Tribune* (October 1998). http://www.tribunes.com/tribune/sel/bell.htm.

Bertolo, Helder. "Visual Imagery without Visual Perception?" *Psicologica* 26, no. 1 (2005): 173–88.

Bérubé, Michael. *The Secret Life of Stories: From Don Quixote to Harry Potter, How Understanding Intellectual Disability Transforms the Way We Read*. New York: New York University Press, 2016.

Biklen, Douglas. *Autism and the Myth of the Person Alone*. New York: New York University Press, 2005.

Blair, R. J. R. "Responding to the Emotions of Others: Dissociating Forms of Empathy through the Study of Typical and Psychiatric Populations." *Consciousness and Cognition* 14, no. 4 (2005): 698–718. doi:10.1016/j.concog.2005.06.004.

Blakeslee, Sarah. "A Boy, a Mother and a Rare Map of Autism." *New York Times*, November 19, 2002. http://www.nytimes.com/2002/11/19/science/a-boy-a-mother-and-a-rare-map-of-autism-s-world.html?pagewanted=all.

Bläsing, Bettina, Beatriz Calvo-Merino, Emily S. Cross, Corinne Jola, Juliane Honisch, and Catherine J. Stevens. "Neurocognitive Control in Dance Perception and Performance." *Acta Psychologica* 139, no. 2 (2012): 300–308. doi:10.1016/j.actpsy.2011.12.005.

Blume, Harvey. "Q&A with William Gibson." *Boston Globe*, August 19, 2007. http://archive.boston.com/news/globe/ideas/articles/2007/08/19/qa_with_william_gibson/.

Bogdashina, Olga. *Autism and the Edges of the Known World: Sensitivities, Language, and Constructed Reality*. London: Jessica Kingsley, 2010.

Brincker, Maria. "Navigating beyond 'Here and Now' Affordances—On Sensorimotor Maturation and 'False Belief' Performance." *Frontiers in Psychology* 5 (2014). doi:10.3389/fpsyg.2014.01433.

Brincker, Maria, and Elizabeth B. Torres. "Noise from the Periphery in Autism." In *Autism: The Movement Perspective*, edited by Elizabeth B. Torres and Anne M. Donnellan. Frontiers, 2015 (eBook). http://journal.frontiersin.org/researchtopic/801/autism-the-movement-perspective.

Broderick, Alicia A., and Christi Kasa-Hendrickson. "'Say Just One Word at First': The Emergence of Reliable Speech in a Student Labeled with Autism." *Journal of the Association for Persons with Severe Handicaps* 26, no. 1 (2001): 13–24. doi:10.2511/rpsd.26.1.13.

Brooks, Cleanth. *The Well Wrought Urn: Studies in the Structure of Poetry*. New York: Harcourt, 1970.

Brown, Lydia X. Z. "Gendervague: At the Intersection of Autistic and Trans Experience." *The Blog* (web log), June 22, 2016. https://thetaskforceblog.org/2016/06/22/gendervague-at-the-intersection-of-autistic-and-trans-experiences/.

Burch, Audra D. S. "He Became a Hate Crime Victim. She Became a Widow." *New York Times*, July 8, 2017. https://www.nytimes.com/2017/07/08/us/he-became-a-hate-crime-victim-she-became-a-widow.html.

Burke, Jamie. "The Power of Communication and Collaboration: When Partnership Supports the Potential." Presentation, "Making Communication Happen" conference, Burlington, VT, 2010.

———. "The World as I'd Like It to Be." In Douglas Biklen, *Autism and the Myth of the Person Alone*, 249–53. New York: New York University Press, 2005.

Carr, Nicholas. "Is Google Making Us Stupid? What the Internet Is Doing to Our Brains." *Atlantic*, July/August 2008. https://www.theatlantic.com/magazine/archive/2008/07/is-google-making-us-stupid/306868/.

Chen, Jacqueline M., and David L. Hamilton. "Natural Ambiguities: Racial Categorization of Multiracial Individuals." *Journal of Experimental Social Psychology* 48, no. 1 (2012): 152–64. doi:10.1016/j.jesp.2011.10.005.

Cherry, Steven. "This Is Your Brain on Metaphor." *IEEE Spectrum* (2012). http://spectrum.ieee.org/podcast/biomedical/imaging/this-is-your-brain-on-metaphor.

Cohen-Rottenberg, Rachel. "Deconstructing Autism as an Empathy Disorder." *Disability and Representation: Changing the Cultural Conversation* (web log), June 25, 2012. http://www.disabilityandrepresentation.com/deconstructing-autism-as-an-empathy-disorder-a-literature-review/.

———. "Unwarranted Conclusions and the Potential for Harm: My Reply to Simon Baron-Cohen." *Autism and Empathy: Dispelling Myths and Breaking Stereotypes* (web log), 2011. https://autismandempathyblog.wordpress.com/unwarranted-conclusions-and-the-potential-for-harm-my-reply-to-simon-baron-cohen/.

Cuddy-Keane, Melba. "Narration, Navigation, and Non-conscious Thought: Neuroscientific and Literary Approaches to the Thinking Body." *University of Toronto Quarterly* 79, no. 2 (2010): 680–701. doi:10.3138/utq.79.2.680.

Cysarz, Dirk, et al. "Oscillations of Heart Rate and Respiration Synchronize during Poetry Recitation." *American Journal of Heart and Circulatory Physiology* 287, no. 2 (2004). doi:10.1152/ajpheart.01131.2003.

Dautenhahn, Kerstin. "Roles and Functions of Robots in Human Society: Implications from Research in Autism Therapy." *Robotica* 21, no. 4 (2003): 443–52. doi:10.1017/s0263574703004922.

Deej. Directed by Rob Rooy. Rooy Media LLC and ITVS, 2017. DVD.

Dick, Philip K. *Do Androids Dream of Electric Sheep?* New York: Del Rey, 1996. Originally published in 1968.

———. *The Exegesis of Philip K. Dick*. Edited by Pamela Renee Jackson and Jonathan Lethem. Boston: Houghton Mifflin Harcourt, 2011.

Djikic, Maja, and Keith Oatley. "The Art in Fiction: From Indirect Communication to Changes of the Self." *Psychology of Aesthetics, Creativity, and the Arts* 8, no. 4 (2014): 498–505. doi:10.1037/a0037999.

Djikic, Maja, Keith Oatley, and Matthew Carland. "Genre or Artistic Merit? The Effect of Literature on Personality." *Scientific Study of Literature* 2, no. 1 (2012): 25–36. doi:10.1075/ssol.2.1.02dji.

Djikic, Maja, Keith Oatley, and Jordan B. Peterson. "The Bitter-Sweet Labor of Emoting: The Linguistic Comparison of Writers and Physicists." *Creativity Research Journal* 18, no. 2 (2006): 195–201. doi:10.1207/s15326934crj1802_5.

Djikic, Maja, Keith Oatley, Sara Zoeterman, and Jordan B. Peterson. "Defenseless against Art? Impact of Reading Fiction on Emotion in Avoidantly Attached Individuals." *Journal of Research in Personality* 43, no. 1 (2009): 14–17. doi:10.1016/j.jrp.2008.09.003.

———. "On Being Moved by Art: How Reading Fiction Transforms the Self." *Creativity Research Journal* 21, no. 1 (2009): 24–29. doi:10.1080/10400410802633392.

Donnellan, Anne M. "The Criterion of the Least Dangerous Assumption." *Behavioral Disorders* 9, no. 2 (1984): 141–50.

Dziobek, Isabel, Kimberley Rogers, Stefan Fleck, Markus Bahnemann, Hauke R. Heekeren, Oliver T. Wolf, and Antonio Convit. "Dissociation of Cognitive and Emotional Empathy in Adults with Asperger Syndrome Using the Multifaceted Empathy Test (MET)." *Journal of Autism and Developmental Disorders* 38, no. 3 (2007): 464–73. doi:10.1007/s10803-007-0486-x.

Edelman, Gerald M. *Second Nature: Brain Science and Human Knowledge.* New Haven, CT: Yale University Press, 2007.

Eye in the Sky. Directed by Gavin Hood. Entertainment One, 2015. Film.

Farmer, Stephen. "The Neurobiological Origins of Primitive Religion: Implications for Comparative Mythology." In *New Perspectives on Myth: Proceedings of the Second Annual Conference of the International Association for Comparative Mythology,* edited by Wim M. J. van Binsbergen and Eric Venbrux, 279–314. Haarlem: Shikanda, 2010.

Fini, Chiara, Flavia Cardini, Ana Tajadura-Jiménez, Andrea Serino, and Manos Tsakiris. "Embodying an Outgroup: The Role of Racial Bias and the Effect of Multisensory Processing in Somatosensory Remapping." *Frontiers in Behavioral Neuroscience* 7 (November 2013). doi:10.3389/fnbeh.2013.00165.

Fisher, Jennifer. "Ballet and Whiteness: Will Ballet Forever Be the Kingdom of the Pale?" In *The Oxford Handbook of Dance and Ethnicity,* edited by Anthony Shay and Barbara Sellers-Young, 585–97. Oxford: Oxford University Press, 2016.

Frank, Arthur W. *The Wounded Storyteller: Body, Illness, and Ethics.* Chicago: University of Chicago Press, 1995.

Fries, Kenny, ed. *Staring Back: The Disability Experience from the Inside Out.* New York: Plume, 1997.

Frith, Uta, Francesca Happé, and Frances Siddons. "Autism and Theory of Mind in Everyday Life." *Social Development* 3, no. 2 (1994): 108–24. doi:10.1111/j.1467-9507.1994.tb00031.x.

Gaither, Sarah E. "'Mixed' Results: Multiracial Research and Identity Explorations." *Current Directions in Psychological Science* 24, no. 2 (2015): 114–19. doi:10.1177/0963721414558115.

Gebauer, Line, Joshua Skewes, Gitte Westphael, Pamela Heaton, and Peter Vuust. "Intact Brain Processing of Musical Emotions in Autism Spectrum Disorders, but More Cognitive Load and Arousal in Happy vs. Sad Music." *Frontiers in Neuroscience* 8 (2014). doi:10.3389/fnins.2014.00192.

Gilligan, Carol. *In a Different Voice: Psychological Theory and Women's Development.* Cambridge, MA: Harvard University Press, 1993. Originally published in 1982.

Gold, Rinat, and Miriam Faust. "Right Hemisphere Dysfunction and Metaphor Comprehension in Young Adults with Asperger Syndrome." *Journal of Autism and Developmental Disorders* 40, no. 7 (2010): 800–811. doi:10.1007/s10803-009-0930-1.

Gowen, Emma, and Antonia Hamilton. "Motor Abilities in Autism: A Review Using a Computational Context." *Journal of Autism and Developmental Disorders* 43, no. 2 (2013): 323–44. doi:10.1007/s10803-012-1574-0.

Grandin, Temple. *Different . . . Not Less.* Arlington, VA: Future Horizons, 2012.

———. "An Inside View of Autism." In *High-Functioning Individuals with Autism,* edited by Eric Schopler and Gary B. Mesibov. New York: Plenum Press, 1992.

———. "My Mind Is a Web Browser: How People with Autism Think." *Cerebrum* 2, no. 1 (2000): 14–22.

———. *Thinking in Pictures*, expanded edition. New York: Vintage, 2006.

Grandin, Temple, and Mark Deesing. *Humane Livestock Handling*. Pownal, VT: Storey Publishing, 2008.

Grandin, Temple, and Catherine Johnson. *Animals in Translation: Using the Mysteries of Autism to Decode Animal Behavior*. New York: Mariner Books, 2006.

Grandin, Temple, and Richard Panek. *The Autistic Brain: Thinking across the Spectrum*. Boston: Houghton Mifflin Harcourt, 2013.

Groner, Rachael. "Sex as 'Spock': Autism, Sexuality, and Autobiographical Narrative." In *Sex and Disability*, edited by Robert McRuer and Anna Mollow, 263–84. Durham, NC: Duke University Press, 2012.

Hacking, Ian. "Autistic Autobiography." *Philosophical Transactions of the Royal Society of London B: Biological Sciences* 364, no. 1522 (May 27, 2009): 1467–73. doi:10.1098/rstb.2008.0329.

———. "Humans, Aliens and Autism." *Daedalus* 138, no. 3 (2009): 44–59. doi:10.1162/daed.2009.138.3.44.

Happé, Francesca G. "Understanding Minds and Metaphors: Insights from the Study of Figurative Language in Autism." *Metaphor and Symbol* 10, no. 4 (1995): 275–95. doi:10.1207/s15327868ms1004_3.

Haraway, Donna. "A Cyborg Manifesto: Science, Technology, and Socialist-Feminism in the Late Twentieth Century." In *Simians, Cyborgs and Women: The Reinvention of Nature*, 149–82. New York: Routledge, 1991.

Hardy, Michael W., and A. Blythe Lagasse. "Rhythm, Movement and Autism: Using Rhythmic Rehabilitation Research as a Model for Autism." In *Autism: The Movement Perspective*, edited by Elizabeth Torres and Anne Donnellan. 2015. http://journal.frontiersin.org/researchtopic/801/autism-the-movement-perspective.

Harris, Lasana T., and Susan T. Fiske. "The Brooms in Fantasia: Neural Correlates of Anthropomorphizing Objects." *Social Cognition* 26, no. 2 (2008): 210–23. doi:10.1521/soco.2008.26.2.210.

Harvey, Graham. *Animism: Respecting the Living World*. New York: Columbia University Press, 2005.

Hermelin, Beate. *Bright Splinters of the Mind: A Personal Story of Research with Autistic Savants*. London: Jessica Kingsley, 2001.

Hoppenstand, Gary, Garyn G. Roberts, and Ray B. Browne, eds. *The Defective Detective in the Pulps*. Bowling Green, OH: Bowling Green University Popular Press, 1983.

Horsley, Jasun. "How Am I Not Myself? Philip K. Dick, the Autism Connection." *Auticulture* (web log), October 28, 2013. https://auticulture.wordpress.com/2013/10/28/philip-k-dick-autistic-time-slip/.

Interactive Autism Network. "Restricted Interests, Obsessions, 'Special Topics,' and Attention Deficits." April 2, 2007. https://iancommunity.org/cs/challenging_behavior/challenging_behavior_restricted_interests.

Irmer, Thomas. "An Interview with Leslie Marmon Silko." *Write Stuff*. http://www.altx.com/interviews/silko.html.

Jabr, Ferris. "How Does a Caterpillar Turn into a Butterfly?" *Scientific American*, August 10, 2012. https://www.scientificamerican.com/article/caterpillar-butterfly-metamorphosis-explainer/.

Järvinen-Pasley, Anna, Gregory L. Wallace, Franck Ramus, Francesca Happé, and Pamela Heaton. "Enhanced Perceptual Processing of Speech in Autism." *Developmental Science* 11, no. 1 (2008): 109–21. doi:10.1111/j.1467-7687.2007.00644.x.

Jaynes, Julian. *The Origin of Consciousness in the Breakdown of the Bicameral Mind*. Boston: Houghton Mifflin, 1976.

Johnson, Dan R. "Transportation into a Story Increases Empathy, Prosocial Behavior, and Perceptual Bias toward Fearful Expressions." *Personality and Individual Differences* 52, no. 2 (2012): 150–55. doi:10.1016/j.paid.2011.10.005.

Johnson, Dan R., Grace K. Cushman, Lauren A. Borden, and Madison S. McCune. "Potentiating Empathic Growth: Generating Imagery while Reading Fiction Increases Empathy and Prosocial Behavior." *Psychology of Aesthetics, Creativity, and the Arts* 7, no. 3 (2013): 306–12. doi:10.1037/a0033261.

Johnson, Nathanael. "Temple Grandin Digs in on the Practical Side of What Animals Want." *Grist*, July 22, 2015. http://grist.org/food/temple-grandin-digs-in-on-the-practical-side-of-what-animals-want/.

Kana, Rajesh K., et al. "Sentence Comprehension in Autism: Thinking in Pictures with Decreased Functional Connectivity." *Brain* 129, no. 9 (2006): 2484–93. doi:10.1093/brain/awl164.

Kang, Sonia K., and Galen V. Bodenhausen. "Multiple Identities in Social Perception and Interaction: Challenges and Opportunities." *Annual Review of Psychology* 66, no. 1 (2015): 547–74. doi:10.1146/annurev-psych-010814-015025.

Kidd, David Comer, and Emanuele Castano. "Reading Literary Fiction Improves Theory of Mind." *Science* 342, no. 6156 (October 18, 2013): 377–80. doi:10.1126/science.1239918.

Klin, A., W. Jones, R. Schultz, and F. Volkmar. "The Enactive Mind, or from Actions to Cognition: Lessons from Autism." *Philosophical Transactions of the Royal Society of London B: Biological Sciences* 358, no. 1430 (February 28, 2003): 345–60. doi:10.1098/rstb.2002.1202.

Klinkenborg, Verlyn. "What Do Animals Think?" *Discover*, May 1, 2005. http://discovermagazine.com/2005/may/what-do-animals-think.

Kolvin, Israel. "Studies in the Childhood Psychoses: Diagnostic Criteria and Classification." *British Journal of Psychiatry* 118, no. 545 (1971): 381–84. doi:10.1192/bjp.118.545.381.

Koshino, Hideya, Patricia A. Carpenter, Nancy J. Minshew, Vladimir L. Cherkassky, Timothy A. Keller, and Marcel Adam Just. "Functional Connectivity in an fMRI Working Memory Task in High-Functioning Autism." *NeuroImage* 24, no. 3 (2005): 810–21. doi:10.1016/j.neuroimage.2004.09.028.

Kuhn, Thomas. *The Structure of Scientific Revolutions*. 3rd ed. Chicago: University of Chicago Press, 1996.

Kuppers, Petra. *Disability Culture and Community Performance: Find a Strange and Twisted Shape*. Basingstoke, UK: Palgrave Macmillan, 2011.

Lacey, Simon, Randall Stilla, and K. Sathian. "Metaphorically Feeling: Comprehending Textual Metaphors Activates Somatosensory Cortex." *Brain and Language* 120, no. 3 (2012): 416–21. doi:10.1016/j.bandl.2011.12.016.

Lang, Martin, Daniel J. Shaw, Paul Reddish, Sebastian Wallot, Panagiotis Mitkidis, and Dimitris Xygalatas. "Lost in the Rhythm: Effects of Rhythm on Subsequent Interpersonal Coordination." *Cognitive Science* 40, no. 7 (2015): 1797–815. doi:10.1111/cogs.12302.

Leach, Michelle. "Deafness with Autism: A School Age Communication Perspective." *Audiology Online*. November 17, 2014. http://www.audiologyonline.com/articles/deafness-with-autism-school-age-13001.

Leonard, Tom. "Temple Grandin: My Autism Made Me a Cowgirl Superstar." *Telegraph*, September 27, 2010. http://www.telegraph.co.uk/news/health/8023603/Temple-Grandin-My-autism-made-me-a-cowgirl-superstar.html.

Lepisto, Tuulia. "Cortical Processing of Speech and Non-speech Sounds in Autism and Asperger Syndrome." PhD dissertation, University of Helsinki, 2008.

Lerner, Matthew D., James C. McPartland, and James P. Morris. "Multimodal Emotion Processing in Autism Spectrum Disorders: An Event-Related Potential Study." *Developmental Cognitive Neuroscience* 3 (2013): 11–21. doi:10.1016/j.dcn.2012.08.005.

Longenbach, James. *Wallace Stevens: The Plain Sense of Things*. Oxford: Oxford University Press, 1991.

Loving Lampposts, Living Autistic. Directed by Todd Drezner. Cinema Libre Studio, 2011. DVD.

Lyman, Rick. "No More Crushes; This Is Serious." *New York Times*, January 29, 2010. http://www.nytimes.com/2010/01/31/arts/television/31danes.html.

Mahoney, John. "A Psychologist Looks Thoreau in the Eye: Did He Meet Criteria for Asperger Disorder?" *Thoreau Society Bulletin*, no. 267 (2009). https://archive.org/stream/thoreausociety2009267unse/thoreausociety2009267unse_djvu.txt.

Malerich, C. S. "Meat." In *Among Animals: The Lives of Animals and Humans in Contemporary Short Fiction*, edited by John Yunker, 55–68. Ashland, OR: Ashland Creek Press, 2014.

Manning, Erin. *Always More Than One: Individuation's Dance*. Durham, NC: Duke University Press, 2013.

Mar, Raymond A. "Simulation-Based Theories of Narrative Comprehension: Evidence and Implications." PhD dissertation, University of Toronto, 2007.

Mar, Raymond A., Maja Djikic, and Keith Oatley. "Effect of Reading on Knowledge, Social Ability, and Selfhood." In *Directions in Empirical Literary Studies*, edited by Sonia Zyngier, Marisa Bortolussi, Anna Chesnokova, and Jan Auracher, 127–37. Philadelphia: John Benjamins, 2008.

Mar, Raymond A., and Keith Oatley. "The Function of Fiction Is the Abstraction and Simulation of Social Experience." *Perspectives on Psychological Science* 3, no. 3 (2008): 173–92. doi:10.1111/j.1745-6924.2008.00073.x.

Mar, Raymond A., Keith Oatley, Maja Djikic, and Justin Mullin. "Emotion and Narrative Fiction: Interactive Influences before, during, and after Reading." *Cognition and Emotion* 25, no. 5 (2011): 818–33. doi:10.1080/02699931.2010.515151.

Mar, Raymond A., Keith Oatley, Jacob Hirsh, Jennifer Deal Paz, and Jordan B. Peterson. "Bookworms versus Nerds: Exposure to Fiction versus Non-fiction, Divergent Associations with Social Ability, and the Simulation of Fictional Social Worlds." *Journal of Research in Personality* 40, no. 5 (2006): 694–712. doi:10.1016/j. jrp.2005.08.002.

Mar, Raymond A., Keith Oatley, and Jordan B. Peterson. "Exploring the Link between Reading Fiction and Empathy: Ruling Out Individual Differences and Examining Outcomes." *Communications* 34, no. 4 (2009): 407–28. doi:10.1515/ comm.2009.025.

Martensson, Frida, M. Roll, P. Apt, and M. Horne. "Modelling the Meaning of Words: Neural Correlates of Abstract and Concrete Noun Processing." *ACTA Neurobiologiae Experimentalis* 71, no. 4 (2011): 455–78. doi:10.3389/conf. fnins.2010.14.00113.

McCullers, Carson. *The Heart Is a Lonely Hunter*. New York: Mariner Books, 2000. Originally published in 1940.

McGilchrist, Iain. *The Master and His Emissary: The Divided Brain and the Making of the Western World*. New Haven, CT: Yale University Press, 2012.

McMurtry, Larry. "Introduction." In Leslie Marmon Silko, *Ceremony*. New York: Penguin, 2007.

McRuer, Robert. *Crip Theory: Cultural Signs of Queerness and Disability*. New York: New York University Press, 2006.

Melogno, Sergio, and Maria Antonietta Pinto. "Enhancing Metaphor and Metonymy Comprehension in Children with High-Functioning Autism Spectrum Disorder." *Psychology* 5, no. 11 (2014): 1375–83. doi:10.4236/psych.2014.511148.

Melville, Herman. *Moby-Dick: A Longman Critical Edition*. Edited by John Bryant and Haskell Springer. New York: Longman, 2006. Originally published in 1851.

———. *The Writings of Herman Melville: Correspondence*. Edited by Lynn Horth. Evanston, IL: Northwestern University Press, 1993.

Miall, David S. "Emotions and the Structuring of Narrative Responses." *Poetics Today* 32, no. 2 (2011): 323–48. doi:10.1215/03335372-1162704.

Mottron, Laurent, Lucie Bouvet, Anna Bonnel, Fabienne Samson, Jacob A. Burack, Michelle Dawson, and Pamela Heaton. "Veridical Mapping in the Development of Exceptional Autistic Abilities." *Neuroscience and Biobehavioral Reviews* 37, no. 2 (2013): 209–28. doi:10.1016/j.neubiorev.2012.11.016.

Mottron, Laurent, and Jacob Burak. "Sensory, Motor and Attentional Characteristics of Autistic Children." In *Encyclopedia on Early Childhood Development (2012–2015)*. http://www.child-encyclopedia.com/sites/default/files/textes-experts/en /572/sensory-motor-and-attention-characteristics-of-autistic-children.pdf.

Mottron, Laurent, Michelle Dawson, Isabelle Soulières, Benedicte Hubert, and Jake Burack. "Enhanced Perceptual Functioning in Autism: An Update, and Eight Principles of Autistic Perception." *Journal of Autism and Developmental Disorders* 36, no. 1 (2006): 27–43. doi:10.1007/s10803-005-0040-7.

Mukhopadhyay, Tito Rajarshi. *Beyond the Silence: My Life, the World and Autism*. London: National Autistic Society, 2000.

———. *How Can I Talk If My Lips Don't Move? Inside My Autistic Mind*. New York: Arcade, 2008.

———. *The Mind Tree: A Miraculous Child Breaks the Silence of Autism*. New York: Arcade, 2003.

———. *Plankton Dreams: What I Learned in Special-Ed*. London: Open Humanities Press, 2015.

Murphree, Julie. "Arizona Agriculture Shares the Full Conversation We Had with Temple Grandin." *Arizona Farm Bureau*, March 25, 2015. https://www.azfb.org/Article /Arizona-Agriculture-Shares-the-Full-Conversation-We-Had-with-Temple-Grandin.

My Classic Life as an Artist: A Portrait of Larry Bissonnette. Directed by Douglass Biklen and Zach Rossetti. Syracuse University, 2005.

Nagel, Thomas. "What Is It Like to Be a Bat?" *Philosophical Review* 83, no. 4 (1974): 435–50. doi:10.2307/2183914.

Nicolaidis, Christina, Dora Raymaker, Katherine Mcdonald, Sebastian Dern, Elesia Ashkenazy, Cody Boisclair, Scott Robertson, and Amanda Baggs. "Collaboration Strategies in Nontraditional Community-Based Participatory Research Partnerships: Lessons from an Academic–Community Partnership with Autistic Self-Advocates." *Progress in Community Health Partnerships: Research, Education, and Action* 5, no. 2 (2011): 143–50. doi:10.1353/cpr.2011.0022.

Nijhof, Annabel D., and Roel M. Willems. "Simulating Fiction: Individual Differences in Literature Comprehension Revealed with fMRI." *PLOS ONE* 10, no. 2 (2015). doi:10.1371/journal.pone.0116492.

Norbury, Courtenay Frazier. "The Relationship between Theory of Mind and Metaphor: Evidence from Children with Language Impairment and Autistic Spectrum Disorder." *British Journal of Developmental Psychology* 23, no. 3 (2005): 383–99. doi:10.1348/026151005x26732.

Nussbaum, Martha. *Frontiers of Justice: Disability, Nationality, Species Membership*. Cambridge, MA: Harvard University Press, 2006.

Obermeier, Christian, Winfried Menninghaus, Martin Von Koppenfels, Tim Raettig, Maren Schmidt-Kassow, Sascha Otterbein, and Sonja A. Kotz. "Aesthetic and Emotional Effects of Meter and Rhyme in Poetry." *Frontiers in Psychology* 4 (2013). doi:10.3389/fpsyg.2013.00010.

"Obsessive Empathy for Inanimate Objects." *Wrong Planet*, last modified March 21, 2006. http://wrongplanet.net/forums/viewtopic.php?t=12187.

Ochs, Elinor, and Olga Solomon. "Practical Logic and Autism." In *A Companion to Psychological Anthropology: Modernity and Psychocultural Change*, edited by Conerly Casey and Robert B. Edgerton, 140–67. Hoboken, NJ: John Wiley and Sons, 2005.

Osteen, Mark, participant. "Neurodiversity and Caregiving: A Roundtable with Parents and Siblings of Children with Autism." *Disability Studies Quarterly* 30, no. 1 (2010). http://dx.doi:10.18061/dsq.v30i1.1061.

Otis, Laura. *Rethinking Thought: Inside the Minds of Creative Scientists and Artists*. New York: Oxford University Press, 2015.

Persicke, Angela, Jonathan Tarbox, Jennifer Ranick, and Megan St. Clair. "Establishing Metaphorical Reasoning in Children with Autism." *Research in*

Autism Spectrum Disorders 6, no. 2 (2012): 913–20. doi:10.1016/j.rasd.2011. 12.007.

Pinker, Steven. *How the Mind Works*. New York: W. W. Norton, 1997.

Pino, Maria Chiara, and Monica Mazza. "The Use of 'Literary Fiction' to Promote Mentalizing Ability." *PLOS ONE* 11, no. 8 (2016). doi:10.1371/journal.pone.0160254.

Prince, Dawn. *Circus of Souls: How I Discovered We Are All Freaks Passing for Normal*. Seattle, WA: CreateSpace, 2013.

———. "The Silence Between: An Autoethnographic Examination of the Language Prejudice and Its Impact on the Assessment of Autistic and Animal Intelligence." *Disability Studies Quarterly* 30, no. 1 (2010). doi:10.18061/dsq.v30i1.1055.

Prince-Hughes, Dawn. *Songs of the Gorilla Nation: My Journey through Autism*. New York: Broadway, 2005.

Purdy, Gilbert Wesley. "Henry David Thoreau and Two Other Lives: Before the Diagnosis Existed." *Virtual Vanaprastha*, 2014. https://www.aane.org/asperger_resources/articles/miscellaneous/henry_david_thoreau_aspergers.html.

Ramachandran, V. S. "Ted Talk: Ramachandran on Your Mind." November 25, 2010. https://brainchemist.wordpress.com/2010/11/25/ted-talk-ramachandran-on-your-mind/.

Ranick, Jennifer, Angela Persicke, Jonathan Tarbox, and Jake A. Kornack. "Teaching Children with Autism to Detect and Respond to Deceptive Statements." *Research in Autism Spectrum Disorders* 7, no. 4 (2013): 503–8. doi:10.1016/j.rasd.2012.12.001.

Rauschecker, Josef, B. Green, J. Salmi, I. Jaakselainen, and M. Sams. "Differentially Recruited Brain Areas for Familiar and Unfamiliar Segments of a Progressively Presented Musical Sequence." Presentation, Neuroscience conference, New Orleans, LA, 2012.

Raymaker, Dora. "Intersections of Critical Systems Thinking and Community Based Participatory Research in Developing a Web Site for Autistic Adults." PhD dissertation, Portland State University, 2015.

Raymond, Midge. "The Ecstatic Cry." In *Among Animals: The Lives of Animals and Humans in Contemporary Short Fiction*, edited by John Yunker, 87–106. Ashland, OR: Ashland Creek Press, 2014.

Richardson, Alan. "Imagination: Literary and Cognitive Intersections." In *The Oxford Handbook of Cognitive Literary Studies*, edited by Lisa Zunshine. Oxford: Oxford University Press, 2015.

Ricks, Daniel J., and Mark B. Colton. "Trends and Considerations in Robot-Assisted Autism Therapy." Robotics and Automation (ICRA), IEEE International Conference, 2010, Anchorage, AK.

Robertson, Scott Michael. "Neurodiversity, Quality of Life, and Autistic Adults: Shifting Research and Professional Focuses onto Real-Life Challenges." *Disability Studies Quarterly* 30, no. 1 (2010). doi:10.18061/dsq.v30i1.1069.

Roth, Ilona. "Imagination and the Awareness of Self in Autistic Spectrum Poets." In *Autism and Representation*, edited by Mark Osteen, 145–65. London: Routledge, 2008.

Russell, Emily. *Reading Embodied Citizenship: Disability, Narrative, and the Body Politic*. New Brunswick, NJ: Rutgers University Press, 2011.

Sacks, Oliver. *An Anthropologist on Mars: Seven Paradoxical Tales*. New York: Vintage, 1996.

Saulny, Susan. "Census Data Present Rise in Multiracial Population of Youth." *New York Times*, March 24, 2011. http://www.nytimes.com/2011/03/25/us/25race.html.

Savarese, Emily T., and Ralph J. Savarese. "'The Superior Half of Speaking': An Introduction." *Disability Studies Quarterly* 30, no. 1 (2010). doi:10.18061/dsq.v30i1.1062.

Savarese, Ralph J. "Cognition." In *Keywords for Disability Studies*, edited by Rachel Adams, Benjamin Reiss, and David Serlin, 40–42. New York: New York University Press, 2015.

———. "I Object: Autism, Empathy, and the Trope of Personification." In *Rethinking Empathy*, edited by Sue Kim and Meghan Marie Hammond, 74–92. New York: Routledge, 2014.

———. "More Than a Thing to Ignore: An Interview with Tito Rajarshi Mukhopadhyay." *Disability Studies Quarterly* 30, no. 1 (2010). doi:10.18061/dsq.v30i1.1056.

———. "Moving the Field: The Sensorimotor Perspective on Autism." (Commentary on "Rethinking Autism: Implications of Sensory and Motor Differences," an article by Anne Donnellan, David Hill, and Martha Leary.) *Frontiers in Integrative Neuroscience* 7, no. 6 (2013). doi:10.3389/fnint.2013.00006.

———. "Neurocosmopolitan Melville." *Leviathan: A Journal of Melville Studies* 15, no. 2 (2013): 7–19. doi:10.1353/lvn.2013.0015.

———. *Reasonable People: A Memoir of Autism and Adoption*. New York: Other Press, 2007.

———. "Toward a Postcolonial Neurology: Autism, Tito Mukhopadhyay, and a New Geo-poetics of the Body." *Journal of Literary and Cultural Disability Studies* 4, no. 3 (2010): 273–90.

———. "What Some Autistics Can Teach Us about Poetry: A Neurocosmopolitan Approach." In *The Oxford Handbook of Cognitive Literary Studies*, edited by Lisa Zunshine, 393–417. Oxford: Oxford University Press, 2015.

Savarese, Ralph James, and Emily Thornton Savarese, eds. "Autism and the Concept of Neurodiversity." *Disability Studies Quarterly* 30, no. 1 (2010). http://dsq-sds.org/issue/view/43.

Savarese, Ralph James, and Lisa Zunshine. "The Critic as Neurocosmopolite; Or, What Cognitive Approaches to Literature Can Learn from Disability Studies." *Narrative* 22, no. 1 (2014): 17–44. doi:10.1353/nar.2014.0000.

Serres, Michel. *The Five Senses: A Philosophy of Mingled Bodies*. London: Continuum, 2009.

Shamay-Tsoory, Simone G. "The Neural Bases for Empathy." *Neuroscientist* 17, no. 1 (2011): 18–24. doi:10.1177/1073858410379268.

Shapiro, Joseph P. *No Pity: People with Disabilities Forging a New Civil Rights Movement*. New York: Crown, 1993.

Sharda, Megha, Rashi Midha, Supriya Malik, Shaneel Mukerji, and Nandini C. Singh. "Fronto-temporal Connectivity Is Preserved during Sung but Not Spoken

Word Listening, across the Autism Spectrum." *Autism Research* 8, no. 2 (2015): 174–86. doi:10.1002/aur.1437.

Sheffer, Edith. "The Nazi History behind 'Asperger.'" *New York Times*, March 31, 2018.

Shore, Stephen. "What We Have to Tell You: A Roundtable with Self-Advocates from AutCom." Edited by Emily Thornton Savarese. *Disability Studies Quarterly* 30, no.1 (2010). http://dsq-sds.org/article/view/1073/1239.

Silberman, Steve. "The Geek Syndrome." *Wired* 9 (2001): 174–83. https:// www .wired.com/2001/12/aspergers/.

———. *NeuroTribes: The Legacy of Autism and the Future of Neurodiversity.* New York: Penguin Random House, 2015.

———. "Was Dr. Asperger a Nazi? The Question Still Haunts Autism." National Public Radio, January 20, 2016. http://www.npr.org/sections/health-shots/ 2016/01/20/463603652/was-dr-asperger-a-nazi-the-question-still-haunts-autism.

Silk, Dennis. "The Marionette Theatre." In *The Next American Essay*, edited by John D'Agata, 168–79. Minneapolis, MN: Graywolf, 2003.

Silko, Leslie Marmon. *Ceremony.* New York: Penguin, 2007. Originally published in 1977.

Silverman, Gillian. *Bodies and Books.* Philadelphia: University of Pennsylvania Press, 2012.

———. "Neurodiversity and the Revision of Book History." *PMLA* 131, no. 2 (2016): 307–23. doi:10.1632/pmla.2016.131.2.307.

Simner, J., and E. M. Hubbard. "Variants of Synesthesia Interact in Cognitive Tasks: Evidence for Implicit Associations and Late Connectivity in Cross-Talk Theories." *Neuroscience* 143, no. 3 (2006): 805–14. doi:10.1016/j.neuroscience.2006.08.018.

Sinclair, Jim. "Why I Dislike 'Person-First' Language." http://autismmythbusters .com/general-public/autistic-vs-people-with-autism/jim-sinclair-why-i-dislike -person-first-language/.

Smilek, Daniel, Kelly A. Malcolmson, Jonathan S. A. Carriere, Meghan Eller, Donna Kwan, and Michael Reynolds. "When '3' Is a Jerk and 'E' Is a King: Personify-ing Inanimate Objects in Synesthesia." *Journal of Cognitive Neuroscience* 19, no. 6 (2007): 981–92. doi:10.1162/jocn.2007.19.6.981.

Smith, Adam. "The Empathy Imbalance Hypothesis of Autism: A Theoretical Ap-proach to Cognitive and Emotional Empathy in Autistic Development." *Psycho-logical Record* 59, no. 2 (2009): 489–510. doi:10.1007/bf03395663.

Speer, Nicole K., Jeremy R. Reynolds, Khena M. Swallow, and Jeffrey M. Zacks. "Reading Stories Activates Neural Representations of Visual and Motor Experiences." *Psychological Science* 20, no. 8 (2009): 989–99. doi:10.1111/j.1467-9280.2009.02397.x.

Stansfield, John, and Louise Bunce. "The Relationship between Empathy and Read-ing Fiction: Separate Roles for Cognitive and Affective Components." *Journal of European Psychology Students* 5, no. 3 (2014): 9–18. doi:10.5334/jeps.ca.

Stephens, Greg J., Lauren J. Silbert, and Uri Hasson. "Speaker-Listener Neural Cou-pling Underlies Successful Communication." *Proceedings of the National Academy of Sciences* 107, no. 32 (2010): 14425–30.

Sturgeon, Theodore. *More Than Human*. New York: Vintage, 1998. Originally published in 1953.

Sullivan, Jenna. "Saving the Black Swan: Responses to Racial Disparity in Classical Ballet." Rhodes Institute for Regional Studies. Unpublished, 2012.

Tammet, Daniel. *Born on a Blue Day: Inside the Extraordinary Mind of an Autistic Savant*. New York: Free Press, 2006.

Temple Grandin. Directed by Mick Jackson. HBO, 2010. DVD.

Thorson, Robert M. "Thoreau and Asperger Syndrome?" *Thoreau Society Bulletin*, no. 262 (2008). https://archive.org/stream/thoreausociety2008262unse /thoreausociety2008262unse_djvu.txt.

Tsur, Reuven. *Playing by Ear and the Tip of the Tongue: Precategorical Information in Poetry*. Amsterdam: John Benjamins, 2012.

———. "The Poetic Mode of Speech Perception Revisited: What Our Ear Tells Our Mind." Lecture, 2010. http://www.tau.ac.il/~tsurxx/Poetic_Mode_Revisited.pdf.

Turner, Fredrick, and Ernst Pöppel. "The Neural Lyre: Poetic Meter, the Brain, and Time." *Poetry* (August 1983): 24. http://munnecke.com/papers/Turner-Neural -Lyre.pdf.

Twain, Mark. *The Adventures of Huckleberry Finn*. New York: Harper & Brothers, 1896. Originally published in 1888.

"2016 Day of Mourning Vigils." *Autistic Self Advocacy Network*. Last modified January 15, 2016. http://autisticadvocacy.org/2016/01/2016-day-of-mourning-vigils/.

van der Kolk, Bessel. "Clinical Implications of Neuroscience Research in PTSD." *Annals of the New York Academy of Sciences* 1071, no. 1 (2006): 277–93. doi:10.1196/annals.1364.022.

———. "Psychobiology of Post-traumatic Stress Disorder." In *Textbook of Biological Psychiatry*, edited by Jaak Panksepp, 319–44. Hoboken, NJ: Wiley & Sons, 2004.

Walker, Nick. *Neurocosmopolitanism*. http://www.neurocosmopolitanism.com.

Ward, Jamie, and Michael J. Banissy. "Explaining Mirror-Touch Synesthesia." *Cognitive Neuroscience* 6, no. 2–3 (2015): 118–33. doi:10.1080/17588928.2015.1042444.

Waytz, Adam, John Cacioppo, and Nicholas Epley. "Who Sees Human? The Stability and Importance of Individual Differences in Anthropomorphism." *Perspectives on Psychological Science* 5, no. 3 (2014): 219–32. dos:10.1177/1745691610369336.

Wetherell, W. D. "Where Melville Paid Homage to a Mountain." *New York Times*, June 7, 1998. http://www.nytimes.com/1998/06/07/travel/where-melville-paid -homage-to-a-mountain.html.

White, William. *Notes and Queries*. Oxford: Oxford University Press, 1905.

Williams, Donna. *Autism and Sensing: The Unlost Instinct*. London: Jessica Kingsley, 1998.

Wojciehowski, Hannah, and Vittorio Gallese. "How Stories Make Us Feel: Toward an Embodied Narratology." *California Italian Studies* 2, no. 1 (2011). http://old.unipr.it /arpa/mirror/pubs/pdffiles/Gallese/2011/california_italian_studies_2011.pdf.

Wolfe, Cary. "Learning from Temple Grandin, or, Animal Studies, Disability Studies, and Who Comes after the Subject?" *New Formations* 64 (Summer 2008): 110–23.

Wretches and Jabberers. Directed by Gerardine Wurzburg. State of the Art Inc., 2011. DVD.

Yergeau, Melanie. *Authoring Autism: On Rhetoric and Neurological Queerness*. Durham, NC: Duke University Press, 2018.

———. "Clinically Significant Disturbance: On Theorists Who Theorize Theory of Mind." *Disability Studies Quarterly* 33, no. 4 (2013). doi:10.18061/dsq.v33i4.3876.

"Yoga and Post-traumatic Stress Disorder: An Interview with Bessel van der Kolk, MD." http://www.traumacenter.org/clients/maginside.su09.p12-13.pdf.

Yunker, John, ed. *Among Animals: The Lives of Animals and Humans in Contemporary Short Fiction*. Ashland, OR: Ashland Creek Press, 2014.

Zeman, Adam, Frazer Milton, Alicia Smith, and Rick Rylance. "By Heart: An fMRI Study of Brain Activation by Poetry and Prose." *Journal of Consciousness Studies* 20, no. 9–10 (2013): 132–58.

Zunshine, Lisa. "Theory of Mind and Experimental Representations of Fictional Consciousness." In *Introduction to Cognitive Cultural Studies*, edited by Lisa Zunshine, 193–213. Baltimore, MD: Johns Hopkins University Press, 2010.

———. *Why We Read Fiction: Theory of Mind and the Novel*. Columbus: Ohio State University Press, 2006.

· index ·

Bogdashina, Olga, 198
Bohr, Niels, 193
Bradbury, Ray, 89
brain, 215; amygdala, 173, 177–78; basal
ganglia, 76–77, 80; cerebellum,
76–77, 80; complex networks, 76;
frontal lobes, 4, 36, 44, 115, 178, 193; as
fully embodied, 80; limbic structures,
74; medial prefrontal cortex (MPFC),
225–26; metaphor, processing of,
40; occipital lobes, 39, 199; parietal
lobes, 39, 115; parietal operculum,
40; plasticity, 21, 80, 85, 90–91, 182;
posterior sensory regions, 4, 38, 43,
72, 74; prefrontal regions, 42–43;
right hemisphere, 43, 198; trauma,
processing of, 74; visual pathways, 68;
of whale, 51–52
Brannon, Biff (character, *The Heart Is a
Lonely Hunter*), 133–34, 136–37, 229
breath, metaphor of, 16–17
Brincker, Maria, 78
Brooks, Cleanth, 164
Brown, Brandon, 97
Brown, Lydia, 139
Burke, Jamie, 9–10, 57, 60, 129, 154,
210, 220; auditory motor cueing, use
of, 79–80; college focuses, 62–63;
concern for others, 65; *The Exchange*
radio show, 75–76, 82; letters, 211–12;
spatial perceptions translated to
language, 67, 69–70, 74
Burke, Mike, 65–66
Burke, Sheree, 62, 82
Burton, Tim, 111

Campbell, John W., Jr., 121
Carlock, William, 164
Carr, Nicholas, 112
Carson, Ben, 195
categories, 72; identity, 125–26, 128–29,
140–41, 147, 191–92; precategorical
sensory information, 47–48, 116, 149,
189, 192; Trump victory and, 194

caterpillars, 96–97
Cather, Willa, 60
central coherence, 78–79
Ceremony (Silko), 9–10, 61–63, 84,
129; multimedia form, 74; mute boy,
as autistic character, 70; pattern in,
73–74, 84–85; spatial visualization
in, 69–70, 74; spiritual priors, 84, 85;
stream of consciousness, 71; trauma,
response to, 66
Charles Mallory Sail Loft, 56
Charles W. Morgan (whaling vessel), 36,
38, 48–49, 56
Chesterton, G. K., 99–100
"Children Selecting Books in a Library"
(Jarrell), 18
Chukovsky, Korney, 170
Circus of Souls (Prince), 90
Clarke, Arthur C., 89
classical autism, 16, 33, 57–59, 65, 76, 81.
See also nonspeaking autistics
"close reading," 54–55
cochlear implant (CI), 126
Coetzee, J. M., 189
cognition, 4–5, 77–78, 205; blind, 5, 199;
embodied, embedded, and extended,
85; letters, processing of, 42–43; metaphor and, 40; social, 78, 113, 148, 172,
225
cognitive literary studies, 178, 232
coincidences, 99–100
Coleridge, Samuel Taylor, 117
community, motor coupling and, 81, 84
Community Based Participatory Research (CBPR), 96, 99
Cook, Frederick Albert, 184
Copeland, Dr. Benedict Mady (character, *The Heart Is a Lonely Hunter*),
143–46
Crip Theory (McRuer), 136
cueing, 80; metronome, 60, 79, 80, 82;
Samonas listening therapy, 58, 80
cultural alienation, 92
cure agenda, 27–28, 49–50

Cure Autism Now (CAN), 27–28, 202
Curious Incident of the Dog in the Night-Time, The (Haddon), 2, 7
cyberpunk, 92
cyborgs, 117

Damasio, Antonio, 177, 240
Damon, Matt, 90
dance. *See* ballet
Danes, Claire, 162, 173, 180
Davison, Richard, 177
Deaf community, 126, 141
deafness, 125, 232; supernatural powers attributed to, 127, 134
decategorization, 148, 232, 235
Deckard, Rick (character, *Do Androids Dream of Electric Sheep?*), 86–88, 103–6, 108
decoding, 72
deficiency, difference interpreted as, 3, 32, 39, 44, 51; "restricted interests," 64
Degler, Claude, 91–92
Delany, Samuel, 92
delayed decoding, 72
demonization, 115
detail, 32, 38, 72, 116; phonemes, attention to, 43–44
DeVos, Betsy, 195
Diagnostic and Statistical Manual of Mental Disorders III, 105
Diagnostic and Statistical Manual of Mental Disorders 5, 201
Dick, Philip K., 121; ambiguity and irony in, 87, 102; *The Martian Time-Slip*, 222; syntax, 100–102. See also *Do Androids Dream of Electric Sheep?*
Dickinson, Emily, 55, 129
Diderot, Denis, 19
digital natives, 119
disability: queerness and, 135–36; supernatural powers attributed to, 127, 134
disability rights movement, 126
disability studies, 6, 88, 94, 136
disagreement, student fear of, 102–3

disclosure, 123, 228
distancing strategies, 20–21
diversity, 213; silico-diversity, 89, 96. *See also* neurodiversity
diversity science, 147–49, 191
Djikic, Maja, 161, 186–87, 235–36
Do Androids Dream of Electric Sheep? (Dick), 10, 86–89, 92, 96, 98–112, 117, 120–21, 129, 222; ambiguity in, 108–9; duality in, 110; electric sheep, 103–4; parody in, 109–10; schizoid humans, 106–7; Voigt-Kampff empathy test, 86, 87, 105–7
Donnellan, Anne, 77–78
drumming, neurological, 58, 60, 79
Du Bois, W. E. B., 144
Duncan, Isadora, 136
Duyckinck, Evert, 55
dyscalculia, 119

Eco, Umberto, 13
"Ecstatic Cry, The" (Raymond), 160, 176–84, 187
Edelman, Gerald, 76
education: inclusion, 16–17, 22, 28, 33–34, 57, 59–60; Skype tutorials, 8, 31–35; special education, 28
Edwards, Mary K. Bercaw, 36
Ehrlich, Greta, 74
Einstein, Albert, 59
embodiment of language, 38, 40–42, 85
emotion: avoidance, 160, 161, 173, 184, 236, 238–39; feeling, thinking in, 124–25, 132–33; integrative capacity of, 177; "mixed," 174–75
emotional prosody, 85
"Emotions and the Structuring of Narrative Responses" (Miall), 177
empathy: absence of display, 106–7; autistics said to lack, 3, 10; cognitive, 107, 171, 238; correctives to, 96; in *Do Androids Dream of Electric Sheep?*, 87, 103, 105–7; emotional, 107, 171, 238; emotional transporta-

tion, 180, 242; identification vs., 179–80; motor, 107; sci-fi treatment of, 86–87; sensory, 171; stereotypes about, 90–91; "Voigt-Kampff empathy test," 86, 87, 105–7

"Empathy Imbalance Hypothesis" (Smith), 107

enfacement illusion, 149

enhanced perceptual functioning (EPF), 37–38, 116, 149, 216–17

entrainment, 79

environmental concerns, 63–64, 214

Erie Canal, 63

"Esthetique du Mal" (Stevens), 100

ET (film), 135

ET effect, 135

Eugenie, 123–54; autism diagnosis, 152, 232; identity enclaves and, 126, 128–29; motion dyslexia, 124, 128; multiraciality, views of, 129–30, 136, 140–43, 146, 153; as parent, 151–52; as skating instructor, 150–51

Exchange, The (radio show), 75–76, 82

Eye in the Sky (film), 168

Ezekiel, Aniekee Tochukwu, 109

facial recognition, ingroup/outgroup perception, 147–49

facilitated communication (FC, supported typing), 60, 65, 211

Farah, Martha, 199

feeling, thinking in, 124–25, 132–33

fiction, as accommodation, 116

figure-eight movements, 58

figures of speech, 40

"filler words," 100

Fisher, Jennifer, 122–23

Fiske, Susan T., 225

Fitzgerald, F. Scott, 168

fractal geometry, 68

Franny and Zooey (Salinger), 175

freak shows, 90

Fries, Kenny, 132

Frost, Robert, 46, 69, 194

functional magnetic resonance imaging (fMRI), 39

functioning, as term, 92–93

future, 78, 81–83

Galaburda, Albert, 60

Gallese, Vittorio, 38

Garcia, Jerry, 128

Garland, Inspector (character, *Do Androids Dream of Electric Sheep?*), 108

"Geek Syndrome, The" (Silberman), 91

gender, 100, 110, 112, 127, 137–39, 229

gendervague, 139

"Gendervague: At the Intersection of Autistic and Trans Experience" (Brown), 139

generalization, 38, 189, 198–99, 206, 238; formal conceptual, 78; move toward from specifics, 149, 158–59, 170; of phonemes, 43–44

genre fiction, 92

Gibran, Kahlil, 77

Gibson, William, 92, 102

Gilles de Rais, 113

Gilligan, Carol, 76

global coherence, 37

Godfather, The (Puzo), 63

Good Morning America, 45

Gorsuch, Neil, 195

Gould, Judith, 26

Graham, Martha, 122, 151

Grandin, Temple, 2–5, 70, 72, 155–90, 232; *Animals in Translation*, 172, 233; *The Autistic Brain*, 67–68, 114, 172; center-track restrainer systems designed by, 170; as conservative literary critic, 188–90; Danes's portrayal of, 162, 173, 180; on emotion, 156–58, 160–61, 164, 171–75, 238; emotional complexity, 174–75; encounters with Mukhopadhyay, 31; film, reactions to, 3–4, 112, 171, 183; *New Yorker* profile, 90; philosophical and ethical questions, 162–63; poetic thinking, 158;

contribution to society, 47; diagnostic assessment of, 25–26; "Harpoons," 52–53; *How Can I Talk If My Lips Don't Move?*, 44–45, 47; hyperfocusing, 38, 72, 193; "I Kept but Sorry Guard," 46–47; India, education in, 204; intellectual property appropriated, 202; lack of inclusive opportunities, 29–30; *The Mind Tree (Beyond the Silence)*, 26–27, 28; Mystic Seaport visit, 36–38, 48–49, 56; personification of nonhuman beings, 112–13; request for tutoring, 30–31; rhythm and rhyme's effect on, 81; Skype tutorials, 31–35; on tactile defensiveness, 31–32

multiraciality, 129–30, 140–43, 147, 153

murder of autistics, 50

music, 172, 217–18; motor system and, 58, 80, 81, 83

Nabokov, Vladimir, 42

Nafisi, Azar, 195

Nagel, Thomas, 238

National Autistic Society (NAS), 25–26

Native Americans: healing, view of, 9, 60–61, 66, 71–74, 84, 220; inclusiveness, 64–65; motor coupling and social bonding, 84; spiritual priors, 84, 85

Nazi T-4 program, 73

Ne'eman, Ari, 45

neural coupling, 219

neural pruning, 116

neurocosmopolitanism, 91, 98, 221

neurodiversity, 75, 85, 121, 189, 194–95; ability/disability divide, 236–37

"Neurodiversity, Quality of Life, and Autistic Adults: Shifting Research and Professional Focuses onto Real-Life Challenges" (Robertson), 75

neurodiversity movement, 92, 195

neurohumanities, 217

neuroimaging, 68, 173, 243

Neuromancer (Gibson), 102

neuroscience, 6, 12, 36; deficiency, difference interpreted as, 3, 39; high- and low-imagery sentence study, 38–39, 42; holistic turn, 85

NeuroTribes: The Legacy of Autism and the Future of Neurodiversity (Silberman), 73, 91, 119

neurotypical bias, 36–37

New Bedford Whaling Museum, 48

New Criticism, 164, 192

Nicolaidis, Christina, 95, 97

nonhuman entities, autistic affinity with, 104–5, 111–13; personification, 112–13

nonspeaking autistics, independent typing, 9, 27, 32, 60, 76, 80, 211

normativity, critique of, 182, 187–88, 209

"Nothing about us without us" adage, 98, 126

novelty, controlled, 81, 218–19

Nussbaum, Martha, 175

Nutcracker, The (ballet), 146, 153

Oatley, Keith, 161, 186–87, 234–36

objectivity, 171–72

object-personality pairings, 115–16

object recognition, 41

object visualization, 68, 124

occupational therapy, 9

"Ode: Intimations of Immortality from Recollections of Early Childhood" (Wordsworth), 11

"Ode on a Grecian Urn" (Keats), 155, 162, 169

oppositional politics, 92

ordinal linguistic personification, 115, 119–20

Osteen, Mark, 182

Otherness, 123, 232, 243

Otis, Laura, 198–99, 214

Pale Fire (Nabokov), 42

paradigm change, 120–21

paradox, 68–69, 167–68, 193

parenting, 10, 70

parody, 109–10
participatory research, 96
particularity, 142, 169, 194, 238
partisan politics, 172
passing, 123, 142, 228
passive voice, 101
pathologization of autism, 44, 51, 189, 198, 220
pattern, 84–85; for motor skills, 80, 82; predictability, 81; pure vs. social, 72
pattern thinking, 68
perceptual functioning, 37–38, 77–79
perseverative behavior, 23, 201
personhood, 182
personification, 112–13, 225–26
personification network, 115
phonemes, 43–44
photographs, as visual aids, 37
picture thinking, 68
Pierre (Melville), 201
Pinker, Stephen, 81, 217–18
plasticity, 21, 80, 85, 90–91, 182
Plath, Sylvia, 97
Playing by Ear and the Tip of the Tongue (Tsur), 192
pleasure, 195
pliant puzzling, 93
poetry, 41, 80–82, 116, 174, 242; autistic, 6–7, 26–27; as corrective, 192; hexameter, 218; as prosthesis, 82; as self-stimulating action, 43
posthuman, 114, 190
precategorical sensory information, 47–48, 116, 149, 189, 192
predictability, 81
prepositional phrases, 101
presuming competence, 182
Prince, Dawn, 89–90
print-rich environment, 83
Pris (character, *Do Androids Dream of Electric Sheep?*), 96, 100, 107, 108–9
probabilistic expectations, 78–79
processing speed, 129
pronouns, 100

prophecy, 84
proprioception, 58
Proust, Marcel, 132, 194
Prozac, 173
psychic breathing, 76
psychopaths, 107
puns, 122, 123
Puzo, Mario, 63

Queequeg (character, *Moby-Dick*), 33, 35–36, 218
queer politics, 135–36, 243

race issues, 143–45
Ramachandran, V. S., 116
rapid prompting method (RPM), 27
Raymaker, Dora, 10, 92–121, 129, 139, 161, 222–23; on AASIRE, 97–98; on androids, 96; dissertation, 99; *Hoshi and the Red City Circuit*, 118–19, 245; life experiences, 104–5; on paradigm change, 120–21
Raymond, Midge: "The Ecstatic Cry," 160, 176–84, 187
reader-response criticism, 178
readers, emotionally avoidant, 160, 161, 173, 184, 236
reading, effects on autism, 111–12
Reagan, Ronald, 75–76
Reasonable People (Savarese), 16, 159
"Reflections of a Community Based Participatory Researcher from the Intersection of Disability Advocacy, Engineering, and the Academy" (Raymaker), 99
repetition, 43, 81, 150
restricted interests, 64, 130, 156, 213
rhythm, 79–80, 219
Rilke, Rainer Maria, 113
Rimbaud, Arthur, 207
ritual slaughter, 169
Roberts, Chief Justice, 145
Robertson, Scott, 75
Rosen, Eldon (character, *Do Androids Dream of Electric Sheep?*), 104–6, 109

Rosen, Rachael (character, *Do Androids Dream of Electric Sheep?*), 104–10; as robot self-advocate, 110
Roth, Ilona, 6
Rottenberg, Rachel, 88
Rubin, Rita, 19
Rubin, Sue, 19
Russell, Bertrand, 155, 182
Russell, Emily, 134–35

Sacks, Oliver, 2–3, 26, 90, 156
Salinger, J. D., 175
Samonas listening therapy, 58, 80
Savarese, DJ, 2, 5–6, 15–21, 76, 150, 159, 178, 199, 236; Burke and, 62, 211–12; on difference, 21–22
Savarese, Emily, 75, 83
Sawyer, Diane, 45
Scarry, Elaine, 39
schizophrenia, 105
science fiction, 10, 89–92, 234; as android, 117; appeal to autistics, 91–92; criticism of, 115; human-robot inversion, 112; mentalizing abilities and, 111
scientific revolutions, structure of, 121
Scott, Michael, 23
Scott, Ridley, 98, 100. See also *Blade Runner*
Sebald, W. G., 159
self-contained classroom, 28
self-determination, 89
self-esteem, 83
self-reliance, fiction of, 85
Senge, Peter, 99
sensing, 37–38
sensorimotor function, 76–77, 215
sensorimotor priors, 78
sensorimotor resonance, 148
sensory-associative thinking, 118, 158
sensory empathy, 171
sensory integration, 57–58, 244
sensory processing, 9, 57–58, 60; motor impairments and, 77–78; nonspeaking autistic communication and,

27; smell, sense of, 24–25, 32; tactile defensiveness, 31–32, 34
sensory thinking, 39, 172
sequencing difficulties, 2–3
Serres, Michel, 40
service dog metaphor, 193
Sexton, Anne, 5
sexuality, autistics assumed to lack, 184
Shackleton, Ernest, 184
Shama-Tsoory, Simone, 107
sheep, electric (*Do Androids Dream of Electric Sheep?*), 103–4, 105
Shelley, Percy Bysshe, 41
Shore, Stephen, 18–19
Sibley, Kassiane, 93
Silberman, Steve, 73, 91, 119
silico-diversity, 89, 96
Silk, Dennis, 113
Silko, Leslie Marmon, 9–10, 61–63
Silverman, Gillian, 183, 207
Sinclair, Jim, 197–98
Singer, John (character, *The Heart Is a Lonely Hunter*), 126–27, 131–34
Skype tutorials, 8, 31–35
slave rebellion concept, 89
smell, sense of, 24–25, 32
Smith, Adam, 107
social world, healing of, 154
Solace of Open Spaces, The (Ehrlich), 74
Song of Myself (Whitman), 67
Songs of the Gorilla Nation (Prince), 89–90
Sontag, Susan, 101
sound waves, 43
spatial visualization, 68
special education, 28–29
spectrum, concept of, 95, 222
speech, 60; in *Moby-Dick*, 52; motor planning, 93; movement tied to, 82–83; pattern and, 84–85; perceptual processing of, 43–44; processing modes, 44; variable relationship to, 93–95
Spielberg, Steven, 135
spiritual priors, 84, 85